NEW PERSPECTIVES ON INTERNATIONAL MIGRATION AND DEVELOPMENT

———

INITIATIVE FOR POLICY DIALOGUE AT COLUMBIA

**INITIATIVE FOR POLICY
DIALOGUE AT COLUMBIA**

**JOSÉ ANTONIO OCAMPO AND JOSEPH E. STIGLITZ,
SERIES EDITORS**

Escaping the Resource Curse, Macartan Humphreys,
Jeffrey D. Sachs, and Joseph E. Stiglitz, eds.

The Right to Know, Ann Florini, ed.

Privatization: Successes and Failures, Gérard Roland, ed.

Growth and Policy in Developing Countries: A Structuralist Approach,
José Antonio Ocampo, Codrina Rada, and Lance Taylor

Taxation in Developing Countries, Roger Gordon, ed.

Reforming the International Financial System for Development,
Jomo Kwame Sundaram, ed.

Development Cooperation in Times of Crisis, José Antonio
Ocampo and José Antonio Alonso

NEW PERSPECTIVES ON INTERNATIONAL MIGRATION AND DEVELOPMENT

EDITED BY

Jeronimo Cortina
and Enrique Ochoa-Reza

COLUMBIA UNIVERSITY PRESS

NEW YORK

Jeronimo Cortina dedicates this book to all past, present, and future migrants.

Enrique Ochoa-Reza dedicates this book to Greta Rojas.

———————————

Columbia University Press
Publishers Since 1893
New York   Chichester, West Sussex
cup.columbia.edu

Library of Congress Cataloging-in-Publication Data

New perspectives on international migration and development / edited by
Jeronimo Cortina and Enrique Ochoa-Reza.
pages cm
Includes bibliographical references and index.
ISBN 978-0-231-15680-6 (cloth : alk. paper) —
ISBN 978-0-231-52749-1 (ebook)
1. Emigration and immigration.   2. Economic development.
I. Cortina, Jeronimo.
JV6035.N49 2013
338.9—dc23   2012049276

Columbia University Press books are printed
on permanent and durable acid-free paper.
This book is printed on paper with
recycled content.

Printed in the United States of America
c 10 9 8 7 6 5 4 3 2 1

Cover image: © Steve McCurry/Magnum Photos
Cover design: Katie Poe

The Initiative for Policy Dialogue (IPD) at Columbia University brings together academics, policymakers, and practitioners from developed and developing countries to address the most pressing issues in economic policy today. IPD is an important part of Columbia's broad program on development and globalization. The Initiative for Policy Dialogue at Columbia: Challenges in Development and Globalization presents the latest academic thinking on a wide range of development topics and lays out alternative policy options and trade-offs. Written in a language accessible to policymakers and students alike, this series is unique in that it both shapes the academic research agenda and furthers the economic policy debate, facilitating a more democratic discussion of development policies.

According to the United Nations, today around 214 million people live outside their countries of birth. Migration between developing countries is now as frequent as migration between developing and more developed countries. The World Bank estimates that remittances—the quintessential by-product of migration—to developing countries account for more than $370 billion, while in the political arena, migration is the ever-present topic both in national and local elections. In sum, international migration has become a key part of globalization, permeating the lives not only of migrants but also of millions more who haven't themselves migrated.

This book focuses on one particular feature of migration: its impact on development. It also examines the various channels through which migration permeates the economic, cultural, social, and political structures in both migrant-sending and -receiving countries. The goal of the book is to highlight the complex nature of the developmental implications of migration by providing new perspectives that address some of the challenges and harness some of the opportunities associated with international migration and development.

The book is divided into three parts. The four chapters in part 1 examine the causal links between demographic and development transitions, the role of the state in shaping migration and how migration shapes politics and the state, and culture and human rights in the migration-development debate. Part 2 focuses on migration, children, women, and development and on how families and local communities are reconfigured as a response to migration. The book closes with a part exploring migration's developmental impacts on various migration corridors, portraying not only a different geographic focus but illustrating the nuanced and context-dependent nature of migration's developmental impacts.

This volume is written for a very diverse set of audiences, from government and elected officials to academics, civil society, and practitioners. Its multidisciplinary nature stresses the need to focus on substantive as well as practical issues needed for designing and implementing migration and development policies that will ensure that migration has the most positive impacts both in the communities that migrants leave behind and in those that become their new homes.

For more information about IPD and its upcoming books, visit www .policydialogue.org.

CONTENTS

ILLUSTRATIONS AND TABLES

FIGURES

TABLES

ACKNOWLEDGMENTS

The initial idea for this book came at the Advanced Graduate Workshop on Poverty, Development and Globalization cosponsored by The Brooks World Poverty Institute at the University of Manchester and The Initiative for Policy Dialogue at Columbia University. There, Joseph Stiglitz gave us his views on the relationship between migration and development and on the challenges and opportunities that international migration presents for the world's developmental prospects. The introduction to this volume reflects this conversation.

Drafts of the chapters in this volume were presented at two conferences: one held at Columbia University in April 2008 and the other held at the Universidad Nacional Autónoma de México (UNAM) in January 2009. We benefited from the comments provided by all the participants who generously gave of their time and expertise. These include Dante Ang, former chairman of the Commission on Filipinos Overseas; Graziano Battistella, director of the Scalabrini Migration Center; Professor Alejandro Canales Ceron at the Centro Universitario de Ciencias Economico Administrativas Universidad de Guadalajara; Benjamin Davis, director of the AFL-CIO Solidarity Center; Christian Dustmann, professor of economics at University College London; Luis Jorge Garay, associate research fellow at the Comparative Regional Integration Studies Programme of the United Nations University; Victoria Garchitorena, president of the Ayala Foundation; Stephany Griffith-Jones, financial markets director at The Initiative for Policy Dialogue at Columbia University; Susan Gzesh, executive director of the Human Rights Program at the University of Chicago; Talip Kilic from the Development Research Group of the World Bank; Jeni Klugman, director of gender and development at the World Bank and former director of the Human Development Report Office of the United

Nations Development Programme; Hyejin Ku, assistant professor of economics at Florida State University; Marcelino Chicano Libanan, former commissioner of the Philippines' Bureau of Immigration; Magdalena Lesinka, deputy director of the Centre of Migration Research at the University of Warsaw; Milena Novy-Marx, program officer at the MacArthur Foundation; Dilip Ratha, lead economist and manager of the Migration and Remittances Unit at the World Bank; John Slocum, director of migration and human mobility at the MacArthur Foundation; Michel Teitelbaum, senior adviser to the Alfred P. Sloan Foundation; Alfredo Thorne, former managing director of economic and policy research at JP Morgan Chase Bank and general director of global markets of Grupo Financiero Banorte; Hania Zlotnik, former director of the Population Division at the Department of Economic and Social Affairs of the United Nations; and Ayman Zohry, chairman of the board of the Egyptian Society for Migration Studies.

We gratefully acknowledge the financial support from the MacArthur Foundation that made the writing of this volume possible. Sarah Green, Mildred Menos, and Farah Siddique from The Initiative for Policy Dialogue provided excellent support. We would like to thank Narayani Lasala-Blanco and Matthew S. Winters for volunteering as rapporteurs for the Mexico City meeting. We are also grateful to Myles Thompson and Bridget Flannery-McCoy at Columbia University Press for their support and patience, as well as the three anonymous referees who provided constructive comments on the volume and the individual chapters.

Finally, our thanks to Joseph E. Stiglitz and José Antonio Ocampo from The Initiative for Policy Dialogue at Columbia University, who offered their wisdom and counsel. This book would not have been possible without their leadership.

INTRODUCTION

Joseph E. Stiglitz, Jeronimo Cortina, and Enrique Ochoa-Reza

The "age of mobility" is here to stay. Never before in human history have so many people been on the move. Today around 214 million people, or approximately 3 percent of the world's population, live outside their country of birth. Women and girls account for half of international migrants, and 16 percent are under the age of 20 (UN/DESA 2011). South–south migration is now as frequent as south–north migration has been in the past, and while 97 percent of the world's population does not move, migration is a global phenomenon that touches millions of lives, including many of those who haven't themselves migrated.

International migration permeates our daily lives. Migration is a key part of globalization, the closer integration of the countries of the world. In many ways, its impacts are greater than any other aspect of globalization, e.g., the movement of goods, services, or capital. It has affected ideas, cultures, even countries' sense of identity. Like other parts of globalization, it has been the center of controversy, but even more so: in many countries, debates about migration have become central to politics. International migration as a transnational and global process has reshaped the meaning of national borders.

Ironically, while migration may have the most profound effects on both receiving and sending countries, it has remained the part of globalization least subject to international regulation. In recent years, though, a number of international forums have been created to understand the migration process better—and to shape the process so that it yields greater benefits to both the recipient and sending countries. These include the Global Forum on Migration and Development (GFMD),[1] the Global Migration Group (GMG),[2] and a wide number of regional consultative processes (RCPs) on migration.[3] Together, they are proof that migration has gained a strong foothold in the international debate and that the dialogue is moving forward.

This book focuses on one particular aspect of migration: its impact on development. We seek to understand the various channels through which migration affects developing countries from which the migrant leaves and what can be done by both the recipient and sending countries to increase the positive impacts on development.

The book grew out of a series of dialogues (the first held in New York City, the second in Mexico City) sponsored by the MacArthur Foundation on migration and development that approached the developmental impacts from a broad perspective, crossing disciplinary lines.

At the time of the first meeting (in April 2008), there was enormous enthusiasm in some circles about the possible positive effects of migration on developing countries. Migration was far more controversial in the recipient countries. But in the ensuing years, controversies have arisen over whether, overall, migration is positive even for development. This book helps us understand the ambiguous perspectives and we hope will lead to policies that will enhance the positive developmental impacts.

BEYOND REMITTANCES

Traditionally, discussions on development and migration focused on remittances. These were celebrated as providing new sources of funding—larger in many cases than foreign direct investment, short-term portfolio flows, or foreign aid. The central question was how to channel the funds toward "productive investments" that would promote development, ensuring the stability of the flow (especially relevant in recent years, with major downturns in some of the recipient countries) and that the flow of remittances is sustained (a worry that, as migrants get integrated into the communities to which they have moved, remittances will drop). The challenge was that money went to individuals, who might be more focused on, say, obtaining good housing than investing money in projects that would promote development.

There is no doubt that remittances have some strong positive benefits, such as stopping further impoverishment, improving families' living standards, and increasing children's access to health and education. But remittances also may create negative externalities, such as economic dependence and an overvalued country's exchange rate, which make other areas of the economy uncompetitive.

A narrow economic analysis of the effects of migration attempts to weigh the positive and negative effects against each other and to ask whether (or how) one can maximize the positive effects and minimize the negative. For instance, can exchange rate intervention ensure that the exchange rate will not be overvalued, and if so, are there adverse ancillary effects?

Economists even more narrowly focused have been aware that there are several other channels through which migration affects development. An earlier literature focused, for instance, on the brain drain. But what happened in some Eastern European countries after the fall of the Berlin Wall was seemingly far more devastating: a hollowing out of their economies and societies, with large fractions of talented young people leaving the country. Implicit in this literature was an understanding that there are benefits to society of, say, a talented individual remaining in the country that go beyond the wage he receives. At the very least, there is his contribution to public revenues. Indeed the existence of these externalities is part of the rationale for public support for education and provides the basis of the criticism of some emerging markets that out-migration of highly educated individuals to developed countries represents a "theft" of intellectual property.

This book argues, however, for taking a broader perspective on development, what it means and what gives rise to it. There are political and broader societal and cultural aspects of development. Migration affects politics and the role of the state in ways that can be either positive or negative for development (see Levitt and Lamba-Nieves and de la Garza in this volume). Migration may lower unemployment and thus reduce the political pressure for economic reforms that would lead to a better-performing economy.

As chapter 3 points out, as important as monetary remittances are cultural remittances: migrations affect the ideas, values, and perceptions of those who migrate, and when they return home (or even in their contacts with those who remain at home) this can have profound impacts on the communities from which they emigrated, impacts that cannot adequately be summarized in terms like an "increase in human capital."

The real issue here is thus not whether migration creates positive or negative externalities through remittances—we know it does both—but whether our definition of development is inclusive enough to provide a comprehensive and meaningful evaluation of migration's developmental impacts (Cortina et al. 2005).

Development is about enhancing individuals' well-being through the advancement of their human rights and life satisfaction. Taking this broader perspective leads to a more nuanced and complex view of the impact of migration on development. The effects of migration are context-dependent: it can speed up development in countries ready to grow—if the macroeconomic and institutional fundamentals are in place—or help sustain underdevelopment. The impacts are neither automatic nor linear and are mediated by culture and by the transnational interactions that arise between migrants and their families back home.

GOAL OF THE BOOK

This volume highlights the complex nature of the developmental implications of migration. Our intention here is to contribute to the migration-development dialogue by broadening the debate and by providing new perspectives that address the challenges and harness the opportunities associated with migration and development. Our analysis strongly suggests that policies *in both the sending and the recipient countries* help shape the developmental impact.

The chapters in this volume bring provocative perspectives to topics that have not yet played a leading role in the debate. Historical and contemporary topics such as the causal linkages between migration and development transitions (going *beyond* remittances), the impact of female migration on development and children left behind, the impact of government policies, and the role of culture in shaping development goals and paths have remained elusive in the international dialogue.

We hope this book will make clear that development in the context of international migration needs to be conceptualized from a holistic and dynamic perspective, one that incorporates not only economic constructs but also the role of the state and its noneconomic policies and of culture. This broader understanding has to be based on an analysis not only of how money and people move across borders but also of how ideas and culture do, and as they do, how these affect individuals and the communities and countries from which and to which they migrate.

A ROAD MAP OF THE BOOK

This book is intended for a very diverse set of audiences: government and elected officials in charge of designing and implementing migration and development policies; civil society and practitioners interested in ensuring that migration has the most positive impacts that it can on the migrants, the communities that they leave behind, and those to which they move; and scholars interested in understanding better the complex relationship between migration and development and deriving better policy prescriptions on the basis of these new perspectives.

This volume is divided into three parts. Each part has a short introduction underscoring the main linkages between each chapter. The four chapters in part 1 are devoted to "big" questions exploring the causal links between demographic and development transitions, the role of the state in shaping migration, and how migration shapes politics and the state, culture, and human rights in the migration-development debate. Part 2 consists of two chapters that focus on migration, children, women, and development. These chapters explore how families and local communities are reconfigured as a response to migration and the developmental implications of destination countries' migration policies on the developmental prospects of migrant-sending countries.

The volume closes with part 3 focusing on migration's developmental impacts on various migration corridors. Migration is a global phenomenon, but the nature of migration and its developmental impacts differ markedly from place to place. The five chapters in this part deal with different geographical areas and topics, illustrate the nuanced and complex nature of the migration-development nexus, and emphasize the context-dependent nature of migration's developmental impacts.

The contributions to this volume demonstrate the rich and global nature of international migration. Migration can speed economic development and reduce poverty, but the effects on development go beyond GDP and incomes more narrowly defined. Ideally, migration benefits migrants, the countries of origin, and the countries of destination; making it easier for migrants to send remittances home is an example. But in some cases, there may be difficult trade-offs.

The central message of this book is that migration *can* have a positive effect on development, though it won't be the "silver bullet" that some had hoped for. But designing policies that maximize the developmental impacts (broadly construed), or even ensuring that the benefits are positive, will not be easy. The relationship between migration and development is complex and will be understood only once we recognize that its impacts go beyond economic indicators and are affected by policies, culture, economics, and politics in both the recipient country and the sending country.

REFERENCES

Cortina, J., Rodolfo de la Garza, and Enrique Ochoa-Reza. 2005. "Remesas: Limites al optimismo." *Foreign Affairs en Español* 5 (July–September): 27–36.

Global Forum on Migration and Development (GFMD). 2011. "Background and Objectives." Geneva, Switzerland: GFMD. Accessed at http://gfmd.org/en/process /background.

Global Migration Group (GMG). 2011. "What is the GMG?" New York: United Nations. Accessed at http://www.globalmigrationgroup.org/en/what-is-the-gmg.

International Organization for Migration (IOM) 2011. "Regional Consultative Processes on Migration" Geneva, Switzerland: GFMD. Accessed at http://www.iom .int/cms/rcp.

United Nations, Department of Economic and Social Affairs, Population Division (UN/DESA). 2011. "Trends in International Migrant Stock: Migrants by Age and Sex." United Nations database, POP/DB/MIG/Stock/Rev. 2010.

NEW PERSPECTIVES ON INTERNATIONAL MIGRATION AND DEVELOPMENT

PART 1

Migration, Development, States, Culture, and Human Rights

This part introduces a mélange of topics that provide a new perspective on the migration-development nexus. The chapters presented here provide a conceptual discussion that seeks to push the migration-development dialogue beyond the traditional remittances-development dichotomy.

In chapter 1, Josh DeWind and Damla Ergun provide a macro-structural, historical, and geographical framework for analyzing the migration-development nexus. Based on the European case, they argue that industrialization has long driven the relationship between development and migration through causal mechanisms that are embedded within four socioeconomic transitions: from agricultural to industrial economies, from rural to urban societies, from high to low levels of fertility, and from emigration to immigration societies. Although they expect that similar transitional processes in other regions of the world are similarly driven by industrial development, they argue that testing this hypothesis will require researchers to draw on theories of global development and world migration systems, which have not yet been synthesized by development and migration specialists.

DeWind and Ergun do not explicitly treat the state as a macrostructural variable, but rather point to the necessity considering the impact of state development and migration policies in accelerating or slowing developmental and migratory processes. This chapter, moreover, raises important conceptual considerations regarding how to frame the role of the state and national boundaries in order to understand transnational migration and development processes and the indicators that are needed to compare development and migration transitions internationally.

In contrast, in chapter 2, Rodolfo de la Garza explicitly analyzes the role of the state and argues that in order to understand the migration-development nexus it is necessary to understand, at the outset, how the state influences development and the consequences of migration on development as it is affected by the state's economic, social, cultural, and political policies.

De la Garza questions governments' efforts to shape development through migration given that states are more constrained in managing their economic variables than they are in shaping political characteristics, which in turn shape economic, social, and cultural variables. Political variables in this context could become more important policy tools for national governments to shape the development-migration nexus. The political capacity of the state is in contrast to the state's limited ability to stimulate or manage the economy.

As conceptualized by de la Garza, the state is a uniquely situated actor that can initiate and implement changes in political practices and policies, which in turn can reduce or increase incentives for migration and development. De la Garza argues that if sending countries stabilize politically and economically, migrants would be among the first to recognize and leverage the resulting new opportunities at home, stimulating growth through investment and circular migration.

Development, however, is not only about economics, and economics is not the whole story. In chapter 3, Peggy Levitt and Deepak Lamba-Nieves take a different but complementary perspective on the migration-development debate by arguing in favor of bringing culture back into the dialogue. Culture permeates all aspects of the development enterprise: it defines how development goals are established, what polices are put in place to achieve them, and how successfully they are achieved. Ideas and practices travel in response to migration, regardless of national boundaries, enabling people to move and create new forms of membership and belonging. Culture then becomes a useful tool to conceptualize the role or lack thereof of national boundaries for framing and understanding the migration-development nexus. More important, culture becomes a unique conceptual anchor to define what kind of indicators will be appropriate in order to measure and compare development between migration systems.

The "blurring" of national boundaries and the creation of a mutual transnational space between sending and receiving countries have implications not only for framing and measuring the impact of migration on development but also for shaping the legal framework of international migration. Khalid Koser in chapter 4 argues that despite a robust legal and normative framework for protecting the rights of migrant workers, protection gaps persist. Part of the answer is that the existing legal framework has not always been adequately implemented because the new dynamics generated by international migration have outstripped the existing legal frameworks. The reality of international migration colored by globalization and the transnational flow of ideas and culture have surpassed the political, economic, and social realities of countries of origin and destination. This gap is particularly evident in three areas (recruitment, the temporal nature of migration, and the growth in irregular migration) that intersect the role of the state with the reality of international migration.

CHAPTER 1

Development and Migration

HISTORICAL TRENDS AND FUTURE RESEARCH

Josh DeWind and Damla Ergun

In recent years, scholars and policymakers have turned their attention to the relation between migration and development, largely due to the recognition that migrants send home remittances that total more than international development assistance (World Bank 2006). Remittances are private, individual funds, while development assistance is chiefly public. For policymakers, enhancing migrants' contributions to development has been a major motivation behind the creation of the Global Forum on Migration and Development, whose member states now meet annually to enhance the contribution of migration to development.

But among scholars there is a growing number of pessimists who doubt that migrants and the resources they bring home have or can have much of an impact on larger structural transformations needed to promote development in many poor, migrant-sending countries (de Haas 2010). The core question was posed by Stephen Castles in a conference[1] paper titled "Development and Migration—Migration and Development: What Comes First?" (2009). In his review of the history of migration and development theories he asserted what he thought was obvious: that "the two are part of the same process and thus are constantly interactive." While the assertion is undoubtedly true, its generality does little to identify or explain the causal relations between migration and development that are central to both social scientific analyses and policy interventions to manage migration or promote development. To understand and explain such relationships it is necessary to identify which aspects of migration, development, and their relations with one another should be considered significant and on what historical and geographic scale those relations can and should be analyzed.

Scholars of migration studies have struggled to evaluate and improve the explanatory and predictive powers of social science theories that focus on both the individuals' decisions to move and the social contexts that motivate and channel movement. In discussing the difficulties of establishing the appropriate scale of micro- and macro-level approaches, Alejandro Portes (1997) warned against not only grand theories that end up being so abstract as to render their predictive power meaningless in specific situations but also narrow theories that, in seeking to take all specific exceptions into account, lose their broader explanatory power. Finding a meaningful level of analysis would seem to require adjusting the scope of a theory and/or the nature and extent of the phenomena to be explained. We make both types of adjustments to refine and advance the contribution of a macro-level approach to explain the relationship between migration and development. In specifying those aspects of the relation between migration and development to be addressed, we hope our approach will not only avoid "such a level of abstraction as to render its predictions vacuously true" (Portes 1997:811) but will also attain advantages and insights that can be strategically derived from tackling "big structures, large processes, and huge comparisons," as encouraged by Charles Tilly (1984).

In what has probably been the broadest and most systematic evaluation of theories of international migration, including relations between migration and development, Douglas Massey and his colleagues (1999) take the position that, far from being contradictory or mutually exclusive, micro- and macro-level theories complement one another in providing a satisfactory theoretical explanation. Pointing to the contributions of macro-level theories, they write, "Our review of research from around the world suggests that international migration originates in the social, economic, and political transformations that accompany the penetration of capitalist markets into non-market or pre-market societies. . . . In the short run, international migration does not stem from a lack of economic development but from development itself" (277). But important as macrostructural contexts may be in shaping migration, the authors suggest that the contributions of macrostructural theories to a broader synthetic understanding remain underdeveloped: "Although the country case studies summarized above highlight the importance of contextual variables in shaping both the determinants of migration and the impacts of migration on development, most suffer from a lack of theoretical and statistical rigour" (251). By specifying the historical and geographic fit between migration and development, we seek to strengthen the contributions of a macrostructural theoretical approach.

To clarify which aspects of development and what kinds of migration are analytically relevant to one another on broad historical and geographic scales, we have begun by focusing on long-term processes and turning points in development and migration processes that seem theoretically related and to fit with one another. With regard to development, this approach emphasizes economic and social transformations in the organization of economic and social reproduction that began with industrialization in Europe at the end of the eighteenth century and the beginning of the nineteenth and has continued to expand across the world until the present day. Thus we focus on long-term secular trends rather than the effects of short-term cyclical fluctuations in production, markets, or trade on migration flows. With regard to migration, we focus on voluntary migration that results in permanent changes of residence, whether internal or international, rather than on forced or circulatory migration. Although both are numerically significant forms of movement, they do not seem as directly responsive as voluntary migration to long-term development trends. In other words, despite the long-term and geographically expansive scope of our approach, we are not attempting to elaborate a theory to encompass all aspects of development or migratory movements but rather to focus on explaining those aspects that are most significantly related to one another.

Scholars from different disciplines have identified four developmental and migratory processes that are increasingly becoming accepted as universal transitions: social transformations that have taken place in the past or are continuing today in all parts of the world, from agricultural to industrial economies, from rural to urban societies, from high to low levels of fertility, and from net flows of emigration to immigration. While analysts have examined how pairs of these processes are related and might affect one another, the long-term and broadly geographical relations between all four of these processes have not yet been proposed as being causally related or systematically examined to specify the sequential nature of their relationships.

In proposing that there are sequentially causal relations between these developmental and migratory transitions, we review contributions that others have made to understanding their interrelations, present empirical evidence that the four transitions have taken place in similar sequences in all world regions, draw on the history of European development and migration to suggest how these processes have been causally related to one another in Europe and can be expected to be similarly related in other regions of the world, and outline issues for future research and analysis to test the extent to which this long-term and geographically broad hypothesis might be tested further to determine its theoretical effectiveness in explaining and predicting contemporary and future migration trends.

RELATIONS BETWEEN MIGRATION AND
DEVELOPMENT TRANSITIONS

The cultural geographer Wilbur Zelinsky (1971) was the first to propose that the ongoing global transition from high to low fertility among women was somehow linked to a transition from low to high, and then back to lower rates of migration. Though he was unable to specify how the two transitions might affect each another, he suggested that "modernization" provides a link. Ronald Skeldon (1990) corrected and refined Zelinsky's descriptive stages of the migration transition, particularly as they take place in underdeveloped countries, and subsequently identified "migration and development units" within a global migration system that linked different types of movement with different modes or levels of economic development and different regions (Skeldon 1997). Manolo Abella (1999), then with the International Labor Organization, focused attention on the transition from emigration to immigration taking place in countries that reach full employment. While each of these scholars explored and advanced understandings of causal relations between some aspects of migration and development, specifically between fertility and migratory transitions or between development and migration transitions, none attempted to identify regular patterns and causal relations between all four of the major socioeconomic and migratory transitions.[2]

We hypothesize that there are causal relationships between these transitions that begin with and are largely driven by the spread of capitalist modes of production and trade. Industrialization disrupts and transforms agricultural production and markets so as to displace rural populations and, together with the demand for labor in urban centers, to stimulate rural–urban migration and urbanization. Access to better health care in cities at first results in population increase, but improvements in health and limited incomes from industrially related employment lead women to reduce the number of children they bear, which results in a decline in population growth. When rural–urban migration and the initial population growth in cities fill the employment needs of local industries, migrants congregate in poverty or, whenever possible, go abroad to find better opportunities. But as local industries grow and urban population growth declines, depleted rural and declining urban populations can no longer fill the demand for labor, industries turn to immigrant workers, and countries of net emigration become countries of net immigration.

To the extent that these transitional processes are universal, we expect to find that the hypothesized relations between them will also be found in all regions of the world. Because the four transitions of industrialization, urbanization, fertility decline, and shift from emigration to immigration first took place within Europe, beginning in Northern Europe and then in Southern and Eastern European subregions, we will test our hypothesis in other parts of the world on a regional and subregional level, though we will also have to consider these transitions on a national level as well. In the end, however, compiling national data to examine what are transnational processes offers insights into the extent and staging of transitions but it will also be shown to have analytic limitations.

TRANSITIONS DATA

To test the hypothesized relations between the four developmental and migratory transitions, we have collected United Nations data that represent the extent to which each transition has progressed within the world's major regions.[3] The data provide only rough indicators of complex processes within each region, but their analytic contributions come primarily from comparisons between regions (see Table 1.1).

- *Agricultural to Industrial Economy:* Transitions from an agricultural to an industrial economy are indicated here by the percentage of gross domestic product (GDP) that derives from industry and services. (The percentage contribution from agriculture is the remaining balance percentage of GDP.) This is a crude indicator, which exaggerates the importance of industry and related services because the contribution of unmarketed subsistence agricultural products is not taken into account, but the resulting distortions seem only to shrink rather than eliminate differences between regions. An alternative indicator might be the allocation of workers between agriculture, industry, and services, but employment data are not as broadly available as GDP data.
- *Rural to Urban Society:* The extent to which a society has experienced a rural–urban transition is represented by the percentage of national populations that reside in urban areas. This too is an imperfect indicator.

While we expect that differences in the percentage of urban populations between regions reflect differences in the extent of rural–urban migration, the percentage of urban populations also reflects population growth from natural increase and differences in how countries define urban areas (United Nations 2007d).

Much rural migration is circular, particularly on the part of workers who seek incomes to sustain their rural livelihoods and to avoid relocating permanently to cities. Our focus is on those migrants who finally make the transition to cities as a result of social transformations that result from industrialization.

• *High to Low Fertility:* Transitions including increases and then declines in fertility are indicated by the average number of children born to women within the countries of each region.

• *Emigration to Immigration:* The net flow of migration out of and into a country is used to measure the extent to which a country has shifted from emigration to immigration. The net flow is calculated by subtracting the total number of emigrants (citizens and noncitizens) from immigrants and representing the remainder as a negative or positive ratio per 1,000 population in the countries of a region.

In the transition from emigration to immigration, migrants are likely to continue to flow in both directions, but the net direction of the flow will reverse and grow larger. Underlying this transition is a changing balance between the supply and demand for labor that results from a decline in labor market entry of new workers as a result of a fertility decline relative to the increasing demand for workers due to economic expansion.

In compiling United Nations' country data into subregional and regional indicators, we have used United Nations' definitions of regions but in a few instances we have placed countries in different subregions, as indicated, to reflect their close developmental relations (United Nations 2007d:viii–x). Within each region, country data are weighted to reflect national population differences in order to eliminate a disproportionate impact that smaller countries would otherwise have on regional averages.

A comparison of the transition indicators for the world's major regions not only reveals that there are differences in the extent to which each of the four transitions have progressed in each region but also suggests that each transition is advancing in tandem with the others. Regions with the lowest levels of industrialization also experience relatively lower levels of urbanization, higher levels of fertility, and net emigration. As the transi-

Table 1.1   Regional Development and Migration Transitions, 2005

Region	Industrialization: Percentage of GDP from Industry and Services	Urbanization: Rural to Urban Society: Percentage Population Urban	Fertility: High to Low Fertility: Average Number of Childbirths per Woman	International Migration: Emigration to Immigration: Net Migration per 1,000 Population
Africa	74.26	38.46	5.09	−0.53
Oceania	84.54	23.88	4.37	−1.37
Asia	84.81	39.66	2.32	−0.37
Americas	94.43	78.64	2.36	0.68
Europe	95.56	72.21	1.42	1.53
Australia and New Zealand	97.00	87.86	1.85	4.92

Data: Figures for each region are calculated as an average of country data weighted by size of populations.

Sources: United Nations 2006, 2007a, 2007b.

tions have progressed, regions attaining higher levels of industrialization have also experienced relatively higher levels of urbanization, decreasing fertility, and a shift from emigration to immigration. That these processes seem to advance together suggests that their progress may be linked. Nonetheless there are some exceptions to this pattern. Relative to industrialization, the levels of urbanization in Oceania and Europe seem to be lagging, and the level of emigration in Oceania seems accelerated. Further, the regional agglomerations obscure additional variations between subregions and countries.

Breaking down regions into subregions reveals patterns of parallel advancement in transitions of industrialization, urbanization, fertility, and international migration that are similar to those found between regions (see Table 1.2). But, despite this seeming general consistency, which might be taken as consistent with our hypothesis, comparisons within and between regions also reveal exceptions that suggest that factors other than relations between transitional processes might be advancing or retarding some transitions in particular subregions. If so, to what extent might these exceptions invalidate the general hypothesis?

Relative to the levels of industrialization within their respective regions, urbanization seems to have lagged in Western Europe and in East Asia, the latter seemingly a result of Chinese policy restrictions on rural–urban resettlement. Similarly, relative to regional levels of industrialization and urbanization, fertility declines seem to have lagged in West Asia and Central America and declined in European regions to varying extents

Table 1.2 Transitions of Development and Migration in World Subregions, 2005

Region	Industrialization: Percentage of GDP from Industry and Services	Urbanization: Rural to Urban Society: Percentage Population Urban	Fertility: High to Low Fertility: Average Number of Childbirths per Woman	International Migration: Emigration to Immigration: Net Migration per 1,000 Population
Central Africa	69.61	33.39	5.81	−0.25
North Africa	82.73	50.85	3.20	−1.61
Southern Africa	96.04	56.16	3.03	−0.04
Melanesia	84.00	19.33	4.48	−0.91
Polynesia	86.00	43.31	3.26	−6.81
Micronesia	86.15	67.80	3.37	−1.57
South Asia	80.33	30.62	2.97	−0.63
South East Asia	85.10	43.90	2.63	−0.63
West Asia	88.59	64.76	3.11	1.13
East Asia	89.15	44.44	1.40	−0.20
Caribbean	82.81	63.45	2.6	−2.86
Central America	92.77	70.13	3.6	−3.39
South America	91.86	81.71	2.2	−0.57
North America	98.81	80.73	1.95	4.26
Eastern Europe	92.89	68.40	1.26	−0.32
Southern Europe	95.26	66.31	1.35	4.14
Northern Europe	98.50	83.90	1.63	2.46
Western Europe	98.54	76.96	1.61	1.92
Australia and New Zealand	97.00	87.86	1.85	4.92

Data: Figures for each subregion are calculated as an average of country data weighted by size of population within each subregion.

Sources: United Nations 2006, 2007a, 2007b.

not seemingly linked to subregional rates of industrialization or urbanization. Finally, relative to levels of industrialization, urbanization, and fertility decline, the rate of emigration seems to be accelerated in North Africa, Polynesia, and Central America and to be lagging in East Asia. Life fertility, immigration in European subregions, seems to vary in ways not precisely linked to different levels of industrialization, urbanization, or fertility.

To what extent might these variations or exceptions to the general pattern be explained within the logic of our hypothesized causal relations between transitional processes, and to what extent need additional factors be considered?[4] One possibility is that in the sequence of causality, the influence of one transitional process has not yet taken effect on the others, which might then result in what seem to be lags in transitions. An alternative possibility is that effects of one transition on another have been exaggerated and will before too long subside to the mean. Reasons for such lagging or acceleration of transitions might include government policy interventions, such as in China, which seems to have delayed migration, while in the Philippines government promotion of emigration has contributed to that country's currently having the highest rate of emigration in South East Asia. Another reason for differences may be that an international economic division of labor between regional and national economies may affect the nature and extent that industrialization and other transitions have taken place. For example, countries whose industrial development is based on extractive industries, such as mining located in rural areas, may attract labor away from urban centers, while countries with assembly operations in port cities might attract urban concentrations but, because of low wages, end up serving as migrant stepping-stones into higher-paid international labor markets, thus accelerating emigration but not providing an industrial basis for a transition to immigration.

Of course yet another possibility is that these variations indicate that our hypothesis is not theoretically sound. Perhaps transitional processes do not affect one another as posited (e.g., declines in fertility might occur simply as a result of access to birth control devices rather than as a response to the limited incomes of industrial employment and pressures of urban life), or perhaps the causal relations posited are not strong enough to account for differences between countries or subregions (e.g., emigration from Mexico to the United States may be the result of differences in wage levels between the two countries that are unrelated to the penetration of capitalist modes of production and commerce into rural areas and the limits of industrial employment in Mexico's urban centers).

In the following pages we first address the issue of causality between transitional processes on regional and subregional levels and then reconsider the extent to which taking into account forces other than the transitions themselves, such as state policy interventions or the international economic division of labor between regions and countries, might be theoretically useful or necessary.

CAUSAL RELATIONS IN EUROPEAN TRANSITIONS

We turn to Europe in order to examine causal relations between developmental and migratory transitions, as this was the first region of the world to undergo industrialization, which in turn seems to have driven rural–urban migration and urbanization, fertility decline, and a shift from emigration to immigration. Although the penetration of capitalist production and commerce into rural areas began considerably earlier, the mechanization of production in factories at the beginning of the nineteenth century initiated a profound transformation that by the third quarter of the twentieth century resulted in the region's having undergone transitions to an industrial economy, an urban society, a low rate of fertility, and a shift from emigration to immigration. In addition to being the earliest region to complete these transitions, Europe is a key case because European colonization from the sixteenth through the twentieth century spread and intensified capitalist modes of commerce and production that initiated similar socioeconomic transformations in other parts of the world. The uneven temporal and geographic expansion and integration of a global capitalist economy seems to provide a basis for explaining variations in the synchronized advance of transitions in different regions and subregions of the world.

HISTORICAL EVIDENCE

Among a number of recent histories of European migration, that by Leslie Page Moch (2003) most explicitly focuses on the progression and interrelations of industrialization with urban, demographic, and migratory processes. Moch divides this history into four time periods, during which she focuses both on macro-level changes in "fundamental structures" (including particularly landholding, employment, demographic patterns, and the deployment of capital) and on micro-level "individual traits" (such as life cycle stage, class, and gender) that affected the likelihood of a person's or family's mobility. "On the most general level," she wrote in summary, "European mobility exists in a world-system in which Europe exploited human and natural resources beginning in the sixteenth century, acted as an exporter of labor to a world labor market in the nineteenth century, and then imported labor in the twentieth century" (6–7).

Moch's analysis of the "large-scale economic frameworks that circumscribed the limits of the possible" (2003:7) begins with the pre-industrial period (1650–1750), when peasant ownership of land, production for consumption, and relatively low levels of urbanization and fertility prevailed. Although in proposing the idea of a migration transition Zelinsky (1971) had claimed pre-industrial European populations were largely sedentary, Moch clarifies that local migration was more common than earlier believed, particularly for the seasonal employment of men and the marriage of women. But permanent migration to cities, where the mortality rate was high due to disease, was limited. Although fertility rates were quite high, the high rate of mortality kept population growth low (Moch 2003:chapter 2).

During the subsequent period of early industrial development (1750–1815), a "capitalist offensive" by urban merchants introduced small-scale industries to rural villages, including the spinning and weaving of woolen textiles and the manufacture of nails for export. During this period, family economies tended to become "hybrids" dependent on both agricultural and industrial incomes. A decline in mortality, which resulted in part from the diminishment of plagues, and marriages at an earlier age, particularly in areas of rural industry, resulted in the expansion of rural populations, which then exceeded the carrying capacity of farmlands. That many landless workers were able to find employment in rural industries reduced labor mobility in some areas, but in others seasonal migration grew, particularly to provincial urban centers of administration, commerce, and production, where nails, textiles, and other products of rural industries were finished and marketed (Moch 2003:chapter 3).

These seventeenth- and eighteenth-century industrial developments and migration patterns set the stage for the major transformations of the "long nineteenth century" that would result from the mechanization of production and centralization of industry in cities (1815–1915). Technological innovations, especially with steam-powered machinery and rail transport, led to the concentration of production in urban factories and the expanded marketing of industrial commodities across the region. Steam engines replaced manual labor in tasks such as spinning, weaving, and nail making and began the displacement of horsepower in transportation. When applied to the planting, harvesting, and processing of agricultural produce, mechanization undermined family farming. By the 1840s only 21 percent of the rural population was composed of peasants, and 79 percent had become proletarian wage laborers. And the marketing of relatively inexpensive factory goods devastated the livelihoods of rural handicraft and industrial workers, leaving many with little alternative but to leave home to find jobs. Seasonal employment both in mechanized agriculture, such as sugar beet planting and harvesting, and in the construction of railroads, canals, and urban buildings grew and reached a numeric peak by midcentury, but an increasing proportion of workers ended up resettling in industrial and commercial cities, particularly where they could find employment in textile mills and heavy manufacturing. As rural populations declined, the number and size of cities grew, a result primarily but not exclusively of rural–urban migration. Another cause of urban growth was natural increase due to a reduction in urban mortality, which resulted from improvements in sanitation and health care. Between 1800 and 1914, the population of Europe grew by 250 percent, seemingly expanding more quickly than opportunities for industrial employment. Rural families who could not find jobs in local urban centers sought and often found alternative opportunities abroad. By the time World War I cut off European emigration, at least 52 million Europeans had migrated to North America (72 percent), South America (21 percent), and Australia, New Zealand, or other destinations (7 percent)—perhaps the largest human migration up to that point in history.

During and between the twentieth century's two world wars, the trends toward industrialization, urbanization, fertility decline, and both internal and international migration continued, even if disrupted and difficult to discern within the chaos and destruction of war. Employment in industry and related services continued to grow compared to that in agriculture. Even after the majority of most European national populations became urban, rural–urban migration continued, and in some areas rural populations experienced absolute declines. Some urban populations expanded into suburban areas and began to form "megalopolises." Fertility also continued to decline, precipitously during the depression of the 1930s. Although wars and depression reduced European emigration to the Americas to insignificant levels, movement within Europe increased, particularly from Southern and Eastern Europe to Northern and Western Europe, where labor shortages appeared. When labor shortages persisted, Western European countries began the transition from net emigration to immigration, first recruiting and then attracting workers from outside the European region. By the mid-1970s over 8 million foreign workers and family members had immigrated to Northwestern Europe.

In sum, the contribution of this history to identifying and clarifying causal relations between European development and migration transitions derives primarily from its analysis of the sequential effects of industrialization on urbanization, population, employment, and internal and international population movements over nearly two centuries. First the displacement of family agriculture and rural handicrafts by industrialization spurred rural–urban migration. Then, although as much as 25 percent of Europe's labor force may have emigrated to the New World, the majority of migrants resettled permanently in European cities, contributing significantly to Europe's urbanization by the end of the nineteenth century. During the nineteenth century increasing numbers of births and improved health care contributed to population increase, urbanization, and emigration. But during the twentieth century the fertility of women declined to below population replacement levels, and by the 1970s employers were facing labor shortages. With rural areas depleted of a sufficient supply of potential migrants, workers were recruited from abroad, particularly from Turkey and North Africa, and European countries began the transition from emigration to immigration.

Notably this sequence of development and migration transitions did not take place simultaneously or uniformly throughout the region but rather began and progressed first in Western and Northern Europe, and then began to take place in Eastern and Southern Europe. Indeed after World War II but before they became destinations of net immigration, Italian, Spanish, Portuguese, and other Southern and Eastern European workers sought employment in Northern and Western European countries. Today, workers from Poland, Albania, and other Eastern European countries continue to emigrate to Western Europe in search of employment. We propose that uneven timing in the introduction and disruptions of industrial production and the circulation of commodities across Europe explain, for the most part, differences in the extent of progression of developmental and migratory transitions between European subregions as reflected in Table 1.2.

DEBATES OVER CAUSALITY

Although our reading of Europe's history of developmental and migratory transitions posits that they were causally interrelated and driven primarily by industrialization, this interpretation is contested by some demographic and economic historians. For example, in analyzing their remarkable compilation of four centuries of European migration data, which show that between 1750 and 1800 and 1850 and 1900 rural-urban migration increased more than 20-fold and emigration from the continent increased nearly 10-fold, Jan and Leo Lucassen (2009:354–56, 359–63, 374) contend that industrialization did not transform the "underlying structural causes of migration" but only accelerated a process that had begun as early as the sixteenth century. While this interpretation seems to ignore Europe's qualitative socioeconomic transformation in the shift from mercantile to industrial capitalism, they say the nineteenth century's dramatic increase in permanent resettlement, compared to the predominantly temporary and circular migration of earlier centuries, was only a quantitative extension of migrants' horizons made possible through the advent of cheaper and faster transportation. Whether part of a quantitative or qualitative transformation, the key question remains: what were the "underlying structural causes" of nineteenth-century European migration?

Debates over the nature of structural causes have largely focused on the relative importance of labor market "push" and "pull" factors. Although Dudley Baines (1995) has helpfully suggested that the two explanations need not be mutually exclusive, neither provides a regionally comprehensive explanation that accounts for internal as well as international migration. Kevin O'Rourke and Jeffrey Williamson (1999) argue that European migrants were attracted to the New World by its relatively higher wages rather than driven by industrialization. After massive migration flows from Europe to the New World, the wage gap slowly narrowed and movement diminished in the twentieth century, they contend, as part of a convergence between the European and North American economies—a result not only of the labor market effects of the migrants themselves but also of international trade and capital transfers within the "Atlantic economy."

Arguing against pull theories of migration, John Bodnar points out that "if immigrants were simply being drawn to America without any compelling reasons for leaving except impoverishment or relative economic advantage, then we would expect to see certain similarities between countries" (1985:3). Examining local rather than regional or subregional histories, he documents in considerable detail not only that migration flows began at different times from different villages, towns, provinces, and countries but also that migration streams from separate areas went through a similar pattern of small beginnings, middle peaks, and declines, which were independent of the American economy. His argument holds that both internal and international migrants were displaced by the same processes of agricultural commercialization, industrialization of commodity production, and population growth.

Preoccupied with international migration, these push or pull theories offer no explanation of why nearly half of nineteenth-century European migrants chose to settle within European urban centers rather than emigrate abroad. International migration data compiled by Imre Ferenczi and Walter F. Wilcox (1929–31) indicate that at least 52 million Europeans emigrated from Europe between 1860 and 1914, but the average number of

Europeans living in cities between 1801 and 1850 and 1851 and 1900 also increased by nearly 50 million people, largely as a result of rural–urban migration (Lucassen 2009:359–361). Other than to point out that rural populations closer to European cities tended to migrate internally and those farther away tended to go abroad, Moch (2003) does not specifically address what shaped migrants' choice of destinations. Focusing on Britain and the United States, Brinley Thomas (1954) proposed that the locations to which migrants were attracted alternated between the two countries as a result of inversely articulated cycles of economic expansion and contraction. That is to say, as capital investments moved back and forth across the Atlantic and created alternating sites of economic opportunities, migrants chose to move accordingly. But even if Thomas were correct that capital and migration flows were cyclically coordinated between Britain and the United States during the second half of the nineteenth century, that a similarly close integration existed between U.S. and other economies would seem unlikely in general. Indeed P. J. O'Leary and W. Arthur Lewis (1955) were unable to find similar economic linkages between the United States and other European countries experiencing internal and international migration during the same time period.

More than other economists in this debate over the causes of migration, Richard A. Easterlin (1961) sought to take into account factors related to urban and fertility transitions. He explored how per capita income, which he took to be an indicator of economic opportunities in Europe, and natural population increased together and affected emigration. He found that, as a secular trend between 1841 and 1910, high levels of international migration from Europe were significantly associated with low per capita income and high rates of natural population increase, while low levels of emigration occurred in association with high per capita incomes and low rates of natural population increases. One possible interpretation of these findings is that workers facing competition for low-wage jobs in Europe chose to emigrate abroad, where they were likely to find better opportunities, while workers experiencing less competition and with access to higher wages tended to choose to stay in Europe. Although Easterlin thought there was insufficient evidence to explain why European migrants would choose between settling in European or American cities, Baines (1995) has pointed out that many international migrants, the majority in some countries, emigrated from urban centers of Europe where internal migrants of childbearing age had earlier settled, had children, and contributed to the growth of the next generation of urban working populations, which then exceeded what local industrial employment could absorb. But the effects of urbanization and initially high fertility on nineteenth-century emigration reversed during the twentieth, when the fertility decline resulted in a shortage of workers and a growing demand for immigrant labor.

Finally, in considering alternative theories of development and migration in Europe, we turn to the issue of the temporal and geographic scales on which explanations have been sought and claimed to have validity. Moch's (2003) history of European migration is unique in focusing on both the processes and time period (1800s–1970s) that embrace the development and migration transitions on which we are focused. Klaus Bade's (2003) history of European migration encompasses the same time period, but focuses more on the role of states and migration policy than on the economic and social processes underlying migration. Because most of the migration researchers cited here were primarily interested in explaining European emigration to the New World, their temporal scope was for the most part limited to the period between 1840 and 1910, when most of the movement occurred, a period too short to take fully into account the progression and interrelations between development and migration transitions.

Within this short temporal limitation, Easterlin (1961) grappled more explicitly than others not only with factors related to development and migration transitions but also with geographic scales and differences between regional, subregional, and country levels of analysis. Stressing the provisional nature of his data and findings, Easterlin expressed confidence in the secular association of international migration with low per capita earnings and high rates of natural population increases for Europe as a whole between 1840 and 1910. But he drew this broad regional conclusion from country-level data that showed wide variations in rates of migration, per capita earnings, and natural population increase. He took these national variations to reflect the uneven extents to which economic transformation had taken place in each of Europe's subregions. Citing Simon Kuznets (1955, 45–46),[5] Easterlin pointed out that variations in "the national origins of the European flow into the United States, in the succession from British, to the German, to the Scandinavian, and then to the South and Southwestern European, reveal the progressive impact of the dislocation in Europe produced by changes in agriculture and by industrialization" (1961:338).

Although causal relations between European development and population movements will no doubt continue to be debated, we believe that this discussion at the least justifies continuing research and analysis of developmental and migratory transitions, between the times that they begin and conclude, as a means by which to further identify the explanatory contributions of a macrostructural approach. That Easterlin found quite consistent patterns in relations between migration, per capita income, and population increase between countries of different European subregions suggests that future analyses of subregional transition data might find similar consistencies on a country level. But Easterlin also found national exceptions, which required explanations that went outside of his theoretical framework. For example, to explain why Russia experienced the lowest rate of emigration of all European countries despite its relatively high rate of population increase and low per capita income, Easterlin pointed to the country's extensive internal frontier, which gave migrants alternatives to emigration, and to legislative restrictions that discouraged emigration. Regardless, he provides a country-level comparative framework that might prove useful with analyses of transitions within broader subregions and regions.

WORLD-SYSTEMS AND TRANSITIONS

Aspects of economic development that suggest European developmental and migratory transitions are relevant to other regions of the world include, first, the introduction and incorporation of all world regions into the global capitalist sphere through European colonization and, second, the resulting, continuing, and intensifying interrelations between development processes in different regions of the world. Unfortunately, theoretical accounts of development and migration on a global scale have for the most part been elaborated independently of one another. Because examining the histories of transitions in each world region, even to the limited extent to which we have been able to consider the European case, lies well beyond the scope of this essay's initial exploration, we instead sketch here part of a macrostructural theoretical foundation on which such a future interpretive investigation might be built. This review focuses particularly on world-systems theories of development and of migration, which, although developed independently, might be brought together to better understand relations between development and migration transitions. Our goal here is to begin outlining a macro-level theoretical synthesis that can guide future international investigations and interpretations of the uneven progress and interrelations between developmental and migratory transitions.

THE WORLD CAPITALIST SYSTEM

The macro-level approach most often cited by migration analysts as contributing to an understanding of relations between migration, or at least international migration, and development is "world-systems theory" (e.g., Massey et al. 1999; Herrera Carassou 2006),[6] the initial formulation of which was lead by Emmanuel Wallerstein. But Wallerstein's analysis of world-systems generally and, more specifically, of the world capitalist system does not "systematically" address migration, which is perhaps a result of how he interprets the spread of capitalism. In explaining his approach, Wallerstein described the post-sixteenth-century world-system as capitalist and defined capitalism by its "priority of *endless* accumulation" (2004:92, emphasis in the original). As Charles Tilly (1984:127) points out, Wallerstein's (1974–1989) histories of capitalism emphasize accumulations taking place through unequal exchange between the core, semiperiphery, and periphery societies that together constitute the world capitalist system, and within this focus on trade of goods, migration has a relatively minor role. Nonetheless, by beginning his history of the capitalist world-system with fifteenth-century Europe's mercantilist global expansion, Wallerstein points to the crucial contribution that the accumulation of capital from the periphery, whether through unequal exchange or other processes, made to amassing assets that financed Europe's subsequent industrialization, an aspect of the European experience not considered in our earlier account of European development and migration transitions. Wallerstein's histories also raise the question to what extent the drain of wealth from the periphery to the center may have altered or slowed development and migration transitions in peripheral regions.

Other analysts of world capitalism have similarly given only limited attention to migration. Rather than unequal exchange, Eric Wolf (1982) emphasized the role of the mode of production in capitalist accumulation. As a result, he was more inclined to give attention to the organization and exploitation of labor—through slavery, indenture, and the free labor market—as part of the spread of capitalist enterprises not only in European factories but also overseas in mines and plantations. But it was Thomas Hylland Erikson's (2010) foreword to a recent edition of Wolf's history, more than Wolf himself, who pointed to the importance and possibility of incorporating world migration, past and present, more fully and systematically into Wolf's analytic framework. Pursing a more explicitly neo-Marxist approach, David Harvey combines both exchange and production in his interpretation of accumulation within capitalism, which he suggests not only survives through but might also be defined as "unequal global development" (2006:115). But even within Harvey's geographical interpretation of the role of labor in the development of global capitalism, he elaborates a relatively abstract model that gives more consideration to the function of exchange and labor than to the systems of global trade and migration, whether internal or international, by which migrant laborers in different regions become incorporated into capitalist production.

THE WORLD MIGRATION SYSTEM

In contrast, historians of world migration have tended to approach migration so comprehensively with regard to time span, geography, and types of movement as to diffuse their ability to establish strong theoretical or analytical links with the causes, structures, and processes of development. In his history of human migration spanning the departure of *Homo sapiens* from Africa 200,000 years ago up to the present, Patrick Manning suggests that, in comparison to the migration of other animals, the long-term dispersion, differentiation, and interactions between human populations generated a "remarkable social evolution" and social convergence (2005:12). To understand the shorter-term impact of migration on development, which he defines broadly as "transformation in human society," Manning provides a model of a "simplified set of circumstances" in which group or individual migrations at different stages of social evolution have enabled societies to adapt to natural resource imbalances. Even though Manning's historical elaboration of this model enables him to identify patterns of migration and development during specific time periods, to the extent that he specifies how this development model applies to migration since 1700, its general focus on adaptation enables a more descriptive narrative of processes and outcomes than an explanation of relations between development and migration.

In addition to the challenge of taking on a broad temporal and geographic scope, histories of world migration tend to encompass a multiplicity of forms of movement whose very diversity defies coherent macro-level explanation. Dirk Hoerder's (2002) compendium covering ten centuries of world migration, for example, takes up a somewhat bewildering array of movements, both local and long-distance, which result from slavery, crusades, conquest, itinerancy, job seeking, marriage, religious pilgrimage, colonization, persecution, trade, disease, nation building, imperialism, and more and which elude a common macro-level explanation. Hoerder seeks to escape this difficulty by proposing a "societal frame of reference" through which he focuses on how people make decisions to migrate in different circumstances (2002:15). As he explains, his analytic focus is primarily on the "meso-level" and on "individuals making conscious choices about perceived opportunities." This "holistic material-emotional approach" to migrants' agency complements but leaves unexplained the macro-level origin and nature of structures and processes that create the opportunities between which migrants choose.

Adam McKeown's (2004) account of the growth of global migration from 1846 to 1940 addresses two central macro-level analytic issues of world migration history: the "periodization" of, and "segmentation" between, migration systems. He argues that an increasingly integrated global economy dominated by European, American, and Japanese industrialization provided the context for the similar and linked intra- and interregional migration flows of Europe, Asia, Africa, and other parts of the world. Although McKeown views industrialization as a driving force in shaping nineteenth- to twentieth-century world migration, he does not analyze the relation between industrialization and migration much more than to note that "migration facilitated more industrial expansion, which encouraged more migration" (166). Although McKeown cites the industrial origin of the world economy in order to criticize exceptionalist views of Asian migration (e.g., of Hoerder [2002] and Williamson [2005]) and to establish the basis of comparability between Eastern and Western migration systems, he also argues that a global history of migration must also recognize not only the independent involvement of non-Europeans in the expansion and integration of the world economy but also the processes of regional "regulation and intervention by which global migration has come to be segmented into distinct systems" (2004:171). As an example, he argues that the integration of South East Asian Chinese and Indian migrants into the world economy as "middlemen" entrepreneurs was the result of regional policies that protected "natives" from exploitative "aliens" rather than integrated migrants into society as citizens, which has generally (though not always for Asians) been the goal of the American immigration policies. But, in the end, although McKeown views the segmentation between world migration systems to be a "structural aspect of the larger global political economy and political intervention" (2004:177), he argues, as do the other historians considered here, that it is primarily micro-level investigations of family networks that provide "keys to understanding broad global patterns of migration" (2008:178).

SYNTHESIS

Perhaps reflecting his view that geography is one of the "great synthesizing" disciplines, the analyst who has most explicitly sought to use a world-systems approach to explain the relation between development and migration has been the geographer Ronald Skeldon (1997). His framework comprises spatial divisions within the global economy, which he labels "development tiers," each of which has a different productive base: primary agricultural or extractive activities, labor-intensive industries, capital-intensive industries, or knowledge-based industries. These development tiers are not coterminous with regions or nation-states, as they tend to be concentrated within rural or urban sectors that constitute only a part of a national territory or that span national borders, an example of the latter being the "blue banana" development corridor that extends across the economic heartland of seven European nations. Skeldon views the global relations between development tiers as dominated by a "system of nested urban hierarchies," with global financial centers, such as New York, London, and Tokyo, standing at the apex and, as a result of 150 years of their extending economic investments and trade across the globe, penetrating less powerful and more peripheral and less dominant urban economic cores located farther down the hierarchy. Skeldon characterizes each tier of this "archipelago" with regard to differences in the centralization of their economic activities and the size and direction of their migration flows.

Skeldon describes the world migration system as both forming and reflecting links between tiers of the global economy during three periods of time over the past 150 years: 1820 to World War I, when the world economy was shaped by colonialism and dominated by the British Empire; from World War I until post–World War II, when mass migratory movements were driven by catastrophes of economic depression and war; and between the 1960s and the present, when decolonization and the consolidation of the world global economy became the context for more diverse and complicated world migration. In summary, through this history countries constituting the "old core" of the world economy in Europe, the Americas, and Australasia were joined by a "new core" located primarily in Asia, and together they became recipient regions of net immigration. Skeldon describes three additional "expanding cores" that are either "extensions" of the core economies (e.g., the *maquiladora* assembly plants built in Mexico by U.S.-based companies), "potential" cores of developing areas, or "restructuring" cores, such as the separate areas formed by the breakup of the Soviet Union. All of these expanding cores are characterized by their mixed flows of both emigration and immigration. Finally, he categorizes areas that offer labor or natural resources to the other core tiers as "frontiers," which are characterized as areas of net emigration (see Table 1.3).

This table's schematic summary of Skeldon's analysis of world economic and migration systems somewhat misrepresents its intended contribution, which is to employ a variety of theoretical perspectives in order to analyze variations and nuances in the relations between development and migration both within and between the development tiers in different parts of the world—an approach that is preoccupied more with interpreting particular places and circumstances than in building or testing an abstract theoretical model. As Skeldon puts it, referring to Charles Tilly's (1984:146) strategies of analytic comparisons, rather than building a universal model:

> The concern in this book is much more with accounting for difference—the variation-finding comparisons that "help us make sense of social structures and processes that never recur in the same form, yet express common principals of causality" . . . [and] to account for the variations in migration from one part of the world to another, encompassing both internal and international movements and covering both more developed and less developed parts of the world. (1997:13)

The "principals of causality" that Skeldon employed in his analyses of development tiers and migration systems included the same notions of development and migration transitions that are the focus of this chapter. But what Skeldon did not look for or expect to find was a sequential pattern of causal relations between development and migration transitions that would progress consistently between and within development tiers. Explaining that his prior work may have "overemphasized universal models at the expense of variation" (1997:13), he states that his current goal is not to formulate or test a universal model or macro-level theory but rather to explain systemic patterns of contemporary migration within and between specific economic contexts. Capturing a key difference between the conceptual and analytic approaches of systems- and model-based ap-

Table 1.3   Development Tiers and Migration Patterns

Tiers	Locations	Economy	Population and Migration
Old core	Western Europe, North America, Australasia	Knowledge-based industries	Urban decentralization; immigration
New core	Japan, Taiwan, Hong Kong, Singapore	Capital-intensive and service industries	Urban decentralization; immigration
Expanding core	China, Malaysia, Thailand, Brazil, Argentina, Venezuela, Mexico, India, Israel, South Africa, Central Asia	Labor-intensive industries	Urban centralization; immigration and emigration
Labor frontier	Latin America, Caribbean, Southern Africa	Agricultural and extractive industries	Urban centralization; emigration
Resource niche	Brazil, East and West Africa, Asia	Peasant agriculture and craft production	Decentralization and centralization; emigration/ immigration and emigration

Source: Skeldon 1997.

proaches, he summarizes his overall conclusions regarding migration thus: "There are transitions in mobility, but not in the sense that all societies are moving uniformly through a sequence of stages. . . . Rather, the transitions are constant shifts in the pattern of mobility that are related to other broad changes in economy and society. These shifts are systematic but not uniform in time and place" (1997:195).

In contrast to Skeldon's goal of identifying and explaining regional differences, our similar but somewhat more abstract preoccupation is first to identify and explain the extent to which uniformity in interrelations between patterns of development and migration transitions do exist and then, after determining the limits of that similarity, to identify those factors that can account for differences. Here we draw from the work of Skeldon and other world-systems analysts in formulating a macro-level model, a theory of progressive causation, and a method to evaluate their limits in global application.

Although world-systems theorists have examined development and migration processes separately, their perspectives offer guidance in advancing the synthetic approach begun by Skeldon. Global economy analysts, such as Wallerstein, Wolf, and Harvey, have aided our efforts by formulating theories to explain the origins and dynamics of a world capitalist system, particularly in identifying evolving processes of capital accumulation that have driven relations between the core and peripheral areas that today constitute migration-receiving and -sending countries. Historians of migration systems, such as Manning, Hoerder, and McKeown, confirm the necessity of understanding the evolution of world migration over long stretches of time, but our own approach to periodization would be based on the beginnings, turning points, and conclusions of interrelated transitional processes rather than on fluctuations of migration flows alone. In linking world-systems approaches to development and migration, Skeldon clarifies the importance of examining how different types of economies underlying development provide a basis for explaining differences between patterns of migration. Finally, the world-systems approach emphasizes the importance of examining relations between both developmental and migratory transitional processes not only between but also within regions and subregions of those broader systems.

FUTURE RESEARCH

In seeking to build the basis for a theoretical explanation of what seem to be recurring sequential patterns in development and migration transitions, which are reflected in regional and subregional indicators, we have examined their history and causal relations within Europe. Then, to explore the extent to which the European experience might be relevant to other regions of the world, we turned to world-system theorists and discovered that those who focus on capital accumulation as the driver of the global economy's expansion and development and those who focus on patterns and differences between migration systems do not yet seem to take into account one another's perspectives. Finally, we found that, although Ronald Skeldon has proposed an initial synthesis between world development and migration system approaches, his focus on identifying and explaining variations in migration patterns within and between different development tiers differs from our own goal of formulating causal model of relations between development and migration transitions that would focus on the extent of universality typically accorded to each transition separately.

The foregoing discussions raise questions regarding conceptual and empirical issues that researchers will have to address in the future in order to formulate a macro-level model and theory and test to what extent it can explain relations between development and migration transitions in different regions of the world. These issues include refining concepts and measures of development and migration transitions, assessing the influence of an evolving international division of labor between regions, taking into account the impacts of state development and migration policies, and distinguishing migration driven by industrialization or development from other types of migration.

Further, any future endeavor to address these difficult questions should be emboldened by Tilly's (1984) endorsement of researchers' taking on "big structures" and "large processes" and employing all four of his strategic methods of "huge comparisons" over time and space. In Tilly's terms, comparing Europe with other regions would provide a basis for both "individualizing" the European case and for "universalizing" the extent to which the model is consistently applicable in other regions. Similarly, comparisons between regions, subregions, countries, and sectors within countries should provide a basis for "variation finding," particularly with regard to the progression of development and migration transitions in each region. Finally, "encompassing" comparisons of transitions as part of an international division of labor within the histories of the global economy and world migration systems might also provide a basis for interpreting variations between them. In recommending Tilly's approach to strategic comparisons between long-term processes, we do not propose research that would focus exclusively on contemporary indicators of transitions; rather we envision research that would take into account regional and temporal differences in the initiation and progression of each transitional process.

1. REFINING TRANSITION INDICATORS HISTORICALLY AND GEOGRAPHICALLY

The conceptual basis for selecting indicators in order to document and compare development and migration transitions in different parts of the world should and can be sharpened. The advantage of the existing definitions and indicators employed above lies largely in their simplicity, but there are likely other data that can be employed more insightfully but equally simply. For example, to measure the transition from agricultural to industrial economies, it might be more helpful to use the number of workers employed in agriculture and industry rather than the percentage of GDP derived from each sector. The sectoral allocation of laborers instead of GDP would seem more pertinent for comparison with the indicators for the other transitions, which refer similarly to the movement and social behavior of people: internal and international migrants, mothers and babies. Using workers' employment as an indicator would also open the possibility for exploring gender differences. We would have used employment data here, but we found available sources to be inconsistent and incomplete compared to GDP data.

One of the fundamental questions raised by the regional and subregional transitions data presented in Tables 1.1 and 1.2 and that a comparative analysis should address is why transitions take place at different times and at different rates in different parts of the world. Addressing this question would be possible were we able to construct sequential regional data that would indicate the initiation and progression of development and migration transitions over time. Our interpretation of regional differences using contemporary data is based on an assumption that regional differences reflect different stages in the temporal progression of transitions. The validity of this claim rests largely on whether the indicators across all four transitions vary in tandem with one another, which suggests that they are causally linked. We have sought to demonstrate there are indeed causal links between transitions by examining the progression of European transitions over nearly two centuries and by arguing that the process of industrialization that drove the European transitions subsequently both penetrated other subregions of Europe and other parts of the world through European colonialism. Finally, we hypothesize that the consolidation of the world economic system and the different timing with which trade, technologies, investments, markets, and production systems spread to different regions across the globe can account for the different rates of progress in transitions in different areas. If so, why did the development and migration transitions, which began about 1800 in Europe, reach conclusion 175 years later while similar processes, which began in South Korea in the 1950s, are now reaching a similar conclusion only sixty years later? (DeWind et al. 2012). Whether the answer is that a faster pace through transitions is resulting from combined and uneven development within a world economic system is an issue that can best be addressed through comparative historical and regional analyses.

While our tables indicate there is correspondence between the European-based model and transitions in other regions, this consistency breaks down when similar indicators are examined on a country level. In examining intraregional transitions, future research should examine whether each of the countries comprising a region are appropriate units of analysis. That available data are produced nationally reflects administrative not analytic priorities. As Skeldon (1997) points out, national borders may incorporate local areas that are each undergoing different stages of transition and national borders may bisect and obscure cross-national or regional processes.

Ideally, perhaps, the geographic unit of analysis would combine the boundaries of development and migration systems. To establish the appropriate geographic scale for any particular case, it would be necessary to refine indicators based on national data to take into account variations in transitions over time and within varying geographies, such indicators for the depletion of rural migrant stock, ratios between the growing demand for industrial workers and the declining rate of population growth, or the shifting composition of immigration and emigration flows. As posed here, however, the causal relations between industrialization, rural–urban migration, urbanization, fertility decline, and the shift from emigration to immigration are only generally formulated. Comparative case studies of appropriate geographic units of analysis can identify commonalities and differences in the progressive stages of transitions as they lead to outcomes that are similar to or different from the overall averages of the broader regions within which they are located.

Where to draw the boundaries of development regions that should become the focus of international comparisons is not obvious. The extent to which the regions within which the United Nations classifies economic and social data are related to development and migration transitions is not obvious. As a result of European colonization, should the North African subregion be analyzed as part of Europe or should North Africa be considered part of the Middle Eastern or sub-Saharan Africa regions? The same question might be asked of most other subregions listed in Table 1.2 and the countries within them. Further complicating these questions, U.N. regional data are based on national sources, but we have already seen in Skeldon's identification of development tiers that individual countries, subregions, and regions often include a mix of productive systems, each with different impacts on rural–urban migration, urbanization, fertility, and international migration. Pragmatically, however, research that is intended to inform policy making by necessity has to analyze development and migration within nationally based regions. Because India and China are so large, do nationally based analyses between internal areas make more sense than in smaller countries? Development and migration

processes differ not only within but also between countries. The economies and migration systems of a city-state, such as Singapore, or of other
largely urbanized states that lack rural hinterlands, such as the oil-rich
Gulf states, are best understood when delimited regionally rather than by
national borders. Perhaps the best way to define the regional boundaries
of development and migration transitions for comparative purposes is on
the basis of combining trade and production with migration networks
that world-systems analysts have sought to identify and suggested evolve
together over time (e.g., Skeldon 1997 and Kritz et al. 1994).

2. ASSESSING THE INFLUENCE OF THE INTERNATIONAL ECONOMIC DIVISION OF LABOR

For Tilly, an "encompassing comparison" is one that examines similarities
and differences between processes and structures as they are affected by
being part of a larger whole (1984:125). How regional migration and development transitions are related as a result of their place in the global economy
is an issue that requires further research. In his critique of theories of the
New International Division of Labor, the migration sociologist Robin
Cohen (2006) adds a historical dimension in order to recognize shifts in
the hegemony of different types of capital over time: mercantile, industrial, imperial, and, most recently, transnational. Cohen argues that, following the post–World War II collapse of the European colonial systems,
changes in the international economic order were reflected in the assertion of competitive transnational capital found in the centralization of
global cities within advanced economies, the relocation of industrial production to newly industrializing regions, the rise of energy-rich economies, and the specialization of more slowly developing countries in providing labor to the centers of growth of more advanced economies.

The cases that Cohen describes to illustrate this new economic order
suggest ways in which a country's role in the international economy can
affect patterns of migration and shape the trajectory of development and
migration transitions. In global cities of de-industrializing advanced
economies, such as New York and Los Angeles, the expansion of financial
enterprises, information-based industries, and the service sector has increased the demand for unskilled and skilled workers, for which local,
industrially trained blue- and white-collar national workers have not been
sufficiently available. The shift of export-oriented manufacturing to Asian
countries created a demand for labor that exceeded the supply of local

rural–urban migrant workers and created a demand for immigrant workers. Without having to go through a process of industrialization, OPEC countries used oil money to launch urbanization projects that exceeded the supply and training of local workers and led to large-scale immigration. These shifts in international production and growth created demands for labor that attracted workers from surrounding regions and across the globe. For many less quickly developing countries in Asia, Latin America, and Africa, but notably the Philippines, one of their key roles in the international economy has become exporting migrant workers.

Within a similar international framework, Bruno Losch (2009) argues that today the primarily agricultural economies of sub-Saharan Africa, the transforming or mixed economies of Asia and South East Asia, and the relatively more highly industrialized economies of Latin America must each cope with "confrontation effects" of competing in global markets on the basis of regional inequalities and policies that can alter the pace or direction of their developmental and migration transitions, though perhaps in complementary ways. He argues, for example, that in the coming decades the continuing population growth within the agricultural economies in sub-Saharan Africa will exacerbate already difficult problems of urbanization without industrial employment. But at the same time, population declines in Asia during rapid industrial growth, particularly in China, largely a result of China's one-child policy, will create a demand for workers that at some point in the not-too-distant future could potentially be filled by the migration of unemployed African workers. Our point is not so much that any particular historical or contemporary scenario may become enacted but rather that the future course of regional developmental and migratory transitions will be shaped by their integration into an evolving world economic order.

While the internationalization of labor markets may facilitate regional complementarities between development and migration, Cohen points out that they would not be the result of the "law of comparative advantages" of free markets, as proposed by David Ricardo in the nineteenth century when state policies played a relatively minor role in regulating international trade. The economist Ha-Joon Chang (2002) goes further to argue that today's advanced economies, which climbed to world market dominance through their earlier industrialization, have now "kicked away the ladder" that would enable other economies to reach advanced industrial development as well. In other words, the imposition on developing countries of orthodox policies and institutions that were the result, rather than the cause, of industrialization now limits the possibility of less developed countries' following similar paths of development. But international investment and trade policies are only part of the influence of states that researchers need to consider when investigating contemporary development and migration transitions. Chang's examination of the limiting effects of contemporary policy restrictions on developing countries' economic growth does not take fully into account the impact of restrictions on labor migration flows, an aspect of international development that has been pursued particularly by political scientists but has not been adequately integrated into economic development studies.

3. TAKING INTO ACCOUNT THE IMPACT OF NATION-STATES AND POLICIES

Our model of development and migration transitions and their history in Europe might seem to suggest we believe that those processes take place independently of political context, but this is not the case. States have clearly taken important roles in promoting industrialization (or deindustrialization), managing rural–urban resettlement, reducing fertility, and controlling immigration. That different national development strategies have different effects on migration has been outlined by Alejandro Portes (1982). States' ability to delay rural–urban migration and affect fertility rates is illustrated dramatically in China by the effects of *hukou* restrictions on rural migrants' access to social services in cities and in limiting births to one child per family (Cai and Wang 2008). Although early nineteenth-century migration within and out of Europe may have taken place without significant policy restrictions, since that time governments have increasingly imposed controls over international movement to suit national economic needs and political priorities (e.g., Zolberg 2006).

Nonetheless the extent to which any particular state might either have wished or been able to alter the relationship between development and migration transitions over extended periods of time is an empirical question that must be addressed case by case. Regardless, consolidation of nation-states across the globe over the past two centuries and their growing assertion of control, individually and collectively, in managing processes of development and migration (e.g., note the now annual meetings of states in the Global Forum on Migration and Development) suggest that the impact of state policies needs to be taken into account in explaining common patterns and inconsistencies in the relations between development

and migration. De la Garza (this volume) argues that the relationship between migration and development is not much mediated by states' direct
involvement in shaping the relationship between migration and development, which may be practically impossible due to states' constraints in
influencing economic variables. Political variables, de la Garza argues,
are far more important policy tools that states may use to shape the
development-migration nexus.

To the extent that states seek to promote national economic development, along with political scientist James Hollified (2008), we hypothesize
that, over the long term, it is in the interest of states to seek, whether
through laissez-faire or positive legislation, a balanced progression between
development and migration. If so, to the extent that industrial development
is desirable, it would be in states' interest to promote transitions that would
be consistent rather than conflict with the transitional patterns we have already identified as having taken place in Europe.

4. IDENTIFYING TYPES OF MIGRATION LINKED TO DEVELOPMENT

Studies of migration theory typically begin with a comprehensive categorization of different types of migrants whose movements they then are
under some obligation to explain. Typical has been the typology devised
by Tilly (1978) in his account of the history of European migration and
that has frequently been adopted not only by historians but also by other
social scientists (e.g., Moch 2003; Skeldon 1997). While Tilly focused on
what he found to be the most frequent types of voluntary migration—
local, circular, chain, and career—he also recognized the significance of
other types of movement, such as coerced and colonizing migrations, and
the possibility of basing typologies on varied criteria. The distinctiveness
of Tilly's typology was that he resisted adopting the administrative categories of migrants created by state bureaucracies for the purpose of managing population movements and favored analytic categories that recognize the geographic or social distance that migrants travel and the extent
to which their movement either extends or breaks social ties between migrants and their networks of families and friends whom they leave behind, whether temporarily or permanently.

Although each of Tilly's types of migration has some relation to processes of development, they are not all equally pertinent to development
and migration transitions. Circular movement for employment is clearly

responsive to the changing location of job opportunities related to development, but among rural populations, it reflects attempts to sustain rurally based lives and resist the fundamental dislocations and transformations of industrialization. In the history of development and migration transitions, it is the migrants who adopt permanent rural–urban resettlement as part of urbanization that are of greatest significance. Similarly, colonizing migrants, who resettle as pioneers in undeveloped territories (often available through the displacement of indigenous populations), are not particularly relevant to the transition from agricultural to industrial economies and urbanization. The coerced flight of refugees from European nations from the sixteenth through the eighteenth century was more the result of processes of social and cultural homogenization related to the building of nation-states than of economic and social transitions of industrialization and urbanization, even though these political and economic processes were related to one another (Zolberg 1983). The massive coerced movement of enslaved peoples from Africa was, at least in the Americas, clearly a response not only to the labor needs of colonial plantation agriculture, which supplied growing urban consumer markets in Europe, but also to the unavailability of local free labor. Crucial as slavery may have been in facilitating the beginnings of capitalist industrialization (Williams 1944; Potts 1990), it was not directly driven by the imperatives of industrialization, urbanization, or fertility decline in Europe. Nonetheless the relation between voluntary and involuntary migrations within the broader context of European colonial expansion and development merits reexamination.

Within Tilly's typology, then, the chain and career migration of voluntary migrants—free laborers for the most part—are the two forms of movement that are most clearly integral to development and migration transitions. But in the future other forms of migration also need to be taken into account. First, as the most advanced economies become based increasingly on information rather than industrial technologies and on employment in the service sector, it will be important to consider not only unskilled but also skilled migration, including that of technicians, managers, executives, professionals, and entrepreneurs. While the highly educated may today constitute only 10 percent of international migrants, they are key to the elaboration and growth of information-based industries and services related to health, education, and commerce in both migrant-sending and -receiving societies. According to the economist Andres Solimano (2010:112), the migrations of contemporary skilled and unskilled workers are likely to follow capital, but whether the relation of both types of migration to development transitions is similar has not yet been empirically or theoretically resolved. Second, the economic ties that transnational migrants and diasporas establish with their homelands, not only through their transferring remittances, investments, and technology but also by opening new and diversified markets, need to be taken into account in order to understand how development and migration are related to one another in international markets. The extent to which these or potentially other types of migrants should be considered pertinent depends on the centrality of their roles in facilitating development transitions.

It was perhaps the great diversity of migrants that migration scholars typically identify as the subject of their field of study that led Portes (1997) to warn against attempts to develop a grand theory of migration. Seeking to explain the relationship between development and migration on the basis of transitions may still require a theory of "big structures" and "large processes," but by focusing on those migrants who are most directly affected by and contribute to such transitions, assessing the significance of macro-level economic and social structures and processes seems a more feasible, though still challenging, undertaking.

CONCLUSION: PROCESS AND OUTCOMES

Macro-level theories of migration have been relatively weak in explaining human movement compared to meso-level theories that largely focus on migrant families and networks across sending and receiving areas and to micro-level theories that focus on the choices and behavior of individuals. Typically surveys and evaluations of migration theory endorse approaches on all three levels of analysis as being necessary for a full understanding of migration, but despite the recognition of the importance of the social structures, large systems, and long processes that shape migrants' motivations and options, macro-level theories are typically used primarily to frame questions but not to answer why and how specific groups migrate from one specific place to another at a particular time.

Focusing on the relation between development and migration transitions highlights some of the theoretical problems of intellectual scope facing the field of migration studies. One problem is that migration scholars tend to focus on trying to explain migration exclusively. That is to say, by beginning with migration defined as the object of study, analysts are tempted to look so comprehensively at the variety of forms of human movement that a meaningful common explanation becomes virtually impossible and is replaced by narrative descriptions of people, places, and periods based on concepts and categories that lack explanatory power. An opposite problem has been that migration studies has also focused too narrowly on specific types of migrants, often on the basis of categories that are perhaps helpful to government administrators but not analytically helpful. The separation between research on internal and international migration flows is a key example. Related, as analysts define migration as their object of study, explaining migration alone becomes the end rather than the means of understanding movement in relation to social context. Examining the relations between development and migration helps resolve these problems by specifying a focus on those internal and international migrants who are similarly driven by processes of development and for whom migration is an adaptive response to social transformation. A macro-structural approach seeks to understand that relationship as the subject of study rather than just migration itself.

Our goal in focusing on the relation between development and migration transitions has been to assess the appropriate temporal and spatial dimensions for understanding how structural transformation in economic and social development are causally linked to processes of internal and international migrations. In this exploration we have identified a two-hundred-year-long relation between development and migration transitions in Europe driven by industrialization. The next step in this project is to determine to what extent similar causal relations and outcomes are repeated in other regions of the world. Such an undertaking will require refinements in current formulations of regions of development, systems of migration, and interregional economic and political relations. Further, it is not entirely obvious how nationally based indicator data can be aggregated to analyze relations between systems of development and migration that are not congruent with the borders of national states. Delineating the contours of interregional economic and migration systems and analyzing their relations with one another remains both a conceptual and empirical challenge.

To the extent that a macro-level approach focuses on creating a model of relations that can be used to explain and predict broad, or even universal, patterns of development and migration transitions, the more likely it will be unable to contribute precisely to more nuanced understandings necessary to explain fluctuations and differentiations in these processes within local circumstances and shorter time periods. In the end, the strength of such a macro-level approach will in part be determined by whether the questions that it raises but cannot answer about development and migration can be answered in conjunction with complementary meso- and micro-level theories and research. Our goal here has been to define more precisely what macro-level approaches can offer to this joint enterprise.

REFERENCES

Abella, Manolo, ed., 1994. "Turning Points in Migration," a special issue of the *Asian and Pacific Migration Journal*, Vol. 3, no. 1:1–202.

——.1999. "Development and the Migration Transition." In *International Migration, Development and Integration: Towards a Comprehensive Approach*, edited by Kristof Tamas and Malin Hansson. Stockholm: Regeringskansliet, Ministry for Foreign Affairs.

Bade, Klaus J. 2003. *Migration in European History*. Oxford: Blackwell.

Baines, Dudley. 1995. *Emigration from Europe 1815–1930*. Cambridge: Cambridge University Press.

Bodnar, John. 1985. "Homeland and Capitalism." In *The Transplanted: A History of Immigrants in Urban America*. Bloomington: Indiana University Press: pp. 1–56.

Cai Fang and Wang Dewen. 2008. "Impacts of Internal Migration on Economic Growth and Urban Development in China." In *Migration and Development Within and Across Borders: Research and Policy Perspectives on Internal and International Migration*, edited by Josh DeWind and Jennifer Holdaway. Geneva: International Organization for Migration.

Castles, Stephen. 2009. "Development and Migration—Migration and Development: What Comes First?" In *Migration and Development: Essays on Future Directions for Research and Policy,* edited by Josh DeWind and Jennifer Holdaway. New York: Social Science Research Council. Accessed online: http://essays.ssrc.org /developmentpapers/wp-content/uploads/2009/08/2Castles.pdf.

Castles, Stephen, and Mark J. Miller. 2009. *The Age of Migration: International Population Movements in the Modern World*. 4th ed. London: Palgrave Macmillan.

Chang, Ha-Joon. 2002. *Kicking Away the Ladder: Development Strategy in Historical Perspective*. London: Anthem Press.

Cohen, Robin. 1987. *The New Helots: Migrants in the International Division of Labor*. London: Avebury.

——. 2006. *Migration and Its Enemies: Global Capital, Migrant Labour and the Nation-State*. London: Ashgate.

de Haas, Hein. 2010. "Migration and Development: A Theoretical Perspective." *International Migration Review* 44, no. 1:227–64.

DeWind, Josh, and Jennifer Holdaway, eds. 2009. *Migration and Development: Essays on Future Directions for Research and Policy*. Geneva: International Organization on Migration

DeWind, Josh, Eun Mee Kim, Ronald Skeldon, and In-Jin Yoon. 2012. "Korean Development and Migration." In *Journal of Ethnic and Migration Studies* 38, no. 3:371–88.

Easterlin, Richard A. 1961. "Influences in European Overseas Emigration Before World War I." *Economic Development and Cultural Change* 9, no. 3:331–51.

Erikson, Thomas Hylland. 2010. Foreword to *Europe and the People Without History*, by Eric R. Wolf. Berkeley: University of California Press.

Ferenczi, Imre, and Walter F. Wilcox. 1929–31. *International Migrations*. Vols. 1–2. New York: National Bureau of Economic Research.

Handlin, Oscar. 1973. *The Uprooted: The Epic Story of the Great Migrations That Made the American People*. 2nd ed. New York: Atlantic Monthly Press.

Harvey, David. 2006. *Spaces of Global Capitalism: Towards a Theory of Uneven Geographical Development*. London: Verso.

Herrera Carassou, Roberto. 2006. *La perspectiva teórica en el estudio de las migraciones*. Mexico City: Siglo Veintiuno Editores.

Hoerder, Dirk. 2002. *Cultures in Contact: World Migrations in the Second Millennium*. Durham, NC: Duke University Press.

Hollifield, James. 2008. "The Emerging Migration State." In *Rethinking Migration: New Theoretical and Empirical Perspectives*, edited by Alejandro Portes and Josh DeWind. New York: Berghahn.

Kritz, Mary, Lin Lean Lim, and Hania Zlotnik, eds. 1992. *International Migration Systems: A Global Approach*. Oxford: Clarendon Press.

Kuznets, Simon. 1955. "Toward a Theory of Economic Growth." In *National Policy for Economic Welfare at Home and Abroad,* edited by Robert Lekachman. Garden City: Doubleday.

Losch, Bruno. 2009. "Migrations and the Challenge of Demographic and Economic Transitions in the New Globalization Era." In *Migration and Development: Essays on Future Directions for Research and Policy,* edited by Josh DeWind and Jennifer Holdaway. New York: Social Science Research Council.

Lucassen, Jan, and Leo Lucassen. 2009. "The Mobility Transition Revisited, 1500–1900: What the Case of Europe Can Offer to Global History." *Journal of Global History* 4:347–77.

Manning, Patrick. 2005. *Migration in World History*. New York: Routledge.

Massey, Douglas S. 1988. "Economic Development and International Migration in Comparative Perspective." *Population and Development Review* 14, no. 3:383–413.

——. 1999. "Why Does Migration Occur? A Theoretical Synthesis." In *The Handbook of International Migration: The American Experience*, edited by Charles Hirschman, Philip Kasinitz, and Josh DeWind. New York: Russell Sage Foundation.

Massey, Douglas S., Joaquin Arango, Graeme Hugo, and Ali Kouaouci. 1999. *Worlds in Motion: Understanding International Migration at the End of the Millennium*. New York: Oxford University Press.

McKeown, Adam. 2004. "Global Migration, 1846–1940." *Journal of World History* 15, no. 2:155–89.

Moch, Leslie Page. 2003. *Moving Europeans: Migration in Western Europe Since 1650*. 2nd ed. Bloomington: Indiana University Press.

O'Leary, P. J., and W. Arthur Lewis. 1955. "Secular Swings in Production and Trade, 1870–1913." *Manchester School of Economic Studies* 23 (May), 113–52.

O'Rourke, Kevin H., and Jeffrey G. Williamson. 1999. *Globalization and History: The Evolution of a Nineteenth Century Atlantic Economy*. Cambridge, Mass.: The MIT Press.

Petras, Elizabeth McLean. 1981. "The Global Labor Market in the Modern World Economy." In *Global Trends in Migration: Theory and Research on International Population Movements*, edited by Mary M. Kritz, Charles B. Keeley, and Silvano M. Tomasi. Staten Island, N.Y.: Center for Migration Studies.

Portes, Alejandro. 1985. "International Labor Migration and National Development." In *U.S. Immigration and Refugee Policy*, edited by M. M. Kritz. Lexington, Mass: Lexington Books.

——. 1997. "Immigration Theory for a New Century: Some Problems and Opportunities." In *Immigrant Adaptation and Native-Born Responses in the Making of Americans*, edited by Josh DeWind, Charles Hirschman, and Philip Kasinitz. Special issue of *International Migration Review* 31, no. 120:799–825.

Potts, Lydia. 1990. *The World Labour Market: A History of Migration*. London: Zed Books.

Pritchett, Lant. 2006. *Let Their People Come: Breaking the Gridlock on Global Labor Mobility*. Washington, D.C.: Center for Global Development.

Skeldon, Ronald. 1990. *Population Mobility in Developing Countries: A Reinterpretation*. London: Wiley.

——. 1997. *Migration and Development: A Global Interpretation*. London: Longman.

Solimano, Andres. 2010. *International Migration in the Age of Crisis and Globalization*. New York: Cambridge University Press.

Thomas, Brinley. 1954. *Migration and Economic Growth*. London: Cambridge University Press.

Thomas, Dorothy. 1941. *Social and Economic Aspects of Swedish Population Movements: 1750–1933*. New York: Macmillan.

Tilly, Charles. 1978. "Migration in Modern European History." In *Human Migration: Patterns and Policies*, edited by William McNeil and Ruth Adams. Bloomington: Indiana University Press.

——. 1984. *Big Structures, Large Processes, Huge Comparisons*. New York: Russell Sage Foundation.

United Nations. 2007a. *International Migration 2006*. United Nations Population Division. Accessed online: http://www.un.org/esa/population/publications/2006Migration_Chart/Migration2006.pdf.

——. 2007b. *Urban Population, Development, and the Environment 2007*. United Nations Population Division. Accessed online: http://www.un.org/esa/population/publications/2007_PopDevt/Urban_2007.pdf.

——. 2007c. *World Fertility Patterns 2007*. United Nations Population Division. Accessed online: http://www.un.org/esa/population/publications/worldfertility2007/Fertility_2007_table.pdf.

——. 2007d. *World Urbanization Prospects, 2007 Revision Highlights*. United Nations Population Division. Accessed online: http://www.un.org/esa/population/publications/wup2007/2007WUP_Highlights_web.pdf.

Wallerstein, Emmanuel. 1974–89. *The Modern World-System*. Vols. 1–3. New York: Academic Press.

——. 2004. *World Systems Analysis: An Introduction*. Durham, N.C.: Duke University Press.

Williams, Eric. 1944. *Capitalism and Slavery*. Chapel Hill: University of North Carolina Press.

Williamson, Jeffrey G. 2005. *The Political Economy of World Mass Migration: Comparing Two Global Centuries*. Washington, D.C.: AEI Press.

Wolf, Eric R. 1982. *Europe and the People Without History*. Berkeley: University of California Press.

World Bank. 2006. "Economic Implications of Remittances and Migration." In *Global Economic Prospects 2006*. Washington, D.C.: World Bank.

Zelinsky, Wilbur. 1971. "The Hypothesis of the Mobility Transition." *Geographical Review* 61:219–49.

Zolberg, Aristide. 1983. "The Formation of New States as a Refugee-Generating Process." *Annals of the American Academy of Political and Social Sciences* 467 (May):24–38.

——. 2006. *A Nation by Design: Immigration Policy in the Fashioning of America*. New York: Russell Sage Foundation and Harvard University Press.

CHAPTER 2

The Impact of Migration on Development

EXPLICATING THE ROLE OF THE STATE

Rodolfo O. de la Garza

Dominant current analyses do not accurately conceptualize the role the state plays in linking migration and development. This is because dominant analytical modes define development in terms of increases in economic characteristics such as gross national income, gross domestic product, or family income. This approach understates or ignores other societal characteristics that influence overall societal well-being, i.e., levels of societal development.

The argument developed here is that development should be understood as progress (Stiglitz 2009:27) and therefore should be defined in terms of changes in economic, social, cultural, and political arenas. The multidimensional perspective presented here argues that changes in these characteristics determine development levels. Therefore to understand how the state influences development it is necessary to examine the consequences of migration as affected by state policies in each of these societal subsections. Furthermore, I argue that the state is more constrained in managing key economic variables than it is in shaping political characteristics that shape economic, social, and cultural characteristics. Therefore political variables are more important policy tools that national governments may use to effect national development than are economic factors.

The chapter begins with a discussion of the demographics and motives of migrants. I then examine migration's economic effects. The third and fourth sections focus on the social and cultural impacts of migration, and the final section targets the link between politics and migration. The conclusion restates the argument regarding the major role that politics plays in the relationship between migration and development.

MIGRANTS: NUMBERS, DISTRIBUTION, AND MOTIVATION

To understand the potential impact of migration on development it is important to know how many international migrants there are, where they go, and the human capital they embody. Currently the United Nations estimates the total number of migrants to be approximately 3 percent of the world's population. This figure is probably a low estimate, as it does not include undocumented immigrants in the United States or the European Union.

Migrants tend to move to proximate states. This is seen in south–south migration as well as in south–north movement, which is roughly similar. In East Asia, South Asia, and sub-Saharan Africa, for example, more than two-thirds of emigrants from poor countries migrate to a poor country in the same region (Page and Plaza 2006:261). Nonetheless migration to industrial countries steadily increased between 1970 and 2000 (Page and Plaza 2006:248–49), but measuring movement between developed and developing countries is difficult because both are labor-sending and -receiving areas, with outflows out of and inflows into Europe and North America and inflows into the Arab Gulf region (Page and Plaza 2006:248–49) and because states vary in how they define *foreign-born*. This is most clearly illustrated in the historical examples of Germany and the colonial experiences of France. In both cases, Germans and French born outside their states' European boundaries were considered native-born citizens upon entering their ancestral homelands. Currently countries granting dual citizenship, such as Spain and Mexico, which grant citizens born abroad citizenship based on familial emigration histories, also blur distinctions between native-born and foreign-born.

The increasing number of undocumented migrants suggests that the number of migrants with low levels of human capital continues to increase, although existing estimates are unreliable (NFIB 2001; Jandl 2003; Martin 2004; Spencer 2004 in Page and Plaza 2006:253). On the other hand, overall trends seem to suggest that the number of skilled migrants has also increased dramatically over the past four decades (UNCTAD 1975; Docquier and Rapoport 2004a, 2004b in Page and Plaza 2006:257). As DeWind and Ergun (this volume) and others (e.g., van Naerssen et al. 2006) argue, different migration categories, whether skilled, less-skilled, voluntary, or forced, will have distinct impacts on development; whether these impacts produce similar developmental externalities is an empirical as well as a theoretical question yet to be answered.

Why does migration occur? Reasons may include positive or negative changes in the economic, social, cultural, or political characteristics of sending states. Each of these may reflect subjective factors, such as the desire for a better, more secure livelihood, a stable society, and transparent democratic elections, or objective issues such as wage differentials, market failures, low income and productivity, unpredictable political processes, and unreliable community environments suffering from institutional corruption (Nyberg-Sørenson et al. 2002; Taylor et al. 1996).

Although migration is associated with efforts to escape poverty, violence, or sociopolitical instability, it often is spurred by positive changes in the national environment, economic development (Massey et al. 1998), or by state initiatives such as enacting dual citizenship laws and institutionalizing programs to serve emigrants, as is particularly evident in Mexico, Ecuador, and Colombia, that are designed to facilitate maintaining links between migrants and the sending state. Migrants thus are not usually the poorest of the poor, nor are they likely to live in isolated places disconnected from world markets (Nyberg-Sørenson et al. 2002:51). Instead they frequently come from regions undergoing economic and sociopolitical transformations that generate increased transnational contact, production, and trade (Olesen 2002:140). Such changes can lead to improved personal resources and greater aspirations that increase the likelihood of more migration. Thus in the short or medium term, economic and sociopolitical improvements may stimulate an increase rather than a decrease in emigration (de Haas 2007b:819).

MIGRATION AND ECONOMIC DEVELOPMENT

Even though development may be defined in economic, social, cultural, or political terms, I focus here on the economic impact of migration on development because this is the perspective that has dominated analyses. Throughout the 1950s and 1960s, theorists argued that through a large-scale capital transfer and industrialization, migration would allow poor countries to jump on the road of rapid economic development and modernization (de Haas 2007a:3; OECD 2007a). In the 1970s and 1980s, this theory was displaced by a historical, structuralist view that argued pessimistically that migration sustains or even reinforces problems of underdevelopment (Almeida 1973; Lipton 1980; Reichert 1981; Rhoades 1979; Rubenstein 1992; Binford 2003 in de Haas 2007a:4). The current dominant perspective, known as the New Economics of Labor Migration (NELM), links causes and consequences of migration more explicitly and maintains that migration can have both positive and negative developmental consequences. This opens the door to analyses of how states influence migration's impact on economic development. This perspective takes into account household dynamics (Stark 1978, 1991), risk-sharing (Stark and Levhari 1982), and overcoming market inefficiencies (Stark 1978, 1991; Stark and Levhari 1982; Taylor 1999; Taylor 1986; Taylor and Wyatt 1996 in de Haas 2007a:5–6). Such evaluations conclude that migration has had a "mixed, but generally positive" impact on economic development (de Haas 2007a:4).

The lack of a clear definition of *economic development* has influenced the evolution of this debate. The conventional criteria used for assessing economic development—increased income, poverty reduction, and improvements in living standards—are vague and can lead to contradictory research results. To overcome such problems, I use a more cogent conceptualization that defines economic development in terms of wealth production and creation that is not dependent on income from remittances (Ellerman 2005).

Remittances to developing countries reached approximately $406 billion in 2012 (World Bank 2012), constituting the largest potential source of funding for economic development in migrant-sending states. However, regardless of the total value in remittances that a state might receive, these funds alone cannot save a strapped economy. They cannot independently generate economic growth or statewide sustainable development nor can they independently trigger economic growth or solve structural problems that stifle economic development, such as bad economic policy controlled by corrupt and unaccountable officials and high levels of economic and social insecurity (Page and Plaza 2006:251–52, 261). As argued by Martin (this volume), economic development instead hinges on government policies and the economic climate across nations, especially in those areas that send migrants, as well as conditions in countries hosting immigrants. If sending countries stabilize politically and economically and growth begins, migrants are likely to be among the first to recognize and leverage the resulting new opportunities, thereby reinforcing growth through investment and circular migration activity, bringing them home to their origin countries (NFIB 2001; Jandl 2003; Martin 2004; Spencer 2004 in Page and Plaza 2006:253; UNHCR 2008).

Remittances can contribute to national economic well-being in a variety of ways. For example, they can affect markets in countercyclical ways. In so doing they can help stabilize an economy spiraling out of control. This was the case during the financial crises in Mexico in 1995 and in Indonesia and Thailand in 1998. The stability provided by remittances may also lessen the probability that investors, anxious in this type of climate, simply pull out their money. However, the 2007 financial and economic crisis proved that when such a crisis is global, remittances' buffering role to absorb income shocks is not so evident (Cortina 2011). Furthermore countries with bad credit ratings are in a position to use future hard currency receivables, such as remittances, as a means of letting investors circumvent sovereign credit ratings (UNCTAD 1975; Docquier and Rapoport 2004a, 2004b in Page and Plaza 2006:257). Still, there is no consensus on the effect remittance-based income has on societal well-being, and controversy remains regarding the overall economic effects these capital flows pegged to migration have on labor-exporting countries and on migrant-producing communities (Cortina and de la Garza 2004; Cortina et al. 2005; de Haas 2007a:25).

Claims that remittances influence economic development are supported by evidence suggesting that these funds are responsive to real exchange rate changes, but results examining whether remittances negatively affect exchange rates are inconclusive. In general, remittances do seem to offer a more stable and sustainable source of income than more volatile sources of foreign exchange such as agricultural exports such as coffee, vegetables, and flowers. Remittances thus tend to protect people to some degree from the destabilizing effects of poorly functioning markets, inept economic policies, and a lack of state-provided social security (de Haas 2007a); however, the degree of protection will depend on the magnitude and where the destabilizing effects are felt simultaneously (Cortina 2011).

Large, sustained remittance inflows can theoretically cause an appreciation of the real exchange rate, whereas the empirical evidence documenting adverse effects of large inflows of foreign exchange is scarce, and it is even scarcer in relation to remittances (El-Sakka and McNabb 1999; Glytsos 1998, 1999 in Page and Plaza 2006:281). However, if the exchange rate is overvalued, migrants send goods rather than cash (Rajan and Subramian 2005 in OECD 2007b:87). Nonetheless a long-term impact of exchange rate appreciation on growth depends more directly on structural economic shifts and the extent to which these affect remittances, savings, investment, and productivity (Page and Plaza 2006:281). Furthermore much of the theoretical and empirical literature regarding the impact of the so-called Dutch disease on growth, which can be stimulated by remittances, relies on externalities such as the loss of technological mastery in manufacturing, especially in nontraditional exports. But this topic remains largely unexplored in the literature (Page and Plaza 2006:281). Finally, the research largely endorses the finding that immigration increases bilateral trade flows (Gould 1990, 1994; United Nations 2004; Light et al. 2002 in Page and Plaza 2006:298–99). This may be because migration helps provide the information businesses in sending countries needed to stimulate trade (Rauch and Trindade 2002 in Page and Plaza 2006:299). Migration may also generate linkages between retailers in sending countries and consumers in communities of destination. Overall the evidence supports that remittances benefit the economies of sending countries. As is subsequently discussed, however, the extent to which state economic policies can influence remittance levels is limited.

The impact migration has on a state's labor market is unclear. Case studies suggest it contributes to reduce unemployment and increase wages (Lucas 2005:150). There is also evidence, however, indicating that the departure of high-skilled workers can stifle employment opportunities for low-skilled workers remaining at home. When departing workers are easily replaced, i.e., when the labor market is slack, emigration does not cause a loss in output or a rise in wages. This is the case in Bangladesh, India, Indonesia, and Sri Lanka. When there is a tighter market with fewer workers, wages tend to rise. This is the case for the skilled construction workers of the Philippines and for those in Pakistan who emigrate to oil-producing states in the Arabian Gulf.

Remittances are intended primarily to support families the migrants leave behind. These monies are part of household strategies designed to diversify familial sources of income and provide additional funds for ongoing expenses. The evidence indicates that this objective is largely realized (Cortina and de la Garza 2004). However, while remittances reduce the depth and severity of poverty by raising household income among those who receive them, their overall effects are not distributed evenly across their countries of origin because migrants are not a representative cross-section of a given country's population (Cortina et al. 2005). Nor is the income distribution of migrants representative of national income patterns (Page and Plaza 2006:281). This is because neither the poorest nor the richest migrate, and the number of lower-income migrants greatly exceeds the number who are wealthy. From an economic perspective, however, lower-skilled migration has a greater impact on reducing poverty among remittance recipients than migration does among more skilled workers, because low-skilled individuals send funds to lower-income households for which remittances are a more vital component of income.

Despite their limited impact, remittances do reduce poverty (de Haas 2007a:25). Nevertheless the impact is mediated by the multiple definitions of *poverty* (Cortina and de la Garza 2004). At the macro- or national level, studies involving 101 countries from 1970 to 2003 found a link between poverty reduction and remittances, regardless of whether poverty was measured in terms of personal income or in terms of national income gaps (Spatafora 2005 in Page and Plaza 2006:284). Similarly, a study using a cross-country data set for seventy-one developing countries shows that official international remittances, i.e., those tabulated by central banks, reduced poverty in the developing world. While this analysis noted that officially tabulated remittances in South Asia have no statistical impact on the level and depth of poverty, it found that when estimating the combined value of official remittance totals and estimates of "unofficial" remittances, the level of poverty in the region was in fact reduced (Munzele 2005 in Page and Plaza 2006:284). Studies focusing on Ghana (Quartey and Blanson 2004 in Page and Plaza 2006:285), Guatemala (Adams 2004 in Page and Plaza 2006:285), Uganda, and Bangladesh show similar results. The size of the poverty-reducing impact of remittances varies across countries, however.

At the household level, the impact of remittances on development and the alleviation of poverty vary with how these monies are spent. Because remittances are mostly used by families to purchase food and clothing and to cover other basic needs, there is little evidence that remittances substantially enhance economic growth (Schiff et al. 2007:6).

Nonetheless migration's impact, including that of remittances, on household production in the sending countries depends on how much the migrant contributed to the overall household income before migrating and while at home. Initially migration is more likely to have a negative than a positive economic effect, since the absence of the migrant is likely to produce small, if temporary, production loss and the migrant is unlikely to immediately earn enough to be able to afford remitting (Taylor et al. 1996:408).

On the other hand, studies since the 1990s suggest that households receiving remittances have a higher propensity to invest than nonmigrant households, when controlling for income and other relevant variables

(Massey et al. 1998; Adams 1991; Taylor 1999; Woodruff and Zenteno 2007; de Haas 2006 in de Haas 2007a:14). Also, ample evidence exists showing that remittances promote conditions amenable to self-employment and increase investment in small businesses (de Haas 2007a:14), which are conducive, eventually, of economic growth. Furthermore, although existing research tends to promote the negative view that remittance-based consumption has little impact on development, there is evidence that the "multiplier effect" of local expenditures funded by remittances provides nonmigrants with jobs and income in the short term (de Haas 2007a:16). It must be noted, however, that what it does not do is generate long-term investments that fund economic development (Alper and Neyapti 2006 in de Haas 2007a:14).

In part, this is because the multiplier effect of productive investment of remittances is constrained by the production capacity available in local communities (OECD 2007b:86). These include poor public services, inadequate infrastructure, and the lack of functioning credit markets (Taylor et al. 1996:403). Further complicating an assessment of the effect of remittances on economic development are the different criteria for determining productive investment, as well as varying value judgments about good uses of money (Taylor et al. 1996:403; de Haas 2007a:17).

How do constraints on production affect migration? If they are truly constrictive, the incentive for migration will be greater and the indirect effects of remittances on family income can be substantially large. In other words, if citizens resort to migration as the most viable economic strategy, the impact of remittances could be very consequential. This is illustrated in research that shows that, at the local level, remittance-induced investment will magnify the positive effects of migration on community income in the long run (Taylor et al. 1996:407). But an important caveat here is that such benefits come at considerable human sacrifice and can have especially negative consequences for children left behind. Furthermore remittance-based economic opportunities and productive investment potentials are often exaggerated. These positive outcomes are more likely to occur if conditions are in place to produce an agenda that benefits both migrants and the state (Nyberg-Sørenson 2007:201). One such condition might be migrant demand for country-of-origin goods and services that, if supplied to countries of destination with large country-of-origin populations, would create the necessary economic infrastructure for influencing state policy, corporate capital, and small-scale business involvement in the participating countries in ways that might benefit send-ing communities. A prime example of such a condition being met is Co-rona beer. Corona's popularity in the United States began with marketing to Mexicans in the United States (Willis 1999). Another example is handi-crafts production in rural Mexico, which expanded to meet migrant de-mand in the United States (Mummert 2001). Two other cases are La Ta-pachulteca, a Salvadorian supermarket chain, which found success in Los Angeles (Guarnizo 2003:683), and La Michoacana markets in Houston.

Migration and remittances do not automatically lead to increased in-equalities between the developed "core" and the underdeveloped "periph-ery," as "dependency" critics have argued historically. Instead the impact of migration on income inequality varies according to the type and the length of migration (de Haas 2007a:12). If migrants are from poorer households, remittances contribute to increasing family income and re-ducing inequality; if remitters are from wealthier households, inequality is likely to increase. There can, however, be indirect effects that occur as a result of various consumption and investment patterns (de Haas 2007a:12). In the short run, remittances can increase inequalities, but such a result is mitigated over time by the development of migrant networks that allow poorer individuals and families to migrate. Their departure increases the average income of those poor families that stay behind and receive remit-tances. Also, in the medium- and long-term migration helps to reduce the proportion of the population living in poverty (Taylor et al. 1996:408).

Another type of migration-based economic effect is the consequence of migration-related brain-drain and brain-gain. Sometimes they occur si-multaneously, and sometimes one wins out over the other. For example, approximately one-third of the most qualified African nationals have settled outside their country of origin; in Mozambique, Ghana, and Tan-zania, almost half of the highly skilled workers in the population leave (World Bank 2000 in Davies 2007:60; Dumont and Lemaitre 2005 in Davies 2007:60). While these numbers point to the devastating effects of brain-drain, it is important to view them in the context of short-term negative effects and the long-term effects of the emigration of the highly skilled, which are often more positive, particularly if these migrants be-come well integrated into the receiving countries and develop economic and knowledge ties to their communities of origin (de Haas 2007a:22).

The contradictory effects of migration on a nation's human capital brain-drain and brain-gain are well established. Brain-drain negatively impacts society by reducing the cadres of a nation's educated and skilled professionals in virtually all fields, which weakens the economy and leads to losses in taxes, corporate earnings, and foreign investment. By contrast, brain-gain produces benefits through knowledge infusion afforded by returnees and networks developed in receiving countries. It also prompts prospective migrants to invest more in education, which will help them get better jobs in their home countries as well as result in better preparing their children for better jobs at home or in the countries to which they might migrate in the future (Page and Plaza 2006:292–93). New data further suggest that in large countries such as Brazil and China migrant networks contribute to brain-gain when they include a large number of relatively well-educated migrants (OECD 2007a:2; Hugo in this volume).

Overall, brain-drain and brain-gain effects seem to hinge on employment opportunities at home. From this perspective, underdevelopment as manifested by limited economic opportunities is a cause more than a symptom of brain-drain (OECD 2007a:2). This suggests that brain-gain occurs when a community is predisposed toward improving its human capital rather than relying on remittances or on returning migrants who have acquired improved skills (Stark 2005:138). Creating such conditions requires stable and accountable policies rather than a particular type of economic regime. Absent the former, the latter cannot be realized (see Martin this volume).

Diasporic communities create networks that often link emigrants socially, economically, and politically to their communities of origin as well as to their conationals in host countries. The trust and solidarity that characterize such communities are limited in developmental impact, however, given that social capital generated by networks generally pertains to the marshaling of resources rather than generating resources (Portes and Landolt 2000:546).

The size of these networks depends on what their common interest is. For instance, the diasporas of Korea, Taiwan, India, China, and Israel, which have well-functioning networks grounded in technology, involve around two hundred members (Pack 1993; Saxenian 2005; Arora and Gambardella 2004; Commander et al. 2004 in Page and Plaza 2006:296). However, generating economic success in developing countries on the basis of technology-based networks remains challenging in that creating a critical mass of skilled and influential participants within any given sector is by no means guaranteed (Page and Plaza 2006:297). Yet these networks have real potential, as evidenced by the Colombian diaspora in the United

States, which has developed organizations and commercial fairs with construction firms to purchase land and build homes for left-behind families and their future retirement (Gomez 2008). Emigrant Africans, by contrast, do not enjoy the same diasporic cohesiveness. While evidence suggests that Africans maintain fragmented and personal links with the continent, such bonds are not strong enough to generate a vibrant diasporic identity with positive developmental ramifications (Davies 2007:72). Furthermore much of the literature on home country relations with its diaspora ignores the potential negative consequences of these networks and home country ties in that it tends to confuse the ability to get resources with the resources themselves (Portes and Landolt 2000:532).

As this section documents, migration affects economic development in a variety of ways. However, its impact is mixed. Most noteworthy is that migration-based remittances, which are the funds states look to finance economic development, contribute so little to immediate economic growth. Indeed the major economic benefit resulting from remittances is the gain in the formation of human capital, which in turn will contribute to economic growth. This is a long-term result, however, and its ultimate effect is open to question for two reasons. First, many of the children who experience such educational gains become migrants when they become adults and thus may contribute more to receiving states than to their countries of origin. Second, the social and psychological trauma experienced by children left behind may prove more damaging than the value of the enhanced education they receive.

Remittances do contribute to reducing poverty among those who receive them, but there is little evidence that such reductions lead to permanent improvements in their standard of living. This is because the great majority of these funds are used for personal consumption rather than for investments in productive activities. The multiplier effect of such expenditures is thus low.

One of the major economic benefits generated by migration through well-established diasporic networks probably results from increased international business ties. These derive from links between home-country businesses and migrant consumers and because of the expertise migrants develop that may benefit the home country and from economic activities initiated by return migrants.

Clearly, from the state's perspective, the economic benefits of migration are tenuous. Remittances, the most important source of funds, are not used to fuel economic development. Moreover they are completely dependent on individual decisions that are in almost all cases beyond the state's control. Human capital formation, which remittances likely fund, often is used to benefit individuals who become migrants and thus does not directly benefit communities of origin. States thus cannot depend on migration to stimulate economic development (also see Martin in this volume for a discussion focusing on Asia).

MIGRATION AND SOCIAL DEVELOPMENT

As indicated previously, migration has the potential to significantly affect social development, which is a key component of overall societal development. Its impact, however, varies with how *social development* is defined. I conceptualize it as the improvement of a wide range of characteristics related to the quality of life of most members of a society. This section examines the impact of migration on health, gender roles, family dynamics, and children's well-being.

Migration is linked to a variety of health outcomes. Case studies of Mexico and Central America (Cortés 2007b) indicate that remittances enable children, especially younger ones, to have greater access to health care (Kanaiaupuni and Donato 1999). Nonetheless negative effects on children's health in general are linked to the early years of parental migration, when family disruption may be at its zenith. The negative health impacts include psychological disturbances (Fletcher-Anthony 2008; see Escobar García and Álvarez Velasco in this volume for a discussion on the impact of parental migration on children left behind for the case of Ecuador) and increased risk of sexually transmitted diseases contracted from returning migrants (Cortés 2007b).

Migration's impact on gender roles depends on patterns in both sending and receiving communities. Although migrants can be exposed to new gender roles, exposure does not automatically result in structural changes to traditional gender roles or to patriarchal customs (King et al. 2006; Hampshire 2006; Taylor 1984; Day and Içduygu 1997 in de Haas 2007a:20; Levitt and Lamba-Nieves this volume). Although migration may positively boost self-esteem and sociopolitical empowerment among women and provide them with new labor market experiences, such benefits must be evaluated in the context of the major caretaking role mothers generally occupy in developing-country households. Moreover, when fathers migrate, life may go on with relatively little disruption for the children. If fathers do not send remittances, their absence becomes more significant. Even when they do remit, their relationship to their children may be severely damaged. Children often define their father's love in terms of the money they receive from him (Fletcher-Anthony 2008). When mothers migrate, however, the family often experiences major disruption, especially if fathers are derelict in assuming broad parental responsibilities. This pattern helps explain how children left behind perceive their parents (Fletcher-Anthony 2008). As shown by Escobar García and Álvarez Velasco (this volume) for the case of Ecuador, young children may become resentful of their migrant mother, who they perceive as not caring for them given her remote status, and of their father when he fails to provide financially for them (Dreby 2008). Nonetheless women whose husbands migrate are particularly affected by migration. Migration's effects depend on a variety of factors that are less significant to men, including gender roles, family organization and cultural practices, and informal institutions that are more rigid for women than for men (Schiff et al. 2007:2–4).

Thus while women migrants often experience empowerment in the form of greater physical and financial independence (OECD 2007b:77), shifts in gender roles are not necessarily positive, as the emotional and physical burdens of increased responsibilities can be substantial. In the long term, however, there may be gains for women through human capital formation, labor market experiences, and expanded roles as decision makers, etc. (de Haas 2007a:20). It should be noted that left-behind men don't always take on traditional roles fulfilled by women, especially domestic responsibilities. Instead they sometimes turn to the extended family for help, regardless of their ability to do the work (Cortés 2007a), creating new responsibilities for extended family members and reshaping the social exchanges among the community (see Escobar García and Álvarez Velasco this volume).

Migration's impact on families and children varies according to the conditions under which the migration occurs. Effects are positive where remittances reduce the effects of poverty or abuse (Gavriliuc et al. 2006). They are especially useful in enabling children to attend better schools (Bryant 2005:5). The overall effect of migration on educational attainment, which is funded primarily by remittances, is mixed. It is evident that migration has a beneficial impact on all key measures of educational attainment, but the results vary by gender and show that girls benefit more than boys in certain contexts (Özden and Schiff 2007:6). On the other hand, children left behind by migrating parents who are not able to financially support them over a long period of time experience psychological problems and often are treated as burdens to their caregivers. In such situations, the feeling of emotional and economic deprivation puts them at a disadvantage relative to children raised in a traditional family (Gavriliuc et al. 2006:21). The problems for children of migrants do not end there, however. Older relatives who often become caregivers can have difficulty effectively communicating with children under their care, which is crucial to providing emotional support. These effects on children are exacerbated by tense relations with peers who resent the benefits they gain from remittances and by community organizations that view these remittance-endowed children as more privileged. It must be noted, however, that these problems are evident in both migrant and nonmigrant households (Bryant 2005:7).

Because of the absence of parental supervision, children of migrant parents are often underprotected or forced to assume adult responsibilities they are not ready to handle. This frequently results in their being less engaged in school and other negative consequences (Cortés 2007a). Younger children face the highest risk of psychological trauma, and their problems tend to be exacerbated by the behavior of migrant fathers, who often lose their sense of obligation toward their children (Cortés 2007a; D'Aubeterre 2000).

Migration has short- and long-term effects on families. One distinctive impact is that migrant families seem more likely to break up than their nonmigrant peers (Frank and Wildsmith 2005). Another migration-related problem is evident in the new norm of the children of migrants who increasingly emphasize consumption of consumer goods and learn to define opportunities in terms of emigration rather than in terms of prospects to be found at home. These changes reflect new familial and general social values induced by the experience of those who migrate (Frank and Wildsmith 2005).

Related or similar negative dynamics may occur when migrants return to reestablish themselves in their communities of origin. Returning is a separate migration decision influenced by social and familial conditions in the receiving and sending communities (OECD 2007a:2). Return requires migrants to sustain themselves, their immediate family, and more distant family members. To meet these demands, returnees must have developed portable economic credentials and skills. If these attributes are lacking or if returnees cannot meet the financial demands made on them, it is counterproductive for them to return. Individually they may have difficulty reestablishing themselves within their old communities, and collectively they could become sources of conflict or instability. Thus they may seek to reduce these risks by migrating again (Nyberg-Sørenson 2007:199–203). The desire to reduce these risks is also suggested by the fact that return to lower-income countries where opportunities may be scarce is less likely than return to more developed countries (Lucas 2005:156). This is why permanent return is rarely a sustainable migratory practice. This circular pattern disrupts family patterns and child rearing. Yet despite the difficulties inherent in return migration, returnees may be more common than theory suggests, even if they subsequently but intermittently migrate again (Cortés 2007a; Nyberg-Sørenson 2007:199–202).

MIGRATION AND CULTURE CHANGE

Anecdotal evidence suggests that migrants learn and often internalize new cultural values of their receiving countries, which they then transmit to their communities of origin. Such "cultural remittances" include ideas and practices regarding gender roles, work, creativity, diet, religion, child rearing, family relations, and class and racial identity (see Levitt and Lamba-Nieves this volume). These are transmitted in person and in the literature and music migrants send home (Nyberg-Sørenson 2007:202). Although there are excellent case studies analyzing this transmission (Levitt 2001), there is no systematic analysis on the extent to which migration-generated values and perspectives take root or on the characteristics of the environments in which they thrive or are disseminated. It should also be noted that if migrants are among the cultural and intellectual elite of a sending community, their exit could have a negative effect on the legitimacy of the cultural characteristic of the sending community (Ellerman 2005:620–21).

On the other hand, there are numerous examples of migration engendering increased corruption and crime in sending countries. The most notorious examples of migration's link to criminal activity are in connection with human trafficking and narcocommerce. Once emigration is institutionalized, it can lead to transnationalizing violent crime, as is increasingly evident in Mexico, El Salvador, Colombia, and many states that were part of the Soviet Union (OECD 2007b:77). Cultural mores in weakly institutionalized sending states, such as those in Central America and sub-Saharan Africa, are especially vulnerable to the impact of transnationalized crime. The instability and insecurity that this produces in sending communities is especially harmful to the children of immigrants who lack the protection that traditional family units normally provide.

Migration thus affects the cultural practices of individual migrants, but how widespread this impact is remains unclear. Furthermore there is little evidence that the state has much influence over the extent or content of cultural remittances.

MIGRATION AND POLITICAL DEVELOPMENT

The effect of migration on political development has been neglected in the research. This lack of attention is puzzling because political development is key to national development and is the arena in which states have the greatest potential to play a major role. States may resort to emigration as a means of forestalling or advancing political and policy change (Hirschman 1970; de la Garza and Szekely 1997; de la Garza and Cortina 2006). Rather than respond to demands for change, sending states have at times developed emigration policies encouraging the resettlement of large segments of their population in immigrant-receiving states. Such a policy can prevent issues such as unemployment from becoming political flashpoints (Ellerman 2005:620–21). Mexico and Cuba have long implemented such policies. States may also encourage the emigration of highly skilled under- and unemployed individuals with the knowledge, vision, and political acumen to mobilize antiregime activity—all for the sake of reducing political risk (Lucas 2005:152). Moldova responded to its domestic crisis in this way (Jandl 2008).

States may reduce migration through the development of policies that increase the accountability of public institutions and serve public needs. This includes stabilizing the economy so that investors and skilled laborers remain at home.

Independent of state intentions, or sometimes in response to them, there are cases of migrants becoming or remaining politically active and gaining political power while living in their host country. Filipino emigrants, for example, contributed to the overthrow of the Marcos regime (Lucas 2005:155). In Colombia, by contrast, emigrants were granted the right to vote as part of the nation's redefinition of who is a citizen. Demands for political representation in sending countries, as has occurred recently in Mexico, illustrate how emigrants continue to attempt to be active in their home countries. Hometown associations in host countries that promote various activities in support of communities of origin, including the financing of local projects and philanthropic programs, also allow migrants to have a voice in hometown politics (Levitt 1997; Landolt

2000 in Guarnizo 2003:678). Colombian emigrants are more directly linked to Colombian public affairs because, in addition to being involved with commercial and social activities in their homeland, they elect their own congressman to the National Assembly, who is formally charged with representing the diaspora's interests.

A related political dynamic is the impact that emigration can have on strengthening long-distance, nationalist support for democracy and peace, or for that matter, for sustained conflict (Nyberg-Sørenson 2007:202). This has been true in Mexico, where the diaspora intensified the call for transparent and free elections, and in Colombia, where the current government's antiguerrilla efforts are strongly supported by its diaspora in the United States and Europe.

***

In sum, the state is uniquely situated to initiate and implement changes in political practices and policies in ways that affect the economy, social arrangements, and cultural practices of migrants. Through its policies, it can reduce or increase the incentives for migration, which in turn reduce pressure for social and cultural change. This political capacity is in contrast to the state's limited ability to stimulate remittances or manage international markets, or to shape gender relations and cultural practices.

It must be recognized, however, that effecting such changes is a formidable challenge. It requires a "transformative" approach (Sabates-Wheeler and Waite 2003:7–8), i.e., the enactment of policies that alter the power imbalances that create, stimulate, and sustain extant conditions such as poverty and the lack of access to health services and education across time and space. Such transformations redirect policymaking away from serving as a mechanism the state can use to mobilize or reward key societal sectors at the expense of others toward an approach that calls for citizens to renegotiate their relationship with the state so as to institutionalize the state's commitment to national development. A transformative approach, in sum, addresses issues of equity, political empowerment, and sociocultural rights. Although migration's impact on development has positive aspects, overall its effects are at best mixed. Therefore there is a need to develop a new understanding for increasing the benefits of migration on development while minimizing its negative externalities. Central to this new perspective is recognizing the importance of political and economic institutions in sending states and the need for institutionalizing the transparency and accountability with which such institutions function. Without implementing such institutional changes, efforts to address the problems associated with migration have little chance for success.

REFERENCES

Adams, R. 1991. "The Economic Uses and Impact of International Remittances in Rural Egypt." *Economic Development and Cultural Change* 394: 695–722.

———. 2004. "Remittances and Poverty in Guatemala." World Bank Policy Research Working Paper No. 3418. Washington, D.C.

Almeida, Carlos C. 1973. "Emigration, espace et sous-développement." *International Migration* 113: 112–17.

Alper, A. M., and B. Neyapti. 2006. "Determinants of Workers Remittances: Turkish Evidence from High Frequency Data." *Eastern European Economics* 445: 91–100.

Arora, A., and A. Gambardella. 2004. "The Globalization of the Software Industry: Perspectives and Opportunities for Developed and Developing Countries." National Bureau of Economic Research Working Paper No. 10538, Cambridge, Mass., June.

Beachy, D. 1998. "A Little Border War over Mexican-U.S. Phone Traffic." *New York Times*, April 11.

Binford, L. 2003. "Migrant Remittances and Underdevelopment in Mexico." *Critique of Anthropology* 233: 305–36.

Bryant, John. 2005. "Children of International Migrants in Indonesia, Thailand, and the Philippines: A Review of Evidence and Policies." Innocenti Working Paper, UNICEF, Innocenti Research Centre, Florence, Italy.

Camacho, Gloria Z., and B. Kattya Hernandez. 2007. *Children and Migration in Ecuador: Situation Diagnostic*. UNICEF, Centre for Social Planning and Research, Quito, Ecuador.

Castles, S. 2004. "The Factors That Make and Unmake Migration Policies." *International Migration Review* 383: 852–84.

Coe, Cati. 2008. "The Structuring of Feeling in Ghanaian Transnational Families." Paper presented at Working Group on Childhood and Migration: Emerging Perspectives on Children in Migratory Circumstances, Drexel University, Philadelphia, June.

Commander, S., M. Kangasniemi, and L. A. Winters. 2004. "The Brain-Drain: Curse or Boon? A Survey of the Literature." In *Challenges to Globalization: Analyzing the Economics*, edited by R. E. Baldwin and L. A. Winters. Chicago: University of Chicago Press.

Cortés, Rosalia. 2007a. "Children and Women Left Behind in Labor Sending Countries: An Appraisal of Social Risks." *Global Report on Migration and Children*. A report submitted to UNICEF.

———. 2007b. "Remittances and Children's Rights: An Overview of Academic and Policy Literature." UNICEF Division of Policy and Planning Working Paper.

Cortina, J. 2011. "Lessons from the Financial Crisis: Remittances and Social Assistance among Left-Behind Children and Women in Mexico." In *Children in Crisis: Seeking Child-Sensitive Policy Responses*, edited by C. Harper, N. Jones, R. U. Mendoza, D. Stewart, and E. Strand. London: Palgrave Macmillan.

Cortina, J., and R. de la Garza. 2004. *Immigrant Remitting Behavior and Its Developmental Consequences for Mexico and El Salvador*. Los Angeles: Tomás Rivera Policy Institute.

Cortina, J., Rodolfo de la Garza, and Enrique Ochoa-Reza. 2005. "Remesas: Limites al optimismo." *Foreign Affaire en Español* 5 (July–September): 27–36.

D'Aubeterre, María Eugenia. 2000. *El pago de la novia: Matrimonio, vida conyugal y practicas transnacionales en San Miguel Acuexcomac, Puebla*. Zamora, Mexico: El Colegio de Michoacán/Benemérita Universidad Autonóma de Puebla/Instituto de Ciencias Sociales y Humanidades.

Davies, R. 2007. "Reconceptualising the Migration-Development Nexus: Diasporas, Globalisation and the Politics of Exclusion." *Third World Quarterly* 281: 59–76.

Day, Lincoln H., and A. Içduygu. 1997. "The Consequences of International Migration for the Status of Women: A Turkish Study." *International Migration* 353: 337–71.

de Haas, Hein. 2006. "Migration, Remittances and Regional Development in Southern Morocco." *Geoforum* 37, no.4: 565–80.

———. 2007a. "Remittances, Migration and Social Development: A Conceptual Review of the Literature." United Nations Research Institute for Social Development Programme Paper No. 34.

———. 2007b. "Turning the Tide? Why Development Won't Stop Migration." *Development and Change* 385: 819–14.

de la Garza, R. 2008. Personal interviews. Quito, Ecuador.

de la Garza, R., and J. Cortina. 2006. "Beyond Networks: The Impact of Politics and Policy on Migration." Paper presented at the Seminar on Migration Politics and Policy, Columbia University, December.

de la Garza, R., and Gabriel Szekely. 1997. "Policy, Politics and Emigration: Reexamining the Mexican Experience." In *At the Crossroads: Mexican Migration and U.S. Policy*, edited by F. Bean, R. de la Garza, B. Roberts, and S. Weintraub. Latham, Md.: Rowman and Littlefield.

Docquier, F., L. Lowell, and A. Marfouk. 2007. "A Gendered Assessment of the Brain-Drain." Preliminary draft. Washington, D.C.: World Bank.

Docquier, F., and H. Rapoport. 2004a. "The Economics of Migrants Remittances." In *Handbook of Economics of Reciprocity, Giving and Altruism*. Amsterdam: North Holland.

———. 2004b. "Skilled Migration: The Perspective of Developing Countries." World Bank Policy Research Working Paper No. 3382, Washington, D.C.

Dreby, Joanna. 2008. "When Gender Matters: Mexican Children's Experiences of Family Separation." Paper presented at Working Group on Childhood and Migration, Emerging Perspectives on Children in Migrator Circumstances, Drexel University, Philadelphia, June.

Dumont, J.-C., and G. Lemaitre. 2005. *Counting Immigrants and Expatriates in OECD Countries: A New Perspective*. Paris: Organisation for Economic Co-operation and Development.

Ellerman, D. 2005. "Labour Migration: A Developmental Path or a Low-level Trap?" *Development in Practice* 155: 617–30.

El-Sakka, M. I. T., and R. McNabb. 1999. "The Macroeconomic Determinants of Emigrant Remittances." *World Development* 278: 1493–1502.

Fletcher-Anthony, Wilma. 2008. "Post-Immigration West-Indian Parent-Child Relationships." Paper presented at Working Group on Childhood and Migration, Emerging Perspectives on Children in Migrator Circumstances, Drexel University, Philadelphia, June.

Frank, R., and E. Wildsmith. 2005. "The Grass Widows of Mexico: Migration and Union Dissolution in a Binational Context." *Social Forces* 833: 919–48.

Gavriliuc, Cezar, Daniela Platon, and Viorica Afteni. 2006. "The Situation of Children Left Behind by Migrating Parents." UNICEF, CIDDC Study Report.

Glytsos, N. 1998. "A Macroeconometric Model of the Effects of Migrant Remittances on Mediterranean Countries." Paper presented at ERF Conference on Population Challenges in the Middle East and North Africa: Towards the 21st Century, Cairo, November.

———. 1999. "Modeling the Growth Generating Capacity of Migrants' Remittances." Mimeo.

Gomez, M. 2008. "Remittances and Home Construction in Colombia." Paper presented at Public Policy Clinic, School of International and Public Affairs, Columbia University, February.

Gould, D. 1990. "Immigrant Links to the Home Country: Implications for Trade, Welfare and Factor Returns?" Ph.D. dissertation, University of California, Los Angeles.

———. 1994. "Immigrants' Links to the Home Country: Empirical Implications for U.S.-Bilateral Trade Flows." *Review of Economics and Statistics* 762: 302–16.

Guarnizo, L. E. 2003. "The Economics of Transnational Living." *International Migration Review* 373: 666–99.

Haan, Arjan De. 1999. "Livelihoods and Poverty: The Role of Migration—A Critical Review of the Literature." *Journal of Development Studies* 36, no. 2: 1–47.

Halter, M. 2000. *Shopping for Identity: The Marketing of Ethnicity*. New York: Schocken Books.

Hampshire, K. 2006. "Flexibility in Domestic Organization and Seasonal Migration among the Fulani of Northern Burkina Faso." *Africa* 763: 402–26.

Hirschman, Albert O. 1970. *Exit, Voice and Loyalty*. Cambridge, Mass.: Harvard University Press.

Jandl, M. 2003. "Moldova Seeks Stability Amid Mass Emigration." Migration Policy Institute, Migration Information Source. Washington, DC: December.

Kanaiaupuni, S., and K. Donato. 1999. "Migradollars and Mortality: The Effects of Male Migration on Infant Mortality in Mexico." *Demography* 363: 339–53.

Ketkar, S., and D. Ratha. 2001. "Securitization of Future Flow Receivables: A Useful Tool for Developing Countries." *Finance and Development: A Quarterly Magazine of the IMF* 38: 1.

King, R., M. Dalipaj, and N. Mai. 2006. "Gendering Migration and Remittances: Evidence from London and Northern Albania." *Population Space and Place* 126: 409–34.

Landolt, Patricia. 2000. "The Causes and Consequences of Transnational Migration: Salvadorans in Los Angeles and Washington, D.C." Ph.D. dissertation, Johns Hopkins University.

Levitt, P. 1997. "Transnationalizing Community Development: The Case of Migration Between Boston and the Dominican Republic." *Nonprofit and Voluntary Sector Quarterly* 26: 509–26.

———. 2001. *The Transnational Villagers*. Berkeley: University of California Press.

Light, I., Zhou, M. and Kim, R. 2002. Transnationalism and American Exports in an English-Speaking World. *International Migration Review*, 36, no. 3: 702–25.

Lipton, Michael. 1980. "Migration from the Rural Areas of Poor Countries: The Impact on Rural Productivity and Income Distribution." *World Development* 81: 1–24.

Lucas, R. E. B. 2004. "International Migration Regimes and Economic Development." Paper presented at the Third Coordination Meeting on International Migration, United Nations, New York, October.

———. 2005. *International Migration and Economic Development: Lessons from Low-Income Countries*. Cheltenham: Edward Elgar Pub.

Martin, P. 2004. "The Challenge of Population and Migration." Paper produced for the Copenhagen Consensus Project, Copenhagen.

Massey, D. S., et al. 1998. *Worlds in Motion: Understanding International Migration at the End of the Millennium*. Oxford: Oxford University Press.

Mummert, G. 2001. "Cultural Production and Consumption in Transnational Social Fields: Exploring Meanings with Rosaries and Flowers." Paper presented at the Research Seminar on Mexico and U.S.-Mexico Relations, Center for U.S.-Mexican Studies, University of California, San Diego, January.

Munzele, S. M. 2005. "Migrant Labor Remittances in the South Asia Region." Report No. 31577 Finance and Private Sector Development Unit. South Asia Region. The World Bank.

NFIB. 2001. "Growing Global Migration and Its Implications for the United States." National Foreign Intelligence Board. Working Paper 2001–02D, March.

Nyberg-Sørensen, Ninna. 2007. *Living across Worlds: Diaspora, Development and Transnational Engagement*. Geneva: International Organization for Migration.

Nyberg-Sørensen, N., N. Van Hear, and Engberg-Pedersen. 2002. "The Migration-Development Nexus: Evidence and Policy Options. State-of-the-Art Overview." *International Migration* 405: 3–48.

OECD. 2007a. "Comments by Jean-Christophe Dumont for Session III." OECD Workshop on More Coherent Policies for More Inclusive Growth and Development, OECD Development Centre, Paris, November.

———. 2007b. *Policy Coherence for Development: Migration and Developing Countries*. Paris: Development Centre of the Organisation for Economic Co-Operation and Development.

Olesen, H. 2002. "Migration, Return and Development: An Institutional Perspective." *International Migration* 405: 125–50.

Özden, Ç., and M. Schiff, eds. 2007. *International Migration, Economic Development, and Policy.* New York: Palgrave Macmillan.

Pack, H. 1993. "Productivity and Industrial Development in Sub-Saharan Africa." *World Development* 211: 152–76.

Page, J., and S. Plaza. 2006. "Migration, Remittances and Development: A Review of Global Evidence." *Journal of African Economies* 15, no. 2:245–336.

Portes, A., and P. Landolt. 2000. "Social Capital: Promise and Pitfalls of Its Role in Development." *Journal of Latin American Studies* 32: 529–47.

Pottinger, A. 2005. "Children's Experience of Loss by Parental Migration in Inner City Jamaica." *American Journal of Orthopsychiatry* 754: 485–96.

Quartey, P., and T. Blankson. 2004. "Do Migrant Remittances Minimize the Impact of Macro-Volatility on the Poor in Ghana?" Final report submitted to the Global Development Network, New Delhi.

Rajan, R. G., and A. Subramanian. 2005. "What Prevents Aid from Enhancing Growth?" IMF Working Paper No. 05/126, Washington, D.C.

Ramirez, C., M. G. Dominguez, and J. M. Morais. 2005. "Crossing Borders: Remittances, Gender and Development." INSTRAW Working Paper. United Nations International Research and Training Institute for the Advancement of Women, Santo Domingo.

Rauch, J., and V. Trindade. 2002. "Ethnic Chinese Networks in International Trade." *Review of Economics and Statistics* 841: 116–30.

Reichert, J. S. 1981. "The Migrant Syndrome: Seasonal U.S. Labor Migration and Rural Development in Central Mexico." *Human Organization* 401: 56–66.

Reis, Michele. 2009. "The Impact of Migration on Children in the Caribbean: Dominica, Bahamas, Belize and Guyana." UNICER-CARICOM Analytical Report.

Rhoades, R. E. 1979. "From Caves to Main Street: Return Migration and the Transformations of a Spanish Village." *Papers in Anthropology* 201: 57–74.

Rubenstein, H. 1992. "Migration, Development and Remittances in Rural Mexico." *International Migration* 30, no. 2: 127–53.

Sabates-Wheeler, Rachel, and Myrtha Waite. 2003. "Migration and Social Protection: A Concept Paper." Working Paper T2, Development Research Centre on Migration, Globalisation and Poverty Sussex.

Sawyer, Adam, and David Keyes. 2008. "Going to School, Going to the USA: The Impact of Migration on the Education of Oaxacan Students." Paper presented at Working Group on Childhood and Migration: Emerging Perspectives on Children in Migratory Circumstances, Drexel University, Philadelphia, June.

Saxenian, A. L. 2005. "The International Mobility of Entrepreneurs and Regional Upgrading in India and China." Paper presented at UNUWIDER Project on the International Mobility of Talent, Santiago, Chile, May.

Schiff, M., A. Morrison, and M. Sjöblom, eds. 2007. *The International Migration of Women.* New York: Palgrave Macmillan, World Bank.

Smith, A., R. Lalonde, and S. Johnson. 2004. "Serial Migration and Its Implications for the Parent-Child Relationship: A Retrospective Analysis of the Experiences of the Children of Caribbean Immigrants." *Cultural Diversity and Ethnic Minority Psychology* 102: 107–22.

Spatafora, N. 2005. "Two Current Issues Facing Developing Countries." In *World Economic Outlook: A Survey by the Staff of the International Monetary Fund.* Washington, D.C.: IMF.

Spencer, D. 2004. "Mexican Migrant-Smuggling: A Cross-Border Cottage Industry." *Journal of International Migration and Integration* 5, no. 3: 295–320.

Stark, O. 1978. *Economic-Demographic Interactions in Agricultural Development: The Case of Rural-to-Urban Migration.* Food and Agriculture Organization of the United Nations, Rome. Report INT/73/P02.

———. 1991. *The Migration of Labor.* Oxford: Blackwell.

———. 2005. "The New Economics of the Brain-Drain." *World Economics* 62: 137–40.

Stark, O., and D. Levhari. 1982. "On Migration and Risk in LDCs." *Economic Development and Cultural Change* 311: 191–96.

Stiglitz, Joseph. 2009. "Progress, What Progress?" *OECD Observer* 272 (April): 27–28.

Stirbu, Mariana. 2006. "Migration and Impact on Child Welfare in Moldova: Assessment of Welfare Policies Against the Rights of the Child." UNICEF-Moldova Working Paper.

Suarez-Orozco, C., and I. Todorova. 2002. "Making Up for Lost Time: The Experience of Separation and Reunification among Immigrant Families." *Family Process* 414: 625–43.

Taylor, E. 1984. "Egyptian Migration and Peasant Wives." *Merip Reports* 124: 3–10.

Taylor, J. E. 1986. "Differential Migration, Networks, Information and Risk." In *Migration Theory, Human Capital and Development,* edited by Oded Stark. Greenwich: JAI Press

———. 1999. "The New Economics of Labour Migration and the Role of Remittances in the Migration Process." *International Migration* 371: 63–88.

Taylor, J. E., and T. J. Wyatt. 1996. "The Shadow Value of Migrant Remittances, Income and Inequality in a Household-Farm Economy." *Journal of Development Studies* 326: 899–912.

Taylor, J. E., et al. 1996. "International Migration and Community Development." *Population Index* 623: 397–418.

UNCTAD. 1975. The Reverse Transfer of Technology: Economic Effects of the Outflow of Trained Personnel form Developing Countries. United Nations Conference on Trade and Development, New York: United Nations.

UNHCR. 2008. "Guidelines on Determining the Best Interests of the Child." UN High Commissioner for Refugees, Geneva: United Nations.

UNICEF-Moldova. 2007. "Migration and Remittances and Their Impact on Children Left Behind in Moldova."

United Nations. 2004. "International Migration." In *The World Economic and Social Survey.* New York: United Nations–Department of Economic and Social Affairs. New York: United Nations.

Van Naerseen T., E. Spaan and A. Zoomers, eds. 2007. *Global Migration and Development.* New York: Routledge.

Whitehead, Ann, and Iman Hashim. 2005. "Children and Migration." Background Paper for DFID Migration Team Brighton. University of Sussex.

Willis, R. 1999. "The King of Imported Beers. Coronas Success: Choice Hops vs. Choice Marketing." *New York Times*, May 28.

Woodruff, C., and R. Zenteno. 2007. "Migration Networks and Micro-enterprises in Mexico." *Journal of Development Economics* 802: 509–28.

World Bank. 2000. *Entering the Twenty First Century: World Development Report 1999/2000*. New York: Oxford University Press.

——. 2006. *International Migration Agenda*. Washington, D.C.

——. 2012. *Migration and Remittances Factbook*. Washington, D.C.

Wuyts, Marc. 2009. "Developing Social Protection in Tanzania Within a Context of Generalized Insecurity." Special Paper No. 06.19, Tanzania Research on Poverty Alleviation (REPOA).

Yeoh, Brenda S. A., and Theodora Lam. 2007. "The Cost of Immobility: Children Left Behind and Children Who Migrate with a Parent." Unpublished paper.

CHAPTER 3

Bringing Culture Back In

OPPORTUNITIES AND CHALLENGES FOR THE
MIGRATION-DEVELOPMENT NEXUS

Peggy Levitt and Deepak Lamba-Nieves

The migration-development nexus, while long studied, is still not well understood. Migrants from the developing world can bring labor, skills, and know-how to the countries where they settle while they promote development in their countries of origin by sending remittances, investing in businesses, introducing knowledge and skills, and contributing to charity (de Haas 2007). But migration can also drive up economic dependency, institutionalize a standard of living that is unsustainable without remittances, and heighten conflicts between increasingly unequal groups. Clearly the impact of migration varies by country and group, over time, and according to whether remittances are used individually or collectively.

Most debates about migration and development privilege the economic at the expense of the social. As noted by de la Garza (this volume), recorded migrant remittances and philanthropic transfers to developing countries amounted to approximately $406 billion in 2012—nearly twice the amount of official development assistance. International aid agencies and governments are hard at work designing policies to tap into and purposefully channel these resources (Wilmaladharma et al. 2004). Against this backdrop, it is not surprising that many scholars and policymakers hail remittances as the next development panacea (see this volume's contributions by de la Garza for a general discussion and Martin and de Haas for a country-level perspective on the impact of remittances on development).

But economics is not the whole story. Culture permeates all aspects of the development enterprise, as a challenge and an opportunity. Ideas and practices travel in response to migration, which in turn enables people to move and creates new forms of membership and belonging. Culture also strongly influences how development goals are established, what policies are put in place to achieve them, and how successfully they are achieved. By privileging the economic, researchers and policymakers overlook an important potential tool and fail to recognize possible barriers to development (Rao and Woodcock 2007).

CONCEPTUALIZING CULTURE

This chapter is part of recent efforts to bring culture back into migration debates. Doing so requires not only looking at the migration *of* culture (or religion, or ideas, or artistic practices) but also seeing *migration as a cultural act*. Because migrants' identities and actions are rich in cultural and social meaning, focusing solely on social networks, positions, or activities comes up short. It is not *when* or *that* these practices or identities *may* be cultural but rather that they *are* inherently cultural.

Scholars of immigrant assimilation have also largely sidestepped culture because they are primarily concerned with immigrant incorporation rather than with how cultural elements were abandoned or adopted. As research shifted "beyond the melting pot" toward acknowledging that diversity would endure as a "salad bowl" or "glorious mosaic," culture was subsumed under the "ethnicity" label. Cultural influences, though everywhere, were characterized as ethnic values, customs, and preferences. And since ethnicity was increasingly deemed optional (Waters 1990), symbolic (Gans 1979), or on the wane (Alba 1990), culture too was relegated to a supporting role. When it was taken into consideration, culture figured in only on a macro level. Modernization theorists and their descendants argued that development would simply follow if we just got culture right. From Edward Banfield's 1958 book, *The Moral Basis of a Backward Society*, to Lawrence Harrison and Samuel Huntington's 2000 book, *Culture Matters—How Values Shape Human Progress*, authors have argued that the wrong kind of culture permanently relegates countries or regions to backwardness. The "dated" and "thin" concepts many of these theorists used fail to recognize the multidimensional and complex picture that emerges when heterogeneous attributes are used to understand culture (Lamont and Small 2008).

But a sea change may already be under way. "It is not culture," wrote Lourdes Arizpe (2004:165), "that is embedded in development. It is development that is embedded in culture." Amartya Sen (2004) also argued that culture is a constitutive part of development. If development is about enhancing well-being and freeing minds, then it has to take into account literature, fine arts, and all else that makes well-being possible. Arjun Appadurai (2004:73) emphasizes the relationship between culture and poverty reduction. "In culture," he writes, "ideas about the future as well as about the past are embedded and nurtured. The capacity to aspire is a cultural capacity. We often focus on culture as some kind of 'past-ness' while development is couched in terms of progress and the future." For culture to be incorporated into the development equation successfully, that gap must be bridged.

Social scientists have struggled with defining culture for decades. Arizpe describes it as

> a flow of meanings that human beings create, blend, and exchange. Cultures are philosophies of life that hold together all the social practices that build and maintain a capable, creative human being. Such practices also hold together well-functioning, balanced societies. In this sense, cultures function as primarily regulating systems that help to keep people's feelings and actions within the bounds of institutionally acceptable behavior. When such systems are ignored in development, they tend to create unsocial behavior. (2004:164)

Sociologist Ann Swidler (1986) proposed the notion of culture as a toolkit. From her perspective, culture is a changing, dynamic bag of tricks that people use to solve problems and interpret their worlds. It is the cognitive, symbolic, and linguistic tools that are in people's heads and the rituals, relationships, and practices they use to express them. Lamont and Small (2008) suggest identifying the frames, repertoires, narratives, cultural capital, and symbolic boundaries people use to analyze more effectively the relationship between culture and poverty.

Our intention is not to resolve these debates (after all, enriching these discussions is what anthropologists do for a living), but we will say what culture is not. First, it is not a cohesive system. Culture's component parts do not have to make sense in relation to each other, nor do the people who belong to the same cultural group necessarily include the same tools in their toolkits. No cultural core exists because the cultural package in place at any point in time grows out of a particular history and political economy (Besserer 2003). The "core" changes in response to changing sociohistorical circumstances. A belief in "cultural holism" is not just misguided; it is harmful. It underlies predictions of civilization clashes because these writers assume that the cultural baggage that migrants bring will automatically clash with those in place.

Cultural fluidity, therefore, rather than the expectation of a static, cohesive cultural package, should be our starting point. According to García Canclini (1995), as traditions become appropriated by globalization, enter into international communication circuits, and move back and forth with transnational migrants, they are both "deterritorialized," or delinked from their localities of origin, and "reterritorialized," or relocalized, mixed, and brought into juxtaposition with modern and postmodern discourse and practices. The end result is *tiempos y espacios mixtos e híbridos,* new spatio-temporal hybrid configurations that transform culture and the public arena, allowing new individuals and collective identities and voices to emerge. What's more, culture is not a discrete social arena but spills over into all other aspects of social life. How it influences the economic sphere is evident in how ethics, rates of entrepreneurship, and risk adversity vary across groups. In politics, viable democratic governance is possible only when a community has prior experience with participation and public debate (Sen 2004).

In sum, culture cannot be artificially lifted out of other social spheres, nor can economics or politics be emptied out of culture. Moreover culture cannot be separated from social structures. All migrations are embedded in particular structural conditions, power relations, and, in particular, socioeconomic contexts of reception (Besserer 2003). Culture and structure are mutually constitutive. What social categories like family, household, and membership actually mean and how they are enacted develop in response to particular economic and social circumstances.

USING A TRANSNATIONAL LENS TO UNDERSTAND MIGRATION

This chapter also sits squarely within the body of work that views migration from a transnational perspective. Acknowledging the strong and interactive links between sending and receiving societies brings to light several things obscured by looking at migration as taking place between two separate nation-states.

First, the migration experience is often as much about nonmigrants as it is about people who move: migrants and nonmigrants, although separated by physical distance, continue to occupy the same sociopolitical space. Because goods, people, money, and social remittances circulate regularly, even individuals who never move are influenced by values and practices from near and far. They have a clear picture of what life is like for their migrant friends and relatives, although it may be quite distorted (see Escobar García and Álvarez Velasco in this volume for the case of Ecuador). Dominicans from the village of Boca Canasta (which provides the empirical data for much of our argument here), for example, who had never visited Santo Domingo, let alone traveled abroad, could describe "El Mozart" and "La Center," a park and a street at the heart of the Dominican community in Boston (Levitt 2001). They had heard enough stories, seen enough photographs, and watched enough videos to imagine themselves in that space even though they had never been there. The social and political organizations they belong to also assumed new forms and functions because their members belonged to the United States and the Dominican Republic simultaneously.[1]

Second, the social fields where migration takes place are multilayered and multisited. The ties between a particular sending community and the urban neighborhood where migrants settle are important. But these connections need to be understood in the context of the broader ties and institutional frameworks within which these develop. To understand the lives of Salvadorans in Los Angeles, what the Salvadoran state and the U.S. government do and what the Salvadoran and U.S. Catholic churches do must be taken into account, for instance. Similarly, understanding the religious lives of Brazilians in Massachusetts requires looking beyond the connections between specific congregations in Boston and Brazil and placing them in the context of the thick, multilayered web of regional and national denominational connections that also link these countries (Levitt 2007).

Third, seeing migrants and nonmigrants as occupying the same social space also drives home dramatic changes in the meaning of incorporation. The immigrant experience that this transnational process embodies is not a linear, irreversible journey from one membership to another (Levitt and Glick Schiller 2004; Smith 2005). Rather, migrants pivot back and forth between sending, receiving, and other orientations at different stages of their lives. The more their lives are grounded in investment and business ventures, health care, and pension systems on both sides of the border, the more likely it is that they will continue to live transnational lives. Increasing numbers of newcomers will not fully assimilate or remain entirely focused on their homeland. Rather, they will craft some simultaneous combination of the two in ways that ebb and flow in response to life-cycle events, elections, economic downturns, and climate disasters. Their lives will be enabled and constrained by multiple cultural repertoires and institutions. As a result, social mobility and inclusion in a new place are strongly connected to social status and inclusion in the old one, and vice versa.

MOVING BEYOND CULTURE AS PRODUCT

Once we acknowledge that immigrant poverty and community development in sending societies are two sides of the same coin and that culture is an important part of its alchemy, where should we look for culture, and what forms does it take? How can it be used effectively as a central piece of this puzzle, and what are the costs and benefits implicit in such an approach?

Most policies treat culture as a *product*, a material and concrete object, such as a dance, a piece of music, folk art, or the tradition of storytelling that is transformed, reinvented, or threatened by migration. Culture is seen as something to be revived and preserved, resuscitated and reinforced, an unconditional good to be protected at all costs. Or it is seen as impeding integration or development: particular groups have negative cultural traits that prevent them from learning to work hard, trust strangers, or govern effectively. Or culture is seen as a tool of empowerment, allowing a group to express its culture and enabling it to assume its place in a new society.

This view is problematic for several reasons. First, cultural products are not set in stone. They are not preserved intact nor completely transformed when people move, but undergo some combination of the two. The power relations surrounding the expression and representation of cultural artifacts also change. Who should decide what dance or song represents some allegedly homogeneous group? Even more misguided, as we have already argued, is the mistaken understanding of culture as a discrete, packageable whole that can be lifted out and analyzed apart from social relations.

A more fruitful approach treats culture as a dimension of all social relations and forms that affects all aspects of immigrant incorporation and sending-community development. Patron saint day celebrations are one example of a cultural performance profoundly shaped by cultural influences. Many Latin American migrants return to their sending communities for their annual patron saint day celebration. Even if they cannot travel, they contribute time, money, and resources to honor their communities, often organizing simultaneous celebrations wherever they are. Some

Mexican communities even send a representative of their village saint (their priest) to attend their festivities in New York (Rivera Sánchez 2004). By extending the feast from Mexico to the United States, the community extends its boundaries of belonging far beyond its actual physical borders. At the same time, it claims space and recognition for itself in New York.

Rather than seeing culture solely as a product, it can also be understood as a *process*. When people participate in and perform cultural representations, they also create and reinvent them. Cultural events are sites of boundary work during which communities affirm who they are to insiders and outsiders around the world.

For instance, patron saint day celebrations are generally sponsored by a *patrón*, or benefactor, a role associated with great respect and responsibility. In fact to retain citizenship in many Mexican indigenous communities, emigrants still have to fulfill certain collective obligations even though they no longer live at home. But migration has changed all that. Since so many community members live in the United States, there are too few men left to sponsor the celebration. As a result, some communities rewrite the rules, allowing people living abroad to be *patrones* who delegate their day-to-day responsibilities to a nonmigrant relative or friend. By so doing the community signals that its territory has expanded to include people living in the United States. It invents new ways for people to fulfill their citizenship obligations so they can still belong. Membership without residence is not only a possibility but a necessity.

The *fiesta patronal* is a performance for outsiders as well as insiders— the community's representation to itself and to the outside world. New kinds of communities are created through cultural performances (Gil et al. 2005). *La Hora Mixteca*, a program on Radio Bilingüe, a station serving indigenous people in Mexico and in the southwestern United States, helped create a pan-indigenous community. When listeners heard programming in their own language for the first time, they felt part of the Mexican nation in ways they had not before. By listening to the broadcast, they also felt a sense of belonging to a pan-ethnic community encompassing members in Mexico and the United States. Listening also reinforced generational ties because family members in Mexico and California could listen "together" (NATC Report 2004a, 2004b).

The *fiesta patronal* is also a site where gender is redefined. Women are allowed and, in some cases, required to assume leadership roles they were previously excluded from simply because there are not enough men to fill the positions. This earns them access to power and decision-making circles that were off-limits in the past. Furthermore, when migrants return to live or visit, they bring with them different ways of managing gender and family, shaped by their experiences living abroad. Smith (2005) writes of the tensions around gender that arise between young second-generation Mexican American men and women when they visit their ancestral villages. What was considered acceptable behavior in New York is considered inappropriate in Mexico. The brother who never thought twice about his sister going out alone in Manhattan feels he is responsible for regulating her behavior back in Mexico. At least two sets of norms compete with each other, and individuals and communities have to figure out how to resolve the conflict.

Some migrants want to be the benefactor of the patron saint day celebration because they want to give back to their community. Others seek the position as a platform from which to display their enhanced status. They spend so much money trying to make that point that sponsoring the festival grows beyond the means of most nonmigrants. As each new *patrón* hosts an even more luxurious celebration than the last, villagers' already inflated consumption aspirations increase even further. What native sons and daughters must do to signal their loyalty is beyond what most residents (migrant or not) feel they can or should be able to afford. Their worth is measured by their financial contributions rather than by their moral authority or leadership. Yet no one seems willing or able to stop this vicious cycle. Toning down the celebration would suggest that the community prospered less than it had led itself to believe or that the benefits of migration do not always outweigh its sacrifices.

Moreover migration forces communities to revisit their narratives about progress and success, about what the goals of development and incorporation should be. Since migrants generally make more money than nonmigrants, they tend to have a louder voice in discussions about what constitutes development. Their motives for contributing to the community and what they hope to achieve through their contributions can grow increasingly distinct from those of the people who stay behind. Migrants see their community as a place to vacation, retire, and eventually die, while nonmigrants see it as a place where they need jobs and health care. Migrant members want to build funeral homes, playing fields, and plazas, while nonmigrant members want to build schools and clinics. A parallel debate emerges vis-à-vis community activism in the country of settlement. While some community members argue for a shift in focus to social and political integration in the United States, others fear this will detract from their efforts to help people back home.

Culture is also a *regime* of norms, power, and status that enables and constrains behavior (Appadurai 2004). Meanings, symbols, and narratives make cultural production possible but also constrain it because the repertoires upon which that production is based contain only certain items. The terms of recognition and possibility underlying these regimes have to shift for any kind of fundamental change to occur.

A close look at ostensibly economic behaviors reveals how cultural regimes work. Some migrants send remittances to friends and family members as a form of social insurance. They keep up relationships with people back home in case things go wrong and they have to return. Bryceson and Vuorela (2002) use the term *relativizing* to describe how individuals establish, maintain, or neglect ties to specific family members or fictitious kinship. They choose strategically which connections to emphasize and which to let slide based on what they think their future needs will be.

How acceptable it is for someone to make these kinds of choices is decided by the normative regimes at play. In some social contexts, individuals feel and are considered by others to be incomplete if they are not part of a family or group. One woman from Gujarat State in India, for example, told Levitt (2007) that her decisions would never be judged outside the context of her family—that her actions would reflect positively or negatively on her family until the day she died. A similar kind of transnational moral economy influences young people's marriage options, lifestyle choices, occupational possibilities, and the level of resources they have to pursue their individual and collective life plans. Because social embeddedness is so thick and dense, individuals cannot make self-interested choices without the risk of being ostracized by the group (Portes and Sessenbrenner 1993).

Take the example of Moreno, a middle-aged man who came back from the United States to his Dominican village to open a small cement factory. His neighbors strongly criticized him when he hired the best workers rather than his relatives and friends. A Pakistani entrepreneur who started a software company in Boston faced similar criticism. His friends and family in Karachi also had lots to say when he decided not to hire every distant acquaintance who came to him looking for a job. How much each man could change his economic behavior was culturally constrained by these social consequences (Levitt 2007).

Changes in gender relations are another arena where cultural regimes are at work. In Karachi, most women do not go to the mosque to pray; in Boston, they not only pray there but actively run its cultural and educational activities. Because the Boston mosque functions as a sociocultural center, women serve as teachers, administrators, and trustees, roles they never would have played in Pakistan. The cultural repertoire shifts, but only so far. Women pray with men but not alongside them. In Karachi, changes also occur but within even more limited parameters. In Levitt's (2007) interviews with the relatives and friends of immigrant respondents in Boston, she found that while most women knew about these changes, they were not all "takers." Some insisted it was "their special privilege" to pray at home, but others wanted to invent ways to pray and study collectively with other women.

Sommer (2005) and her colleagues conceptualize culture as *agency*. Art, she argues, has the capacity to "interrupt" or to "unblock" habits. It unsettles regimes through "defamiliarization," or the surprise inspired by new artistic techniques or encounters. Cultural engagement nudges actors outside their comfort zones and normal ways of doing and thinking and thus can lead to positive, purposeful social change. According to Sommer, we are all cultural agents, in that small shifts in perspective and practice can turn artists, teachers, and religious and community leaders into catalysts of collective change. It's not a question of whether we exercise agency but how self-consciously we do so, to what end, and with what effect.

Throughout the world, creative arenas have long been vehicles for agency. Without the *Teatro Campesino,* labor organizers who worked with César Chávez argue, there would have been no United Farm Workers' Union. From the beds of pickup trucks, loudspeakers called pickers to watch and join plays that poked fun at bosses and celebrated workers' solidarity. At the Gujarati Social Forum in India, a sexuality rights NGO launched its campaign with a street play (also a familiar art form in India) about the *hijra*s, castrated biological males who consider themselves to be women inside. Many consider the places where *hijra*s live to be pure and thus sites of justice. Rights workers talked about Shikhandi, a great warrior from the epic *Mahabharata* who was allowed to sit next to Lord Krishna in his chariot in honor of his bravery. Some people believe that Shikhandi was impotent; others claim that he was gay. Whatever one believes, he was undoubtedly a great warrior (Rajaram and Zakaria 2009). This narrative revealed to audience members that acceptance of same-sex relationships is not merely a Western import but something with deep Indian roots. Facilitators presented new ideas about homosexuality using English words but then explained them using familiar elements from paintings, dances, and epics.

The example of the village *banda* in Mexico is also useful. The *banda* is important not just during the *fiesta patronal* but is also an integral part of collective mourning when someone passes away. When listeners recognize changes in the music because nonmigrants have replaced musicians now living in the United States and because new musical styles and instruments have been imported, they also experience their community differently. Incorporating new elements signals to them that something has shifted, that who and what the community is has expanded in some small way. Moreover when communities ask musicians from neighboring villages to fill in for absent migrant musicians, neighbors cooperate where they may have competed in the past.

But culture is also about *profit*. Neither the underlying economic interests that shape cultural enactments nor the economic benefits that flow from them can be overlooked. The markets created by transnational migration build upon already well-developed ethnic and nostalgia markets in many immigrant communities. A successful *fiesta patronal* requires costumes, instruments, souvenirs, and food. Even places get marketed. One of the fastest-growing religious shrines in Mexico, for example, is Santa Ana de Guadalupe in Jalisco State, believed to be the birthplace of Mexico's patron saint of migrants, St. Toribio. It was not economic development that transformed this former backwater into a thriving community but the many tourists who make a pilgrimage there each year (Levitt 2007).

The potential for profit is not lost on the state. Governments produce their own versions of tradition for public consumption and worldwide dissemination, which often differ significantly from the community's account. The *chilena*, originally considered a dance of the poor, became legitimate and profitable after the Mexican government appropriated it (Revilla López 2000). The state pushed a commercial tourist spectacle, displaying the splendor of Mexico to its urban residents and foreigners. In contrast, *grupos chilenos* and *technobandas* used the form to invoke a strong sense of belonging among Mixtecos. Because *chilenas* do not consist of a fixed set of elements, musicians could incorporate new instruments and rhythms, producing an alternative national self-representation outside the reach of the state.

Cultural products such as dances, music, and radio transmissions are created in the context of cultural processes and regimes that strongly influence how they develop and the impact they have. The *fiesta patronal* gets reinvented so that less powerful actors, like women or poorer community members, assume positions of power and replace people who have migrated. Who is actually allowed to do so, however, is strongly influenced by cultural regimes about what is appropriate. The *chilena* does a different kind of symbolic work now that it incorporates elements from the North and because it has been anointed by the Mexican state. Here again regimes of power strongly shape how cultural products are deployed and to whose advantage. Without embedding them in the social relations and power hierarchies in which they are produced and used, we fail to exploit a potential development tool and also fail to recognize potential obstacles.

The final piece of this puzzle, to which we now turn, is *cultural circulation*. We need to understand the relationship between the movement of people and the circulation of ideas and practices.

SOCIAL REMITTANCES AND THE MIGRATION-DEVELOPMENT NEXUS

In her book *The Transnational Villagers* (2001) Levitt coined the term *social remittances* to call attention to the fact that, in addition to money, migrants also export ideas and behaviors back to their sending communities. She observed at least four types of social remittances—norms, practices, identities, and social capital—circulating in the Dominican village of Boca Canasta. Social remittance exchanges occur when migrants return to live in or visit their communities of origin, when nonmigrants visit those in the receiving country, or when migrants exchange letters, videos, cassettes, emails, blog posts, and telephone calls with nonmigrants. Social remittances are distinct from but reinforce and are reinforced by other forms of global cultural circulation.

While the idea of social remittances has gained some traction in the literature, it is not without critics, who argue that the "social" should also include the "cultural" and that social remittances do not move in just one direction. They also caution against seeing all social remittances as positive. We completely agree. However, to study how social remittances travel and to evaluate their impact, one has to look in one place at one time. While this methodological imperative might suggest that ideas and practices travel only one way, there is clearly a continuous, ongoing process of exchange. What migrants bring with them and continue to receive from their homelands affect their experiences in the countries where they settle. This, in turn, affects what they remit back to nonmigrants, who then adopt ideas and behaviors that are transformed in the process and eventually re-remitted back to the migrants, who adopt and transform them yet again. These exchanges include a wide range of social and cultural elements.

We have already alluded to cases in which social remittances challenge gender and generational dynamics. When migrant men and women work and share responsibility for housecleaning and child care, they talk about and model a different kind of gender relations when they visit or return home. Levitt (2001) found that young Dominican women no longer wanted to marry men who had never migrated because they thought the men would "play by the old rules." They saw their migrant mothers and sisters as having better, more equal relations with their partners, which was the kind of relationship they now wanted for themselves.

Social remittances affect a lot more than gender and generation, however. They also shape health and educational outcomes. Because Dominican migrants earned more money and got more education in the United States, we found that they were more conscious about taking care of their health. They were more likely to drink bottled water, to keep animals out of living spaces to prevent the spread of disease, or to recognize the importance of annual checkups (because they were entitled to one through their medical insurance in the United States).

Social remittances also challenge people's ideas about politics and democracy. Everyone in the United States has to wait in line to cash their check at the bank on Fridays, whether they wear a suit and a tie or overalls covered with sawdust and paint, Dominican returnees told us. They said that young people get into college on the basis of their grades, not on the basis of whom they know. Return migrants to Governador Valadares in Brazil had a lot to say about Brazilian politicians and lawyers based on their experiences abroad (Levitt 2007). "We have a democracy in Brazil," said sixty-five-year-old Gilberto, "but it doesn't work as it should. You have a system of checks and balances there. When the President gets too powerful, the Senate can rein him in. When Bill Clinton was accused of committing a crime, he was prosecuted." Every time a streetlight went out or the garbage wasn't collected, Gilberto went down to City Hall. "I learned this in the United States—that governments can do what they're supposed to do and that citizens should make sure that happens. I'm trying to get people here to understand that they don't have to accept business as usual."

High-tech professionals and entrepreneurs from Pakistan and India send back not only new technology and skills but also new ideas about how business should be conducted. Working in the United States emboldened them to take chances: challenging superiors rather than always deferring to them, changing the box rather than always trying to fit within it. "The first thing my boss taught me," recalled Amir, a thirty-five-year-old engineer from Karachi, "was not to stand up when he came into the room or to call everyone 'Sir'"(Levitt 2007:95).

COLLECTIVE SOCIAL REMITTANCES

Lamba-Nieves's (2009) fieldwork in Boca Canasta and Villa Sombrero, two villages in the southern region of the Dominican Republic, has led us to distinguish between individual and collective social remittances. While our examples thus far have illustrated how social remittances challenge interpersonal and family dynamics, we also find that they are harnessed collectively in organizational settings. We focus on two hometown associations (HTAs): Modebo (Movimiento para el Desarrollo de Boca Canasta) and Soprovis (Sociedad Progresista de Villa Sombrero), based in Boca Canasta and Villa Sombrero, respectively.

Most of the people Lamba-Nieves interviewed in the Dominican Republic and the United States agreed that the opportunity to travel and live abroad has transformed migrants' general attitude and "vision" in several ways. One theme mentioned repeatedly was what people referred to as "outlook," shifts in the contours and ideological ethos of the geographies where people imagine themselves. How they think about that space and their goals for its transformation radically changed. Samuel Sánchez, a forty-two-year-old male who migrated from Boca Canasta to Boston in 1989, explained, "People who have been here [in the United States] do not have the same mentality. One learns many things here. . . . We see the world differently, there is a different culture." When asked about the differences, Samuel pointed out that, unlike his father, he regularly attends parent-teacher meetings at his child's school. Since migrating, he has also had to learn to wait his turn at public offices and adapt to different workplace norms, such as stricter supervisors and rules. While it took him a while to get used to these differences, he now considers them positive. The fact that people are accountable for their actions in the United States is something he likes and does not see replicated in the Dominican Republic.

The different "vision" that our respondents alluded to is also reflected in the projects proposed by migrant HTA members. In the early years of migration, most of the group's projects were selected and administered by nonmigrant members. As the U.S. members grew in number and fundraising capacity, however, they started to design projects that grew out of their experiences in the United States. These included opening a local fire station with its own fire truck, building different kinds of sports facilities, purchasing an ambulance, and organizing AIDS awareness and sexual health campaigns. Most projects were negotiated between Boston, New York, and island-based members. Normally a compromise between migrant and nonmigrant concerns was achieved. But there were instances when migrants' views and needs prevailed simply because, more and more, they controlled the purse strings.

A sports complex, slated to include a softball and Little League field, clubhouse, pool, and basketball court that Soprovis is now building, is one example of the impact of migrants' different vision. Carlos Melo, the current president of the Soprovis Boston chapter, explained what drew them to the project:

> We saw that we had not done much to promote sports activities, and that there weren't places in the community where we could spend leisure time with our families. . . . When we traveled there [back to Villa Sombrero], we had to go to other communities [to enjoy family-oriented places]. . . . We had to do something related to sports because they say that sports can discourage the youth from vices. . . . There's going to be a youth baseball field to teach the children [how to play]. Big league players can come out of there.

In other words, community members had grown accustomed to these kinds of facilities in Boston. They saw them as keeping families together and helping youth and as potential breeding grounds for new baseball talent. They also wanted to be able to use them during their vacations back home.

The motivation behind this project also reflects members' changing notions of the meaning of development and their aspirations for their community. The sports complex is the biggest project Soprovis has undertaken. Its total cost is estimated at 7 to 8 million pesos (approximately $200,000). The former president of Soprovis in Villa Sombrero, a forty-nine-year-old who has never been to Boston, explained that the Boston members are very sports-oriented. He also recalled, "Because they are in a developed country, they are looking at other types of constructions, edifices, other sports complexes and they want to bring those ideas to their community. . . . Boston has always thought big." He also recalled a conversation with the Boston leaders during which they proposed building a paved road from Villa Sombrero to the sports facility (which is far from the town's center) and an avenue leading to the nearby beach. The projects are part of efforts to increase tourism in the area. "They have a futuristic idea, with a vision that I said: 'that's not for now,' but we have to start thinking about those things. Now we see it as difficult, but we have to start somewhere, then it gets easier. . . . Because they're in big countries, they're teaching us to think big. Many times we do not share that view, because one thinks as one is. We think smaller."

Soprovis's stateside chapters have taken on other projects inspired by the public services they became accustomed to in the United States. In 2004 the Boston chapter sent a fire truck to Villa Sombrero and supported the creation of a community fire squad that could respond quickly to local emergencies. They also introduced the idea that the government should share some of the burden of support. At a meeting of Soprovis Boston in March 2009 during which the government's contribution was discussed, Carlos Melo stated, "I have been reading that in all places [in the United States] the firemen are supported by the authorities." Until now, the community funded all of these activities, but they now expect the local mayor to assume some of the cost.

The New York chapter has focused on supporting the local health clinic with medicines and equipment and has organized numerous health drives for local residents. The health drives are an opportunity to provide checkups, distribute medicines, and offer educational workshops on topics that are generally not discussed in the community, including teenage pregnancy, reproductive health, and AIDS awareness. William Pimentel, the current president in New York, explained that while many of these topics are taboo on the island, it is important to talk openly about them, especially to young people. New York's commitment to addressing sexual health and AIDS awareness led them to distribute condoms and informational literature during the community's patron saint festivities. They also made sure that some of the bars and bodegas offered free condoms to their patrons.

The knowledge and skills people acquire working in the United States are also applied to business ventures. Such is the case of Bolivar Dumé, who founded Soprovis New York and has been its president several times.

As he neared retirement and prepared to spend extended periods in Villa Sombrero, he joined a group of local investors building a gated community in the town center. The project, he says, will be built according to the rules and codes so it will not turn into a "slum." There will be no mixed-use commercial properties. The houses cannot exceed two stories and must be built using certain materials. The rules are included in the sales contracts and apply equally to all buyers. He got the idea for this, he explains, from contracts in the United States that include riders or addenda specifying certain conditions. He hopes that future projects both in and outside the community will follow suit.

For Dumé, Villa Sombrero's rapid growth needs to be more orderly and purposeful so that infrastructure projects such as access roads are not afterthoughts. Villa Sombrero, he says, needs to live up to its reputation as a modern town: "We have to think about tomorrow." His approach represents the "big thinking" and change in "outlook" alluded to earlier. It also reflects a respect for rules and laws observed in the United States and different ideas about town planning and development. Bolivar wants things to work as they are supposed to and for the community to proactively plan its future rather than have it happen haphazardly. His efforts, however, are also likely to increase the social inequality between better-off migrants who can afford to purchase a house in a gated community and those who cannot.

SCALING UP AND OUT

Migrants to the United States brought with them a strong commitment to work for the collective good through active social, political, and religious organizations. They also brought technical and organizing skills that aided their efforts in New York and Boston. Their experiences abroad challenged and expanded how they did things and why they did them, and the types of projects they took on and how they implemented them reflected these changes. As groups in the United States matured, assumed the lion's share of responsibility for fundraising, and learned how to work transnationally, they took the lead in proposing ventures that were consonant with their new "vision" of what hometown development should entail.

Projects like the sports complex, the fire station, and the ambulance are examples of the chapters' growing organizational capacity. They reflect migrants' heightened concern with safety and health and their assumption that living in a developed community means living somewhere where these services are part and parcel of what good governments do. They stimulate "state-society synergies," or collaborations between social actors and government entities that bridge public-private divides (Evans 1996). These ideas can scale out as residents apply them to other domains of practice. They expect the government not only to share the cost of public safety but also to partner with them in providing education and health. They can also scale up as community members change their expectations of local government as well as provincial and national governments.

For example, Soprovis Boston members pursued projects inspired by the public services they used in Boston. They sent a fire truck and supported the creation of a community fire squad to respond quickly to emergencies. After the fire truck was delivered to Villa Sombrero, residents formed a committee to train volunteer firefighters and found a place to build a fire station. Because migrants were unwilling to fund these efforts indefinitely, they pressured the government to assume some of the burden of support. Continuous claims made by migrants and nonmigrants have swayed the mayor to assume more responsibility, and led to larger public investments in firefighting services and the upkeep of the truck. Thus a project conceived by migrants as a way to modernize the town's public safety infrastructure has become a sustainable joint citizen-state effort that has rewritten the rules of state and citizen responsibility. Most residents are very satisfied with the fire squad and expect that other partnerships can be developed to provide basic services that are still lacking.

Another example involves social remittances scaling out to other associations in ways that promote organizational learning. This was the case when the Modebo Boston chapter decided to create an ambulance service. Several months after Villa Sombrero received their ambulance, Modebo decided to follow suit. Once they bought a used vehicle from a nearby state, leaders began figuring out how to ship it to the Dominican Republic. They needed a large sum of money for fees and taxes since the vehicle was registered under an individual's name and was therefore not tax-exempt. (Soprovis's vehicle was registered as a municipal government vehicle, so they did not face this problem.) Modebo's leaders feared that if they entered into a similar agreement with a politician or a government leader, they would risk losing control of the vehicle.

Once the vehicle arrived, leaders need to figure out how it would be used. Who would drive the passengers? Where would it be stationed?

Who would pay for the maintenance and insurance? Leaders in Boston had not anticipated these issues and were frustrated by what they perceived as island-based leaders' unwillingness to take responsibility. Finally, Carlos Melo, who headed the Soprovis Boston chapter when the ambulance was purchased, was called in. He explained the legal and administrative requirements and helped Modebo members see how they needed to adjust Soprovis's strategy to the Boca Canasta reality. They agreed to form a trust to draft a series of regulations to govern vehicle use that they modeled after their neighbors' policies but also customized to meet their needs. After several months of trial and error, the ambulance began operating. But the service was eventually shut down due to maintenance issues and management problems. Despite the adverse outcome, leaders in Boston and Boca Canasta argue that the project provided important learning opportunities that will ensure success in future ventures.

Another interesting example of scaling out involves Soprovis's attempt to increase accountability and transparency in the management of the town's patron saint festivities. Usually organized and administered by a special committee, the festivities are an important community activity that generates substantial economic activity and revenues for the community. According to Soprovis's leaders, before 2008 the festivities were run by a group of residents who were suspected of cheating because so little money was generated. In 2008 Soprovis took over and established a series of administrative practices that stressed transparency and increased accountability. They established stricter reporting guidelines and other measures such as requiring each kiosk to submit sales figures. The net revenues that year were well over 200,000 pesos (over $5,000). They also produced a detailed financial report for community members. The following year, a financial report was posted on the Internet. According to Carlos Melo, Soprovis instituted these measures in Villa Sombrero because its members had grown accustomed to reporting financial matters to members in the United States who wanted to know how their money was being used.

Demands for greater transparency and accountability also scale out into the private sector. According to Ismael Díaz Melo, people who have lived abroad or who work closely with migrants make firmer commitments regarding time and money. They demand project contracts and schedules and expect them to be honored. But, he says, these practices carry benefits and risks. They formalize business transactions but suggest to participants that if no signed paper exists, then no one is responsible. Likewise, when migrants wanted to invest in Bolivar Dumé's gated community project and asked a local lawyer to serve as their proxy, hometown investors interpreted their request as a lack of trust. Their reticence led those from Boston to pull out of the project.

Social remittances also scale up to other levels of organization and governance. When Levitt did her fieldwork in the 1990s, for example, many of the people she talked to did not consider the state responsible for providing basic services. They said that there was too much poverty for the government also to build roads. Now residents see these activities and institutional frameworks as part and parcel of what constitutes good governance. The more people adopt this stance and the more they demand contracts and their compliance to them, the more these social remittances will scale up to other levels of governance. Similarly the more people demand accountability and transparency in community projects, the more likely they are to demand that of political parties and businesses as well.

A funeral home renovation project is another example of scaling up. When Soprovis rebuilt its funeral home, it did so in partnership with Procomunidad, a national government program that supports community projects. The government financed 75 percent of the project, and Soprovis raised the rest from migrant contributions. Because the organization had a financial stake in the project, it requested that Ismael Díaz Melo, a native and well-known architect and developer, be put in charge. When the project stalled because Procomunidad held up the funds, the community used its contacts in the national government to restart it. The funeral home was rebuilt in record time and within budget. As Modebo and Soprovis gain experience developing projects and become more skilled at dealing with politicians and government agencies, these types of ventures become increasingly common. The expectation of public-private partnerships brokered locally is replicated nationally. Residents, empowered to actively engage in the public domain, demand greater accountability from national as well as local government agencies.

Scaling up also occurs when organizations are able to make their demands heard at the national level and eventually take control of important community services. For years, Soprovis lobbied the central government and INAPA (the National Water Supply and Sewage Institute) to solve the growing water problem in Villa Sombrero. After countless efforts, the agency responded favorably, even going a step further and delegating to the community the power to run the water system. This move was part of a government initiative, in conjunction with the United States

Agency for International Development, to expand potable water provision in the Dominican Republic and develop pilot initiatives in which communities participated actively in the management of the water infrastructure. Soprovis's willingness to fully finance the system from the outset with the help of stateside chapters, their ability to convince residents that paying the water fees would ensure better service, and their political savvy and previous successes in partnering with state entities were major factors behind the government's decision to build the system and cede control. Since 1997 an elected community board has run the service. Their success serves as a model that the state has tried to replicate in other parts of the country.

We cannot stress enough that social remittances produce both positive and negative impacts. Many people fear that the flow of ideas from the United States devalues family and deifies consumerism. In small villages throughout the Dominican Republic, a generation is being raised on remittances. These young people dream of making a home in the United States rather than in their communities of origin. Instead of going to school or trying to find a job, they spend their days waiting for their monthly check or for the magical day when their visa finally arrives. It is not worth it to them to work in a factory or on a farm, if such work is even available, because their parents send money anyway. Not only do their skills and discipline waste away while they wait to leave, but the economic base of their communities continues to deteriorate. Constructing gated communities, while an attempt to achieve more orderly, planned development, exacerbates the class stratification that has already worsened because of migration. Migrants and nonmigrants also worry about deportees who committed crimes in the United States and get into similar trouble when they return. Residents blamed the deportees for introducing "bad habits" and increasing crime and insecurity and felt they set a bad example for local youth and compromised immigrants' reputation abroad. They also held the deportees responsible for introducing new criminal technologies and contacts with international crime syndicates.

We also warn against the dangers of what Levitt (2007) has elsewhere called "the Ossification Effect." This happens when major social and economic changes occur in the homeland, but the homeland remains frozen in time in migrants' minds. Migrants often need the homeland to be a bastion of traditional values because it counteracts the racism and overly liberal values they experience in the countries where they settle. Most of the Gujarati migrants Levitt interviewed left India before the economic liberalization and the rise of the Indian middle class. They often clung to the India of their memories, in which modesty, civility, and the collective prevailed over the individual. But their homeland moved on at top speed. In many parts of India, the consumer is now king. The billionaire high-tech entrepreneur, rather than the Gandhian humanitarian intellectual, is today's hero. Yet migrants still held fast to their old images of India. They were shocked and deeply disappointed when they realized that things had changed. Their relatives, in turn, looked at them as Rip Van Winkles who had been asleep while the world kept turning. The migrants' children not only had to figure out how to be hyphenated Americans and members of the homeland simultaneously; they also had to do so with contradictory information. The Ossification Effect also deepens the wedge between migrants' and nonmigrants' goals for their community and nation.

Thinking big is also not enough to make dreams a reality. Ideas have to be realized and sustained, the biggest challenge facing HTAs. Development is not just about delivering an ambulance or building a park. These projects require upkeep and maintenance. They require moving from isolated, discrete projects to ongoing, integrated long-term development plans.

Culture pervades all aspects of the migration-development nexus and is at once a resource and a curse. In all of our examples, the definition of development and progress, who gets to define them, and the methods the community uses to achieve its goals are culturally informed. What's more, what migrants bring with them deeply informs their interactions with the host society, and therefore what they adopt from their native-born neighbors and the political and social systems they encounter. A sports complex will seem to some like a step in the right direction because it encourages tourism, keeps families together, and teaches youth good values. Others will say it is frivolous in a context where there are still basic needs to be met. Either way, how the project was conceived, implemented, and used takes place within a set of culturally informed processes and regimes that strongly shaped its evolution and impact.

CONCLUSION

This chapter is a call to bring culture seriously and creatively into migration debates. It is also a call for scholars and policymakers primarily concerned about immigrant incorporation in host countries and those working on home-country development to see themselves as part of the same conversation. Finally, it is a call to all stakeholders to use language that makes interdisciplinary research and policymaking truly possible.

Our research reveals the many ways cultural processes, regimes, and products inform the migration-development nexus. How communities perceive themselves, what they want, who defines these goals, and how they try to achieve them are all culturally informed. Culture enables and constrains possibilities. Without factoring culture into the migration-development equation, policymakers overlook both important opportunities and potential obstacles.

Future research needs to look more carefully and systematically at how ideas and values travel and under what circumstances idea change contributes to behavioral change. When does local-level change in something like gender relations, for example, scale up to produce broader shifts in reproductive behavior and labor market participation? What is the time frame within which this occurs? Under what circumstances can local-level democratic capacity-building scale up to produce stronger provincial and national governance?

There is a clear divide between the scholars most concerned about what happens to immigrants once they arrive in a new place and those most concerned about what happens in the places where they come from. This is a false dichotomy. These processes were never disconnected, and they certainly are not today. Continuing to speak about them and organize research around them separately is counterproductive. It reifies an artificial separation that neither reflects migrants' lives nor allows us to respond creatively to the challenges they face.

As we said at the outset, many academics and policymakers see economic remittances as the next development panacea. Migrants clearly make major contributions to community development. We are concerned, however, that despite improved living conditions and infrastructure, such projects disproportionately burden migrants and make them responsible for functions that rightfully belong to states. Although remittances significantly contribute to economic development and family survival, they can also be a tremendous burden for those who send them. Family and kinship links, while providing network support, can also be a source of never-ending obligations. Such demands can work against migrants' social mobility in the host country and also make accumulating capital for return or investing back home very difficult. They falsely and unfairly pin the prospects of future development on the backs of migrants, raising concerns both for the short and the long term.

Development agencies should be careful that their renewed focus on diasporas and remittances does not place additional stress on already vulnerable groups. A way out of this conundrum could be to build capacity, strengthen organizations, and increase skills so that migrants can protect their interests more effectively and to equip nonmigrants to work with migrants on a playing field that is as level as possible. Another strategy would include fostering cooperation between grassroots groups so that communities could work cooperatively, leaving no community disproportionately burdened. Whatever one's stance on these debates, cultural factors have to be taken into account.

We especially hope that this chapter helps to facilitate truly interdisciplinary conversations with economists and political scientists. There is an important lesson here. Socially and culturally oriented social scientists have to make arguments that are comprehensible and compelling to people working outside their disciplines. If future research can show, as we have intimated here, that culturally driven changes in gender relations could scale up to changes in fertility and reproductive health, then demographers may be more convinced by our arguments. If we can show how these same changes could lead to greater female integration into different sectors of the labor market, then economists might also listen. But such research agendas require partnerships across disciplines and across methodological divides. The work of translation goes both ways.

REFERENCES

Alba, Richard. 1990. *Ethnic Identity: The Transformation of White America*. New Haven: Yale University Press.

Appadurai, Arjun. 2004. "The Capacity to Aspire: Culture and the Terms of Recognition." In *Culture and Public Action: A Cross-Disciplinary Dialogue on Development Policy*, edited by Vijayendra Rao and Michael Walton. Palo Alto, Calif.: Stanford University Press.

Arizpe, Lourdes. 2004. "The Intellectual History of Culture and Development Institutions." In *Culture and Public Action: A Cross-Disciplinary Dialogue on Development Policy*, edited by Vijayendra Rao and Michael Walton. Palo Alto, Calif.: Stanford University Press.

Banfield, Edward C. 1958. *The Moral Basis of a Backward Society*. New York: Free Press.

Besserer, F. 2003. "Contesting Community: Cultural Struggles of a Mixtec Transnational Community." Ph.D. dissertation, Stanford University.

Bryceson, D. F., and U. Vuorela. 2002. *The Transnational Family: New European Frontiers and Global Networks*. Oxford: Berg.

de Haas, Hein. 2007. "Remittances, Migration and Social Development: A Conceptual Review of the Literature." Programme Paper No. 34. New York: United Nations Research Institute for Social Development.

Evans, Peter. 1996. "Government Action, Social Capital and Development: Reviewing the Evidence on Synergy." *World Development* 24, no. 6: 1119–1132.

Gans, Herbert. 1979. "Symbolic Ethnicity: The Future of Ethnic Groups and Cultures in America." *Ethnic and Racial Studies* 2, no. 1: 1–20.

García Canclini, Néstor. 1995. *Hybrid Cultures: Strategies for Entering and Leaving Modernity.* Minneapolis: University of Minnesota Press.

Gil, Rocio, et al. 2005. "Informe de Investigacion #1 Etnografía Transnacional de Santa María Tindú Circuito Oaxaca, Sub-circuito Mixteca." Unpublished manuscript.

Harrison, Lawrence, and Samuel Huntington, eds. 2000. *Culture Matters—How Values Shape Human Progress.* New York: Basic Books.

Lamba-Nieves, Deepak. 2009. "Furthering the Discussions on the Migration Development Nexus: A Closer Look at Dominican Hometown Associations and Their Development Impacts." MIT Department of Urban Studies and Planning. Unpublished paper.

Lamont, Michele, and Mario L. Small. 2008. "How Culture Matters: Enriching Our Understanding of Poverty." In *The Colors of Poverty: Why Racial and Ethnic Disparities Persist*, edited by Ann Lin and David Harris. New York: Russell Sage Foundation.

Levitt, Peggy. 2001. *The Transnational Villagers.* Berkeley: University of California Press.

———. 2007. *God Needs No Passport: Transnational Religious Life.* New York: New Press.

Levitt, Peggy, and Nina Glick Schiller. 2004. "Conceptualizing Simultaneity: A Transnational Social Field Perspective on Society." *International Migration Review* 38, no. 3: 1002–39.

North American Transnational Communities Program (NATC). 2004a. "The Cultural Dimension of Transnational Communities." Meeting report, Oaxaca City, Mexico, August. Internal Rockefeller Foundation document.

———. 2004b. "Translocal Flows in the Americas." Bellagio Workshop report, October. Internal Rockefeller Foundation document.

Portes, Alejandro, and Julia Sensenbrenner. 1993. "Embeddedness and Immigration: Notes on the Social Determinants of Economic Action." *American Journal of Sociology* 98, no. 5: 1320–50.

Rajaram, N., and Vaishali Zakaria. 2009. "Translating Women's Human Rights in a Globalizing World: The Spiral Process in Reducing Gender Justice in Baroda, India." *Global Networks* 9, no. 4: 462–85.

Rao, Vijayendra, and Michael Walton. 2004. "Conclusion: Implications of a Cultural Lens for Public Policy and Development Thought." In *Culture and Public Action: A Cross-Disciplinary Dialogue on Development Policy*, edited by Vijayendra Rao and Michael Walton. Palo Alto, Calif.: Stanford University Press.

Rao, Vijayendra, and Michael Woodcock. 2007. "Global Insights: The Disciplinary Monopoly in Development Research at the World Bank." *Global Governance* 13: 479–84.

Ratha, Dilip, Sanket Mohapatra, K. M. Vijayalakshmi, and Zhimei Xu. 2007. "Remittance Trends 2007." Migration and Development Brief 3, Development Prospects Group, Migration and Remittances Team, World Bank. Accessed at http:// siteresources.worldbank.org/EXTDECPROSPECTS/Resources/476882 -1157133580628/BriefingNote3.pdf.

Revilla López, Ulises. 2000. "La chilena mixteca transnacional." Master's thesis, La Universidad Autónoma Metropolitana, Iztapalapa Campus, Mexico.

Rivera-Sanchez, Liliana. 2004. "Expressions of Identity and Belonging: Mexican Immigrants in New York." In *Indigenous Mexican Migrants in the United States*, edited by Jonathan Fox and Gaspar Rivera-Salgado. La Jolla, CA: Center for U.S. Mexican Studies, UCSD.

Sen, Amartya. 1999. *Development as Freedom.* New York: Knopf.

Smith, Robert. 2005. *Mexican New York.* Berkeley: University of California Press, 2005.

Sommer, Doris. 2005. "Art and Accountability." Unpublished manuscript.

Swidler, Ann. 1986. "Culture in Action: Symbols and Strategies." *American Sociological Review* 51: 273–86.

Waters, Mary. 1990. *Ethnic Options.* Berkeley: University of California Press.

Wilmaladharma, J., D. Pearce, and D. Stanton. 2004. "Remittances: The New Development Finance?" *Small Enterprise Development Journal* 15: 2–19.

World Bank. 2009. *Migration and Remittances Factbook.* Washington, D.C.: World Bank.

CHAPTER 4

Protecting the Rights of Migrant Workers

Khalid Koser

There is a comprehensive legal and normative framework for the protection of the rights of migrant workers and a wide variety of international, regional, and national organizations and institutions dedicated to safeguarding these rights. Yet around the world migrant workers continue to experience violence, abuse, and exploitation. A 2010 report by Human Rights Watch (HRW) documents the rising incidence of abuse of domestic workers in Kuwait. Maids are reported to have minimal protection from employers who withhold salaries, force them to work long hours with no days off, deprive them of adequate food, or abuse them physically or sexually. In 2009 domestic workers from Sri Lanka, Indonesia, the Philippines, and Ethiopia filed over ten thousand complaints with their embassies (HRW 2010b). Another HRW report documents the killing, torture in detention, extortion, and sexual abuse of migrant workers in Thailand from Burma, Cambodia, and Laos (HRW, 2010a). An Amnesty International Report, also published in 2010, reports that Central American migrant workers in Mexico have virtually no access to justice and face reprisals and deportation if they report abuse to the authorities. Meanwhile a series of reports by the International Organization for Migration suggests that working and living conditions for migrant workers around the world have deteriorated as a result of the effects of the recent global financial and economic crisis (IOM 2009a, 2009b). Although it is by definition more difficult to document their circumstances, it is likely that migrant workers in an irregular situation—and there may be as many as 30 million of them worldwide—are often even worse off than the migrants with legal status addressed in these and other reports. This chapter asks why the current regime for protecting the rights of migrant workers appears to be failing and considers alternative approaches.

The first part of the chapter outlines the scale and scope of the problem, identifying categories of migrant workers who appear to be at particular risk. The second part describes the current legal and normative framework, including institutional arrangements, for protecting migrant workers' rights. The remainder of the chapter explains why, despite a robust legal and normative framework for protection, gaps persist. I suggest that part of the answer is that the existing law has not always been adequately implemented, and I consider options for more effective implementation. At the same time the dimensions and dynamics of international migration have in some regards outstripped existing legal frameworks, and recognizing that lawmaking can be a lengthy process, there is also a role for national and regional policies to more effectively address the protection of migrant workers' rights. There are likely to be many more migrant workers in the next few decades, often arriving in countries that do not yet have significant experience with immigration, and so it is important to put effective instruments for protection in place now.

THE SCALE AND SCOPE OF THE PROBLEM

There are no published estimates of the number of migrant workers in the global economy, but it is generally accepted that the majority of the world's 214 million international migrants are migrant workers or their families (IOM 2010). It is important to emphasize that this number refers to international migrants, the focus of this chapter. There are far more workers in the world who have moved within their own country (an estimated 115 million in China alone), and their rights are probably less well-protected, and certainly less well-researched, than those of international migrant workers.

Traditionally migrant workers have been men. But as an increasing number of countries have extended the right of family reunification to migrants, they have been joined by their spouses and children. Family reunification is an important reason why almost half of the world's migrants today are women. (See Cortina and Ochoa-Reza in this volume for a discussion of family reunification migration and its developmental consequences for sending and receiving countries.) An increasing proportion of women among migrants have moved to work, and often independently of their families, rather than to join their husbands abroad. The feminization of labor migration has become more visible over the past few decades for three main reasons. First, the demand for labor, especially in more developed countries, is becoming increasingly gender-selective in favor of jobs typically filled by women, for example, in services, health care, and entertainment. Second, changing gender relations in some countries of origin, for example, across the Maghreb and in Latin America, mean that women have more independence to migrate than they did previously. (See Escobar García and Álvarez Velasco in this volume for a discussion focusing on the case of Ecuador.) Third, and especially in South East Asia, there has been growth in the migration of women for domestic work (sometimes called "the maid trade"), organized migration for marriage (sometimes referred to as "mail-order brides"), and the trafficking of women into the sex industry (Koser 2007).

Another important consideration in any discussion of the rights of migrant workers is that a significant proportion of migrant workers are in an irregular situation. (Different states and stakeholders use different terminology, including *irregular, undocumented, unauthorized*, and *illegal migrants*; see Koser 2005.) By definition irregular migrants are hard to count, and many of those included in the figures may not be workers but family members (Koser 2010). Still, it is estimated that there are between 10 and 20 million irregular migrants in the United States alone (Terrazas et al., 2007) and between 1.5 and 10 million irregular migrants in the Russian Federation (Vitkovskaia 2004). In 2007 the Council of Europe reported an estimate of 4.5 million irregular migrants in the European Union, which by then encompassed twenty-seven states (Council of Europe 2007a, 2007b). Turning to global estimates, the International Labour Organization estimated in 2004 that between 10 and 15 percent of the world's immigrant stock were in an irregular situation (ILO 2004). Today this would amount to some 21 to 32 million irregular migrants.

Some migrants are highly skilled and work at the upper end of the labor market; indeed there is growing competition for a limited pool of global talent among both states and corporations. But most migrants (including some who are highly skilled) work in low-skilled occupations and the informal sector and engage in so-called 3D jobs that are dirty, dangerous, and difficult, for example, in heavy industry, agriculture, mining, and forestry. This is particularly the case for irregular migrants. In a discussion about rights, it is migrant workers at the lower end of the labor market who are of most immediate concern.

Within this wide range of migrant worker profiles, certain categories are of particular concern with regard to the protection of their rights: children, domestic workers, and those involved in "forced labor." Domestic workers, for example, are estimated to compose up to 10 percent of total employment in some countries, and half of them are migrants, yet almost every country excludes domestic work from its national labor laws (ICMC 2010). The conditions of concern typically include threat or physical harm to the worker, restriction of movement and confinement to the workplace or to a limited area, debt bondage, withholding of payment or excessive wage reductions, retention of passports and identity documents, and threat of denunciation to the authorities when the worker has an irregular immigration status. Migrant workers with irregular status, including the victims of migrant smuggling and human trafficking, are especially vulnerable to exploitation in work. Women constitute a substantial proportion of the many migrants with irregular status. Because they are confronted with gender-based discrimination, female migrants with irregular status are often obliged to accept the most menial informal sector jobs. Such can be the level of abuse of their human rights that some commentators have compared contemporary human trafficking with the slave trade (O'Connell Davidson 2010). Women in particular also face specific health-related risks, including exposure to HIV/AIDS. More generally migrants with irregular status are often unwilling to seek redress from authorities because they fear arrest and deportation. As a result, they do not always make use of the public services to which they are entitled, such as emergency health care. In most countries, they are also barred from using the full range of services available to citizens and migrants with regular status. In such situations, already hard-pressed NGOs, religious bodies, and other civil society institutions are obliged to provide assistance to migrants with irregular status, at times compromising their own legality (GCIM 2005).

The recent global financial and economic crisis has also impacted the rights of many migrant workers (Koser 2010). Job losses for migrant workers have been recorded around the world, especially in the employment sectors that are most sensitive to economic cycles, such as construction, manufacturing, financial services, retail, and travel and tourism. Unemployment rates for foreign nationals have increased in the Russian Federation, Spain, Taiwan, the United Kingdom, and the United States. In Malaysia and Singapore labor market policies have been put in place to encourage employers to fire migrant workers first and to replace them with unemployed nationals. More significant than unemployment, however, working and living conditions for migrant workers have been rapidly deteriorating. There have been press reports from the Russian Federation, Malaysia, and Singapore of nonpayment of wages for foreign workers as well as reductions in wages, working days, and the availability of overtime. Sporadic instances of discrimination against migrant workers and a rise in xenophobia have also been recorded in Malaysia, Russia, Singapore, Spain, the United Kingdom, and elsewhere.

THE LEGAL AND NORMATIVE FRAMEWORK

International migrants have rights under two sets of international instruments. The first are the core human rights treaties currently in force, namely, the International Covenant on Civil and Political Rights, the International Covenant on Economic, Social, and Cultural Rights, the Convention against Torture, the Convention on the Elimination of All Forms of Racial Discrimination, the Convention on the Elimination of All Forms of Discrimination against Women, the Convention on the Rights of the Child, and the Convention on the Rights of Persons with Disabilities. The second instrument is the U.N. Convention on the Protection of the Rights of All Migrant Workers and Members of their Families, adopted by the U.N. General Assembly in 1990. This Convention is intended to reinforce the international legal framework concerning the human rights of migrant workers by adopting a comprehensive instrument applicable to the whole migration process and regulating the legal status of migrant workers and their families. The Convention protects the basic rights of all migrant workers and their families and grants regular migrants a number of additional rights on the basis of equality with nationals. It further provides a framework for interstate cooperation on migration issues.

Migrant workers are also provided rights under international labor law, which includes two specific ILO conventions concerned with the protection of migrant workers (Nos. 97 and 143). The trafficking and smuggling protocols, supplementing the U.N. Convention against Transnational Organized Crime, also make reference to protecting the human rights of trafficked victims and smuggled migrants. ILO labor standards have also had a significant impact, especially on domestic law in ILO member states. Migrants' rights are also protected under regional treaties (e.g., under the European Court of Human Rights and the Inter-American Court of Human Rights). In addition, national courts are increasingly applying international human rights law and case law and advisory opinions from regional treaties to cases that come before them.

A whole range of institutions and organizations at the international, regional, and national levels have responsibility for implementing this legal framework and safeguarding the rights of migrant workers. The ILO is the only U.N. agency with a constitutional mandate to protect migrant workers, and this mandate has been reaffirmed by the 1944 Declaration of Philadelphia and the 1998 ILO Declaration on Fundamental Principles and Rights at Work. The ILO has developed a series of international conventions to guide migration policy and protection of migrant workers. In all of its work the ILO adopts a "rights-based" approach to labor migration and promotes tripartite participation (governments, employers, and workers) in migration policy. While the IOM does not have a specific protection mandate, its guiding principle is to promote humane migration, and it supports numerous projects aimed at protecting the rights of migrant workers around the world.

The protection of migrant workers is also a significant focus for regional organizations and regional consultative processes (RCPs) on international migration around the world. They are addressed through provisions in numerous bilateral labor agreements between sets of states (although these provisions are not always effectively implemented). At the national level numerous government agencies are dedicated to promoting the legal rights of migrants and protecting them in the workplace. Civil society organizations are also very active in this arena. In the Philippines and Sri Lanka, for example, civil society organizations have lobbied effectively for standard contracts as a means to enforce minimum wages for their migrant workers (IOM 2010). Trade unions are active as well. In Spain, for example, the Unión General de Trabajadores has recently undertaken high-profile work.

IMPLEMENTATION GAPS

Certainly the legal and normative framework for protecting the rights of migrant workers is not perfect, and equally the institutional infrastructure for its implementation has weaknesses. It is generally agreed, however, that there exists a sufficient legal framework to protect the rights of most migrant workers and sufficiently robust institutional responsibility to do so. Nevertheless many migrant workers continue to experience violence, abuse, exploitation, and discrimination.

One problem relates to the ratification of existing instruments. There is a particularly vigorous debate surrounding the Convention on Migrant Workers, ratified by only forty-six states as of January 2013, none of which is a major developed country of destination for migrants. Some of the main reasons provided for nonratification include the Convention's breadth and complexity, the technical and financial obligations it places on states that have ratified, the view that it contradicts or adds no value to existing national migration legislation, concerns that it provides migrants (especially those with irregular status) rights that are not found in other human rights treaties, and claims that it generally disallows for differentiation between regular and irregular migrants. However, the Convention has recently received further endorsement within the United Nations system: in December 2010 the U.N. Committee on Migrant Workers approved formal jurisprudence that elaborates the rights of migrant domestic workers on the basis of an interpretation of the 1990 Convention. At a conference to mark the twentieth anniversary of the Convention on Migrant Workers, the U.N. Office of the High Commissioner for Human Rights called for those states that have not yet done so to ratify the Convention. The Global Migration Group, an interagency conglomerate of U.N. and international organizations, also called for the ratification and implementation of the Convention during the 2011 one-day Informal Thematic Debate on International Migration and Development convened by the General Assembly at its sixty-fifth session (A/RES/63/225).

Nevertheless significant problems persist in making the rights guaranteed in the Convention a reality, even for those states that are party to it, arising at times from a lack of political will but also from a lack of capacity and resources. Neither is there a sufficient infrastructure for monitoring or enforcing state compliance. To help fill this gap it has been suggested that capacity building is especially required in civil society to increase its effectiveness in lobbying for the rights of migrants and migrant workers, monitoring and reporting on conditions for migrant workers, and providing migrant workers with services. Effective practice also stresses empowering migrants by providing them with information about their rights in the labor market, giving them the identification and rights needed to access banks and other institutions abroad, and developing incentives to encourage migrants to report the worst abuses of their rights.

For those states that are not yet party to the Convention, the emphasis has been on trying to ensure that domestic law and regulations conform to international human rights standards. It has been suggested that one way to facilitate this is to articulate the legal and normative framework—which is currently dispersed across a number of treaties, nonbinding agreements, and policy understandings—in a single compilation of all treaty provisions and other norms that are relevant to international migration and the human rights of migrants (GCIM 2005).

EFFECTIVE NATIONAL POLICIES

Another reason for the gap between legal provisions and empirical realities in protecting the rights of migrant workers is that the dynamics and dimensions of labor migration have changed since the main labor standards and conventions were adopted. Three areas where this has become particularly problematic recently are (1) decreasing significance of the state in the recruitment of migrant labor and the increasing importance of private agents and intermediaries, (2) the increasingly short-term nature of migration and the expansion of temporary migrant worker programs, and (3) the growth in irregular migration and the need to balance control measures with measures to facilitate labor migration and to protect migrant workers. Given the time it takes to develop a new law and the political and economic domestic realities that need to be balanced between all sending and receiving states, there is a need for national and regional dynamic policies to address the gaps that have emerged as a result of these sorts of changes.

REGULATING RECRUITMENT AGENCIES

Destination states, especially in the more developed world, increasingly depend on private recruiters to identify foreign workers and match them with job openings in the labor market. Their functions can range from a straightforward matching service to a comprehensive hiring package consisting of recruitment, skills testing, travel, visa, and living arrangements. Criticism of private recruitment agencies occurs mainly when there is evidence of corruption in some agencies that do not provide socially protected jobs. Such agencies have been accused of requiring excessively high commissions and providing unsafe and unsanitary work and living conditions. (See Martin in this volume for a discussion of this issue in the Philippines.) The method for recruiting workers for the United Kingdom's Sector-Based Scheme, for example, involves private agencies sending workers to countries with unregulated operations and matching them with individual employers with no reference to state institutions until the employer applies for the work permit. Even in the case of legitimate recruiters, there has been a tendency to shift the costs of recruitment from employers to workers, such as with upfront costs for obtaining information, documentation, health checks, predeparture orientation and training, and paying for transportation.

There are three broad government responses to regulating private recruitment agencies (Martin 2007). One is to step up enforcement to eliminate unscrupulous agents, for example, by requiring recruiters to identify themselves to authorities via registration, ensuring they can meet minimum standards by requiring them to pass tests, and generating some financial security for migrants by having agents post bonds that can be tapped if agents do not fulfill their promises. A second is to encourage more legitimate agents to become involved in the migrant brokerage business so that competition gives migrants options and leads to effective self-regulation and ratings to guide migrants toward better agents. A third approach is to increase the role of public employment service agencies in moving workers over borders in the hope that public agencies are most likely to ensure that minimum standards are satisfied in recruitment and deployment.

Responsibility for reducing labor migration costs lies with origin countries as much as with destination countries. The Philippines is considered a leader in regulating recruiters (see Martin this volume). The government operates three agencies to serve and protect migrants: the Philippine Overseas Employment Administration (POEA) regulates recruitment and provides predeparture orientation; labor attachés stationed at consulates abroad provide assistance to migrants while they are abroad; and the Overseas Workers Welfare Administration (OWWA) operates centers in areas with concentrations of Filipinos that cover the cost of emergency repatriation and provide various services to families left behind. These activities are financed by fees collected from migrants, including a P 3,000 (USD 60) processing fee charged by the POEA, whose governing board includes representatives of the recruitment industry, and a USD 25 fee paid to the OWWA (Abella 2004). While the Philippine system is often considered a model for regulating recruitment and protecting migrants abroad, there is an active debate among migrant organizations, some of which allege that overregulation of recruitment raises the costs of Filipino migrants to foreign employers, reducing the number of foreign jobs for Filipinos. Most recruiters as well as the Union of Filipino Overseas Contract Workers want less government regulation of recruitment, arguing that it increases the costs of sending migrants abroad at a time when other countries in the region that offer lower-wage workers are aggressively expanding deployment.

An initiative proposed in Bangladesh, an important sending country for labor migrants, is aimed at reducing predeparture loan costs for migrants. At the Global Forum on Migration and Development in Brussels in 2007, the Bangladeshi government proposed that donors consider expanding the country's active microfinance industry to migrants leaving the country (IOM 2010). Predeparture loans for Bangladeshi migrants would go primarily to men who leave, and the benefit of the loan would come in the form of remittances and the return of migrants with experience gained abroad. One proposal is for a partnership of banks and NGOs that could assess risks, make low-cost loans, and ensure repayment as NGOs with a presence in the villages from which migrants originate form partnerships with banks seeking to expand their customer base.

PROTECTING THE RIGHTS OF TEMPORARY MIGRANT WORKERS

There is a wide range of experiences relating to the conditions attached to employment permits as regard their duration and renewability, occupational mobility, procedures governing migrants' rights upon loss of employment, possibilities for permanent residence, family reunion, and other social rights. As a generalization, better conditions are attached to long-term permits for skilled workers than to those for temporary and less skilled workers, with the result that at times the rights of temporary migrant workers may be jeopardized (Koser 2009).

The length of time a work permit is valid needs to be considered carefully as it can have important consequences. One often-cited criticism of the U.K. Sector-Based Scheme for temporary labor migration is that it permits entry for only one year initially, which some argue is not sufficient time for most labor migrants to generate the net financial gains necessary to make migrating financially worthwhile (Ruhs 2005). This is especially the case for migrants traveling long distances, who normally incur greater initiation costs than those moving shorter distances. In addition, short-term entries increase costs for employers as well, for once a migrant overcomes the job-related learning curve, he or she has to return home. A number of commentators have proposed that longer contracts should be offered not only to make temporary labor in another country a worthwhile proposition for migrants but also to try to reduce the likelihood of migrants overstaying their visas. While most commentators appear to agree that one year is too short a period, there is no consensus about what is an appropriate period. Some of the factors that are likely to influence the extent and rate at which migrants can save are their salary, employment flexibility, initial settlement costs, living costs, and pressures to remit. The balance to strike is between permitting migrants to stay long enough to generate savings but not so long that the likelihood of return diminishes. From a rights-based perspective, liberal democracies should not maintain migrants indefinitely without extending to them broad integration rights, including access to permanent residence and the right to family reunion (Black 2004).

In general, entrants under highly skilled migration programs can be "free agents" with uninhibited access to the labor market, either immediately upon entry or after a certain number of years. Low-skilled migrants, in contrast, tend to be tied to particular employers either for the duration of their permit or for longer periods than is the case for highly skilled migrants, and the rules governing their access to other jobs are more rigorous. Advocates frequently argue that freedom to change jobs in destination-country labor markets can be an important protection for lower-skilled migrants, allowing them to escape abusive employers, for example, in the context of domestic work in some of the Gulf countries (Shah 2007a). In this regard the Live-in Caregiver Programme in Canada is often cited as an example of good practice, as it allows temporary migrant workers to change employers while in the country, provided that the new employment offer is confirmed by the authorities.

Recognizing the reluctance of most governments to provide total labor market flexibility for temporary migrants, one proposal is to more systematically facilitate the portability of temporary work permits within a defined job category after a certain period of time (Ruhs 2006). The duration could be determined on the basis of a realistic assessment of the time needed for employers to recover at least part of their original migrant worker recruitment costs. Even where unskilled migrant workers do have limited rights regarding occupational mobility, they have been found in various studies either to not fully understand their rights or to be nervous about asserting them. Various strategies, including the right to trade union membership and collective bargaining, information dissemination, and access to NGOs, have been proposed to try to bridge this gap (Koser 2009).

A related vulnerability for temporary migrant workers arises when they are expected to leave the country if they lose their job, which exposes them to the possibility of exploitation and abuse by their employers, who can hold over them the threat of firing. There is a consensus that a reasonable period (not less than six months) to seek employment in the event of the termination of previous employment and equality as regards access to core benefits are basic rights that should be granted even to temporary migrants to empower their rights and protect them from exploitation.

Another issue that arises in this context is the extent to which any contributions made by migrant workers to social security systems are portable back to their origin country. The consensus is that best practice for benefit portability is bilateral social security agreements, preferably based on multilaterally agreed standards (OSCE/IOM/ILO 2006).

REGULATING EMPLOYMENT

Much of the exploitation of migrant workers takes place in the workplace, and this is particularly the case for irregular migrants. To the extent that irregular migration is fueled by the demand for labor, enforcement at the worksite is as an important deterrent (Martin 2008). Many countries impose sanctions on employers who hire irregular migrants. The standard differs as to the level of knowledge that an employer must have about the worker's immigration status. In countries where systems to verify identity are weak, employers are often able to skirt sanctions because they have not "knowingly" hired the irregular migrant who poses as an authorized worker. In countries in which there are rigorous systems to verify identity, any hiring of a person unauthorized to work may be a violation.

In addition to immigration status verification, enforcement at the worksite includes basic labor standards: payment of minimum or prevailing wages, health and safety standards, overtime payment, child labor restrictions, and so on (Martin 2008). Employers may also be investigated for failure to pay required taxes on wages. The logic behind this broader set of enforcement actions is to identify employers who are hiring irregular migrants because they are more vulnerable to labor standards abuses or they are more willing to work in the underground, cash economy because of the precariousness of their immigration status.

A comprehensive approach to irregular migration provides alternative avenues for employers to hire foreign workers when domestic workers are unwilling or unable to perform the jobs that irregular migrants hold. There is an important caveat on this statement, however. Often domestic workers are unwilling to take the jobs held by irregular migrants at the wages and under the working conditions offered. Or jobs that are held by irregular migrants could be performed offshore (bringing the jobs to the workers rather than the workers to the jobs) or could be mechanized. Indeed there is a difference between a demand for foreign workers and a true need for those workers.

Even with these stipulations, however, there are likely to be jobs that cannot be mechanized or sent offshore and for which domestic workers are unavailable even at higher wages; an example is the labor shortages recently experienced by the agricultural sector in Alabama and Georgia. Establishing legal work programs or increasing the number and types of work permits issued would present an alternative to irregular migration for some migrants. The extent to which legal programs will offset irregular migration will be determined by a number of factors, including the sanctions and incentives in place for employers to hire legal workers rather than maintain an irregular workforce, the eligibility of those with irregular status for the legal work programs, the relative size of the work programs (whether the number of visas matches the demand for workers and the supply of would-be migrants), the procedures used to process applications from employers, and the requirements imposed on would-be workers to obtain visas (Koser 2008).

Another option for regulating the employment of irregular migrants is regularization. Regularization and amnesty programs vary widely in terms of the populations they target, their scope, their overall intentions, and procedures (Martin 2008; Shah 2007b; Skeldon 2008). Regularization is an important strand of responses in East and South East Asia to irregular migration (Skeldon 2008), as well as in the countries of the Gulf Cooperation Council (Shah 2008). However, regularization may place constraints on migrants (Skeldon 2008) and have the unintended consequence of attracting more irregular migrants (Shah 2008). Thus it may be counterproductive if implemented without adequate measures to prevent future flows (Martin 2008). Technical assistance may therefore be required in developing countries to design programs that are appropriate for the local context and that are implemented effectively.

While the removal of some irregular migrants is generally in the best interest of destination countries, the capacity to identify, detain, and deport irregular migrants is limited even in developed countries. Policies and processes for detention and deportation vary widely, and a particular area for capacity building is to ensure that national laws and policies conform to international standards, are implemented with due regard to the rights of migrants, and do not undermine the right to asylum (Crisp 2008; Martin 2008).

CONCLUSIONS

This chapter has shown that around the world migrant workers continue to suffer violence, exploitation, discrimination, and other abuses of their human rights, despite a well-established legal and normative framework that defines those rights and clear institutional responsibilities for protecting them. I have identified some of the reasons for this protection gap, from poor ratification of legal instruments through their ineffective implementation to new dynamics in international migration, and have suggested some solutions, ranging from a better articulation of the legal and normative framework to more robust national policies and monitoring mechanisms. It is important to get this right now, as the problem will not be going away.

After a temporary dip during the global financial and economic crisis, labor mobility is expected to resume worldwide and even to exceed prior levels (IOM 2010). The combined effects of factors such as "youth bulges," structural unemployment, agricultural intensification, and industrial restructuring are likely to lead to a growing labor surplus in many developing countries and demands for greater access to labor markets in the developed world and emerging economies. While demand for migrant labor is likely to grow across much of the developed world in the short term, for example, in response to the effects of the "demographic crisis," as well as in emerging economies, it will not be at a level sufficient to meet supply. Furthermore the demand for migrant labor is likely to be selective, focusing primarily on migrants with skills in short supply in destination countries (e.g., in health care) and on highly skilled migrants and students, although low-skilled migration will still be required (IOM 2010).

The anticipated accentuation of the global mismatch of labor supply and demand places pressures on destination and origin countries to develop the capacity effectively to assess foreign labor demand while protecting the domestic labor force, to regulate admissions, and to ensure migrant workers' rights. It will increase the need to train migrants, strengthen bilateral labor mobility agreements, and develop capacities for return and reintegration. It is also expected to result in an increase in irregular migration, often exploited by migrant smugglers and human traffickers. Mixed flows, combining labor migrants with asylum seekers, the victims of trafficking, and others, are also expected to increase in scale and frequency.

Furthermore it has been predicted that new patterns of mobility may be observed, in particular as the emerging economies of Asia become even more important countries of destination for labor migrants. In response, emerging countries of destination and origin will need to develop new capacities to cope with new labor migration. At the same time more traditional countries of destination may also need to strengthen existing capacities to cope with changes in labor mobility.

REFERENCES

Abella, M. 2004. "Best Practices to Manage Migration: The Philippines." *International Migration Review* 38, no. 4: 1544–64.

Amnesty International (AI). 2010. *Invisible Victims: Migrants on the Move in Mexico.* London: Amnesty International.

Black, R. 2004. "Migration and Pro-Poor Policy in Africa." Working Paper C6, Development Research Centre on Migration, Globalization and Poverty, Brighton, U.K.

Council of Europe. 2007a. "The Human Rights of Irregular Migrants in Europe." Issue Paper 1, Brussels.

———. 2007b. "Regularisation Programmes for Irregular Migrants." Document 11350, Brussels.

Crisp, J. 2008. "Mixed Migratory Movements: A UNHCR Perspective." Background paper prepared for Civil Society Roundtable 2.2 at the 2008 Global Forum on Migration and Development, Manila, October.

Global Commission on International Migration (GCIM). 2005. *Migration in an Interconnected World: New Directions for Action.* GCIM: Geneva.

Human Rights Watch (HRW). 2010a. *From the Tiger to the Crocodile: Abuse of Migrant Workers in Thailand.* New York: HRW.

———. 2010b. *Walls at Every Turn: Exploitation of Migrant Domestic Workers Through Kuwait's Sponsorship System.* New York: HRW.

International Catholic Migration Commission (ICMC). 2010. "ICMC Hails New Protection for Migrant Domestic Workers." Press release, December 3.

International Labour Organisation (ILO). 2004. "Towards a Fair Deal for Workers in the Global Economy." Report IV, International Labour Conference, 92nd Session, ILO, Geneva.

International Organization for Migration (IOM). 2009a. "IOM Policy Brief." Geneva, January.

———. 2009b. "IOM Policy Brief." Geneva, March.

———. 2010. *World Migration Report 2010. The Future of Migration: Building Capacities for Change.* Geneva: IOM.

Koser, K. 2005. "Irregular Migration, State Security and Human Security." Paper prepared for the Policy Analysis and Research Programme of the Global Commission on International Migration, GCIM, Geneva.

———. 2007. *A Very Short Introduction to International Migration.* Oxford: Oxford University Press.

————. 2008. "Managing Migration and Minimizing the Negative Impacts of Irregular Migration." Synthesis paper for Civil Society Roundtable 2.2 at the 2008 Global Forum on Migration and Development, Manila, October.

————. 2009. "Study of Employment and Residence Permits for Migrant Workers in Major Countries of Destination." International Migration Papers No. 95, ILO, Geneva.

————. 2010. "Dimensions and Dynamics of Irregular Migration," *Population, Space, and Place*, 16: 181–93.

Martin, P. 2007. "Towards Effective Temporary Worker Programs: Issues and Challenges in Industrial Countries." International Migration Papers No. 89, ILO, Geneva.

————. 2010. "The Future of Labour Market Costs." Background paper for the World Migration Report 2010, IOM, Geneva.

Martin, S. 2008. "Unauthorized Migration: U.S. Policy Responses in Comparative Perspective." Background paper prepared for Civil Society Roundtable 2.2 at the 2008 Global Forum on Migration and Development, Manila, October.

O'Connell Davidson, J. 2010. "New Slavery, Old Binaries: Human Trafficking and the Borders of 'Freedom.'" *Global Networks* 10, no. 2: 244–61.

Organization for Security and Cooperation in Europe (OSCE), International Organization for Migration (IOM), International Labour Office (ILO). 2006. *Handbook on Establishing Effective Labour Migration Policies in Countries of Origin and Destination.* Vienna: OSCE/IOM/ILO.

Ruhs, M. 2005. "Managing the Immigration and Employment of Non-EU Nationals in Ireland." Studies in Public Policy No. 19, The Policy Institute/Trinity College, Dublin.

————. 2006. "The Potential of Temporary Migration Programmes in Future International Migration Policy." *International Labour Review* 145, nos. 1–2: 7–36.

Shah, N. 2007a. "Irregular Migration and Some Negative Consequences for Development: Asia-GCC Context." Background paper prepared for Civil Society Roundtable 2.2 at the 2008 Global Forum on Migration and Development, Manila, October.

————. 2007b. "Recent Labor Immigration Policies in the Oil-Rich Gulf: Some Difficulties in Effective Implementation." Paper presented at the Regional Symposium on Population and Foreign Workers in Arab Gulf States: Towards a Common Strategy, Doha, Qatar, April.

Skeldon, R. 2008. "Managing Irregular Migration as a Negative Factor in the Development of Eastern Asia." Background paper prepared for Civil Society Roundtable 2.2 at the 2008 Global Forum on Migration and Development, Manila, October.

Terrazas, A., J. Batalova, and V. Fan. 2007. "Frequently Requested Statistics on Immigrants in the United States." Migration Information Source (MPI), Washington, D.C.

Vitkovskaia, G. S. 2004. "Irregular Migration to and Through Russia: Situation, Trends and Policies." Paper presented to the Annual Meeting of the International Studies Association, Montreal.

PART 2

Migration, Development, Children, and Women

The next two chapters focus on migration, children, and women. Escobar García and Álvarez Velasco explore in greater detail what Levitt and Lamba-Nieves refer to as "cultural fluidity," that is, the exchanges in the form of social and monetary remittances and practices that occur between migrant-sending and -destination countries. By focusing on two communities in the Ecuadorian highlands, Escobar García and Álvarez Velasco are able to trace both the creation of these transnational communities and its impacts on basic social structures such as the family and the school. The formation of these transnational communities reconfigures many of the communities' social practices by handing new roles to old players. Caretakers, teachers, and children left behind undertake a new set of responsibilities to maintain newly minted family structures while negotiating the new challenges and inequalities created by international migration.

The chapter by Cortina and Ochoa-Reza studies how naturalization and family reunification policies in countries of destination impact home countries' developmental prospects. Using the cases of Turkey, Poland, and Mexico, Cortina and Ochoa-Reza argue that once family members (women and children) are united in the host country, migrants will likely stop remitting or at least will substantially decrease the frequency and amount sent home given that the contract by which migrants and family members left behind were obliged becomes obsolete. Instead of remitting, immigrants then will potentially increase the level of consumption or savings in the host country.

To a certain degree Cortina and Ochoa-Reza illustrate de la Garza's argument by focusing on the role of destination countries' migration policies that determine who is able to enter and form part of the polity. They highlight that destination countries' immigration and naturalization policies may create unintended developmental consequences for migrant-sending countries. These unintended consequences may be quite harmful both at the family and national levels, especially in those cases in which families and governments are dependent upon some of the clearest by-products of migration: remittances. As de la Garza, Levitt and Lamba-Nieves, and other contributors to this volume illustrate, remittances are not the panacea to solve countries' developmental problems; instead countries need to focus on privileging the rule of law, accountability, and effective governance in order to stimulate development for all its citizens.

CHAPTER 5

Family and School Reconfiguration

THE CASE OF ECUADORIAN HIGHLAND MIGRATION TO SPAIN

Alexandra Escobar García and Soledad Álvarez Velasco

No, I won't leave; because Oyacoto is beautiful and small. I know everyone. . . . I am afraid of leaving.

—Ángela, ten years old
Ecuadorian, daughter of emigrants
Oyacoto, February 2007

I wouldn't leave to Spain because here [in Cañar] I have my family, who are mainly my grandparents, and the land we sow.

—Jorge, fourteen years old
Ecuadorian, son of emigrants
Cañar, September 2008

One of the main consequences of globalization is the increase in the quantity and complexity of international migration. As noted by Levitt and Lamba-Nieves (this volume), the movement of millions of men and women across international borders has caused significant social, economic, political, and cultural transformations that have affected the micro- and macrosocial aspects of life in countries of origin, transit, and destination (Sassen 2008).

In flux with this global process, the reality of Ecuadorian migration at the end of the twentieth century has been altered, and its social and economic complexity has increased dramatically during the first decade of the twenty-first century. The Ecuadorian development and migratory transitions (see DeWind and Ergun this volume) took the country from having a moderate unidirectional out-migration system to a tripartite system in which it became a *sending, receiving,* and *transit* country simultaneously.

In this context and focusing only on Ecuador as a sending country, migration of Ecuadorians to Spain has been undoubtedly one of the processes that have had major impacts, both in Ecuador and Spain. Ecuadorian migration to Spain constitutes one of the most significant movements of population in the past ten years that has not been caused by an armed conflict or by a natural disaster (UNFPA-FLACSO 2008:63). According to the Spanish Institute of National Statistics, between 1998 and 2003 the number of Ecuadorians in Spain increased by 1,000 percent, from 7,406 to 470,090 (INE 2004 in OIM 2008:29). Just between 1999 and 2000, around 57 percent (267,030) of Ecuadorians left the country (National Migration Direction in UNFPA-FLACSO 2008:16). In those years, Spain also registered an unprecedented increase in the arrival of Ecuadorians. In 1999 there were 8,793 Ecuadorians registered in Spain; a year later the number increased thirteen times; by 2000, 91,120 Ecuadorians were listed in the Spanish registries (UNFPA-FLACSO 2008:63). Even though this trend has slowed since 2004 due to Spain's adherence to the Schengen Treaty, which imposes visa restrictions on Ecuadorian citizens, and the Euro economic and financial crisis, migration has continued via family reunification initiated by the first wave of immigrants who changed their migratory status. (See Cortina and Ochoa-Reza in this volume for a discussion of the impact of family reunification on development.) In less than a decade, this exodus has led 450,000 Ecuadorians to reside in Spain, of which around 51 percent are women and 49 percent are men (UNFPA-FLACSO 2008). The composition and magnitude of this migratory flow have triggered several sociopolitical, cultural, and economic transformations in both countries.

Among the most analyzed and publicly highlighted issues, apart from the obvious demographic change that both countries have been facing over the past two decades, is the economic impact that migration has had both in Ecuador and Spain. Spain's economic growth during the 1990s would not have been possible without migrant labor, which revitalized certain sectors, such as construction and agriculture, and also impacted the domestic labor force by increasing the labor and economic mobility among Spanish workers (Pajares 2009). Simultaneously the entrance of Ecuadorian workers in Spain's labor market, especially in the informal sector (domestic service, child and elder care, construction, agriculture, among others), has created a permanent remittance market from Ecuadorian workers in Spain to their families left behind in Ecuador. As in other migrant-sending countries, monetary remittances have had a significant and direct impact on Ecuador's national economy. At the national level, remittance flows constitute the third largest source of income in the state's annual budget. According to the Banco Central del Ecuador

(2009), remittances from Spain constitute around US$1.025 billion, with 2007 being the year in which remittances peaked significantly, with a total amount of 1.287 billion. Even though this influx of money has significantly affected local development, migration impacts at the micro level go beyond economic indicators. Migration affects the social and cultural life of migrant-sending and -receiving communities mainly in the daily life of migrants and those left behind: sons, daughters, husbands, wives, grandparents, cousins, and uncles, among others. Certainly remittances have changed the way we understand the relationship between migration and development; however, our understanding of the impact of migration beyond economic indicators is still nebulous at best and demands immediate responses from the state as well as from civil society. (See Levitt and Lamba-Nieves, this volume, for a discussion on how migration creates a transnational space that establishes a unique development and migration culture.)

The outflow of Ecuadorian men and women to Spain has transformed private spaces. New family arrangements have been configured; new social roles and forms of care have been established; and clearly one of the most complex but yet unseen impacts has been on those children who have been left behind. The out-migration of adults necessarily implies that an increasing number of children and adolescents have been affected in diverse ways by the departure of mothers and fathers. In addition, parental migration has transformed some of the traditional social institutions in charge of children's daily lives.

The main purpose of this chapter is to contribute to the understanding of the impact that Ecuadorian migration to Spain has had in the microsocial sphere. We are interested in analyzing the relationship between migration and childhood and in exploring the ways families and schools in Ecuador have been reconfigured and have assumed new social roles and, above all, how they have adopted new forms of care in response to the high mobility of Ecuadorians to Spain. How has the Ecuador–Spain migration process affected the microsocial domain? What types of reconfigurations have taken place inside families and schools? How does migration affect the lives of children and adolescents who are left behind? What are public policies' challenges for Ecuador and Spain in response to children affected by migration? What is the possible impact of migration on Ecuadorian and Spanish local development?

In order to shed some light on these questions, we explore the impact of Ecuadorian migration to Spain in two highland provinces where migration into Spain is among the highest: Oyacoto in the province of

Pichincha and Cañar in the province of Cañar. We analyze the impact of transnational migration—particularly from Ecuador to Spain—on children, mainly through ethnographic research highlighting the voices of local actors involved in this process.

This chapter has four sections. In the first section we present our theoretical approach in which we discuss the main contributions that have emerged from the transnationalism literature in order to study the relationship between transnational migration and the impacts on families, schools, and children. Then we offer a brief historical review of the sociopolitical and economic contexts in Ecuador during the past decade, in which this complex contemporary migration process is taking place. In the third section we discuss the results of two case studies, one conducted in Oyacoto and the other in Cañar. These case studies allow us to weigh the impact of transnationalism on the microsocial arena, particularly at the household and school levels. In the last section we stress the importance for local development in the analysis of migration and its transnational implications to establish a course of action to confront the impact of migration on children, their development, and the exercise of their rights. Understanding the effect of transnational migration on the daily life of boys, girls, adolescents, grandparents, cousins, teachers, and classmates should be a priority for states and civil society to respond to youth affected by migration who are growing more isolated in the midst of a transnational migration process.

THEORETICAL REMARKS

Based on sociological and anthropological theoretical approaches, the transnational perspective has made important contributions to the understanding of contemporary migration. Glick-Schiller and Levitt (2004:1003) point out the need to consolidate a new paradigm for the analysis of migration, rejecting the view of nation-states and societies as monolithic and "natural" institutions with an a priori existence or given set of functions. They propose the reformulation of these concepts by considering them part of a social process that is constantly fluctuating, that is, a process that simultaneously occurs within and between national boundaries, thus creating a transnational space. A transnational theoretical approach is necessary to broaden and deepen our understanding given that social actors, the immigrants in this case, cross borders daily, migrate internally, and interconnect and transform societies both at origin and destination countries simultaneously (1003). This, in turn, has significant impacts on each country's political systems.

This critique does not exclude recognizing the crucial role of nation-states as noted by de la Garza (this volume), but emphasizes that any approach should not be confined to the limits of states and instead should prioritize the leading role of migrants in the creation of this simultaneous space as well as the social interactions and life experiences that are established with those left behind. It is essential, then, to analyze the interaction between origin and destination societies—in our case, between Ecuador and Spain—to understand the modus operandi of transnational social networks and the way they exchange ideas, identities, experiences, strategies, and migration knowledge. In short, it is essential to analyze the production, transfer, and reception of social remittances (Levitt 1998), which will reconfigure the social, political, cultural, and economic dynamics at the local level and thus the impact of migration on development (Glick-Schiller and Levitt 2004:1009; Levitt 1998).

Analyzing migration as part of a transnational process that impacts other social institutions also requires considering such institutions as dynamic entities that are reconfigured constantly. Without a doubt, improvements in communication technologies have accelerated the multiplication of networks that shape the way institutions are reconfigured. In fact the main characteristic of this most recent migration wave is the permanent and simultaneous communication between migrants and those left behind and its impact on the countries of origin and destination (Mummert 1999; Glick-Schiller and Levitt 2004). The exchange of social remittances has had a crucial impact on this transnational process. (See Levitt and Lamba-Nieves in this volume for a discussion of how social remittances coupled with culture shape policy outcomes.) On the one hand, the advances in communication and the transnational dynamics it generates have kept migrants interconnected, creating a cross-border migration network that, among other things, has blurred national borders, allowed the movement of thousands of migrants (documented and undocumented), putting into question state migratory policies (see Koser in this volume for a discussion), and has also promoted their insertion into receiving societies. On the other hand, it has modified the traditional role of families and schools, both at home and in host societies (Glick-Schiller et al. 1995; Glick-Schiller and Levitt 2004).

In the particular case of the family, the continuous and accelerated mobilization of men and women has caused direct effects on the role of this social institution. The concept of family has been a cornerstone of the debate. Recognizing that families are neither homogeneous nor fixed units, researchers have investigated how the process of social reproduction, understood as a process that sustains or transforms the inherited characteristics of a social institution, in this case the family, happens at a distance (Sørense 2005; Thorne 1997; Hondagneu-Sotelo and Avila 1997; Salazar Parreñas 2001, 2005; Pribilsky 2004). The analysis has been centered on understanding how the so-called *transnational family*, that is, those families that live separated most of the time, are configured. Despite being separated by thousands of miles, they remain "united," giving way to a collective feeling of well-being and unity that transcends national borders (Bryceson and Vuorela 2002:3).

The new care arrangements, derived from the transnational family, have been analyzed from the transnational approach, especially to "bring gender" into the debate. This has implied that, on the one hand, women are seen as participants at all levels and phases of the migration process (Mahler and Pessar 2006). In contrast, despite women's presence in this process, power and social inequalities between men and women, configured in home societies, end up being reproduced in some cases and abolished in some other. (See Levitt and Lamba-Nieves in this volume for a discussion of gender roles.) Hence including a gender perspective when researching the reconfiguration of families in a transnational setting is of the outmost importance. Often, and despite migration, those inequalities determine the way women relate to global processes of social reproduction (Herrera 2006:284).

The decision to migrate that thousands of women make every day, with their particular emotions and stories, has impacted the way families are organized and to some extent has raised questions about the traditional conception of maternity within a transnational framework (Salazar Parreñas 2001, 2005; Pessar and Mahler 2006; Hondagneu-Sotelo and Avila 1997). When mothers migrate, they change the ancestral matriarchal system that gives them the exclusive role of caregiver. These women break from the idea of maternity as a sort of "epoxy glue" holding together the family and, ultimately, society (Blum and Deussen 1996; Scheper-Hughes 1992). The continuous mobility of women has transformed the interactions between mother and child, as well as the modes of social reproduction, which now occurs at a distance.

Contemporary "transnational maternity" has affected not only the family as a structure but also schools as institutions. This social institution has taken over new roles and experienced significant transformations. And, as we shall exemplify further, the school has been inserted into the global scaffolding of caregiving to those children and adolescents who stay behind, affecting the traditional social roles (Parreñas 2001; Hondagneu-Sotelo and Avila 1997; Glick-Schiller and Levitt 2004).

This contemporary social process has directly affected the lives of boys, girls, and adolescents. Frequently these social actors stay with a relative or start their own migration journey. However, while women (especially mothers) have been widely recognized within this process, children have not. Even though the relation between children and migration is included in the theoretical debate, their presence and participation continue to be passive, silent, and marginal because there is a prevailing adult-centric perspective that extends to all aspects of social life and thus to the migration process (Horton 2008; Huisjman 2006; Camacho 2006; James and Prout 1997). The peripheral status of children is clearly evident in their recent recognition as social actors (the U.N. Convention on the Rights of the Child was approved only in 1990), and children have been subsumed under the binomial "mother-child" (Mayall 2001:243; Mahler and Passar 2006).

Even if the decision to migrate remains an adult or household responsibility, the children who do not migrate reconfigure their parents' role and constantly delineate their migration decisions. Since children are the last link in the chain, if there are no family reunification policies at the countries of destination, they face the greatest impacts because they have to stay under the care of relatives, and sometimes they even live independently (Dreby 2007; Salazar Parreñas 2005; Faulstich Orellana et al. 2001). Within this process, both the ones who stay and the ones who leave must deal with a complex family situation which is exacerbated by geographical separation. However, migration scholars focus disproportionately on the lives of adults and, with very few exceptions, don't take into account the children's role in the context of transnational families. The importance of highlighting what happens to children and adolescents through their own voices, while recognizing their autonomy and ability as active social actors of the migration process, is a crucial task that remains underresearched.

Three institutions shape the development of children and adolescents: family, schools, and the media. The first two have traditionally gained major attention as brokers or agents that transfer dominant relations and where social codes are established (Bustelo 2005:254). Despite the obvious relevance of understanding how these relations are established, especially during children's developmental stages, the majority of the analysis about globalization and transnationalism focuses on the production side rather than on how it was created in the first place. This is particularly important given that the reproduction of social relations and codes constitute an important cornerstone of transnationalism, which in turn is an essential part of any migratory experience.

As a response to the new social fabrics knitted by transnational migration, schools have also modified their role in society. Schools have adopted new strategies to receive children from migrant households or have been forced to face the situation of students with absent parents. Despite the immediate impact that migration has had on school systems, very little research has been done on this issue from a transnational perspective. In what follows we discuss the importance of analyzing schools as a part of the transnational fabric of care. First, however, we present a migration profile of Ecuador.

THE SCENARIO OF CONTEMPORARY ECUADOR

During the first decade of the twenty-first century, Ecuadorian migration has been transformed. Today Ecuador is a place in which three different but interlinked realities conflate within the same space and time: outflow, inflow, and transit of migrants. On the one hand, the difficult socioeconomic and political situation since the mid-1990s and during the first years of the new millennium positioned Ecuador as the main migrant-sending country in the Andean region to Europe and the United States. According to demographic projections, between 10 and 11 percent of the total population (1.4 to 1.7 million) lived outside Ecuador (CEIEME 2008:3; UNFPA-FLACSO 2008:15). The work these men and women do abroad represents the third largest source of income that sustains Ecuador's economy. It is estimated that remittances amount to US$2.5 billion (World Bank 2011). On the other hand, Ecuador has become an attractive destination, either temporary or permanent, for immigrants, the majority coming from Colombia, Peru, Haiti, Cuba, and China. Among the main reasons that explain this fact is that since 2000 Ecuador's economy has been dollarized (an attractive factor for new immigrants who want to send remittances in dollars to their countries of origin); the country is less violent and thus much safer than other countries in the region; and since approving its new Constitution at the end of 2008, Ecuador advocates for universal citizenship and free mobility, making the acquisition of refugee status and the regularization of migratory status a simple matter.[1] Additionally, between the end of the twentieth century and the first years of the twenty-first, Ecuador received increasing inflows of migrants from South America, Asia, and Africa. Many arrive in order to contact or pay "coyotes" (migrant smugglers) and continue their transit along highly violent and dangerous paths with illegal crossings to the borders of Guatemala, crossing the southern and northern Mexican borders, to finally attempt entering the United States (UNFPA-FLACSO 2008:11–13; OIM 2008; Ramírez Gallegos and Álvarez Velasco 2009). As expected, this complex reality, produced by the tripartite migration system, has impacted the state and society in different ways, not only in Ecuador but also in all the origin and destination countries where Ecuadorians go or whence they came. Even though this condition presents us with a range of possibilities to reflect on the Ecuadorian migration process, in this chapter our analysis is framed by the outflow of Ecuadorians and its effects on social processes.

Our analysis focuses on the second migratory wave, which started in the mid-1990s. Demographic figures estimate that between 1996 and the first years of the new millennium, around 700,000 Ecuadorians left the country (UNFPA-FLACSO 2008). The migratory process that covers this new stage corresponds to global transformations that interacted with the economic and political national context; combined, these resulted in a continuous increase of out-migration to northern countries, changing the profiles of the migrant population and multiplying the migrant destinations.

Ecuador ended the twentieth century with an unprecedented social, economic, and political crisis that continues to radically influence the economic and social capacity of thousands of Ecuadorian families. In 1995 the last armed conflict with Peru triggered a profound economic crisis that was intensified in 1997 due to the ecological disasters caused by El Niño (especially among the population of the coastal urban areas of the country).[2] Unemployment and underemployment were massive, and consequently household income fell dramatically. The Ecuadorian state exacerbated the situation with the implementation of neoliberal policies and reduced investments in health, education, development, and housing (Acosta 2006:12). Furthermore in 2000 the banking system collapsed, leading to the "banking holiday" that ended in the dollarization of Ecuador's economy. As a consequence unemployment, social inequality, and poverty increased even more.[3] Throughout the decade a continuous degradation of the rule of law coupled with an increase in corruption left a wide segment of the population feeling disenchanted with whatever was left of Ecuadorian democratic institutions and political parties (Bustamante et al. 2006:27). Ultimately these "critical events," as Sassen (1998) refers to them, to a large extent impelled the emigration of thousands of Ecuadorian men and women.

During this second cycle, the classic pattern of migration shifted in terms of points of origin, characteristics, and destinations. Three-quarters of the migrants who left during this period came mainly from urban areas (INEC 2008), and their origin extended to all provinces from the three regions of the country. Migrants were young men and mainly women, with educational levels above the national average, who belonged to the working and middle classes (Herrera et al. 2005:19–20). The prominence of migrant women is indicative of their relevant role in the migration process. Even though more men continue to migrate nationwide, in some parts of the country the proportion of women is higher. Given the age composition of this second migratory group, many of them were or are parents: 37 percent left their children living in Ecuador (INEC 2008). Finally, destination countries also changed: Italy and, above all, Spain emerged as new receiving countries. The magnitude and frequency of Ecuadorian migration to Spain is astonishing: in only five years, around 500,000 Ecuadorians migrated there (Observatorio Permanente de la Inmigración 2009).

The consolidation of Spain as a main destination in this second migratory wave, from our point of view, is based on four causes: (1) the existing migrant networks, (2) the binational policies that agreed on the free mobility of migration flows between both countries along with the increase of economic costs and the risks that clandestine migration to the United States implied, (3) the socioeconomic transformations produced by the acceptance of Spain into the European Union, and (4) the cultural and language similarities between Ecuador and Spain.

The increase in Ecuadorian out-migration since 1999 forms part of an increase of Latin American migration to Spain. Even though Ecuadorian migration to Spain peaked during this second wave, it is not a story that began at the end of the 1990s. Historical data show a slow but sustained Ecuadorian emigration from 1960 until 1990. For instance, if we compare the four Andean countries (Bolivia, Colombia, Ecuador, and Peru) in 1995, Ecuadorian migration to Spain was consistently the largest, followed by Colombia and Peru. During this period the trend remained stable. At the beginning of 1990 Ecuadorians were already the second-largest group in Spain after Moroccans, and the first among South Americans allowing the consolidation of social networks that pulled their families and friends to Spain during this period (Herrera et al. 2005).

Second, until 2003 Ecuadorians were able to enter Spain as tourists without any visa requirements whatsoever, which explains why the annual outflow of 5,000 migrants during the 1990s increased to 150,000 annual migrants after 2000 (Gratton 2005:43). Also, given the economic crisis and the increase on restrictive migratory policies, the cost of migrating to the United States illegally basically meant using networks of coyotes. As a result, the costs of migrating to the United States increased four times. In 1980, for instance, an emigrant paid between US$1,500 and US$3,000 to get into the United States through a coyote. In contrast, in 2002 the cost increased between US$8,500 and US$12,000—three times higher than Ecuador's GDP per capita. The economic crisis and the increase on restrictive measures were reflected not only in higher prices but also in the risks that migrants faced (Gratton 2005:41; Durand 2007).

Third, the insertion of Spain into the European Union promoted the implementation of structural macroeconomic changes that modernized and boosted the Spanish economy and as a consequence improved the living standards of Spaniards. One of the main measures adopted during this economic boom was the increased flexibility of the labor market that led to a reduction of production costs and unemployment. The deregulation of the labor market, however, hampered the rights of Spanish workers and worsened the work conditions in low-productivity sectors, which allowed the creation and consolidation of new labor niches that required a labor force willing to meet the needs of a precarious secondary labor market; migrant workers were the only ones willing to fill this niche. Their insertion into the labor market helped to accelerate the modernization of the Spanish economy, generated a massive incorporation of women into the labor market, and allowed the native-born population to increase their human capital through investments in education. Both transformations affected the socioeconomic structure of families and modified the needs of the labor market, as they delayed the entry of young people into formal employment and indirectly created a demand for domestic workers and care services to support the role of women in their homes who were now being incorporated into the labor market.

Finally, the cultural closeness between Ecuador and Spain also favored the selection of this destination by many migrants. The language, the historical proximity, and the cultural practices within Spanish society, such as the need for domestic employees and care services for the elderly, religious celebrations, beliefs, and other practices, influenced individuals' selection of Spain as a destination. This cultural closeness and the possibility of earning salaries two or three times higher than in Ecuador (Gratton 2005:45) explain why Spain was the main destination for Ecuadorian migrants during this second wave.

Although migration flows show a steep decline after visas were imposed to restrict the entry of Ecuadorians into Spain—and consequently into the European Union—as well as after the recent European sovereign debt crisis, the Ecuadorian community is still the biggest group of Latin American immigrants living in Spain (UNFPA-FLACSO 2008). The regularization processes encouraged by Spain resulted in an estimated 440,000 Ecuadorians with legal residence in the country and a total of 86,000 with Spanish nationality (OPI 2009). Currently the profile of the Ecuadorian population in Spain is characterized by a majority of women versus men (51 percent are women, 47 percent are men) and is also relatively young: 66 percent of Ecuadorians are between twenty-five and forty-four, and 22 percent have children under sixteen years, of whom 87 percent live in their country of origin (INE 2007). A large proportion of the Ecuadorian community is settled in Madrid (32 percent), followed by Cataluña (19), Valencia (12), Murcia (11), and a minor proportion in other communities (UNFPA-FLACSO 2008). In Madrid and Cataluña, the proportion of women is higher given the demand for domestic and caregiving work. The majority of Ecuadorian migrants work in the service sector (61 percent), followed by agriculture (9) and industry (8); and more than 70 percent are incorporated into the labor market (UNFPA-FLACSO 2008). It is estimated that around 86 percent of Ecuadorian migrants in Spain remit money to their families, becoming the second-largest remitting group after the Dominican community (BENDIXEN 2007).

Since 2008 the Spanish economy suffered a terrible setback due to the global economic crisis, which was exacerbated by the European sovereign debt crisis. The most affected sectors were the ones in which migrant labor tended to be overrepresented, such as the service and construction industries. Although the greater part of Ecuadorians already had legal status by that time due to the regularization process of 2005, Ecuadorians nonetheless experienced unemployment rates as high as 20 percent, making them the third-largest group of unemployed immigrants in Spain (Pajares 2009). The effect of the economic crisis is manifested by a decline in the number of Ecuadorians reuniting with their family members living in Spain through either family reunification or employment. The repercussions of the global economic crisis are also felt in Ecuador, where negative income shocks due to a reduction in the amount and frequency of remittances reduced overall household income. According to Ecuador's Central Bank, while in 2006 remittances coming from Spain were approximately US$1.29 billion, by 2009 that amount decreased to US$1.032 billion. While part of this reduction can be attributed to successful reunification processes or to the return of some migrants back to Ecuador (see Cortina and Ochoa-Reza in this volume for a discussion of family reunification for the case of Turkey and Mexico), a significant number still live in Spain but are unemployed and therefore cannot remit as much or as frequently as they did in the past.

FROM MACRO TO MICRO

Analyzing the migratory process between Ecuador and Spain and its impacts at the local level implies a methodological challenge. Glick-Schiller and Levitt (2004) and Massey and Capoferro (2006), among others, suggest that when studying simultaneous social processes like the ones we endeavor to explore in this chapter, the primary methodological resource should consist of a multisited ethnography. Even though the ideal scenario would be to concentrate on both contexts, that is, on sending and receiving countries, these authors suggest that it is still possible to study the impact of the transnational dynamics that arise due to the interactions between sites by focusing on those who stay behind. This assumes that the interactions occurring within a particular social context are reconfigured interactively between those who stayed behind and those who migrated.

In what follows, we present and explore the impacts of Ecuadorian emigration to Spain in Oyacoto and Cañar in the Ecuadorian highlands. Our main focus is an ethnographic analysis on families and schools. Several reasons explain why we chose these two research sites for our analysis. First, both localities have a historical record of internal migration (inflow and outflow). In the case of Oyacoto, it is known that migrants arrived during the 1970s from the southern provinces of the country, mainly from Azuay and Loja, due to its proximity to the nation's capital.[4] In the case of Cañar, during the 1960s its population migrated to the Ecuadorian coast. This allows us to assume, following Portes (2001), that previous migratory experiences at the community level served as a catalyst for today's migratory flows.

Second, as a direct result of that experience, both localities experienced out-migration during the latest migratory wave. Even though the United States is an important destination for migrants from Oyacato and Cañar,

Spain is still preferred. Third, emigration to Spain has affected the lives of those who stayed behind in Oyacoto and Cañar. Due to the small size of both rural localities, however, very little is known about the impact of migration, not only on development but on the lives of children who stayed behind.

Despite the fact that in both localities it is possible to identify the impacts of migration on families and on schools, in the case of Oyacoto we have prioritized the analysis of schools, given that there is only one school that plays a predominant and dynamic role in the lives of those who stayed behind. This case illustrates what happens with this particular social institution and the contemporary changes as a by-product of migration and its transnational dynamics. For the case of Cañar, we focus on the family in order to illustrate the changes brought by migration in terms of how child care is organized and regarding the creation and promotion of transnational family ties and the role that the community plays to ensure the maintenance of children.

CAÑAR: CHANGES WITHIN THE FAMILIES

Cañar canton (municipality) has some important features that enable us to track migration's microsocial impacts. It is a rural municipality located in the southern part of Ecuador, a region in which migration is a prevalent phenomenon.

Migration has shaped the way the community and families are organized. In a twenty-year span, for instance, household composition experienced significant changes due to the increase in out-migration. While the number of extended households at the national and Latin American level underwent a clear decrease, in Cañar the number increased gradually over the same period. With or without a parent-child core, these households incorporated other relatives. Currently extended households in Cañar represent around 41 percent of all households in the canton and 63 percent among migrant households (Escobar 2008).

Jorge is a fourteen-year-old boy from Cañar who, like the other eight thousand children in the canton, has been part of his family's international migration practices since his parents moved to Spain in 2000. When we asked him what family meant to him, he said, "For me, family is the place where you are taken care of, protected and loved. . . . It is comprised of a father, a mother, brothers, grandparents, uncles and cousins" (September 2008). Jorge makes a simple and accurate description of what family represents within the local conceptualization, especially among children in rural communities. Family, especially in rural communities such as Cañar, is essential to the development and organization of community life because it provides solidarity and protection within the community. In Cañar the reorganization of the family from extended to transnational as a response to parental international migration has been crucial to guarantee that the traditional conceptualization of family as a social structure and the fundamental principles—outlined by Jorge—are kept intact and transmitted generation after generation.

The decision to migrate made within a family rarely incorporates children in the process. This, however, creates a number of family tensions, especially between parents and their children, that should be constantly monitored in order to ensure the survival of the family when facing the geographical separation of its members. For example, Jorge mentioned that he was never asked by his parents about their decision to migrate: "I would have liked to be asked what I thought about it, because if they did, I would have asked them not to leave and to stay here to take care of us."

Even though adults try to implement some transition strategies to mitigate the impacts of physical separation on children, these don't always work. In the case of Jorge, his father was the one who initially migrated to Murcia and found a job at a swine farm. During this first stage, as Jorge says, the changes in their lives were not so significant: "We were at our house in Ger [community of origin]; we had our land, we went to school, and my mom took care of us; but, of course, we were always close to my grandparents." However, three years later, after his father managed to improve his migratory status and his conditions in Spain, his mother also traveled as part of the family reunification process. From that moment on, interactions within Jorge's family changed.

On the one hand, Jorge's new family, made up of his younger sister (age ten) and his maternal grandparents, moved to the main town in the canton in order to give him and his sister access to secondary education, thus fulfilling their parents' dream of giving them the opportunities they did not have in their community. On the other hand, his mother entrusted them to her parents to guarantee their care. A key point to differentiate the caring arrangements inside these families is the social construct of gender that regulates the division of reproductive and productive labor within households: care and socialization, the reproductive sphere, are functions conferred on women, while men deal only with the productive sphere (Salazar Parreñas 2005). The task of taking care of Jorge and his sister, therefore, was transferred specifically to the maternal grandmother, who now assumes the role of mother and organizes her grandchildren's lives according to the instructions sent by their parents.

Jorge has had close ties with his grandparents since he was a child, and he respects and loves them very much, especially now that they take care of him. They represent authority, even more so than his parents. He shares with them the activities that should be undertaken with his biological parents. In his words, "My grandparents are my parents now because they take care of us and love us. . . . Together with my grandfather, we plant, harvest, and keep the land clean. . . . And I help my grandmother with household chores."

Even though kinship ties have helped to keep the family organization in Cañar, the departure of fathers and mothers has left clear emotional wounds upon their children. Jorge's voice reveals the consequences of what it means to be a son from afar: "Now that they are there, I don't feel much love for them . . . because I think they left us, first my dad when I was only six years old, and then my mom when I was nine. . . . I am feeling resentful towards them and I do not think I can do anything to change that." Resentment and emotional pain are some of the feelings that children like Jorge experience once they are separated from their parents. Here a question arises: How are these feelings mediated through the social reproduction of transnational families like Jorge's? Bryceson and Vuorela (2002) suggest that the new notion of family—the notion of a transnational family—as well as the emotional and economic ties that this reconfiguration brings is handled by the members of the newly reconfigured family: migrant parents, children, and caregivers.

Jorge's mother, who tries to maintain contact with him and his sister and mitigate the resentment by exercising her maternal role from a distance, apparently negotiates the burden of raising children in a distant family. From Murcia, she uses a number of mechanisms to maintain close relationships despite the distance in order to decrease her children's pain. These mechanisms include the monthly sending of remittances, gifts, constant communication via cell phone, and even visits home. Even though they help to strengthen family ties, they can also create tension between children and parents.

The money sent home—administered by his grandmother—has allowed Jorge and his new family to remain in Cañar, to have a new house, and to buy more land and for the children to attend school. It is clear that the education of Jorge and his sister is very important to the whole family and is necessary for the children to have access to different opportunities, which would be difficult to achieve in Cañar if not for their parents' migration. Jorge explains, "My parents and grandparents say that I will go to the university in Riobamba, where I can pursue the studies that I want. . . . I want to be a school teacher." Although Jorge recognizes and values his parents' efforts, it is very difficult for him to understand their decision to depart and leave them behind: "My parents send money for the education and well-being of my sister and I, but I would have preferred if they had stayed with us and to be together."

Similarly the use of phones helps maintain contact, familiarity, and intimacy despite the distance. Jorge and his parents use mobile phones to negotiate some of the emotional tensions involved in being a son, a mother, and a father from afar. His mother calls every week to talk to her children in order to maintain their relationship. However, Jorge has decided to avoid the calls: "My mom calls every week to hear from us, but I don't really want to talk to her, I prefer if she talks to my grandmother and tells her what to do with us."

Visiting has been another mechanism employed by Jorge's parents, yet he finds the visits unsatisfactory and sometimes conflicting to deal with the physical presence of his parents: "They have been here twice since they left, but it is a weird feeling to have them by my side because I'm not used to it; ultimately, for me, they are like strangers."

Social remittances also influence parents' and children's decisions and ways of thinking. According to Jorge, while his parents would like to reunite the family in Spain, he doesn't believe that is a possibility. When we asked him about what his parents said about the place where they live and why they made the decision to migrate, he replied that his parents did not talk about it with him. However, the stories his cousins tell about what it means to be a migrant child in Spain did make Jorge think that he wouldn't want to live there, even if he was with his parents: "My cousins say there is no place to go out, that they stay inside their homes and alone because there is no family. And the family you have is far away so you can't see them every day. That's why I'd rather stay here with my grandparents; it would be better if my mom and dad returned."

Experiencing international migration at a very young age leaves a mark on many of these children. In Jorge's case, not only are his parents gone, but several of his uncles have migrated to the United States. While Jorge now shows clear resentment about his parents' decision, the possibility of migrating abroad when he becomes an adult is a potential reality. Despite his intentions to be a schoolteacher, get married, and have a family, he says, "If things don't work well here [in Cañar], I will have to go, but I will go to the United States because—as my uncles say—there you can really find a job." Apparently, due to the lack of opportunities and exclusion in this canton, families from Cañar and their children will continue facing challenges and responding to what it means to be a child from afar.

SAN FRANCISCO DE OYACOTO:

CHANGES WITHIN THE SCHOOL

The Oyacoto commune has two characteristics that make it particularly interesting for our analysis: it is located in Calderón, one of the urban parishes with the highest migration rate within the Metropolitan District of Quito, and it is one of the few rural communities within the district that, despite the push of the metropolis, still survives.[5]

International migration in Oyacato started in the mid-1990s and has changed the lives of thousands of people. Proof of this is in the record kept by the Atahualpa School, the only school in Oyacoto: out of 140 students in total, 60 have one or both parents living abroad. By the time this study was conducted, only fifteen cases had complete data, and the remaining forty-five were disclosed only as "children of emigrants." The reasons that explain this lack of information are discussed in the following section.

We focus here on households with complete data. Spain was the main destination for 73 percent of the cases, followed by the United States. In 67 percent of the cases both parents moved to another country (in five of the fifteen cases only the father migrated abroad), leaving their children under the care of their grandmother.

Atahualpa School is an elementary public school with an enrollment of 140 students between six and eleven years of age. Most of the students come from working-class families. Upon graduation, students have two options: continue their secondary (middle school) education in other schools located in Calderón or the Metropolitan District of Quito or migrate abroad via family reunification either formally or by informal means. Formal migration of children usually happens when their parents have already regularized their migratory status and when, thanks to Spain's governmental programs, migrants are able to "pull" their children into the country. Irregular migration, on the other hand, occurs mainly in those cases in which children's parents are living in the United States. In these cases parents pay a *coyote* to bring their children across the border. Both situations have been identified by the principal and the teachers of Atahualpa School, who have started to pay significant attention to children affected by parental migration. As the principal said, "From one day to the next they stop attending classes. Weeks passed and we knew nothing. Then we were concerned and went looking for the children in their homes. So we learned they were gone. On other occasions, very few though, the grandmothers came to tell us and ask for advice. But this is recent" (February 2007).

Only in the past four years had Atahualpa School become aware of the impact that international migration has had on its students and the new role that it is assuming as an institution. Although the permanent absence of one of its students due to a family reunification process is strong evidence of the impact of migration, many other students remain home without their parents, living under the care of their grandmother along with their cousins, sisters, or brothers who are in a similar situation. This may not be the worst-case scenario, but that does not necessarily mean that it has no direct consequences on their lives and on the community. A second-grade teacher described the situation: "The majority [of parents] leave without saying anything. We don't realize what is going on until we notice that some of the children seem concerned, when they don't bring their homework, or when the grandmothers come to school, if they do. For these children, it's hard. . . . We can tell just by observing children's behaviors when he or she has his parents living abroad because that face of sorrow does not change, it stays the same" (March 2007).

Teachers and the school's principal share the same perception: children of migrant parents seem to be going through a period of grief and seem to be sadder than children of nonmigrant parents. Teachers have identified several behaviors: sometimes students become quieter in the classroom; they are regularly absent as the roles of authority within their new families are often blurred; sometimes their personal hygiene and their diet deteriorate, evident when they tend to fall asleep easily while in class; also, they seem to "be in pain" (seventh-grade teacher, Atahualpa School, February 2007). These issues have slowly become more apparent as more men and women are emigrating from Oyacoto. As a response, the principal and the teachers are assuming a more active role in identifying the impacts of migration among their students.

Teachers have interestingly noticed that the children of migrants do not necessarily exhibit lower academic performance. On the contrary, they maintain or even improve their performance. According to the seventh-grade teacher, "This happens because these children are aware of the sacrifice their parents are making. *Los guaguas* [the children] are responsible and know they have to get good grades." The children seem to believe that the best way to thank the parents who have gone abroad is by obtaining good grades and behaving well at home. Ten-year-old Angela, whose father migrated to Madrid five years earlier, says, "My grades are the best gift that I can give to my dad who is so far and who is making some sacrifices for me" (February 2007). On the other hand, eight-year-old Esteban, whose parents live in Murcia, says, "One day when we spoke, my parents told me: if I have good grades, I will be able to see them sooner. So I have to study" (February 2007).

Teachers have also noticed that in the classroom, and particularly during social studies class, a special dynamic has emerged. It has become a space where children can process what it means to be the sons and daughters of migrant parents. The class curriculum addresses issues related to population, geography, and national and international history, which seem to encourage children to ask questions and debate migration. The seventh-grade teacher explained:

> Most of my students have a relative who has migrated; it may not be close, but nonetheless still a relative. Then, during social studies class, they discuss about experiences they know. That's very good because the kids realize that there is nothing wrong or different with them and that many other children are going through the same issues. They talk about their life experiences; the places where their parents are, and they always talk about or show the things their parents have sent them.

Children also frequently ask about the country where their parents are residing. According to the teachers, the children want to know about Spain, about Madrid, Spanish culture and people, and the things one can buy there. They ask about why people migrate and especially if it ever will be possible for their parents to return home.

To sum up, the weekly hour-long social studies class has become a kind of collective therapy in which children attempt to process their emotions and feelings about migration. Teachers, however, have expressed that they don't feel entirely qualified to answer certain questions. To fulfill children's needs not only implies that teachers possess greater knowledge about Ecuadorian migration (causes, processes, destinations) and about countries of destination, but also that they have the tools to help the children process their feelings. Most of the time, teachers talk to students based on their perceptions or personal experiences without any psychological toolkit that would allow them to approach migration and its impacts holistically.

Another school dynamic occurs outside the classroom, during breaks, when students show one another the gifts they've received from abroad (candies, shoes, colored pens, toys, etc.). Children eagerly await the arrival of the "package from Madrid or New York" (second-grade teacher, February 2007). The gifts (part of social remittances) become a synonym for affection and a kind of temporary physical parental replacement. But the gifts can also create distinctions and rivalries among children.

Not all children receive gifts; some get gifts frequently; some don't get nice things. If they are lucky, they get something nice and they bring it to the social studies class to show it (second-grade teacher, February 2007). Teachers are concerned about this situation because they perceive that these distinctions can affect children in the long term. They insist, however, that they are not well prepared to deal with it. Teachers cannot forbid children to bring gifts; they also cannot tell parents to stop sending them. Teachers have simply chosen not to intervene and hope that these distinctions won't affect the children significantly. A more holistic approach to these issues created as a by-product of parental migration is necessary to reduce the inequalities not only among children from migrant households but also between children from migrant and nonmigrant households.

Having so many students affected by international migration has helped the teachers understand the need to embrace certain changes in the classroom and in the curriculum. A first step is keeping track of the migratory status of the parents. Obtaining information from families, however, is not a simple task due in part to the limited availability of communication channels established between schools and families. On the other hand, parents tend to hide their decision, preventing schools from anticipating and adequately addressing this complex situation. In fact this same issue was observed in the case of Cañar. Many schoolchildren there claimed that the decision to migrate was not communicated and, even less, agreed among family members. From one day to the next, parents disappeared and their children were left under the care of other relatives. It is unlikely, therefore, that fathers or mothers who have a migration plan will tell the school. The school knows that this situation demands much more creativity on their part to communicate more with parents before they leave and to build trust with the new families so they will let the school know about what is happening.

Another significant change occurred in the school's curriculum, particularly in the social studies class in which the process of migration to Spain is addressed but with the constraints that teachers themselves identify. It is worth noting that the school also adopted a policy in which children of migrant households do not receive any preferential treatment. Both the principal and the teachers agree that such treatment could end up stigmatizing the children. Everyone, however, is convinced of the need to constantly monitor these children in order to have a better understanding of the conditions under which they live, their needs, their concerns, whether or not they communicate with their parents and mothers, and even if they plan to migrate. In most cases the situation is beyond teachers' control since they don't have the necessary tools to pursue the best interests of the child in these situations.

Additionally the school has become a place for community gathering. When migrants return for holidays, they organize parties on the grounds of the Atahualpa School. Despite the fact that parents hardly ever inform the school when they are leaving and don't communicate while abroad, apparently school parties are expressions of gratitude to the school for taking care of their children. Parties have also become a space to show off migrants' new, improved status. These celebrations are recent, and the ones who organize them are the emigrants who left more than five years earlier and already have regularized their migratory status in Spain. The principal said, "At the School they have already organized three of these parties. Some migrant parents who come on vacations come to the school to tell me they want to throw a party in gratitude. But they are really using the party to show off how they're doing in Spain [economically]. They provide food, sodas and give presents to the people from the community who come." The seventh-grade teacher added, "The *mamitas* [mothers] arrive very different[ly]. First, they cannot speak well and they speak with [a] Spanish accent. And second, their clothes are different, they paint their hair and look different; they can't even eat the food from here."

These celebrations are intended for those who stayed, to demonstrate that despite harsh consequences for the children the migrants are successful. This display of success directly shapes the conceptualization of a social and cultural reality about the benefits of migration and how attractive Spain would be as a possible destination. Without a doubt, the social perception of the destination society greatly impacts the decision to migrate and could end up pulling more potential migrants from Oyacoto. These are dynamic answers that most likely will change over time because, as noted by the principal of Atahualpa School, "We have recently become aware that migration directly impacts the school. Previously, it was thought that [migration] only brought consequences to households." The departure of parents not only affects the family, but also what happens at the school and community levels. Actions must then focus comprehensively on distinct but interconnected social institutions.

CONCLUSION

The daily life at Atahualpa School and in Jorge's transnational family demonstrates that there are a number of nonmigrant stakeholders involved in the migration process between Ecuador and Spain. Teachers, children, and their new caregivers have clearly become salient actors in transnational migration. All of them, in various ways, directly or indirectly, play specific roles and are also impacted positively and negatively by migration. The nature of migration and its transnational reach make evident the complexity and multidimensionality of migration's impact on migrants and those who stay behind.

Families and schools have negotiated new interactions and reconfigured the traditional roles that these institutions play in society. From the perspective of the family, however, kinship ties become essential to cope with disruptions and to mitigate the changes that the departures of parents cause in children's lives. Also, securing the protection of their children through the child care arrangements in the country of origin depends on the sensitivity of their new caregivers, as shown in Jorge's story, but this does not always happen in the new families of those who are left behind. From a microsocial point of view, the school in Oyacoto and Jorge's family in Cañar are very interesting examples of responses to migration's negative externalities. It is here that the state, through inclusive and participative public policies, could play a very important role in achieving the full developmental potential of children left behind.

The analysis presented in this chapter shows that indeed it is not just the family that assumes the care of children who are left behind but also other nontraditional institutions, such as schools. The school in Oyacoto, while functioning as a space of learning and socialization, became a place where students were able to express and vent their feelings about migration in general and about the departure of their parents in particular. Atahualpa's school has taken on this new task because children are demanding spaces that go beyond traditional concepts of education. As we were able to witness during our fieldwork, small initiatives have been adopted to counter the effects of migration, such as keeping immigration records, making changes in the social studies class, creating a space for dialogue between children of migrants, holding parties by returning migrant parents. However, the demands from the children left behind go beyond these measures and challenge the school in ways that the teachers themselves recognize. These challenges indicate to the teachers that the situation is far more complex and that sometimes they lack the appropriate tools to deal with these issues. Although the roles that Atahualpa School and Jorge's family have assumed are recent, they require immediate public policy interventions. In the domestic sphere, while the relationship between social policy and family is not always clear due to the common conceptualization that the issue of migration lies within the space of "private relationships," there is not a complete disconnection between what happens within the family and what happens outside it. Somehow, in the end, state actions always impact the private sphere and vice versa. Even if we do not intend to support a set of state interventions on family matters, we do believe the state must be responsible for the effects caused by the absence of care, exclusion, and lack of protection of its citizens, even more if they are boys, girls, and adolescents. Moreover the state's actions must be aimed at the well-being of communities in order to avoid the constant outflow of its citizens.

To confront the tensions within family relationships caused by migration, state actions cannot claim family reunification as the sole mode of public policy intervention. Jorge's example shows that daily problems and conflicts go beyond the simple reunification of family members either in the country of origin or in the country of destination. The emotional scars caused by parental migration demand the implementation of specific actions such as the activation of safety nets that provide psychological assistance to families in order to restore the emotional well-being of children, as well as of caretakers.

Schools can become an ally for both the state and families to effectively achieve the full development of children affected by migration. Some of their most visible requirements are new teaching resources, new course curricula that incorporate the topic of migration, psychological support to children, and ongoing training for teachers on how to cope with the effects of migration on children. The last is a key issue, as it is in the classroom's daily activities that children's emotional scars come to the surface and where the differences between them are pointed out. It is essential, then, that teachers know how to act in such cases in order to help children avoid the stigmatization of being left behind.

Teachers and family members affected by migration, in turn, must process their new roles and experiences within transnational migration. Education policy should include spaces to promote awareness and dialogue among teachers in relation to what it means to teach sons and daughters of migrants in communities where emigration rates are high. It is not a matter of implementing contingent measures to counter this problem. State actions should be permanent and must be recalibrated continually; they must be inserted into the context of a transnational reality and should be able to respond constantly to this particular process. Schools are a prime area for cooperation between countries of origin and destination. Spanish international aid policies could help to improve the response of Ecuador's educational system to the children of migrants. Much has been said about codevelopment between countries of origin and destination; here is an area that needs a creative policy intervention.

The transnational reality of Oyacoto and Cañar has given us a framework to appeal for new social and educational policies prioritizing the cooperation between schools and families. Migration policies go beyond issues of enforcement and population management. They should be inclusive and allied with educational and social policies. Above all, they need to consider that microsocial spaces are where the impacts of these macro processes are primarily felt. The challenge that lies ahead of us is to design policies that minimize the negative impacts of migration while maximizing its positive impacts in both countries of origin and destination.

REFERENCES

Acosta, A. 2006. *Impacto de la migración: Una lectura desde la experiencia ecuatoriana.* Quito: UNICEF.

Banco Central del Ecuador (BCE). 2009. "Remesas en el Ecuador." Quito. Accessed at http://www.bce.fin.ec/frame.php?CNT=ARB0000985.

BENDIXEN. 2007. "Remesas de España a Latinoamérica." Madrid: Bendixen y Asociados, Ministerio de Economía.

Blum, L., and T. Deussen. 1996. "Negotiating Independent Motherhood: Working-Class African American Women Talk about Marriage and Motherhood." *Gender and Society* 10: 199–211.

Bryceson, D., and U. Vuorela. 2002. "Transnational Families in the Twenty-First Century." In *The Transnational Family: New European Frontiers and Global Networks,* edited by D. Bryceson et al. Oxford: Oxford University Press.

Bustamante, F., et al. 2006. "La sociedad civil en el Ecuador: "Una sociedad civil eficaz más allá de sus debilidades." Quito: CIVICUS–Fundación Esquel [*Mimeo*].

Bustelo, E. 2005. "Infancia en indefensión." *Salud Colectiva* 1, no. 3: 253–84.

Camacho, A. Z. 2006. "Children and Migration: Understanding the Migration Experiences of Child Domestic Workers in Philippines." Institute of Social Studies research paper, The Hague.

Comisión Especial Interinstitucional de Estadísticas de Migraciones en el Ecuador (CEIME). 2008. "Apuntes sobre la emigración internacional del Ecuador." Quito.

Constitución de la República del Ecuador. 2009. Montecristi. Accessed at http:// www.asambleanacional.gov.ec/documentos/constitucion_de_bolsillo.pdf.

Dreby, J. 2007. "Children and Power in Mexican Transnational Families." *Journal of Marriage and Family* 69: 1050–64.

Durand, J. 2007. "Otra vez en primavera los inmigrantes salen a las calles." *Revista Migración y Desarrollo* 1, no. 8: 108–22.

Escobar, A. 2008. *Niñez y migración en el cantón Cañar*. Quito: ODNA-UNICEF-FLACSO.

Faulstich Orellana, M., et al. 2001. "Transnational Childhoods: The Participation of Children in Processes of Family Migration." *Social Problems* 48, no. 4: 572–91.

Glick-Schiller, N., L. Basch, and C. Szanton Blanc. 1995. "From Immigrant to Transmigrant: Theorizing Transnational Migration." *Anthropological Quarterly* 8, no. 1: 48–63.

Glick-Schiller, N., and P. Levitt. 2004. "Transnational Perspective on Migration: Conceptualizing Simultaneity." *International Migration Review* 38, no. 3: 1002–40.

Gratton, B. 2005. "Ecuador en la historia de la migración internacional ¿modelo o aberración?" In *La migración ecuatoriana: Transnacionalismo, redes e identidades*, edited by G. Herrera et al. Quito: FLACSO.

Herrera, G. 2006. "Mujeres ecuatorianas en las cadenas globales del cuidado." In *La migración ecuatoriana: Transnacionalismo, redes e identidades*, edited by G. Herrera et al. Quito: FLACSO.

Herrera, G., et al. 2005. *La migración ecuatoriana: Transnacionalismo, redes e identidades*. Quito: FLACSO-Plan Migración, Comunicación y Desarrollo.

Hondagneu-Sotelo, P., and E. Avila. 1997. "I'm Here, but I'm There." *Gender and Society* 11, no. 5: 548–71.

Horton, S. 2008. "Consuming Childhood: 'Lost' and 'Ideal' Childhoods as a Motivation for Migration." *Anthropological Quarterly* 81, no. 4: 925–43.

Huijsmans, R. 2006. "Children, Childhood and Migration." Institute of Social Studies Working Paper Series No. 427, The Hague.

Instituto Nacional de Estadística y Censos (INEC). 2001. *Censo de Población y Vivienda*.

———. 2008. *Sistema Integrado de Encuesta de Hogares*. December.

Instituto Nacional de Estadísticas de España (INE). 2004. *Anuario Estadístico de España 1998 y Anuario Estadístico de España 2004*. Madrid. Accessed at http:// www.ine.es/prodyser/pubweb/anuarios_mnu.htm.

———. 2007. *Encuesta Nacional de Inmigrantes, 2007*. Accessed at http://www.ine.es/ jaxi/menu.do?type=pcaxis&path=/t20/p319&file=inebase&L=.

———. 2008. *Perfil migratorio del Ecuador 2008*. Geneva. Accessed at http://publica
tions.iom.int/bookstore/free/ecuador_profile.pdf.

James, A., and A. Prout. 1997. "A New Paradigm for the Sociology of Childhood?
Provenance, Promise and Problems." In *Constructing and Reconstructing Child-
hood: Contemporary Issues in the Sociological Study of Childhood*, edited by A.
James and A. Prout. London: Falmer Press.

Levitt, P. 1998. "Social Remittances: Migration Driven Local-Level Forms of Cultural." *International Migration Review* 32, no. 4: 926–48.

Mahler, S., and P. Pessar. 2006. "Gender Matters: Ethnographers Bring Gender from
the Periphery toward the Core of Migration Studies." *International Migration
Review* 40, no. 1: 27–63.

Massey, D., and C. Capoferro. 2006. "La medición de la migración indocumentada."
In *Repensando las migraciones*, edited by A. Portes and J. Dewind. Mexico City:
Editorial Miguel Ángel Porrúa, Universidad Autónoma de Zacatecas, Secretaría
de Gobernación.

Mayall, B. 2001. "The Sociology of Childhood in Relation to Children's Rights."
International Journal of Children's Rights 8: 243–59.

Mummert, G. 1999. "Fronteras fragmentadas: Indentidades múltiples." In *Fronteras
Fragmentadas*, edited by G. Mummert. Zamora, Mexico: El Colegio de Michoacán, Centro de Investigación y Desarrollo del Estado de Michoacán Zamora.

Observatorio Permanente de la Inmigración (OPI). 2009. "Extranjeros con certificado
de registro o tarjeta de residencia en vigor y Extranjeros con autorización de estancia
por estudios en vigor a 31 de diciembre de 2009." Informes trimestrales OPI. Accessed at http://extranjeros.mtas.es/es/InformacionEstadistica/Informes/Extranje
ros31Diciembre2009/Archivos/Informe_Trimestral_31diciembre_2009.pdf.

Organización Internacional para las Migraciones (OIM). 2008. *Perfil Migratorio del
Ecuador 2008*. Ginebra: Organización Internacional para las Migraciones.

Pajares, M. 2009. *Inmigración y mercado de trabajo: Informe 2009*. Madrid. Accessed at
http://extranjeros.empleo.gob.es/es/observatoriopermanenteinmigracion/publicaciones
/archivos/Inmigracixn_y_mercado_de_trabajo. Informe_2009.pdf.

Pedone, C. 2006. "Tu siempre jalas a los tuyos, Cadenas y redes migratorias de las
familias ecuatorianas hacia España." In *La migración ecuatoriana: Transnacionalismo, redes e identidades*, edited by G. Herrera et al. Quito: FLACSO.

Pessar, P. R., and S. J. Mahler. 2003. "Transnational Migration: Bringing Gender."
International Migration Review 37, no. 3: 812–46.

Portes, A. 2001. "Inmigración y metrópolis: Reflexiones acerca de la historia urbana."
Migraciones Internacionales 1, no. 1 (2001). Accessed at http://redalyc.uaemex.mx
/pdf/151/15100106.pdf.

Pribilsky, J. 2001. "Nervios and Modern Childhood: Migration and Shifting Contexts of Child in the Ecuadorian Andes." *Childhood* 8, no. 2: 251–73.

———. 2004. " 'Aprendamos a Convivir:' Conjugal Relations, Co-parenting and Family Life among Ecuadorian Transnational Migrants in New York City and the
Ecuadorian Andes." *Global Networks* 4, no. 3: 313–34.

PROREDES. 2006a. "Calderón donde el agua es vida." In *Imágenes de Nuestra Iden-
tidad*. Quito: Fundación Esquel.

———. 2006b. *Plan de revalorización cultural de la parroquia de Calderón*. Quito: Fundación Esquel.

Ramírez Gallegos, J. P., and S. Álvarez Velasco. 2009. "Del Austro a Nueva York: Migración ecuatoriana en tránsito." In *Estudios fronterizos: Migración, sociedad y género*, edited by A. Grijalva et al. Baja California, Mexico: Universidad Autónoma de Baja California, Cuerpo Académico de Estudios Sociales, Instituto de Investigaciones Sociales, Mexicali.

Rojas, G. 2007. Interview in *Revista Líderes, Diario El Comercio*, May 14.

Salazar Parreñas, R. 2001. "Mothering from a Distance: Emotions, Gender, and Intergenerational Relations in Filipino Transnational Families." *Feminist Studies* 27, no. 2: 361–90.

———. 2005. *Children of Global Migration: Transnational Families and Gendered Woes*. Stanford: Stanford University Press.

Sassen, S. 1998. *Globalization and Its Discontents*. New York: New Press.

———. 2008. *Territory, Authority and Rights: From Medieval to Global Assemblages*. Princeton: Princeton University Press.

Scheper-Hughes, N. 1992. *Death Without Weeping: The Violence of Everyday Life in Brazil*. Berkeley: University of California Press.

Sørense, N. 2005. "Transnational Family Life across the Atlantic: The Experience of Colombian and Dominican Migrants in Europe." In *Migration and Domestic Work in Global Perspective*. The Netherlands: Wassenar.

Thorne, B., ed. 1997. "Feminism and the Family: Two Decades of Thought." In *Rethinking the Family: Some Feminist Questions*, ed. B. Throne et al. Boston: Northeastern Univerity Press.

United Nations Population Fund and Facultad Latinoamericana de Ciencias Sociales (UNFPA-FLACSO). 2008. *Ecuador: La migración internacional en cifras*. Quito: UNFPA-FLACSO.

Vela, M. P. 2006. "Remesas, motivo para emigrar, motor para la economía." *Revista Gestión*, no. 148: 25–30.

World Bank. 2011. *Migration and Remittances Factbook, 2011*. Washington: The World Bank.

CHAPTER 6

Women, Children, and Migration

DEVELOPMENTAL CONSIDERATIONS

Jeronimo Cortina and Enrique Ochoa-Reza

This chapter addresses the question, what are the potential developmental consequences of the international migration of women? Our specific aim is to analyze the relationship between female migration and development by paying attention to emigration originating in developing countries. After introducing some empirical and theoretical elements related to migration and development, we will discuss some of the impacts of female migration on development. This is followed by two case studies on Mexican migration to the United States and on Turkish and Polish migration to Germany.

Women have been no strangers to international migration. At the global level, female migrants have accounted for almost half of the total migrant stock since 1960 (United Nations 2011; see Table 6.1). At the regional level, the proportion of female migrants is larger in more developed regions (51 percent) than in less developed regions of the world (45 percent), suggesting the existence of a "gender push-pull" gap between more and less developed migrant destinations due to the characteristics of the labor market (see Escobar García and Álvarez Velasco in this volume for a discussion on Ecuadorian migration to Spain) on the one hand and, on the other, the immigration laws and regulations of destination countries.

In terms of growth, the female migrant stock in Africa, Latin America and the Caribbean, and Oceania grew above that of the male migrant population (8 vs. 7 percent in Africa; 3 vs. 1 percent in Latin America and the Caribbean, and 11 vs. 9 percent in Oceania). In Europe and North America female migrants have grown side by side with their counterparts (12 percent in Europe and 13 percent in North America), while in Asia the

Table 6.1   Female and Male Migrants among the Total Number of International Migrants, 1960–2000

Year	Total	Female	Male	Percent Female	Percent Male	Percent Female Growth	Percent Male Growth
1960	77,114,679	36,245,832	40,868,847	47.0	53.0	0	0
1965	80,796,968	38,240,525	42,556,443	47.3	52.7	6	4
1970	84,460,125	40,204,253	44,255,872	47.6	52.4	5	4
1975	90,368,010	43,149,598	47,218,412	47.7	52.3	7	7
1980	101,983,149	48,681,481	53,301,668	47.7	52.3	13	13
1985	113,206,691	53,869,213	59,337,478	47.6	52.4	11	11
1990	155,518,065	76,385,633	79,132,432	49.1	50.9	42	33
1995	165,968,778	81,761,249	84,207,529	49.3	50.7	7	6
2000	178,498,563	88,256,349	90,242,214	49.4	50.6	8	7
2005	195,245,404	96,074,285	99,171,119	49.2	50.8	9	10
2010	213,943,812	104,794,962	109,148,850	49.0	51.0	9	10

Source: United Nations, Department of Economic and Social Affairs, Population Division, 2011.

growth of the female migrant population has been slightly slower than that of the male migrant population (6 vs. 7 percent; see Figure 6.1).

Despite the fact that women have represented practically half of the global migrant population for more than fifty years and that awareness of the specificity of women in contemporary research has increased (Castles and Miller 2009; Donato et al. 2006), female migration remains an elusive topic in migration and development research. One reason for this is the scarcity of individual-level data on the incidence and magnitude of international migration of women. Another reason for the paucity of research to assess the full developmental implications of women and international migration is the lack of a gender perspective to understand migration's developmental potentials. Until the 1970s, for instance, most research on migration implicitly assumed that all migrants were male. This "assumption was particularly prevalent when attention was focused on the economic aspects of international migration; because it was widely believed that the participation of women in international labor migration was negligible" (Zlotnik 2003:1); when women's migration was acknowledged, it portrayed them as accompanying dependents (Boyd 1989; Chant and Radcliffe 1992). Since the late 1980s, however, there has been a vast body of literature on issues related to gender and migration (see Donato et al. 2006 for a review), as well as a tidal wave of research on development and gender (see Boserup 1970; Harcourt 1994; McDonald 2000) that has generated a number of theoretical approaches to gauging the role of gen-

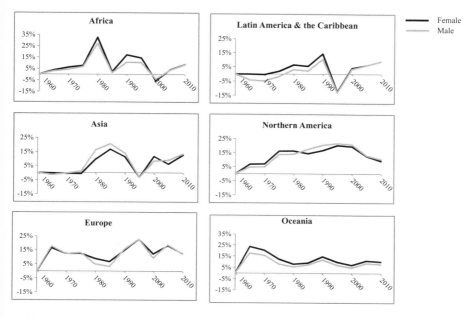

Figure 6.1   Growth of the international migrant stock by region.

der differences in development. While much work has been done to ascertain the role of gender on migration and development as separate fields of inquiry, not enough attention has been paid to assessing the impact of female migration on development as a unique paradigm (though see, among others, Bjeren 2007 and United Nations 2006 for exceptions).

Why, then, the need to analyze the impact of female migration on development? A gendered perspective is necessary in order to understand both the structural causes and the impacts of migration in sending and receiving societies. The structural divides between migrant sending and receiving countries, especially the North-South divide but also within the South, continues to grow, and it appears to remain firm for future generations. Gender inequality can be a "powerful factor in precipitating migration, particularly when women have economic, political and social expectations that actual opportunities at home do not allow them to meet" (United Nations 2006:1); that is, for many women, migration may be a strategy that provides them with access to educational and employment opportunities to become social actors in their own right (Zlotnik 2003).

In a similar vein, family reunification can also be a powerful migration-inducing factor for women.[1] Both categories (women as primary migrants and women as secondary migrants) have important implications for development that are not readily apparent from a gender-blind perspective. (See Escobar García and Álvarez Velasco in this volume for a discussion on Ecuadorian women migrating to Spain.) For instance, women migrating in search of employment (i.e., as primary migrants) and who remit money back home are more likely to send money for basic consumption items such as food and clothing in comparison to men (Chant and Radcliffe 1992; Curran and Saguy 2001; Tacoli 1999). In contrast, migration due to family reunification could potentially lead to a significant reduction of both supply and demand of remittances. As families reunify in the host country, both the original and the new migrant will have fewer relatives to send their remittances to.

Gender differences among remittance recipients are also associated with how remittances are spent. Women tend to prioritize family needs (food, clothing, home, education, and health), while men often use resources for saving and investments to prepare for their "potential" return home (Cortes 2007).

The relationship between migration and development, however, is neither always positive nor always negative; it depends, among other factors, on the demographic composition of the migratory flow, as well as on the banking and immigration policies that are seldom analyzed comprehensively by scholars or policymakers (some exceptions are Bauer and Sinning 2006; Cobb-Clark and Hildebrand 2002; Amuedo-Dorantes and Pozo 2002).

With these initial considerations in mind, in what follows we briefly discuss some empirical and theoretical elements related to migration and development from a gender and age perspective; we then discuss some of the links by which female and child migration may affect development. Given the dearth of global micro-level data on female and children migration per se—which limits our generalizations—we pay particular attention to the potential impacts of female migration on remittance flows using the Mexican, Turkish, and Polish cases to illustrate our argument, as well as on the psychosocial impacts of migration on children left behind, a topic intimately related to female migration.

WHY DO PEOPLE MIGRATE?

Thousands of pages have been devoted to answer the very simple question, Why do people migrate? There is no single satisfactory answer, as it is evident that people migrate for many different reasons. In fact the push-and-pull factors that motivate people to move from one place to another vary by migratory system; depending on the circumstance, people move for economic, political, ethnic, and even environmental reasons. Push factors that prompt individuals to migrate include economic crises, disparities in income and opportunities, political and religious persecution, natural disasters, and population pressures, among others. Some of the factors that pull people out of their countries of origin may include higher wages, better job opportunities, religious and political liberties, and better standards of living. In one word: *differences*. Differences between countries of origin and destination stimulate migration whether it is south–north or south–south migration.

In the literature we find a significant number of theories on the migratory phenomenon from various perspectives, such as neoclassical economics, segmented labor market theory, world-systems, social capital, and cumulative causation (see Massey 1999 for a theoretical review). Piore (1979) initiated a series of theoretical revisions that culminated with a "gendered transnationalism" perspective about migration (Grasmuk and Pesar 1991; Pessar 1995); however, traditional immigration theories largely focus on the labor aspect of the phenomenon and are largely gender-blind (although Ravenstein [1885] hinted at a migratory gap between men and women). Gender in migration research nonetheless has grown considerably since the 1984 special issue of *International Migration Review*, "Women in Migration" (Morokvasic 1984), as documented by the 2006 special issue of *International Migration Review*, "Gender and Migration Revisited" (Gabaccia et al. 2006). In this chapter, however, we center our attention on the New Economics of Labor Migration (NELM; Stark and Bloom 1985) in an attempt to bridge the migration and development literature from a gender and age perspective. This theory centers on the individual as the unit of analysis. Here researchers are concerned with individual values and future expectations of migrants and potential migrants.

The particular focus of this theory is on how the migration decision process is made. According to NELM, migration decisions are not made in a vacuum by isolated migrants but are made within families or even communities in order to maximize their future income and to minimize their financial risks (Stark and Bloom 1985). Here it is possible to focus on the gender division of labor in productive as well as reproductive activities within the household. Following Thadani and Todaro (1984)[2] and incorporating one of the basic premises derived from NELM (that of maximizing future family income via remittances, which perhaps is the clearest mechanism by which migration maximizes future earnings), female migration and its impact on development can be summarized into two broad categories:

1. Primary Migrants: Women (married and unmarried) who migrate for employment reasons.
2. Secondary Migrants: Women (married or attached) who primarily migrate for family reunification purposes.

The question that arises now is: How do these variants of female migration help us understand their impacts on development? To answer this question, it is necessary to understand immigrants' remitting behavior in order to assess migration's and development's links within NELM's framework. Even though the literature is partially silent on the potential differences in remitting behavior between migrant men and migrant women, several studies have concentrated on the remitting behavior of the migrants who send money home (Banerjee 1984; Cortina and de la Garza 2004; Durand et al. 1996; Lucas and Stark 1985; Osaki 2003; Stark and Lucas 1988). Immigrants remit for a large number of reasons that can be encompassed into at least two conceptual perspectives. The first deals with remittances as interfamilial transfers for family maintenance and insurance (Amuedo-Dorantes and Pozo 2002; Durand et al. 1996; Massey 1999; Lucas and Stark 1985). These include transfers for basic consumption and asset accumulation. The second considers remittances as personal or community-oriented investment in the home country (see Goldring 2004 for a comprehensive discussion). In a recent attempt to summarize the literature, Chami et al. (2008) describe these two basic motivations as altruistic and as self-interested exchanges in which the remitter exchanges remittances for goods and services back home that may provide utility to him or her.

Even though migrant women tend to earn less on average than migrant men, a number of studies seem to suggest that women tend to remit more of their income to their families than their male counterparts for reasons primarily related to their roles within their families (Chant and Radcliffe 1992; Cortes 2007; Curran and Saguy 2001; United Nations 2006; Tacoli 1999).

In this chapter we concentrate on the first conceptual category, that is, on interfamilial transfers. A common denominator that helps explain why immigrants send money home in light of the NELM theory seems to be altruistic reasons, which are sustained by an explicit or implicit contractual agreement between the migrant and those family members left behind and sometimes between the migrant and her or his community of origin

(Cortina and de la Garza 2004; Dustmann and Mestres 2007; Lucas and Stark 1985; Stark and Lucas 1988). In particular, some studies have argued that the most significant predictors that explain why immigrants remit are two: having direct family members and/or children living in the home country and having the expectation of returning to the home country someday (Cortina et al. 2005; Sana and Massey 2005). Somehow following this literature, others argue that altruism is going to be strongest in cohesive traditional families and weaker in nontraditional families with unstable bonds (Sana and Massey 2005).

To put it simply, once an individual has migrated, he or she has an implicit or explicit contract to send money home to those family members left behind, suggesting that among migrants, women tend to remit more of their income due to their family roles. Within this framework, we would expect that women as primary migrants would send more of their income back home for basic purposes. As a consequence, remittances sent by women may reduce even more the depth and severity of poverty. In addition, since women presumably have closer ties to those left behind, especially their children, remittances may have more positive effects on education and health in terms of providing better access to services of higher quality.

Now the question that arises here is what happens when women migrate as secondary migrants. That is, what happens once migrants' family members are reunited with the primary migrant in the host country? Do immigrants continue to remit? If so, do they remit at the same rate? Some argue that given immigrants' transnational behavior they will continue to send money back home even if they have settled (Glick Schiller 1999; Guarnizo 2003). We will argue that the opposite is true.

Once family members who had been left behind are reunited in the host country as secondary migrants, the contract by which migrants and family members left behind were obliged becomes obsolete (Sana and Massey 2005). Migrants then will stop remitting to the home country or at least will substantially decrease the frequency and amount sent home (see Massey and Sana 2003 for the Mexican case). This of course does not mean that migrants have reduced their level of income. This means that instead of remitting, immigrants will potentially increase the level of consumption or savings they hold in their host country. They have been transformed indeed from remitters to savers.

To illustrate the potential developmental impacts once women migrate for family reunification purposes, we look at the cases of Turkish and Polish migration to Germany and Mexican migration to the United States.

MIGRATION AND REMITTANCES FROM TURKS
AND POLES IN GERMANY

The German case offers an interesting puzzle to the academic literature on the relationship between migration and remittances, especially as the cases of Turkish and Polish immigrants are analyzed in comparative terms. Turks have been the largest population of nonnationals living in Germany for most of the past three decades. Still, although the Turkish population in Germany has been increasing almost every year since 1973, their remitting behavior has not been as predicted. Remittances have grown consistently for most of the decades of the 1980s and 1990s, reaching a high mark of $5.5 billion for the year 1998. Since then, however, remittances have fallen in a staggering way, amounting to levels similar to that of 1974. This is a bigger puzzle indeed, as we realize that on average almost 2 million Turks during this decade were remitting similarly to what less than 1 million Turks were remitting thirty-five years before, back in 1974 (see Figure 6.2).

At the opposite end of the comparative framework, Polish immigrants in Germany were remitting around $1 billion in 1998, only one-fourth of what Turkish immigrants in Germany were remitting in that same year. By 2009, however, these numbers changed. That year almost 1.1 million

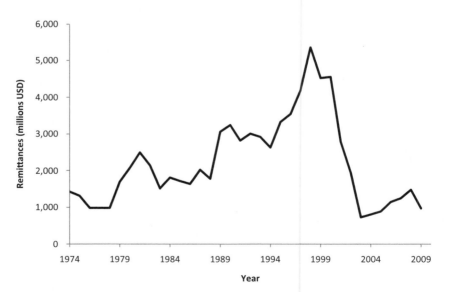

Figure 6.2   Remittances to Turkey by year.

Source: World Bank 2011.

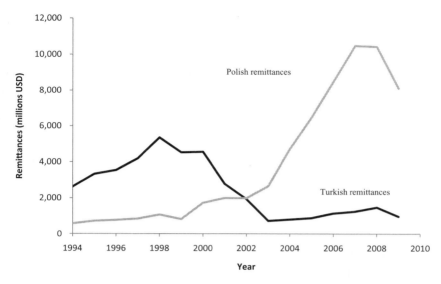

Figure 6.3   Remittances to Turkey and Poland by year.

Source: World Bank 2011.

Polish in Germany (OECD 2011) were remitting $8 billon, even during the economic crisis ($10.5 billion in 2008), in comparison to 1.4 million Turks who were remitting $970 million (see Figure 6.3).

All in all, it seems that for the Polish case, more migration has meant more remittances, but for the Turkish case in the past decade, more migration has meant fewer remittances. What explains these opposite effects?

IMMIGRATION POLICY MATTERS

Despite the evidence, Germany used to envision itself as a country in which immigration played no role. In an often quoted academic nutshell: "Germany was not a country of immigration." (See Green 2003 for an extended list of sources. See also ICMG 2001.) This belief was demystified in 2001 by a governmental commission that addressed the German immigration phenomenon (see ICMG 2001). To begin with, Germany has had several recent waves of internal migration. Since 1945 and up until 1961 there were around 11 to 12 million ethnic German expellees and refugees from the lost eastern part of the former Reich and from the German Democratic Republic (Castles and Miller 2009; Oezcan 2004).

Second, and more important for this chapter, Germany has also had several waves of foreign migration in the past half century. In the mid-1950s the German government began to recruit foreign labor through bilateral guest worker programs as Germany's economic miracle was in need of a larger labor force. These programs were established with Italy, Spain, Greece, Morocco, Portugal, Tunisia, Yugoslavia, and, most important, Turkey. Consequently the number of foreign workers in Germany increased substantially in the following two decades. By 1956 there were around 95,000 foreign workers in the country. Almost twenty years later, in 1973, this number had climbed to 2.7 million (63 percent male, 47 percent female). After two decades, these programs came to an end. Since November 23, 1973, no permanent labor recruitment from outside the EU has been permitted in Germany (Castles and Miller 2009).

Different work programs had different specifications, but generally they granted temporary work permits for an individual for a period of one to two years. At the end of this short stay, guest workers were then required to return to their home countries so that new workers could come in. The rationale of the "rotation principle" was twofold: first, to prevent immigration settlement in Germany; second, to expose to industrial work the largest possible number of workers from sending countries (Oezcan 2004). The guest worker program also established special restrictions, such as limited labor and social rights, no path to citizenship, and no formal mechanisms for family reunification. Despite the formal rules and the restrictive design of the labor programs, many of their beneficiaries (especially Turkish guest workers) decided to stay in Germany permanently (Bauer et al. 2005). Moreover, despite immigration restrictions, in the following decades new immigrants continued arriving regularly.

Once the work programs had been suspended, the path for new Turkish immigrants to Germany was reduced to two options: seeking asylum or applying for family reunification. For those Turkish workers who had decided to stay in Germany after their work programs had come to an end, the path for naturalization was mostly closed.

In 1977 the Guidelines on Naturalization (*Einbürgerungsrichtlinien*) were enacted, which explicitly defined naturalization as an exceptional act. The policy of the German state toward its immigrants followed the notion that "Germany was not a country of immigration," so the logic behind immigration policy was to request the immigrant to integrate first and apply for naturalization second.

In that order of ideas, dual citizenships were established as an exception. The rule was that immigrants were required to surrender their original nationality in order to receive German citizenship. This policy, in addition to the requirement of ten years of residence previous to application and a high monetary fee for the bureaucratic process, proved to be too much for those who were applying for naturalization.

The restrictive Guidelines on Naturalization worked as planned. "As late as 1988, when over 60 per cent of Turks had residence periods of at least ten years, the proportion of Turkish citizens gaining citizenship each year (the naturalization rate) was an almost unbelievable 0.08 per cent" (Green 2003:239). In addition, following a long-standing tradition back to the Prussian Empire, the German state did not recognize citizenship as a birthright (*jus soli*); instead the mechanism to achieve citizenship was through *jus sanguinis*, by which nationality or citizenship can be granted to any individual born to a parent who is a national or citizen of that state. The outcome of this tradition was that by the end of 2000, over 700,000 Turkish children born in Germany were not German citizens. (If we include other nationalities, approximately 1.6 million inhabitants of Germany were still nonnationals, although they had been born in Germany.)

New immigrants faced problems of their own. Asylum seekers soon found that Germany was a more difficult point of entry than other European countries. A high number of Turks applied for asylum following the coup d'état in Turkey on September 12, 1980. At the time, German bureaucrats suspected that a large number of applicants were not genuine political refugees but were trying to get around the 1973 ban on labor recruitment (Pirkl 1982). However, one must point out that although many Turkish asylum seekers were denied their request, they were not sent back to Turkey. German law allows for Temporary Humanitarian Residence permits, which could then be renewed. This became an additional way for Turkish immigrants to stay in Germany and begin their process of integration.

Altogether Germany's immigration policy produced an ironical result. On the one hand, Turks (as well as other nationals) had a very difficult time either obtaining German citizenship or receiving political asylum. On the other hand, the legislation was not strong enough to expel Turkish citizens from German soil in a recurrent and significant way. Moreover, as working permits and residence requests were two different bureaucratic processes, which were allocated independently from each other, although Turkish immigrants were not receiving naturalization or asylum status, it became possible for them to get a work permit or a residence permit, which allowed them to stay in Germany legally. In addition, all benefits from the German welfare state, besides income support, are allocated to inhabitants regardless of their nationality or immigration status. These benefits created a safety net for Turkish immigrants while they struggled through their process of assimilation. Finally, as a by-product of an Association Agreement that Turkey signed with Germany in 1964, and an interpretation by the European Court of Justice, Turkish citizens enjoy the same protection from expulsion as EU nationals (Green 2003).

By 1990, seventeen years after the last labor program came to an end, there were around 1.7 million Turks living in Germany, many of whom had been residents for an extended period or had been born on German soil. That same year also saw a dramatic change for immigrants: the Foreigners Law (*Ausländergesetz*) was enacted, which made it easier for family reunification and for naturalization to be approved. This shift in immigration policy would change the dynamics of migration and remittances of the Turkish community in Germany for the next decade.

The 1990 Foreigners Law established the requirements under which dependents may immigrate to Germany in order for families to reunify. Spouses are allowed to immigrate if

1. the pioneer migrant has a full residence permit
2. the resident is able to provide for the whole family
3. there is adequate living space (12 square meters per person age six and older).

In addition, minors were allowed to immigrate to join their non-German parents up to age sixteen; moreover before 1996 they were granted visa-free entry and were exempt from holding a residence permit (Green 2003). Those seeking naturalization also benefited from the 1990 Foreigners Law. A simplified naturalization procedure was enacted for those with over fifteen years of residence and for nonnationals ages sixteen to twenty-three. All these changes led to a significant increase in naturalizations. From 1993 onward, the naturalization rate for Turks consistently exceeded that of the nonnational population as a whole. Indeed from 1995 to 2009, around 748,000 Turks were naturalized, compared to just 14,600 for the entire period between 1972 and 1990 (see Figure 6.4). Moreover, at the end of 2008 the largest decrease of the foreign-born was among the Turkish population. According to the Federal Statistical Office (Destatis), the population with Turkish passports decreased by 1.5 percent, from 16.7 to 16.9 million, as a result of naturalizations of Turkish citizens.

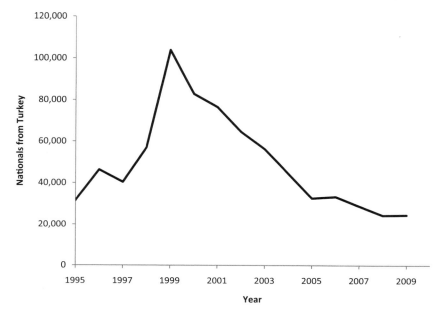

Figure 6.4   Acquisition of citizenship by nationals from Turkey.
Source: OECD 2011.

In general, birth in Germany does not confer German citizenship if neither parent is German. However, children born on or after January 1, 2000, to non-German parents acquire German citizenship at birth if at least one parent has a permanent residence permit (and has had this status for at least three years) and has been residing in Germany for at least eight years. Such children will be required to apply to retain German citizenship by the age of twenty-three. Assuming the laws are not changed prior to 2023, they will also be required to prove they do not hold any foreign citizenship.

In 1993 the asylum law was reviewed to become even stricter. New Turkish immigrants now have a tougher time getting in, unless they are coming in the process of family reunification. In 1997, for example, Germany sheltered 254,000 refugees from the war in the former Yugoslavia, 95,000 "quota refugees" (*Kontingentflüchtlinge*) from other regions, and 360,000 de facto refugees who either had not applied for asylum or were allowed to remain in Germany on humanitarian grounds after their asylum applications had been turned down.

Family reunification has been strictly controlled, and Germany's recognition rates for asylum seekers are generally much lower than in other high-volume asylum destinations. Thus gross immigration of Turks has been almost halved, from over 80,000 in 1992 to 48,000 in 1999. Moreover, at the end of 1998, for example, 45.7 percent of the resident aliens holding Turkish passports were women and girls, which we presume are mothers and daughters of first-wave immigrants.

We argued in the first section of this chapter that there are two main reasons for immigrants to remit: first, immigrants are more likely to remit if they have a family member that has been left behind in the home country; second, immigrants tend to remit if they have the intention to go back home in the future. As family reunification and naturalization increased in Germany, the two main reasons to remit have been reduced in importance. On the one hand, the family members who were left behind have left their home country and are now living in the host country with the original immigrant; on the other hand, naturalization creates an additional incentive to make the host country the new home country. Put it differently, there are fewer reasons for the immigrant to go back home now that he is a citizen in his residential country. As we can see in Figure 6.5, the level of remittances has been decreasing as the number of nationalizations has been increasing. Due to the reforms in the immigration laws, Turkish immigrants have become less prone to remit. In 2008, at the peak of the financial and economic crisis, remittances went up, presumably to help out families and friends back home. In 2009, however, remittances went back to their previous downward trend.

Similar to Turkish migration, Polish migration started at the beginning of the 1990s with a temporary guest worker program. This time, for geopolitical reasons (see de la Garza, this volume, for a discussion of the impact of political variables on development) as well as to spur economic growth in the region (Oezcan 2004), the countries that were chosen were Yugoslavia, Hungary, and Poland. In 2002, for instance, around 374,000 temporary work permits were extended. Of these, around 12 percent were for Polish contract workers; around 298,000 permits were issued for seasonal work, of which almost 240,000 were awarded to Polish citizens. When Poland became an EU member in May 2004, there were fears that the new EU citizens would promptly move to Germany, saturate the labor market, and take advantage of the German welfare state. However, as Figure 6.6 shows, those fears were unfounded, at least in the short run. The stock of Poles living in Germany actually decreased considerably in 2004–5, especially that of male migrants.

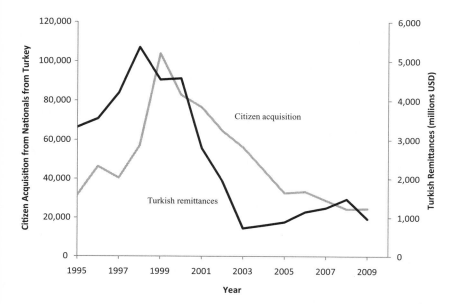

Figure 6.5   Turkish citizenship acquisition (left *y*-axis) and Turkish remittances (right *y*-axis) by year.

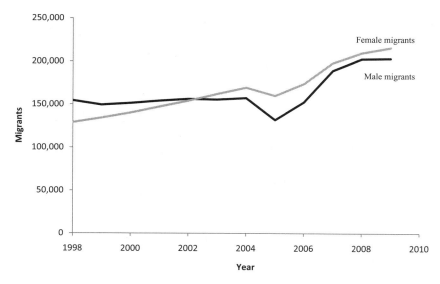

Figure 6.6   Stock of Poles in Germany by gender.

Source: OECD 2010.

MIGRATION AND REMITTANCES FROM MEXICANS
IN THE UNITED STATES

Mexican migration to the United States has been the subject of a vast policy and academic literature (see Massey et al. 1994). Even though international migration from Mexico to the United States is of long standing, it wasn't until the early 1940s, with the Bracero (farmhand) program, a temporary guest worker program between the United States and Mexico, that the current migratory system was born (Cornelius and Rosenblum 2005).[3]

The Bracero program started in 1942, right after the U.S. entry into World War II. During the war, around 168,000 *braceros* were recruited to the United States as guest workers; from 1955 to 1960, annual *bracero* migration oscillated between 400,000 and 450,000 (Massey et al. 2002). By the end of the program, "nearly 5 million Mexicans [had] entered the United States, a figure that dwarfs the combined total of legal and contract labor between 1900 and 1929" (Massey et al. 2002:39).

The Bracero program created new aspirations. Potential migrants in Mexico no longer attempted to earn a predetermined amount of money through a fixed contract in the United States and then return to Mexico as soon as the contract was over. Moreover potential migrants, especially those who did not taste the American dream through the Bracero program, sought to migrate in order to have access to some of the new consumption patterns that the program made available to some Mexican families (Reichert 1981).

In 1986 the U.S. Congress passed a law to "fix" the immigration problem that started with the passage of the Hart-Celler Act of 1965, which abolished the quota system of the 1920s by eliminating nationality as an admission criterion. The Immigration Reform and Control Act (IRCA) was signed into law by President Reagan and took effect in January 1987. IRCA legalized around 2.3 million formerly undocumented Mexican migrants who were already in the country before January 1, 1982, and allowed the newly minted naturalized U.S. citizens to bring their families legally from Mexico to the United States.

In 1996 the immigration law was reformed again. This time the law had tougher provisions, including increases in criminal penalties for immigration-related offenses, and it authorized increases in enforcement personnel and enhanced their enforcement authority. In addition, other acts of Congress (welfare reform and antiterrorism legislation) reduced undocumented immigrants' access to social services and denied them some

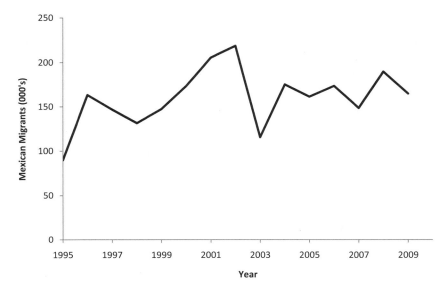

Figure 6.7 **Inflows to the United States of Mexican nationals by year.**

Source: OECD 2011.

opportunities to legalize their status. Right after the terrorist attacks of September 11, 2001, the U.S. Congress passed the U.S.A. Patriot Act, and the Department of Homeland Security put in place certain measures such as the Special Registration Program that had a negative effect on the immigration flows. Figure 6.7 shows that just after the 1996 immigration reform and in 2002 inflows to the United States of Mexican migrants decreased significantly.

Historically, Mexican migration to the United States was mainly composed of single males; however, nowadays this is no longer the case. In 2005 one in every six Mexican undocumented immigrants was a child, and one of every three was a woman. Altogether the immigrant population is composed of 1.8 million children and 4 million women. Figure 6.8 illustrates the total of Mexican migrants (documented and undocumented) in the United States for the 1994–2009 period, clearly showing the growth of Mexican-born female immigrants in the United States.

The question now is whether the Turkish migratory pattern and its impact on Turkish immigrants' remitting behavior is being replicated by Mexican migrants in the United States. In other words, is there a change in the demographic composition of the migratory flow, as a by-product of

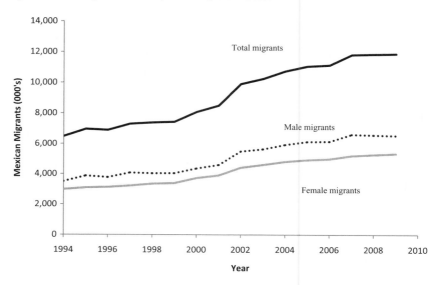

Figure 6.8   Stock of Mexican-born migrants in the United States by year.
Source: OECD 2011.

immigration policies in the United States, which could lead to more migration but fewer remittances?

The available data suggest three complementary phenomena. First, family reunification as a by-product of IRCA has increased. Second, after the immigration reforms of 1996 it became increasingly difficult to cross the border due to border control policies (Donato and Patterson 2004) and also due to the economic and financial crisis, though presumably the latter would have a temporary effect. Third, border crossing has become even more difficult after September 11 and the enactment of the U.S. Patriot Act. In recent years, migrants minimize crossing back to Mexico and tend to stay for longer periods in the United States. Are these changes in the migratory flow affecting remitting behavior?

Remittances from the United States to Mexico have been growing over the past several decades. According to the World Bank and Mexico's Central Bank, between 1980 and 2007 remittances increased at a speedy rate, and by 2007 they accounted for more than $26 billion (see Figure 6.9). This amount of money is the highest flow of foreign currency to Mexico for the year, second only to oil revenues.

However, the annual growth rate of remittances reveals a very interesting pattern (see Figure 6.10): it peaks and decreases in particular periods

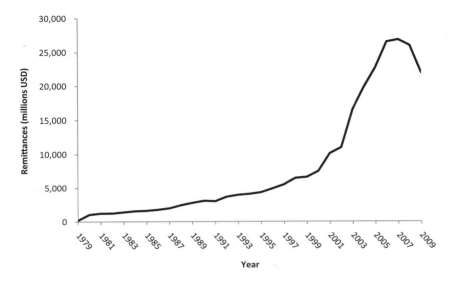

Figure 6.9   Annual remittances flow to Mexico.

Source: World Bank 2011.

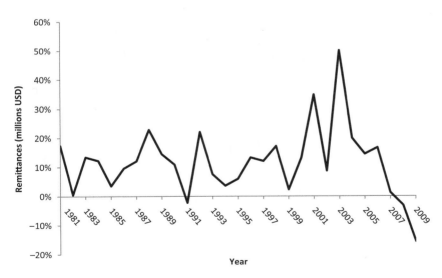

Figure 6.10   Remittances' annual growth rate.

Source: Authors' calculations with data from World Bank 2011.

that closely follow Mexican naturalization rates. The relationship seems to be clear: as naturalization rates increase, the growth of remittances slows down or even decreases; likewise, as naturalization rates decrease, the rate of growth of remittances increases.

For instance, between 1986 and 1996 the naturalization rate increased significantly; however, as Figure 6.11 shows, in 1997 the naturalization rate fell as "the cohort of Mexicans legalized under IRCA passed and the former [Immigration and Naturalization Service] bureaucracy staggered under the administrative load" (Massey 2005:6). The administrative reforms implemented during the mid-1990s helped reduce the 1998 backlog, and, as a consequence, the number of Mexicans acquiring citizenship once again increased significantly in the following year. It is worth noting that after 1999 remittances began to increase until 2007, while the number of Mexicans acquiring citizenship began to decrease. Between 2000 and 2003 the number of Mexicans acquiring citizenship was importantly reduced; the amount remitted from the United States to Mexico started to grow at a very fast pace. After 2003, however, the number of naturalizations increased dramatically and started to fall in 2008 with the economic crisis.

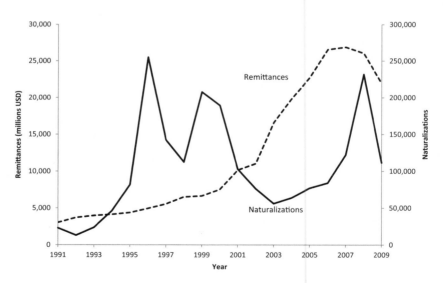

Figure 6.11   Mexican remittances (left *y*-axis) and citizenship acquisition (right *y*-axis).

Source: OECD 2011.

Family reunification plays a double catalytic role. On the one hand, it reduces the demand for remittances because family members are no longer living in the home country. On the other hand, family reunification reduces the supply of remittances; that is, migrants do not need to send money home as frequently and presumably not in the same amounts.

POLICY IMPLICATIONS

The findings of this chapter have important policy implications. First, migrant-sending countries that may be starting to be or are already dependent on their diasporas' monetary flows may start to see their remittances-based developmental aspirations truncated by a deceleration of these flows as a by-product of family reunification and other policies, which are exacerbated by the slow global recovery from the financial and economic crisis.[4] Second, migrant-receiving countries may benefit economically from family reunification given that at least some of the money that was sent home before is now spent or saved in the host country.

The positive and potentially negative effects of family reunification are most evident at the micro and macro levels, respectively. At the micro level, the obvious positive effect (which outweighs most if not all of the costs) is that families are reunited. Family reunification will eliminate some of the psychological costs that arise when families are apart. At the macro level, family reunification for migrant-sending countries would imply a loss in future human capital, especially when children are reunited with their parents. A considerable proportion of future generations will be leaving their countries of origin, diminishing the human capital potential of migrant-sending countries. This loss of human capital would translate into a gain for host countries, particularly for those countries in which the fertility rate is low. An inflow of women and children will have a positive impact in the labor market once these children are incorporated into it.

Family reunification may benefit migrant-sending countries by relieving them of political pressures that may arise with the demands for the provision of public goods such as education and health. In contrast, for migrant-receiving countries, an increase in the migratory flow may exert some pressures in the provision of these same public goods. These pressures would be most evident at the local level; however, as previous studies have shown at the national level, immigrants contribute more to the generation of wealth in the host country than they may consume in public services (e.g., Edmonston and Lee 1996; Fix and Passel 1994).

Finally, once families are reunited in migrant-receiving countries, the need to send money home will decrease; thus those migrants who once were remitters will become the new savers in their host countries.

REFERENCES

Amuedo-Dorantes, Catalina, and Susan Pozo. 2002. "Precautionary Saving by Young Immigrants and Young Natives." *Southern Economic Journal* 69, no. 1: 48–71.

Banerjee, Biswajit. 1984. "The Probability, Size, and Uses of Remittances from Urban to Rural Areas in India." *Journal of Development Economics* 16: 293–311.

Bauer, Thomas K., and Mathias Sinning. 2006. "The Savings Behavior of Temporary and Permanent Migrants in Germany." Paper presented at the Verein für Socialpolitik, Universität Bayreuth.

Bauer, Thomas K., Barbara Dietz, Klaus F. Zimmermann, and Eric Zwintz. 2005. "German Migration: Development, Assimilation, and Labor Market Effects." In *European Migration: What Do We Know?*, edited by K. F. Zimmermann. Oxford: Oxford University Press. 197–261.

Bjeren, Guinilla. 2007. "Gender and Reproduction." In *International Migration, Immobility and Development*, edited by Tomas Hammar, Grete Brochmann, Kristof Tamas, and Thomas Faist. Oxford: Berg.

Boserup, Ester. 1970. *Women's Role in Economic Development*. London: George Allen & Unwin.

Boyd, Monica. 1989. "Family and Personal Networks in International Migration: Recent Developments and New Agendas." *International Migration Review* 23: 638–71.

Castles, Stephen, and Mark J. Miller. 2009. "The Age of Migration: International Population Movements in the Modern World." Basingstoke: Palgrave MacMillan.

Chami, Ralph, Adolfo Barajas, Thomas Cosimano, Connel Fullenkamp, Michael Gapen, and Peter Montiel. 2008. *Macroeconomic Consequences of Remittances*. Washington, D.C.: International Monetary Fund.

Chant, Sylvia, and Sarah A. Radcliffe. 1992. "Migration and Development: The Importance of Gender." In *Gender and Migration in Developing Countries*, ed. Sylvia Chant. London: Belhaven Press. 1–29.

Cobb-Clark, Deborah, and Vincent Hildebrand. 2002. "The Wealth and Asset Holdings of U.S.-Born and Foreign-Born Households: Evidence from Sipp Data." SSRN online.

Cornelius, Wayne, and Marc R. Rosenblum. 2005. "Immigration and Politics." *Annual Review of Political Science and Politics* 8: 99–119.

Cortes, Rosalia. 2007. "Remittances and Children's Rights: An Overview of Academic and Policy Literature." New York: United Nations Children's Fund.

Cortina, Jeronimo, and Rodolfo de la Garza. 2004. "Immigrant Remitting Behavior and Its Developmental Consequences for Mexico and El Salvador." Los Angeles: Report for The Tomas Rivera Policy Institute.

Cortina, Jeronimo, Rodolfo O. de la Garza, and Enrique Ochoa-Reza. 2005. "Remesas: Límites Al Optimismo." *Foreign Affairs en Español* 5, no. 3: 27–36.

Curran, Sara R., and Abigail C. Saguy. 2001. "Migration and Cultural Change: A Role of Gender and Social Networks?" *International Women's Studies* 2: 54–77.

Donato, Katherine M., and Evelyn Patterson. 2004. "Women and Men on the Move: Undocumented Border Crossing." In *Crossing the Border: Research from the Mexican Migration Project*, edited by Jorge Durand and Douglas S. Massey. New York: Russell Sage Foundation.

Donato, Katherine M., Donna Gabaccia, Jennifer Holdaway, Martin Manalansan, and Patricia R. Pessar. 2006. "A Glass Half Full? Gender in Migration Studies." *International Migration Review* 40: 3–26.

Durand, Jorge, William Kandel, Emilio A. Parrado, and Douglas S. Massey. 1996. "International Migration and Development in Mexican Communities." *Demography* 33, no. 2: 249–64.

Dustmann, Christian, and Josep Mestres. 2007. "Remittance and Saving Behaviour of Migrants: Theory and Evidence." Working Paper. London: University College London and Centre for Research and Analysis of Migration.

Edmonston, Barry, and Ronald Lee, eds. 1996. *Local Fiscal Effects of Illegal Immigration*. Washington, D.C.: National Academy Press.

Fix, Michael, and Jeffrey S. Passel. 1994. "Immigration and Immigrants: Setting the Record Straight." Washington, D.C.: Report. Urban Institute.

Gabaccia, Donna, Katherine M. Donato, Jennifer Holdaway, Martin Manalansan, and Patricia R. Pessar (eds.). 2006. "Gender and Migration Revisited." *International Migration Review* 40: 3–256.

Gelman, Andrew, and Jennifer Hill. 2006. *Data Analysis Using Regression and Multilevel/Hierarchical Models*. New York: Cambridge University Press.

Glick Schiller, Nina. 1999. "Transmigrants and Nation-States: Something Old and Something New in the U.S. Immigrant Experience." In *The Handbook of International Migration: The American Experience*, edited by Charles Hirschman, Philip Kasinitz, and Josh DeWind. New York: Russell Sage Foundation.

Goldring, Luin. 2004. "Family and Collective Remittances to Mexico: A Multi-Dimensional Typology." *Development and Change* 35, no. 4: 799–840.

Grasmuck, Sherri, and Patricia R. Pessar. 1991. *Between Two Islands: Dominican International Migration*. Berkeley: University of California Press.

Green, Simon. 2003. "The Legal Status of Turks in Germany." *Immigrants & Minorities* 22: 228–46.

Guarnizo, Luis Eduardo. 2003. "The Economics of Transnational Living." *International Migration Review* 37, no. 3: 666–99.

Harcourt, Wendy. 1994. *Feminist Perspectives on Sustainable Development*. London: Zed Books.

Independent Commission on Migration to Germany (ICMG). 2001. "Structuring Immigration: Fostering Integration." Report. Berlin: Federal Ministry of the Interior of the Federal Republic of Germany.

Lucas, Robert E. B., and Oded Stark. 1985. "Motivations to Remit: Evidence from Botswana." *Journal of Political Economy* 93, no. 5: 901–18.

Massey, Douglas S. 1999. "Why Does Immigration Occur? A Theoretical Synthesis." In *The Handbook of International Migration: The American Experience*, edited by Charles Hirschman, Philip Kasinitz, and Josh DeWind. New York: Russell Sage Foundation.

———. 2005. *Strangers in a Strange Land: Humans in an Urbanizing World*. New York: Norton Publishers.

Massey, Douglas S., Jorge Durand, and Nolan J. Malone. 2002. *Beyond Smoke and Mirrors: Mexican Immigration in an Era of Economic Integration*. New York: Russell Sage Foundation.

Massey, Douglas S., Luin Goldring, and Jorge Durand. 1994. "Continuities in Transnational Migration: An Analysis of Nineteen Mexican Communities." *American Journal of Sociology* 99, no. 6: 1492–533.

Massey, Douglas S., and Mariano Sana. 2003. "Patterns of U.S. Migration from Mexico, the Caribbean and Central America." *Migraciones Internacionales* 2: 5–39.

McDonald, Peter. 2000. "Gender Equity, Social Institutions and the Future of Fertility." *Journal of Population Research* 17: 1–16.

Morokvasic, Mirjana. 1984. "Birds of Passage Are Also Women." *International Migration Review* 18: 886–907.

OECD. 2006. "International Migration Outlook: Sopemi 2006 Edition." Paris: Organization for Economic Co-Operation and Development.

———. 2010. "International Migration Outlook: Sopemi 2010 Edition." Paris: Organization for Economic Co-Operation and Development.

———. 2011. "International Migration Outlook: Sopemi 2011 Edition." Paris: Organization for Economic Co-Operation and Development.

Oezcan, Veysel. 2004. "Germany: Immigration in Transition." In *Migration Information Source*. Washington, DC: Migration Policy Institute.

Osaki, Keiko. 2003. "Migrant Remittances in Thailand: Economic Necessity or Social Norm?" *Journal of Population Research* 20, no. 2: 203–22.

Pessar, Patricia R. 1995. *A Visa for a Dream: Dominicans in the United States*. Needham Heights: Allyn and Bacon.

Piore, Michael J. 1979. *Birds of Passage: Migrant Labor and Industrial Societies*. New York: Cambridge University Press.

Pirkl, Fritz. 1982. "Berufliche Eingliederung Ausländischer Jugendlicher in Der Aktuellen Ausländerpolitischen Diskussion." *Zeitschrift für Ausländerrecht* 1: 12–14.

Ravenstein, Ernest G. 1885. "The Laws of Migration." *Journal of the Statistical Society* 48: 167–235.

Sana, Mariano, and Douglas S Massey. 2005. "Household Composition, Family Migration, and Community Context: Migrant Remittances in Four Countries." *Social Science Quarterly* 86, no. 2: 509–28.

Shadish, William R., Thomas D. Cook, and Donald T. Campbell. 2002. *Experimental and Quasi-Experimental Designs for Generalized Causal Inference*. Boston: Houghton Mifflin.

Stark, Oded, and David E. Bloom. 1985. "The New Economics of Labor Migration." *American Economic Review* 75, no. 2: 173–78.

Stark, Oded, and E. B. Robert Lucas. 1988. "Migration, Remittances, and the Family." *Economic Development and Cultural Change* 36, no. 3: 465–81.

Tacoli, Cecilia. 1999. "International Migration and the Restructuring of Gender Asymmetries: Continuity and Change among Filipino Labor Migrants in Rome." *International Migration Review* 33: 658–82.

Thadani, Veena N., and Michael P. Todaro. 1984. "Female migration: A conceptual framework." In *Women in the Cities of Asia: Migration and Urban Adaptation,* edited by James T. Fawcett, Siew-Ean Khoo, and Peter C. Smith. Boulder: Westview Press: 36–59.

United Nations, Department of Economic and Social Affairs. 2006. "2004 World Survey on the Role of Women in Development: Women and International Migration." New York: United Nations.

United Nations, Department of Economic and Social Affairs, Population Division (DESA). 2011. Trends in International Migrant Stock: Migrants by Age and Sex. POP/DB/MIG/Stock/Rev. 2011: New York: United Nations.

World Bank. 2006. "Global Economic Prospects." Report. Washington, D.C.: World Bank.

——. 2011. "Outlook for Remittance Flows 2011–13." Report. Washington, D.C.: World Bank.

Zlotnik, Hania. "The Global Dimensions of Female Migration." Migration Policy Institute. Accessed at http://www.migrationinformation.org/feature/display.cfm?ID=109.

PART 3

Migration and Development

COUNTRY EXPERIENCES

The five chapters in this last part of the book, while focusing on different migration corridors, clearly highlight the multidimensional and complex relationship between migration and development. The common denominator of these chapters is nuance, subtle differences in geography, economic development, and migration flows, all of which mediate the relationship between migration and development.

In his contribution, Hein de Haas raises a fundamental question: Does the shift toward optimistic views that migration will speed development reflect a real change or a general paradigm shift from dependency and state-centrist to neoclassical and neoliberal views? De Haas uses the case of Morocco to show that, in some regions and countries, migration has reinforced positive development trends, sustaining and improving the livelihoods of migrants and their families, but has done little to encourage national development and may even have reinforced sluggish economic growth and maintained the political status quo. He shows that the impact of migration on development is multifaceted, and that this impact depends on the general institutional context and investment conditions of each region. Despite migration's considerable development potential, he concludes that migration and remittances cannot independently set in motion more general, nationwide development processes.

In their contribution Loren Landau and Aurelia Wa Kabwe Segatti examine the impacts of migration on South Africa. They focus on two core issues: the integration of international migrants into local communities and the local governance of migration when there is extreme vulnerability and resource competition.

They conclude that some common distinctions, such as those between documented and undocumented migrants, voluntary and forced migrants, and international and domestic migration, impede effective policymaking by creating silos with little coordination among agencies charged with law enforcement, social assistance, and local development.

In his chapter, Graeme Hugo focuses on migration from Asia to Australia, exploring the nexus between student migration and eventual permanent settlement. Hugo's data show that there is a significant north-to-south flow of skilled workers from Australia to Asia, but the dominant permanent flow is still toward Australia. This two-way movement, north–south–north, illustrates the strong circular dimension encountered in many of the world's migration systems, which opens up considerable potential for the positive developmental effects of migration to be enhanced in both countries of origin and countries of destination. The circular, reciprocal, and complex nature of the Asia–Australia migration system forces us to reconceptualize the whole notion of south–north migration as well as its categorization as temporal or permanent in order to recognize the fundamental complexity of the population flows involved.

Philip Martin focuses on the developmental consequences of Asian migration to the United States by highlighting the three Rs of the migration-development nexus: recruitment, remittances, and returns. Similar to de Haas's contribution, Martin argues that there is no automatic link between more migration and faster development. Migration can accelerate development in countries ready to grow or can perpetuate underdevelopment. Remittances can speed up development when the macroeconomic fundamentals are in place; that is, the implementation of sound economic policies can give all residents, not only migrants, incentives to save and invest. Return migration, even when migrants bring home human and financial capital, cannot reverse per se the effects of deficient development policies.

Migration and its by-products are by no means the silver bullet to solve migrant-sending countries' developmental problems. The best way for a migrant-sending country to maximize migration's developmental potentials is to get the economic and institutional fundamentals right, which means having a growing economy, an appropriate exchange rate, a climate that fosters small investments, and respect for the rule of law and the rights of workers. S. Irudaya Rajan and K. C. Zachariah tackle this issue by analyzing the impacts of Indian migrants to the Gulf on the southern state of Kerala. Using household-level survey data, they find an interesting pattern seldom discussed in the literature: the interaction between migrant self-selection and migration's developmental impacts. A significant proportion of workers who migrate to the Gulf countries are Muslim. This has important implications. On the one hand, it shows that culture plays an important role in shaping who migrates and thus migration's future developmental impacts. On the other hand, cultural and migrant self-selection may have important social and political ramifications back home, especially in India, where social stratification is still present in Indians' daily lives. The creation of new inequalities and social elites on the basis of income derived from remittances, which help reduce poverty and unemployment among Muslims (given that they are more likely to migrate than any other religious group), creates a new paradigm that illustrates the impact of culture on development as argued by Levitt and Lamba-Nieves.

CHAPTER 7

Migration and Development

LESSONS FROM THE MOROCCAN EXPERIENCE

Hein de Haas

THE MIGRATION AND DEVELOPMENT DEBATE

After decades of pessimism and concerns about brain drain and disbelief in the development role of remittances, since 2000 there has been a truly remarkable renaissance in optimism and the overall interest in the issue of migration and development among governments, development agencies such as the U.K. Department for International Development, and international financial institutions such as the World Bank. Also, governments of developing countries have put renewed hopes on migrants as potential investors and actors of development. Surging remittances in particular are often believed to be a more effective instrument for income redistribution, poverty reduction, and economic growth than large, bureaucratic development programs or development aid (de Haas 2010; Jones 1998; Kapur 2003; Ratha 2003).

This raises the fundamental question whether the recent shift toward more optimistic views in policy and academia reflects a veritable change in development impacts of migration, the use of better or other methodological and analytical tools to analyze this impact, or a general paradigm shift in research and policy away from dependency and state-centrist to neoclassical and neoliberal views. In fact it seems hard to deny that ideological factors have played a major role, and it is certainly not the first time that the pendulum has shifted between pessimistic and optimistic views and that these were driven by parallel ideological shifts.

Over the past five decades, the impact of migration on development in migrant-sending communities and countries has been the subject of heated debate, opposing views of the "migration optimists" and "migration pessimists" (cf. Taylor 1999). This divide in views on migration and development reflects deeper paradigmatic divisions in social theory (i.e., functionalist versus structuralist paradigms) and development theory (i.e., balanced growth versus asymmetric development paradigms) and in terms of how development is conceptualized (de la Garza this volume). To a considerable extent, this also reflects ideological divisions between state-centrists and what is usually referred to as "neoliberal" views.

The debate on migration and development has swung back and forth like a pendulum, from optimistic views in the 1950s and 1960s, to neo-Marxist pessimism over the 1970s and 1980s, toward more nuanced and pluralist views in the 1990s. Such shifts in the migration and development debate should be seen primarily as part of more general paradigm shifts in development theory. It is important to note, however, that shifts in academic thinking have been paralleled by ideological shifts; such shifts question the "scientific" underpinnings of what can be characterized as mood shifts in migration and development thinking.

Within regard to this new migration and development optimism, Kapur (2003) has pointed to the ideological roots of recent "remittance euphoria." He argues that remittances strike the right cognitive chords and fit in with a communitarian, "third way" approach, exemplifying the principle of self-help: "Immigrants, rather than governments, then become the biggest provider of 'foreign aid'" (10). This has certainly increased the attraction of remittances for neoliberal development ideologies prescribing less state intervention and more room for market forces. Curiously, the idea of migrants helping themselves also fits well with ideas about "development from below," which is traditionally more associated with left-wing agendas. Some scholars question this approach on the premise that it is some of the world's most exploited workers who need to carry the burden of their countries' failed development policies (Castles and Miller 2009).

On the other hand, the quality and quantity of empirical research on migration, remittances, and development have enormously improved over the past decades. New evidence has challenged prior work, which has been "unduly pessimistic about the prospects for development as a result of international migration, largely because it has failed to take into account the complex, often indirect ways that migration and remittances influence the economic status of households and the communities that contain them" (Taylor et al. 1996a: 397). Over the previous decades, a growing number of empirical studies have countered pessimistic views on migration and development. Earlier (Taylor et al. 1996a, 1996b) and more recent (cf. Agunias 2006; Katseli et al. 2006; Özden and Schiff 2005; Rapoport and Docquier 2005; UNDP 2009) reviews of the literature have pointed to the *potentially* positive role of migrants and remittances in social, economic, and political development in origin communities and societies.

For instance, the universality of the brain drain hypothesis has been seriously questioned, making room for a much more nuanced picture. Not all migrants are highly skilled, and the brain drain seems to be truly massive only in a minority of generally small and/or very poor countries. Furthermore a brain drain *can* be accompanied by a significant brain gain, because the prospect of moving abroad may stimulate the incentive to study among stay-behinds (Lowell and Findlay 2002; Stark et al. 1997; World Bank 2005). And remittances do not *necessarily* lead to dependency and economic decline in origin communities and countries; under favorable circumstances, remittance expenditure can not only improve living standards but also stimulate broader economic growth in origin countries.

If anything, the accumulated evidence points to the diverse nature of migration impacts, and in particular their contingency on *more general development conditions*. In some regions and countries, migration has reinforced already positive development trends. Elsewhere, migration might have contributed to sustaining and even improving the livelihoods of migrants and their families, but it has done little to encourage national development or has even reinforced economic stagnation and maintained the political status quo frequently dominated by authoritarianism and misguided development policy.

This chapter uses the Moroccan migration and development experience to further explore and illustrate this point. The international debate on migration and development is mainly based on the Mexican experience and, to a lesser extent, the experiences of some Asian countries such as the Philippines, China, and India. This is unfortunate because Morocco is an emigration country and emigration state par excellence. Since the 1960s, Moroccan migration has gained momentum, and since the late 1990s Morocco has overtaken Turkey as the prime source country of migrants to Europe (see Figure 7.1). Over 3 million people of Moroccan descent (out of a total population of about 32 million) are currently believed to live abroad, although this includes the second generation holding Mo-

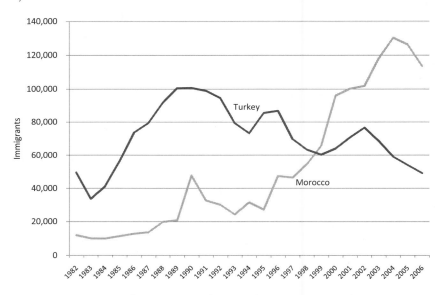

Figure 7.1   Registered immigration from Turkey, Morocco, and Egypt to Germany, France, the Netherlands, Belgium, Sweden, Spain, and Italy, 1982–2006.

Source: United Nations Population Division: *International Migration Flows to and from Selected Countries: The 2005 and 2008 Revisions* (inflows until 1993 exclude France).

roccan citizenship. At an estimated $7.3 billion in 2011, remittances account for about 7 percent of Morocco's GDP and cover over half of the country's trade deficit.

The Moroccan experience is also interesting because migration has been an integral part of the Moroccan government's national development strategy for decades. Since the 1960s, Morocco has integrated migration into its national development policies, including policies aiming to increase remittances and migrant investments and create ties with the burgeoning Moroccan diaspora. What makes the Morocco-EU case also interesting is that, since the 1970s and 1980s, many EU countries have taken an active interest in migration and development policies. These policies, which are also known as *codevelopment* policies (cf. Lacroix 2005), have taken diverse forms but generally link return and temporary or circular migration to development. Unfortunately the successes and particularly failures of such past policies are systematically ignored in the current migration and development debate. This chapter assesses the diverse ways in which Moroccan migration has impacted upon and interacted with wider processes of social and economic development and, in particular, how public policies of receiving and sending states have affected development impacts in positive, negative, or perhaps rather insignificant ways.

MOROCCAN MIGRATION:
FROM "GUEST WORKERS" TO SETTLERS

Over the past four decades, Morocco has evolved into one of the world's leading emigration countries. Since the mid-1960s, it has experienced large-scale migration of mostly low-skilled migrants to Western Europe. Moroccan labor migration to France was rooted in migration patterns that emerged in colonial times. The French occupation of Morocco (1912–56) marked the beginning of emigration to France. Yet this colonial migration was only modest compared with the 1962–72 decade, when the magnitude and geographical scope of Moroccan emigration dramatically expanded. Strong economic growth in Western Europe in the 1960s resulted in great demand for low-skilled labor. Morocco signed labor recruitment agreements with the former West Germany (1963), France (1963), Belgium (1964), and the Netherlands (1969). This was the onset of a spatial diversification of Moroccan emigration, increasingly away from France.

Although the Moroccan state, most receiving states, and most migrants themselves expected that this migration was going to be temporary, many "guest workers" did not return but ended up settling permanently. The 1973 oil crisis radically changed political and economic conditions in Morocco and receiving countries. Morocco suffered even more than the European countries from the global economic downturn. The economic situation in Morocco deteriorated and, following two failed coups d'état against King Hassan II in 1971 and 1972, the country also entered into a period of increasing political instability and repression. Simultaneously confronted with a progressive tightening of immigration policies in Europe, many migrants decided to stay on the safe, European side of the Mediterranean. Large-scale family reunification marked this shift toward permanent settlement. The recruitment freezes and restrictive immigration policies following the 1973 oil crisis and economic recessions in the early 1980s did not curb immigration. Ironically immigration restrictions have instead led to decreased return and circular migration and have effectively pushed migrants into permanent settlement.

To illustrate this trend toward permanent settlement, return migration rates among Moroccans are among the lowest and naturalization rates are among the highest of all immigrant groups in Europe (de Haas 2007b).

A second consequence of the restrictive immigration policies combined with renewed economic growth in Europe in the 1990s was an increase in undocumented migration after the 1990s, which was particularly directed at the new destination countries of Italy and Spain, where there was a high demand for unskilled migrant labor. An increasing proportion of independent labor migrants to Southern Europe is women who work as domestic workers, nannies, or cleaners or in agriculture and small industries. Undocumented migrants have often managed to obtain residence permits through legalizations or marriage with partners in the destination countries. Between 1980 and 2010 the combined Moroccan population officially residing in Spain and Italy increased from about 20,000 to 1.2 million according to the latest population census.

While family reunification was largely complete at the end of the 1980s, family formation as the result of new marriages between the second generation and native Moroccans gained significance as the major source of new migration from Morocco to the classic destination countries in northwestern Europe over the 1990s (Reniers 1999, 2001). While networks have continued to facilitate family and undocumented migration, there is sustained demand for labor migration, particularly in Italy and Spain. These factors help to explain why policies by receiving states aiming to curb migration seem to have had only a limited effect.

The combined effects of family reunification, family formation, natural increase, undocumented migration, and new labor migration to Southern Europe explain the tenfold increase in the number of Moroccan citizens living abroad, from 300,000 in 1972 on the eve of the recruitment freeze to at least 3 million at the turn of the century. This does not include undocumented migrants as well as at least 280,000 Moroccans living in Arab countries and the approximately 700,000 Jews of Moroccan descent living in Israel. Figure 7.2 illustrates the remarkable increase in the Moroccan migrant stock living in the main European receiving countries since the late 1960s as well as the decreasing spatial focus on France. Between 1974 and 2004 Moroccan expatriate communities in Europe increased at an average rate of 72,000 people per year in defiance of the increasingly restrictive immigration policies, although part of this increase represents natural growth.

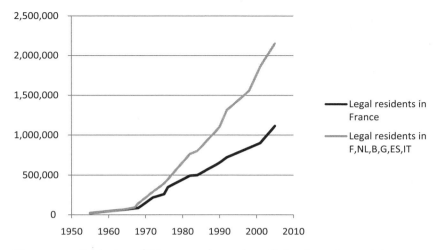

Figure 7.2 Evolution of Moroccan descendants living in main receiving countries, 1955–2004.

Source: Various sources in de Haas 2007b.

Table 7.1 Moroccan Citizens Residing Abroad, 2004

Country		Country	
France	1,113,176	Algeria	79,790
Netherlands	300,332	Libya	120,000
Germany	102,000	Tunisia	25,637
Belgium	293,097	Other Arab countries	57,345
Spain	671,669	U.S.	100,000
Italy	486,558	Canada	77,713
U.K.	35,000		
Other European	50,384	Other	11,734
Total	**2,616,871**	**Total**	**472,219**

Source: Consular data in Fargues et al. 2005:231–32.

Nowadays Moroccans form not only one of the largest but also one of the most dispersed migrant communities in Western Europe. In 2004 France was still home to the largest legally residing population of Moroccan descent (more than 1.1 million), followed by Spain (424,000), the Netherlands (300,000), Italy (299,000), Belgium (293,000), and Germany (102,000). Smaller but rapidly growing communities of higher-skilled migrants live in the United States (100,000) and Canada (78,000; consular data cited in Fargues et al. 2005; see Table 7.1).

MOROCCAN MIGRATION AND DEVELOPMENT POLICIES

MIGRATION AND REMITTANCES AS A NATIONAL DEVELOPMENT STRATEGY

Ever since the start of large-scale migration, Morocco has pursued a persistent policy of openly or, sometimes, tacitly stimulating migration as a development tool. Throughout the postindependence period, the Moroccan state has actively stimulated international out-migration for political and economic reasons. International migration was seen as a "safety valve" to prevent political tensions in certain rural, predominantly Berber areas (Rif, Sous, and southeastern oases), which have a rebellious reputation vis-à-vis the central "Arab" state. These policies were mainly pursued through selective passport issuance policies and directing recruiters to these areas (de Haas 2007a; De Mas 1978).

Besides a political instrument, migration was also seen as a tool for national economic development. The utility of migration was primarily seen through the skills and knowledge that migrants were expected to acquire by working and studying abroad. Migration was initially thought to be temporary; as a consequence, return migrants were widely expected to play a key role in modernizing the Moroccan economy and triggering investments. The belief that migrants would be particular actors of change, however, gradually faded over the 1970s. Efforts to stimulate returned migration and migrants' investment programs largely failed, mainly because of an unfavorable investment climate and a general distrust among migrants in government agencies (Berriane and Aderghal 2009; Fadloullah et al. 2000; Obdeijn 1993). This declining faith in migrants as development actors echoed a broader international mood shift characterized by increasing skepticism, leading public officials to claim, "Migration and development, nobody believes that anymore" (cf. Taylor et al. 1996a:401).

This did not refute the fact that, in the meantime, remittances had become increasingly important in sustaining the livelihoods of millions of Moroccans, particularly in rural areas. The Moroccan state saw this as vital to maintaining political stability and preventing popular unrest. However, because the Moroccan government gradually realized that most migrants would not return, it increasingly focused on policies aimed at securing remittances, stimulating investments by migrants, and fostering bonds between migrants and the real or imagined Moroccan "homeland."

In contrast to policies aiming to stimulate investments by migrants, policies to increase remittance transfers through the creation of a network of consulates, post offices, and bank branches abroad over the 1970s and 1980s were rather successful. At the same time, the Moroccan state attempted to maintain tight control on migrant communities in Europe through control and spying networks abroad. Until the early 1990s the state actively discouraged migrants' integration in the receiving countries, out of a fear that migrants would form a political opposition "from outside." Integration was also perceived as endangering the vital remittance transfers (de Haas and Plug 2006; also see Cortina and Ochoa-Reza in this volume for the case of Mexican and Turkish migration to the United States and Germany, respectively).

FROM CONTROLLING EMIGRANTS TO COURTING THE DIASPORA

An ominous stagnation in remittances in the 1990s and a growing consciousness that repressive policies alienated migrants rather than bound them closer to the Moroccan state prompted the Moroccan state to adopt a more positive attitude toward migrants (de Haas and Plug 2006). This concurred with a process of relative political liberalization and a certain improvement in Morocco's human rights record. Furthermore a neoclassical turn in economic policies implied partial deregulation and the opening of the Moroccan economy. After years of skepticism, this also created renewed hope in the role that migrants might play in encouraging foreign direct investment.

This broader political shift toward liberalization also created room for more positive attitudes toward naturalization, dual citizenship, and debates about voting rights for migrants abroad. In a rather striking reversal of views, integration of migrants was officially seen no longer as a danger but as a potentially beneficial process that enables migrants to send more money home and to invest. Increasing general civil liberties also implied more freedom for migrants to establish Berber, cultural, and "hometown" associations (cf. Lacroix 2005). However, the Moroccan state has not given up a number of policy instruments to exert a certain level of control. This is most evident in its systematic opposition against Moroccan descendants in Europe relinquishing Moroccan citizenship.

Besides establishing a ministry for Moroccans residing abroad, the Moroccan state also created the *Fondation Hassan II pour les Marocains*

Résidant à l'Étranger, which aims to reinforce its links with Moroccan emigrants. In the 1990s the state also started to clamp down on the long delays, corruption, and harassment by state officials that migrants on vacation experienced at the borders and inside Morocco. This likely contributed to the enormous increase in the number of migrants entering Morocco's northern harbors during the summer holidays, from 848,000 in 1993 to 2.2 million in 2003. On the economic side, new monetary policies have been applied in Morocco since the end of the 1980s, involving the lifting of restrictions on exchange and on the repatriation of money. Remittances have further been encouraged through fiscal policies favoring migrants (Refass 1999).

At first glance, the new Moroccan policies toward migrants and remittances seem to have reversed the earlier stagnation in remittances. In 2001 a spectacular increase in remittances occurred, amounting to $3.3 billion, up from $2.2 billion in 2000. After a minor relapse in 2002, remittances have shown a continuing steep upward trend in subsequent years, to reach an unprecedented level of $7.0 billion in 2011 (see Figure 7.3). However, the structural solidity of Moroccan remittances should *primarily* be explained by the unforeseen persistence of migration to northwestern Europe,

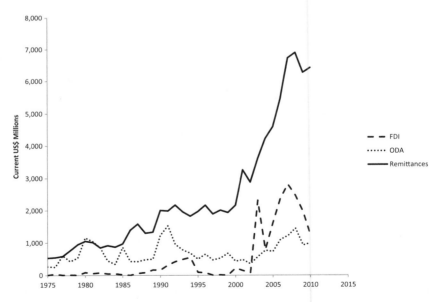

Figure 7.3   Total volume of official remittance, ODA and FDI flows to Morocco, 1975–2010.

Source: World Development Indicators database, World Bank.

the strength of transnational links between migrants and stay-behinds (see Levitt and Lamba-Nieves in this volume for a discussion on transnational links), and, last but not least, new labor migration to Spain, Italy, and North America. Also, the huge increase in the number of migrants visiting Morocco is likely to have contributed to increasing remittances, as remittance figures include cash changed against Moroccan dirhams by migrants during visits home.

REMITTANCES POLICIES AS A SAFETY VALVE

Thus, for the Moroccan government, the encouragement of new out-migration and holiday visits and other forms of largely circular mobility have turned out to be effective instruments for securing remittances. While the Moroccan government has been encouraging new out-migration since the 1980s by lifting restrictions on passport issuance, it has also started encouraging migrants to obtain foreign citizenship while retaining their (dual) Moroccan citizenship as a strategy to optimize circulation while simultaneously preventing the alienation of migrants and their descendants. The targeted policies to attract remittances, the expansion of financial services, low inflation, and the absence of a large black market for foreign exchange have also stimulated remittances. This explains why Morocco has been relatively successful in directing remittances through official channels.

For the Moroccan state, remittances are a crucial and relatively stable source of foreign exchange and have become a vital element in sustaining the country's balance of payments. Remittances have proven to be a substantially higher and less volatile source of foreign exchange than official development assistance (ODA) and foreign direct investment (FDI; see Figure 7.3). However, the observation that Moroccan emigration *and* remittances have steadily increased over the past fifty years does not say anything about the *impacts* of remittances. We have already seen that the general migration and development debate offers two diametrically opposed hypotheses. After all, from a theoretical point of view, migration and remittances can lead to both positive and negative development outcomes. On the one hand, one can argue that remittances and migrants' investments stimulate economic growth or national development. Alternatively, one might also argue that remittance dependency can postpone necessary reform and reinforce unfavorable investment conditions.

However, in reality the developmental impacts of migration and remittances are likely to be more diverse across places, regions, social groups, and time. In order to understand the factors explaining this diversity of impacts for the case of Morocco, we have to turn to the empirical literature.

EMPIRICAL EVIDENCE ON MOROCCAN MIGRATION IMPACTS

MIGRATION AS AN ACCELERATING FORCE IN REGIONAL ECONOMIC DEVELOPMENT

For migrants and their families, international migration is often an extremely effective way of improving their financial situation and living conditions. It has been estimated that 1.17 million out of 30 million Moroccans would fall back to absolute poverty without international remittances (Teto 2001). In regions with high international out-migration, the contribution of remittances to household income growth can be far higher (Berriane and Aderghal 2009; Schoorl et al. 2000). In several communities in Morocco's three traditional migration belts—the Rif Mountains, the Sous Valley, and southern oases—between one-fifth and over a half of all households have at least one member who has migrated abroad (Berriane and Aderghal 2009; de Haas 2006; Schoorl et al. 2000).

As in the international literature, pessimism has long pervaded the Moroccan literature. It is often stated that remittances are primarily used for daily expenses, conspicuous consumption, and "nonproductive" investments, such as the construction of palatial houses, and, most important, that such expenses spur inflation and do little to generate employment and economic growth. In many instances, it is argued, migrant households even withdraw from productive activities in and outside agriculture. This is believed to lead to a dangerous passive dependency on remittance income (Fadloullah et al. 2000; Hamdouch et al. 1979; Lazaar 1987; Mezdour 1993).

However, the empirical and analytical basis of such assertions seems to be rather uncertain. Claims that remittances are mostly spent for conspicuous consumption (e.g., luxury houses, videos, television, satellite dishes, cars) are often not based on systematic data collection and analysis (cf. Aït Hamza 1988; Kagermeier 1997). If we look at the pertinent empirical data that *are* available, a considerably more positive picture arises.

Several surveys have indicated that among migrant households willingness to invest is higher than among nonmigrant households (de Haas 2006; Hamdouch 2000; Heinemeijer et al. 1977; McMurray 1992; Nyberg-

Sorensen 2004). It has been commonly argued in the literature that international migration has contributed to agricultural decline. The "lost labor" of able-bodied (migrated) men is ascribed a key role in the process of agricultural decline (De Mas 1990b; Ferry and Toutain 1990; Kerbout 1990). However, this pessimistic perspective is challenged by empirical work showing that although the "lost labor effect" might initially have a disruptive effect in the agricultural sector, particularly in the long term, international remittances can also play a key role in facilitating agricultural investments and an intensification of agricultural production. A key observation is that such impacts are not uniform across different sending regions and seem mainly to occur in favorably located regions with road connections to main population centers and favorable institutional and agro-ecological conditions (Bencherifa 1996; Bencherifa and Popp 1990, 2000; Bonnet and Bossard 1973; de Haas 2003; Pascon 1985; Popp 1999).

Over the past decades, and parallel with changes in the national economy, there has also been diversification in the economic activities of migrants, partly shifting away from investments in subsistence agriculture, small-scale commerce, and housing toward investment in commercial agriculture, enterprises in the tourist sector, trade, transport, and small and medium-size industries in food processing, and the supply of building materials (Bencherifa and Popp 1990, 2000; Khachani 2009; Nyberg-Sorensen 2004).

REMITTANCES, HOUSING, AND URBAN GROWTH

The recent literature has also questioned traditionally negative judgments about migrants' priority for investment in housing. The majority of researchers lament housing investments, which is seen as a form of "irrational" and "unproductive" investment behavior that does not contribute to development (Agoumy 1988; Aït Hamza 1988; Ben Ali 1996; Kaioua 1999). However, there is ample reason to question these assumptions. The importance attached to housing should primarily be explained by the legitimate and well-being-enhancing quest for space, safety, privacy, fewer conflicts, and better health (Hajjarabi 1988). It also enables women to live in nuclear families and to be more independent from their in-laws (Aït Hamza 1988, 1995; Berriane 1996; de Haas and Van Rooij 2010; De Mas 1990a; Hajjarabi 1988). In fact dismissing such aspects of well-being as "nondevelopmental" reflects rather narrow views of development. Housing can also be seen as a relatively secure investment in an insecure investment environment (cf. Adams 1991), by which households can potentially generate income through lease arrangements (Ben Ali 1996; Charef 1986).

In migrant-sending areas throughout Morocco, a remittance-fueled building fever has transformed certain villages into towns, where migrants also prefer to locate other investments (Berriane and Aderghal 2009; Fadloullah et al. 2000). In this way, migration and remittances have also accelerated (albeit not initiated) the more general long-term trends toward livelihood diversification, decreasing dependence on agriculture and urbanization. This can be seen as a largely positive development, as it has made people's livelihoods less dependent on vagaries of the climate and agricultural markets. Partly due to remittances, in large parts of rural Morocco agricultural activities have now become an activity of secondary economic importance. In other words, migration has accelerated the already ongoing process of decreasing importance of agriculture for Morocco's national income. At the macroeconomic level, diversification of the Moroccan economy away from the one-sided dependency on agriculture can be seen as one of the cornerstones for creating the conditions for rapid and sustainable economic growth.

This process of "de-agrarianization" has coincided with the rapid growth of urban centers *within* rural areas, in which more and more internal migrants and returning international migrants settle and invest in nonagricultural enterprises. The urban allocation of migrants' investments and the fact that many return migrants prefer to resettle in towns in their native regions have spurred the development of new urban centers and "migrant boomtowns" within or near migrant-sending areas themselves (Agoumy 1988; Berriane 1996; Berriane and Aderghal 2009; Bounar 1993; Lazaar 1989; McMurray 2001). Through urban-based housing and business investments, international migrant households simultaneously capitalize on and actively contribute to the accelerated urban growth and concentration of economic activities in existing urban centers and migrant boomtowns and the overall process of what Berriane (1996) has aptly termed the "micro-urbanization" of rural Morocco.

In this light, there is also reason to put migrants' expenditure on housing and consumption in a more positive light. Provided that most goods and services are produced regionally or nationally, consumption and so-called nonproductive investments in housing and the service sector can have multiplier effects and create employment and income among nonmigrants as well. Although there is no hard micro-level empirical evidence that can shed a more precise light on the economic impacts, we know from research conducted in Mexico and elsewhere that such positive effects can be considerable (Adelman et al. 1988; Taylor et al. 1996a).

There is ample descriptive evidence suggesting that similar processes have affected several Moroccan sending regions. In the Sous and Rif, urban-oriented consumption and investments by international migrants have created a surge in the demand for laborers, particularly in housing construction, which cannot be met locally or even regionally. In fact the cumulative effect of decades of remittance expenditure and investments has transformed some established regions of international out-migration into thriving destinations for internal migrants coming from poorer areas of the country (Berriane and Aderghal 2009; de Haas 2006).

MIGRATION, DEMOGRAPHIC CHANGE, AND EDUCATION

The traditional policy and research focus on migrants' business investments has coincided with a lack of attention on the effects of migration on children's education. This is unfortunate in light of the crucial role of education in development processes, as well as the rather poor performance of Morocco (in comparison with other countries in the region) with regard to literacy rates and overall levels of schooling. Although more research is needed on this issue, the available evidence suggests that international migration has positive effects on higher school enrollment rates and that international migration might have played an accelerating role in closing the gender gap in education (Bencherifa 1996; de Haas 2003).

It has been frequently argued that migration has contributed to a slow-down in population growth or even depopulation of rural areas (Kerbout 1990). However, the commonly employed metaphor *exode rurale* to indicate this process is misleading, since absolute rural depopulation seems to occur only in particularly marginal, isolated areas (de Haas 1998). Leaving aside the question of why population stagnation or decline should necessarily be interpreted as negative—certainly given the fact that the same observers lamenting the *exode rurale* often also commonly express concerns about rural *overpopulation*—several studies have indicated that international migration and remittances have often enabled families *to stay* in rural areas and have actually prevented the depopulation of regions such as the Rif, Anti-Atlas, and southern oases (Berriane and Aderghal 2009; De Mas 1990a; Fadloullah et al. 2000; Heinemeijer et al. 1977; Mter 1995). This is in line with the new economics of labor migration, which have interpreted migration not as an individual income-maximizing strategy but as a livelihood strategy pursued by households to diversify their income and minimize their risk exposure (Stark and Bloom 1985; Taylor 1999). As Heinemeijer et al. (1977) aptly put it, migration is a form of family behavior aiming at *"partir pour rester."*

MIGRATION, REMITTANCES, AND INEQUALITY

Migration has also changed the social and ethnic structure of sending communities. Migration is not only an economic attempt to secure better livelihoods but also a clear avenue of upward social mobility and a way to decrease relative deprivation. This shows that it is artificial to separate the social and economic dimensions and functions of migration. Migration and the associated access to remittance income have also accelerated the breakdown of ancient socioethnic hierarchies and the emergence of new social stratifications in migrant-sending communities (Fadloullah et al. 2000; Mter 1995), with international migrant households often forming a new kind of "migration elite." The new socioeconomic dividing line in Moroccan migrant-sending communities now is often between households with and without international remittance income (de Bree et al. 2010; de Haas 2003).

However, from this we should not conclude that migration has "thus" increased inequality in migrant-sending communities, as this depends on the nature of historical inequalities. In this context, it is important to realize that "traditional," premodern agrarian communities tended to be intrinsically unequal (de Haas 2003; Ensel 1999; Ilahiane 2001). What has often happened is that new forms of inequality, based mainly on access to monetary resources, which are to a considerable extent defined along lines of access to international migration and remittances, have been largely superimposed upon the traditional forms of structural, hereditary inequality based on kinship, complexion, and land possession.

By offering new livelihood opportunities, migration and remittances have thus enabled members of formerly subaltern socioethnic groups to escape the constraints that traditional society imposed upon them. In some cases, this has coincided with a declining relative status of traditional land-based elites (de Haas 2003; Ensel 1999; Ilahiane 2001). Formerly landless migrants now often earn wages that allow them to buy land and gain increasing influence in local affairs (Crawford 2001; Otte 2000). This exemplifies the ambiguity and subjectivity in judging whether such migration-induced shifts should be regarded as positive or negative, also because any judgment will partly depend on the weight attached to distributional versus average income objectives (cf. Stark et al. 1988:309). It is also important to realize that such shifts are usually part of more general processes of social change. So they are not the unique result of migration, although migration often has an accelerating role in such processes.

Nevertheless the middle- and higher-income classes profit relatively more from remittances than the lowest income groups because migration itself has proven to be an (increasingly) selective process (Schiff 1994; Teto 2001). This is directly linked to the increasing migration restrictions that European states started to implement during the 1980s and 1990s. Rather than curbing migration, this appeared to have coincided with an increasing selectivity of migration. In the "guest worker" era, when direct recruitment took place and Moroccans could travel more or less freely to Europe, relatively poor (although generally not the *poorest*) peasants and workers were able to migrate, which also explains evidence that in the 1960s and 1970s migrants from rural areas were not better educated or wealthier than the population average within their age groups (Heinemeijer et al. 1977). However, due to tougher immigration restrictions, access to international migration has become increasingly selective according to wealth and dependent on access to largely kinship-based international migrant networks. This is likely to have reduced the poverty- and inequality-reducing potential of migration.

MIGRATION AND THE POSITION OF WOMEN

Large-scale out-migration has also affected the position of migrant and nonmigrant women. While migrant women have generally been able to improve their social, legal, and economic status vis-à-vis men through migrating internationally (de Bree et al. 2010), the impact of male migration on women left behind is much more ambiguous. Traditionally, migrants leave their wives and daughters behind with their extended family (De Mas 1990a). However, nuclear family households have increasingly become the norm over the past decades. In Morocco migration-related tensions on remittance use between migrants' wives and their in-laws have played an accelerating role in the breakdown of extended families and have accelerated the more general processes of nucleation of family life (de Haas 2003; Fadloullah et al. 2000; in contrast, see Escobar García and Álvarez Velasco in this volume for a discussion of the creation of extended families in the case of two Ecuadorian communities).

It is commonly asserted that migration of men has encouraged the emancipation of women. In the absence of their husbands, women's responsibilities, autonomy, and power are said to increase (Aït Hamza 1988; Bouzid 1992; Fadloullah et al. 2000). Nevertheless a limited number of available targeted studies have challenged this hypothesis (de Haas and Van Rooij 2010; Steinmann 1993). The lives of migrants' wives often remain largely confined to housekeeping, child rearing, and agricultural work. Although the women tend to have more control over the use of their husbands' earnings and in child rearing, this gain in authority is mainly temporary, since migrants tend to resume their position as patriarchs as soon as they return. Furthermore migrants' wives do not necessarily appreciate the sudden increase in responsibilities and tasks, which were not theirs within the normative context of traditional society and to which they do not always aspire (de Haas and Van Rooij 2010; Hajjarabi 1995). Migration itself apparently has no direct influence or only a limited one on such norms, and gradual changes in these and the improving position of women therefore reflect general processes of cultural change within Moroccan society rather than that they are the particular effect of migration.[1]

However, there might be some more indirect positive effects, as international migration and remittances have the potential to encourage the schooling of girls in migrant families. Furthermore there is some evidence that—besides factors such as higher age of marriage, increased female labor force participation, and improved education—the migration of Moroccan families to European countries has contributed to the diffusion and adoption of European marriage patterns and small family norms, and so has played an accelerating role in the demographic transition (Courbage 1994; Fargues 2006). This exemplifies the potentially developmental role of what Levitt (1998) has called *social remittances*.

THE NEED TO REFRAME THE MIGRATION AND DEVELOPMENT DEBATE

What lessons can we draw from this review of the Moroccan migration and development case? First and foremost, I have illustrated that the impact of migration on development processes is complex and multifaceted. Second, the nature of this impact is highly dependent on the general institutional context and investment conditions. For instance, it is not surprising that migrants prefer to invest in towns and rural areas that already boast favorable development conditions. This directly leads us to the third lesson: despite their considerable positive significance for the livelihoods of families and communities, migration and remittances cannot independently set in motion more general, nationwide development processes.

The evidence from Morocco and other emigration countries such as Mexico and Turkey points to the diverse nature of migration impacts and in particular their contingency on more general development conditions (cf. de Haas 2010; Castles and Delgado). This exemplifies the need to see migration as an integral part of development processes rather than an "exogenous" force impinging upon development processes that can change the overall direction of development. The specific role of migration and remittances is unlikely to be a radical course-shifting one; instead they seem to accelerate or deepen preexisting, more general development trends, whether of rapid growth, stagnation, or decline. Therefore migration can trigger a vicious as well as a virtuous development circle.

Depending on the general investment and development conditions, migration may enable people to retreat from, just as much as to engage and invest in, social, political, and economic activities in origin countries. After all, it is the very capabilities-enhancing potential of migration (which can be seen as micro-level development) that also increases the freedom of migrants and their families to effectively withdraw from such activities. It is therefore not very surprising that in countries affected by violence, insecurity, and dismal investment conditions, few migrants will invest. However, if general development trends take a positive turn, if trust in governments increases and economic growth is high, migrants are likely to be among the first to recognize such new opportunities, join in, and reinforce these positive trends through investing in and circulating and returning to their origin countries. Such mutually reinforcing migration-development processes seem to have occurred in several former emigration countries as diverse as Spain, Taiwan, South Korea, and, recently, Turkey.

The inference is that the development impacts of migration are highly *contextual*. Although this might sound like a rather commonplace generalization, it is worth emphasizing, because all too often migration and remittances still get blamed for a lack of development (cf. the critique by Cohen et al. 2005), while the real cause should be sought in generically unfavorable investment conditions that are not the consequence of migration as such. In designing sensible and realistic policies, it is important to keep in mind that *legitimate* individual and family needs primarily drive migrants' remittance expenditure. Only secondarily are migrants perhaps interested in promoting the development of entire communities or regions, and it would also be highly naive to expect that they would be able to trigger nationwide development. Any policy attempting to shift the responsibility of national development onto the shoulders of individual migrants is therefore doomed to fail.

The context-dependency of migration impacts also explains why migration does not have a fixed impact on development. It is important to stress that what is involved is a development *potential*, not an automatic mechanism. The extent to which migrants will spend in, invest in, and return to their origin countries depends on general investment conditions, political stability, and overall trust in future development. Paradoxically, development is therefore a *prerequisite* for investment and return by migrants rather than a consequence of migration. This provides a warning against naively optimistic views on migration and development by pointing at the real but fundamentally limited ability of individual migrants to overcome structural development constraints.

Unfavorable economic and political conditions make investments and development projects difficult to design and implement and often lead to their failure. In Morocco studies have indicated that although migrants do not generally indulge in conspicuous consumption and are more prone to invest in nonhousing sectors of the local economy than was previously assumed (Khachani 1998; Refass 1999), investment opportunities remain limited. So we may conclude that the development potential of migration is not fully realized due to several structural development constraints.

In the 1970s Heinemeijer et al. (1977) had already concluded on the basis of a large-scale survey in two main migrant-sending areas (the Rif and the Sous) that although migrants actually had a relatively high *propensity* to invest, the investment opportunities for migrants in their regions of origin are often limited (see also Bonnet and Bossard 1973). This, combined with the insecure political situation and the severe curtailing of civil liberties in Morocco over the 1970s and 1980s, helps to explain why many migrants chose not to return and to cancel or at least downsize their original investment plans.

The Moroccan experience also suggests that it can take many decades before positive development impacts of migration and remittances gain full momentum, that "integrated" and settled migrants possess greater capabilities to remit and invest, and that migrants possessing residency rights or (dual) citizenship have a higher propensity to return and circulate. This casts serious doubt on the common policy assumption that temporary migration programs—*if* states succeed in enforcing return at all—will favor development in sending countries.

The Moroccan case also shows the importance of distinguishing between impacts on the individual or family, regional, and national level. In general, impacts tend to be more positive at lower (individual, household, and community) levels of aggregation, while the potential role of migration and remittances in stimulating national development is much more ambiguous. While international migration and remittances have the real capacity to substantially improve livelihoods and economic activity in migrant-sending regions, it would be naive to expect that migration alone can lead to structural reform needed for nationwide development.

This shows the need to reframe the debate on migration and development. Because development is a condition for attracting migrants' income-generating investments rather than a consequence of it, policymakers would be wise to reverse their perspective on migration and development. Rather than asking what migrants can do to support development, governments would be better off identifying how to make investment and general development conditions attractive for migrant investments. In many ways, governments of sending and receiving countries have become overly obsessed with maximizing remittances while generally ignoring the basic necessity to first create a fertile soil where the remittance seeds can be sown.

Again, the Moroccan case provides a useful illustration of this more general point. While Moroccan policies to increase remittances have been successful, this does not mean that the impact of remittances has necessarily become more positive, as this will depend on the way money is ultimately spent, or is not spent at all. The crucial point is that public policies that improve the functioning of social, legal, economic, and political institutions, that increase the access of ordinary people to basic amenities and markets, and that restore trust in governments are crucial not only for creating fertile ground for development *in general* but also for compelling more migrants to return to and invest in origin countries. As argued by de la Garza (this volume), governments are better situated to manage and shape political variables that in turn will shape economic development. Policy and scholarly discourses celebrating migration, remittances, and transnational engagement as self-help development "from below" shift attention away from structural constraints and the real but limited ability of individuals to overcome these constraints. This exemplifies the crucial role *states* have to play in shaping favorable conditions for human development to occur.

While migrants can potentially accelerate development at home, they can neither be blamed for a lack of development nor be expected to generate development in unattractive investment environments. Destination countries have an important role here as well. During the most recent global economic crisis, European countries in particular have attempted to encourage the return of migrants. But when return policies require migrants not to come back, destination countries are actually pushing migrants into semipermanent settlement. By deterring the relatively poor from migrating and by marginalizing migrants and impeding return and circulation, restrictive immigration policies also damage the poverty-alleviating and overall development potential of migration.

From this we can draw clear lessons for policy. First, targeted remittance and diaspora policies will have limited effects if they are not accompanied by general reform and progress. The only way of genuinely releasing the development potential of migration and migrants' resources is by creating attractive investment environments, generating economic growth, and building trust in political and legal institutions of sending countries, along with sensible, demand-driven immigration policies that do not deter migrants from circulating or push them into undocumented migration.

This also reveals that the stated development intentions of newly advocated temporary, return, or "codevelopment" migration policies are discursive tools to justify an agenda of marginalizing and depriving migrants of their rights and to forcibly expel irregular immigrants and rejected asylum seekers. Such policies are misguided because they not only fail to stop migration but will also considerably decrease the potential of migration for development in origin countries.

REFERENCES

Adams, R. H. 1991. "The Economic Uses and Impact of International Remittances in Rural Egypt." *Economic Development and Cultural Change* 39: 695–722.

Adelman, I., J. E. Taylor, and S. Vogel. 1988. "Life in a Mexican Village: A SAM Perspective." *Journal of Development Studies* 25: 5–24.

Agoumy, T. 1988. "Retombées de l'Emigration et Croissance Urbaine: Le Cas de Taza." In *Le Maroc et La Hollande: Actes de la Première Rencontre Universitaire*. Rabat: Université Mohammed V.

Agunias, D. R. 2006. "Remittances and Development: Trends, Impacts, and Policy Options," Migration Policy Institute. Report. Washington D.C.

Aït, Hamza M. 1988. "L'émigration, Facteur d'Intégration ou de Désintégration des Régions d'Origine." In *Le Maroc et La Hollande: Actes de la Première Rencontre Universitaire*. Rabat: Université Mohammed V.

———. 1995. "Les Femmes d'Emigrés dans les Sociétés Oasiennes." In *Le Maroc et La Hollande: Une Approche Comparative des Grands Interêts Communs*. Rabat: Université Mohammed V.

Ben, Ali D. 1996. "L'Impact de Transferts des Résidents Marocains à l'Etranger (RME) sur l'Investissement Productif." In *Séminaire sur "La Migration Internationale," 6–7 juin 1996*. Rabat: Centre d'Etudes et de Recherches Démographiques (CERED).

Bencherifa, A. 1996. "L'Impact de la Migration Internationale sur le Monde Rural Marocain." In *Séminaire sur "La Migration Internationale," 6–7 juin 1996*. Rabat: Centre d'Etudes et de Recherches Démographiques (CERED).

Bencherifa, A., and H. Popp. 1990. *L'Oasis de Figuig: Persistance et Changement*. Passau, Germany: Passavia Universitätsverlag.

Bencherifa, A., and H. Popp. 2000 *Rémigration Nador III: Le Développement Agricole dans la Province de Nador (Maroc) sous l'Effet de l'Emigration Internationale du Travail*. Passau, Germany: L. I. S. Verlag.

Berriane, M. 1996. "Migration Internationale et Extension du Cadre Bâti: Le Cas des Villes du Maroc Nord." In *Séminaire sur "La Migration Internationale," 6–7 juin 1996*. Rabat: Centre d'Etudes et de Recherches Démographiques (CERED).

Berriane, M., and M. Aderghal. 2009. "Etat de la recherche sur les migrations internationales à partir, vers et à travers le Maroc." Prepared for the program on African Perspectives on Human Mobility. Université Mohammed V and International Migration Institute, University of Oxford.

Bonnet, J. J., and R. Bossard. 1973. "Aspects Géographiques de l'Emigration Marocaine vers l'Europe." *Revue de Géographie du Maroc* 23, no. 245–50.

Bounar, A. 1993. "L'Urbanisation dans un Milieu d'Oasis Présahariennes (La Vallée du Draa et le Pays de Ouarzazate)." Ph.D. dissertation, University of Poitiers.

Bouzid, N. 1992. "Espace et activités au féminin dans une vallée présaharienne du Sud marocain: La vallée du Todra." Ph.D. dissertation, Paris-Sorbonne.

Castles, S., and Delgado-Wise, R. 2007. *Migration and Development: Perspectives from the South*. Geneva: International Organization for Migration.

Castles, Stephen, and Mark J. Miller. 2009. "The Age of Migration: International Population Movements in the Modern World." Basingstoke: Palgrave MacMillan.

Charef, M. 1986. "L'émigration Internationale Marocaine et son Role dans la Production du Logement au Maroc." Ph.D. dissertation, University of Poitiers.

Cohen, J., R. Jones, and D. Conway. 2005. "Why Remittances Shouldn't Be Blamed for Rural Underdevelopment in Mexico—A Collective Response to Leigh Binford." *Critique of Anthropology* 25: 87–96.

Courbage, Y. 1994. "Demographic Change in the Arab World: The Impact of Migration, Education and Taxes in Egypt and Morocco." *Middle East Report* 24: 19–22.

Crawford, D. 2001. "How 'Berber' Matters in the Middle of Nowhere." *Middle East Report* 219: 21–25.

de Bree, J., T. Davids, and H. de Haas. 2010. "Post-Return Experiences and Transnational Belonging of Return Migrants: A Dutch-Moroccan Case Study." *Global Networks—A Journal of Transnational Affairs* 10: 489–509

de Haas, H. 1998. "Socio-Economic Transformations and Oasis Agriculture in Southern Morocco." In *Looking at Maps in the Dark: Directions for Geographical Research in Land Management and Sustainable Development in Rural and Urban Environments of the Third World*, edited by L. D. Haan and P. Blaikie. Utrecht: KNAG/FRW.

——. 2003. "Migration and Development in Southern Morocco: The Disparate Socio-Economic Impacts of Out-Migration on the Todgha Oasis Valley." Ph.D. dissertation, Radboud University.

——. 2006. "Migration, Remittances and Regional Development in Southern Morocco." *Geoforum* 37: 565–80.

——. 2007a. "Between Courting and Controlling: The Moroccan State and 'Its' Emigrants." Centre on Migration, Policy and Society Working Paper No. 54, University of Oxford.

——. 2007b. "Morocco's Migration Experience: A Transitional Perspective." *International Migration* 45: 39–70.

——. 2010. "Migration and Development: A Theoretical Perspective." *International Migration Review* 44: 227–64.

de Haas, H., and R. Plug. 2006. "Cherishing the Goose with the Golden Eggs: Trends in Migrant Remittances from Europe to Morocco 1970–2004." *International Migration Review* 40: 603–34.

de Haas, H., and A. Van Rooij. 2010. "Migration as Emancipation? The Impact of Internal and International Migration on the Position of Women in Rural Morocco." *Oxford Development Studies* 38: 43–62.

De Mas, P. 1978. *Marges marocaines: Limites de la cooperation au développement dans une région périphérique: Le cas du Rif.* 's-Gravenhage: NUFFIC/IMWOO/Projet Remplod.

——. 1990a. "Overlevingsdynamiek in het Marokkaanse Rif-Gebergte: De Samenhang tussen Circulaire Migratie en Demografische Structuur van Huishoudens." *Geografisch Tijdschrift* 24: 73–86.

——. 1990b. "Regroupement Familial Marocain aux Pays-Bas 1968–1987: Un Aperçu Quantitatif." In *Le Maroc et La Hollande: Actes de la Deuxième Rencontre Universitaire*. Rabat: Université Mohammed V.

Ensel, R. 1999. *Saints and Servants in Southern Morocco*. Leiden: E. J. Brill.

Fadloullah, A., A. Berrada, and M. Khachani. 2000. *Facteurs d'Attraction et de Répulsion des flux Migratoires Internationaux. Rapport National: Le Maroc.* Rabat: Commission Européenne.

Fargues, P. 2006. "The Demographic Benefit of International Migration: Hypothesis and Application to Middle Eastern and North African Contexts." World Bank Policy Research Working Paper No. 4050, Washington D.C.

Fargues, P., J.-P. Cassarino, and A. Latreche, eds. 2005. *Mediterranean Migration—2005 Report*. Florence: EUI-RSCAS, CARIM Consortium.

Ferry, M., and G. Toutain. 1990. "Concurrence et Complementarité des Espèces Végétales dans les Oasis." In *Les Systèmes Agricoles Oasiens*. Paris: Centre Internationale de Hautes Études Agronomiques Méditerannéennes (CIHEAM).

Hajjarabi, F. 1988. "Femmes et Emigration: Cas de la Région d'Al Hoceima." In *Le Maroc et La Hollande: Actes de la Première Rencontre Universitaire*. Rabat: Université Mohammed V.

——. 1995. "Femmes, famille et changement social dans le Rif." In *Le Maroc et La Hollande: Une Approche Comparative des Grands Interêts Communs*. Rabat: Université Mohammed V.

Hamdouch, B., ed. 2000. *Les Marocains résidant à l'étranger: Une enquête socio-économique*. Rabat: INSEA.

Hamdouch, B., et al. 1979. *Migration de Développement, Migration de sous-développement?* Rabat: INSEA, REMPLOD.

Heinemeijer, W. F., et al. 1977. *Partir pour rester, une enquête sur les incidences de l'émigration ouvrière à la campagne marocaine*. The Hague: NUFFIC.

Ilahiane, H. 2001. "The Social Mobility of the Haratine and the Re-working of Bourdieu's Habitus on the Saharan Frontier, Morocco." *American Anthropologist* 103: 380–94.

Jones, R. C. 1998. "Introduction: The Renewed Role of Remittances in the New World Order." *Economic Geography* 74, no. 1: 1–7.

Kagermeir, A. 1997. "Migration Internationale et Changements Sociaux dans le Maghreb: Colloque international, Hammamet-Tunis, 21–25 Juin 1993." In *Migration Internationale Et Changements Sociaux Dans Le Maghreb*, edited by Centre d'études maghrébines à Tunis. Tunis, Faculte Des Sciences Humaines Et Sociales.

Kaioua, A. 1999. CPlace des Emigrés Marocains en Europe dans l'Investissement Industriel à Casablanca." In *Migrations Internationales entre le Maghreb et l'Europe*, edited by M. Berriane and H. Popp. Rabat: Université Mohammed V.

Kapur, D. 2003. "Remittances: The New Development Mantra?" United Nations Conference on Trade and Development G-24 Discussion Paper No. 29. Geneva.

Katseli, L. T., R. E. B. Lucas, and T. Xenogiani. 2006. "Effects of Migration on Sending Countries: What Do We Know?" OECD Working Paper No. 250, Paris.

Kerbout, M. 1990. "Les Mutations des Campagnes du Moyen Atlas Oriental: Le Cas des Beni Yazgha et des Marmoucha." In *Le Maroc: Espace et Société*, edited by A. H. P. Bencherifa. Passau, Germany: Passavia Universitätsverlag.

Khachani, M. 1998. "Migration from Arab Maghreb Countries to Europe: Present Situation and Future Prospects." *Economic Research Forum for the Arab Countries* 5, no. 9.

——. 2009. "The Impact of Migration on the Moroccan Economy." *Journal of Ethnic and Migration Studies* 35: 1609–21.

Lacroix, T. 2005. *Les réseaux marocains du développement: Géographie du transnational et politiques du territorial*. Paris: Presses de Sciences Po.

Lazaar, M. 1987. "International Migration and Its Consequences in the Central Rif (Morocco)." *European Review of International Migration* 3: 97–114.

————. 1989. "La migration internationale de travail et ses effets sur les campagnes du Rif (Province d'Al-Hoceima—Maroc)." Ph.D. dissertation, Université de Poitiers.

Levitt, P. 1998. "Social Remittances: Migration Driven Local-Level Forms of Cultural Diffusion." *International Migration Review* 32: 926–48.

Lowell, L. B., and A. Findlay. 2002. "Migration of Highly Skilled Persons from Developing Countries: Impact and Policy Responses." ILO/DfID, Geneva.

McMurray, D. A. 1992. "The Contemporary Culture of Nador, Morocco, and the Impact of International Labor Migration." Ph.D. dissertation, University of Texas at Austin.

————. 2001. *In and out of Morocco: Smuggling and Migration in a Frontier Boomtown.* Minneapolis: University of Minnesota Press.

Mezdour, S. 1993. "Economie des Migrations Internationales." *Revue Française des Affaires Sociales* 47: 179–99.

Mter, M. A. 1995. "La population ksourienne du sud du Maroc et l'émigration internationale: Le cas des vallées du Dadess et du Draa dans la province de Ouarzazate." Ph.D. dissertation, University of Rouen.

Nyberg-Sorensen, N. 2004. "Migrant Remittances as a Development Tool: The Case of Morocco," Danish Institute for Development Studies Working Paper 2004/17. Copenhagen.

Obdeijn, H. 1993. "Op Weg naar Werk ver van Huis: Marokkaanse Emigratie in Historisch Perspectief." *Migrantenstudies* 4: 34–47.

Otte, C. 2000. "Playing with the Essence of Life: MA Thesis about Organisation Control and Disputes over the Interrelated Issues of Water and Land in a Moroccan Oasis Village." University of Amsterdam.

Özden, Ç., and M. Schiff, eds. 2005. *International Migration, Remittances, and the Brain Drain.* Washington D.C.: World Bank.

Pascon, P. 1985. *La Maison d'Iligh et l'Histoire Sociale de Tazerwalt.* Rabat: SMER.

Popp, H. 1999. "Les Effets de la Rémigration sur l'Agriculture Irriguée: Etude de Cas dans la Plaine de Zébra (Maroc du Nord-Est)." In *Migrations Internationales entre le Maghreb et l'Europe,* edited by M. Berriane and H. Popp. Rabat: Université Mohammed V.

Rapoport, H., and F. Docquier. 2005. "The Economics of Migrants' Remittances." Institute for the Study of Labor (IZA) Discussion Paper No. 1531. Bonn.

Ratha, D. 2003. "Workers' Remittances: An Important and Stable Source of External Development Finance." In *Global Development Finance 2003.* Washington, D.C.: World Bank.

Refass, M. A. 1999. "Les Transferts des Ressortisants Marocains à l'Etranger." In *Migrations Internationales entre le Maghreb et l'Europe,* edited by M. Berriane and H. Popp. Rabat: Université Mohammed V.

Reniers, G. 1999. "On the History and Selectivity of Turkish and Moroccan Migration to Belgium." *International Migration* 37: 679–713.

————. 2001. "The Post-Migration Survival of Traditional Marriage Patterns: Consanguineous Marriages among Turks and Moroccans in Belgium." *Journal of Comparative Family Studies* 32, no. 1: 21–35.

Schiff, M. 1994. *How Trade, Aid, and Remittances Affect International Migration.* Washington, D.C.: World Bank, International Economics Department.

Schoorl, J., et al. 2000. *Push and Pull Factors of International Migration: A Comparative Report.* Luxembourg: Eurostat, European Communities.

Stark, O., and D. E. Bloom. 1985. "The New Economics of Labor Migration." *American Economic Review* 75: 173–78.

Stark, O., C. Helmenstein, and A. Prskawetz. 1997. "A Brain Gain with a Brain Drain." *ECOLET* 55: 227–34.

Stark, O., J. E. Taylor, and S. Yitzhaki. 1988. "Migration, Remittances in Inequality: A Sensitivity Analysis Using the Extended Gini Index." *Journal of Development Economics* 28: 309–22.

Steinmann, S. H. 1993. "Effects of International Migration on Women's Work in Agriculture." *Revue de Géographie du Maroc* 15: 105–24.

Taylor, J. E. 1999. "The New Economics of Labour Migration and the Role of Remittances in the Migration Process." *International Migration* 37: 63–88.

Taylor, J. E., et al. 1996a. "International Migration and Community Development." *Population Index* 62: 397–418.

——. 1996b. "International Migration and National Development." *Population Index* 62: 181–212.

Teto, A. 2001. "Contribution des Transferts à la Solidarité Sociale et Familiale, à la Consolidation des Filets de Sécurités et de Protection contre la Pauvrété: Cas du Maroc." Paper presented at the Analysis of Poverty and Its Determinants in the MENA Region, Economic Research Forum, Sana'a, Yemen, July 31–August 1.

United Nations, Department of Economic and Social Affairs, Population Division. "International Migration Flows to and from Selected Countries: The 2005 Revision," edited by United Nations. New York, 2006.

——. "International Migration Flows to and from Selected Countries: The 2008 Revision," edited by United Nations. New York, 2009.

United Nations Development Program (UNDP). 2009. *Overcoming Barriers: Human Mobility and Development.* New York.

World Bank. 2005. *Global Development Finance 2005.* Washington, D.C.: World Bank.

CHAPTER 8

The Southern Crossroads

HUMAN MOBILITY, GOVERNANCE, AND DEVELOPMENT IN SOUTH AFRICA

Loren B. Landau and Aurelia Segatti

The challenge for South Africa is to formulate policy that takes advantage of the positive aspects of globalization, including the unprecedented movement of people with skills, expertise, resources, entrepreneurship and capital, which will support the country's efforts at reconstruction, development and nation-building.

Republic of South Africa, White Paper on International Migration (Sec. 4.2, 1999)

South Africa and its urban centers are primary nodes in a regional migration system. Unlike countries in the Maghreb or West Africa, South Africa is neither a major source nor a transit country for low-skilled labor en route to the European Union or North America. Rather, the country's wealth and relative stability attracts people, cash, goods, and information from neighboring countries—Mozambique, Zimbabwe, and especially Lesotho—and from those as far away as Cameroon, Nigeria, Somalia, and increasingly China and South Asia. In many instances these ties build on decades of carefully orchestrated guest worker programs (see, e.g., Harries 1994). However, it is impossible to understand the relationships between contemporary forms of international migration and development without carefully considering the country's domestic population dynamics. Here we find a remarkably mobile population whose spatial distribution, skills, health, and wealth have been shaped by elaborate regulations on human mobility. Indeed from South Africa's colonial foundation, the majority of its residents, citizens and nonnationals, faced stark limitations on where they could live and own land and when and how they could move (see Posel 1997).

Whether it is the commercial farming areas near the Zimbabwean and Mozambican borders or in the prosperous urban province of Gauteng, human mobility in all its forms continues to transform the country's population and economy as never before. With the country's first democratic elections in 1994, South Africa's previously forbidden cities became primary destinations for migrants from around the country. There they have encountered international migrants from around the continent and beyond, seeking profit, protection, and the possibility of passage elsewhere. Given its economic and political importance to neighboring countries and the continent, South Africa holds a critical position in the region's development.

Migration in southern Africa must be understood alongside its complex political context and institutional effects. While a magnet for the region, South Africa has consistently struggled to retain its educated middle class, who have gone elsewhere to improve their economic and physical security. As such, the country cannot meet its short-term development targets without significant in-migration of skilled and semiskilled labor. But despite the evident need to build an effective system to monitor and address human migration, the South African government and civil society possess perilously limited capacity to improve migration management and ensure the peaceful integration of migrants into the development process. Rather than see the domestic and regional benefits of mobility, official discussions have largely continued to center on citizens' economic and physical security and the human rights of a relatively small number of refugees and asylum seekers. Efforts to reframe the debate in developmental terms have met limited success in large part due to vital anti-immigration sentiment that remains widespread within and outside of government (see Crush 2007). As if to emphasize the point, the outbreak of antiforeigner violence in May 2008 and the continued threat of violence in the years that followed starkly illustrate the fact that the developmental effects of human mobility, as all of my fellow contributors to this volume highlight, cannot be understood solely in economic terms (see Misago et al. 2009; on the continued threat of violence, see Brown 2010; Landau 2011).

This chapter attempts to capture a number of the dynamics and contradictions associated with human mobility into and within South Africa. We begin by providing a broad overview of the demographic and socioeconomic data available, appraising the quality of knowledge this offers on contemporary migration flows to and within South Africa. We then approach issues of migration and development from an explicitly political perspective by focusing on two core issues: the integration of international migrants into local communities and the local governance of migration in contexts of extreme vulnerability and resource competition. Along the way, we highlight the challenges of developing effective policies in the presence of prevailing anti-immigrant attitudes within and outside government and the influence of a strong antitrafficking lobby, which further complicate efforts to achieve progressive, development-oriented reforms.

We conclude with three recommendations for improving migration policy and management: first, to reconsider the analytical and policy divisions between documented and undocumented migrants; between voluntary and forced migrants; and between international and domestic migration. Such divides have produced policy silos with little coordination among agencies charged with law enforcement, status determination, documentation, social assistance, or local development. With South Africa's patterns of mixed migration, there is a need to develop bureaucratic and planning mechanisms to address human mobility more broadly. Second, we call for an analytical respatialization in future planning and management scenarios. While recognizing national government's role, we suggest that positive development outcomes will be maximized only by enhancing the role of local governments and regional bodies in evaluating, designing, and implementing an approach to human mobility. As migration and development vary across both space and time, any policy approach that fails to disaggregate migration according to these variables is unlikely to fully realize its objectives. We end by arguing that there is much to learn from situating discussion on migration and its management within the broader global debate over governance and development. With a move away from universally prescriptive approaches to governance among bilateral and multilateral institutions, there is widespread recognition that pragmatism must carry the day. However, few international actors (let alone the South African government) have applied this approach of governance to migration, an area still dominated by security concerns, which is ill-adapted to development challenges. If nothing else, we suggest that foreign assistance and domestic policy reforms push for "migration mainstreaming" into all aspects of governance. In a region where international and domestic mobility remains so demographically and politically important, the success of any development initiative must overtly consider the country's population dynamics.

DATA SOURCES AND APPROACH

This study embeds demographic and economic trends within broader sociopolitical formations by drawing on an ecumenical set of data in illustrating the intersections between human mobility and development in South Africa. In a number of instances, it calls on the African Centre for Migration Studies (ACMS—formerly, the Forced Migration Studies Programme) surveys conducted with 847 respondents in seven central Johannesburg neighborhoods. Of these, 29.9 percent (253) were from the Democratic Republic of Congo (DRC); 24 percent (203) from Mozambique; 22 percent (186) from Somalia; and 22.4 percent from South Africa (190). (The remaining 1.8 percent were from other countries mistakenly included in the sample.) The sample was 59.7 percent male, generally reflecting official estimates of the inner-cities demographic composition (SACN 2006). These data are by no means representative of South Africa's "migrant stock" or of the host population. However, they do provide critical illustrations of trends and points where migration and development intersect. To make broader claims, we also draw on the 2001 South African Census and the 2007 National Community Survey, both conducted by Statistics South Africa. The latter generated a nationally representative sample of all South African residents but does not provide all of the spatial and demographic details afforded by the 2001 census.[1] In all instances, we work from the position that social and political understandings of human mobility are as important as actual movements and economic activity in determining development outcomes. Indeed this chapter benefits from extensive participant observation in national, local, and regional migration-related discussions and interviews with migrants, service providers, advocates, and local and national government representatives in Johannesburg, Pretoria, Cape Town, and elsewhere.

By way of both qualification and appeal, it is worth noting that one of the greatest challenges in tracing the link between human mobility and development in South Africa is poor data quality. Without improved national data there is little way of knowing how many migrants there are in South Africa, how long they stay, what motivates them to move, or what they do after moving. As a consequence, South African discussions around migration policy during the 1990s and early 2000s have struggled over the evidence needed to make sound choices and evaluate the impact of past decisions. Despite our best efforts, the data used here are similarly compromised.

CONTEMPORARY MOBILITY INTO
AND WITHIN SOUTH AFRICA

Scholars often explain migration with reference to the 3Ds: demography, development, and disparities. A more nuanced analysis of migration motivations and trends points to the 3Ps. While the majority move in search of *profit*, others are after *protection* from political or domestic persecution, natural disasters, or violence. Others seek *passage*, onward movement elsewhere. These divergent trajectories have important implications for migrants' experiences in and contributions to development. They also help to explain both international and domestic migration within, into, and through South Africa.

Although domestic mobility accounts for the vast majority of the country's migrants, international migrants are at the center of political and popular debate. The most recent available data from the South African Census (2001) estimated between 500,000 and 850,000 nonnationals in the country. These numbers have climbed due to South Africa's relative economic strength and the ongoing Zimbabwean crisis. In 2007 Statistics South Africa estimated that the total number of foreign-born residents is just over 1.2 million, or 2.79 percent of the total population. In 2011 the percentage climbed to 3.2, topping 1.6 million (Statistics South Africa 2012). That is higher than many South Africans would like, but is low compared with, for example, Gabon (17.9 percent), the United States (13.0 percent), Ivory Coast (12.3 percent), France (10.6 percent), the United Kingdom (9.7 percent), Ghana (7.6 percent), and Namibia (6.6 percent). Although not by much, it remains below neighboring Botswana (5.8 percent).

As in destination countries around the world, the nonnationals living in South Africa are a mix of documented and undocumented migrants along with refugees and asylum seekers. The number of temporary work, study, business, and tourist permits granted annually has consistently increased since the end of apartheid. (The overall number of temporary permits and visas went from 3.0 million to 9.9 million between 1992 and 1999; Department of Home Affairs 1992–99.) During the same period, permanent immigration permits went from 1,400 a year in 1990 to 4,000 at the end of the 1990s. The number then jumped to around 10,000 a year by 2004 (Department of Home Affairs 1990–2004). Temporary permits and visas are also increasingly granted to Africans. There has also been a largely unsuccessful effort to increase the number of "exceptionally skilled" migrants to South Africa through the general work permit, a (skills) quota work permit, an intracompany transfer work permit, treaty permits, and corporate permits. (The government's recruitment efforts are discussed later in the chapter.)

In addition to what might be termed voluntary migrants, South Africa also hosts a relatively small but expanding number of refugees and asylum seekers. Whereas elsewhere in Africa refugees are held in refugee camps, South African law encourages self-settlement and grants the immediate right to work upon application for asylum. Because of the employment rights associated with becoming a refugee or asylum seeker—and the limited options for international job seekers to regularize their stay in other ways—many people from around the region use asylum as a kind of work permit. Indeed only about one in ten asylum applicants is ultimately successful in gaining refugee status, although, due to the poor quality of adjudication, many who are rejected likely should qualify (see Consortium for Refugees and Migrants in South Africa 2009). Somewhat unsurprisingly given these conditions, South Africa was the global leader in new asylum applications in both 2010 and 2011. In 2011, 81,708 people applied for asylum while only 5,556 people were granted status and another 28,641 were rejected. In total this contributes almost 50,000 new people to the asylum-seeker population (Department of Home Affairs 2012, p. 68). Officials estimated that by mid-2012 there were 219,368 asylum seekers in the country (in Allison 2012).

Understanding international migration dynamics in South Africa also draws attention to the long-standing and elaborate (if expensive and ineffective) system of arrests and deportations (see Figure 8.1). Under the 2002 Immigration Act, police or immigration officers may remand people to custody without a warrant if they have reasonable grounds to believe they are not entitled to be in the Republic of South Africa. Immigration officers are also empowered to arrest illegal foreigners and deport them.

There are theoretical limits on these activities, and the government has halted the deportations of Zimbabweans since mid-2008. The significant decrease between 2008 and 2009 is due to a moratorium on the deportations of Zimbabwean nationals introduced by the South African Department of Home Affairs in 2009 under pressure from a range of human rights and migrant organizations. (For a detailed analysis of the moratorium and regularization program, see Segatti and Landau 2011.) This moratorium was subsequently lifted in 2011 following a regularization program for Zimbabweans. Although South Africa is unlikely to achieve its 2007 figures in 2011, the numbers of deportations continue to increase and will certainly return to levels comparable to the mid-2000s in 2012 (see Figure 8.1).

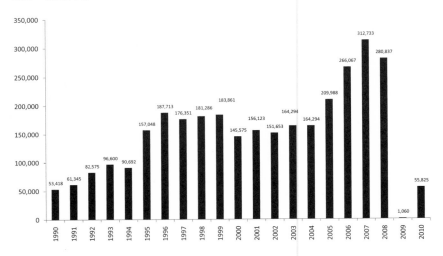

Figure 8.1   Deportations from South Africa, 1990–2010.

Source: Department of Home Affairs, 2012. Data reproduced in *Consortium for Refugees and Migrants in South Africa* (C.oRMSA).

Although less controversial than international migration, domestic mobility is South Africa's big development story. Even if international migration attracts the most political attention and popular opprobrium, domestic mobility is far more significant in numeric and developmental terms. Research by the South African Cities Network and others clearly illustrates the spatial dynamics of migration to particular urban centers (SACN 2006:16). In Metsweding, a small municipality in Gauteng Province, more than 10 percent of the total population has recently moved there. In contrast, in Durban, the figure is less than 1 percent. And while discussions of urbanization typically focus on primary cities, the fastest-growing parts of Gauteng are not Johannesburg and Pretoria but smaller communities beyond the "urban edge." The most notable and controversial effect of this growth has been the expansion of poorly serviced informal settlements (i.e., shantytowns) encircling more established and well-serviced formal settlements. As a result of these internal movements, out-migration is also significantly shifting population profiles of a number of the country's smaller and less prosperous communities. For example, Chris Hani municipality in the Eastern Cape has lost more than 8.5 percent of its population over the past decade (SACN 2006:18). Many of those who left are young men heading for the Western

Cape (Dorrington 2005). Consequently there are significant distortions in population pyramids in both sending and receiving communities (see Kok and Collinson 2006).

These population dynamics raise clear issues for municipalities in terms of planning in a context of annual target programs based on the most recent census population estimates. This means that as late as 2012, allocations were on 2011 figures. This is aggravated by a fiscal redistribution system that uses the same source, further widening the gap between needs and allocated resources. Overall this internal mobility quite logically increases the degree of heterogeneity (in terms of origins, languages, housing structures, and income) in a society already driven by socioeconomic and historically inherited racial divides. This is taking place in a highly volatile context marked by xenophobic repertoires and violent protests against whomever the population considers responsible for a lack of service delivery. In their current state, South African local government structures are ill-equipped on the one hand to produce and use more appropriate mobility data and, on the other, to care for increasingly heterogeneous populations with huge social and economic needs.

South Africa is also seeing a great diversification in its population's migration trajectories. Whereas apartheid-era South African migration policy promoted permanent white immigration and temporary black migration, the postapartheid period is characterized by a mix of circular, permanent, and transit migration. Indeed such impermanence is encouraged by the current policy frameworks, the difficulties migrants have in accessing secure accommodation, and the rapid rate of deportations (see above). Linked to these trajectories and other factors, people regularly move *within* South Africa as well as into and out of it. According to the 2007 Community Survey, 18 percent of Gauteng's inhabitants had moved within the province since 2001. According to ACMS data for the inner city of Johannesburg, the South African–born population has, on average, moved twice since coming to the city, usually within the previous decade. For foreigners, typically in the city for a shorter period, the average is slightly above three times (see Jacobsen and Bailey 2004).

EFFECTS ON DEVELOPMENT

Given the limited data available on transnational and translocal transfers of money, goods, and information, it is difficult to make firm conclusions regarding the relationship between mobility and development in southern and South Africa. There are clearly a range of issues and debates that deserve attention, although few are likely to be settled without considerably more research. Take, for example, concerns over the degree to which migration is motivated by (or improves) access to health care or other services (see, e.g., Chikanda 2007). As far as cash transfers and other forms of translocal socioeconomic investments, there is not the evidence base to say much more than that they are a critical livelihood strategy for both domestic and international migrants throughout southern Africa (see Table 8.1). The Southern African Migration Project goes so far as to argue that for most migrant-sending households, migrant remittances represent the main source of household income, but we are left to presume their long-term impacts at their individual, household, or community level (see also Maphosa 2007).

ACMS research provides additional dimensions to migrants' remitting behavior. While remittances remain important, the 2006 survey in central Johannesburg found that just over 45 percent of international migrants sent money or goods to people outside the city. This compares broadly with the percentage of South Africans who also report regularly sending resources to friends and family elsewhere. However, this figure ranged widely among national groups. Among the Congolese who send money home, only 33 percent reported sending money, usually to parents (63 percent) or other close relatives (38 percent). The percentage rises to 56 percent among Somalis, who send primarily to parents (89 percent) and siblings (24 percent). In almost all cases, the Somalis relied on community-based remittance systems; those from the DRC depended most frequently on MoneyGram, while Mozambicans typically rely on friends of family members to transport remittances. There seems to be little evidence to suggest that legal status or income is closely connected to remittance rates. Importantly, the study found that over a third of Congolese and almost a fifth of Somalis and South Africans report regularly receiving money from outside the city. In the case of the Congolese, most of these transfers originated outside Africa, suggesting a complex web of multisited families and livelihood strategies. Qualitative research suggests that these transnational or translocal transfers are often related to establishing or supporting migrants in the city in order to invest, get an education, or take care of financial and administrative needs in order to move elsewhere. However, given the limited scope of the study, it is impossible to

Table 8.1 Estimated Intraregional Remittance Flows (in ZAR million)

Sending country	Receiving Country							
	Botswana	Lesotho	Malawi	Mozambique	RSA	Swaziland	Other SADC	Total
Botswana	—	2.59	3.65		29.64	0.55	51.42	87.87
Lesotho	0.61	—						0.61
Malawi	0.18		—					0.18
Mozambique				—				
RSA	133.28	1,675.84	57.19	2,241.71	—	432.29	1,531.85	6,072.15
Swaziland	0.39					—		0.39
Total	**134.46**	**1,678.43**	**60.84**	**2,241.71**	**29.64**	**432.84**	**1,583.27**	

Note: ZAR = South African Rand; SADC = Southern African Development Community.

Source: Genesis calculations from various sources. Table reproduced from Pendleton et al. 2006.

understand the impacts on Johannesburg, on South Africa, or on the areas from which money is being sent and received.

International migration is also closely connected with South Africa's efforts to address the acute skills gap produced by decades of intentionally undereducating the country's black majority and the extensive flight of skilled professionals. In 2003–4, South Africa acknowledged a deficit of 57,574 nurses, 200 of them leaving the country every month. Since 2004, no figures are available for emigrated South African citizens' whereabouts. However, comparing stocks of South African migrants in receiving countries and self-declared emigrants, Statistics South Africa (2003) came to the conclusion that approximately 322,499 South Africans had emigrated between 1970 and 2001 (see also Southern African Migration Project n.d.). As the Roy model would predict, it is often the highly skilled migrants who have moved (Heckman and Honore 1990).

While suffering remarkable losses, the country has increasingly become a source country for highly skilled professionals—notably in the medical professions, mine and mechanical engineering, and information and communication technology—from across Africa. (For a detailed study of African elites in South Africa, see Bourgouin 2006.) Much of this is the result of spontaneous moves driven by economic interests and commercial recruitment that are helping to reinforce South Africa's centrality to the continent's service and financial sectors. Other moves come as a partial consequence of government and private sector initiatives. Foreseeing a skills gap of 1.2 million persons by 2014, the Mbeki administration created the Accelerated and Shared Growth Initiative for South Africa and, subsequently, the Joint Initiative on Priority Skills Acquisition (JIPSA). A more recent survey by the Harvard Center for International Development advocates for a proactive high-skill immigration policy as a remedy for a high unemployment rate, arguing that economic growth is capped at far below the desired target by the lack of skills (Levinsohn 2008). In supporting the cause, First National Bank initiated the "Homecoming Revolution" to attract patriotic South Africans back to the country. The bank's funding for the program has waned, but the campaign continues its efforts to attract South Africans now residing in the United Kingdom, Australia, and elsewhere.

Although undoubtedly appealing to some, neither the Homecoming Revolution nor JIPSA has made much progress in addressing South Africa's skills gap.[2] JIPSA reports from 2007, for example, suggest that there will continue to be severe skills shortfalls in all five of the high-profile areas identified when the initiative was founded in 2006. JIPSA's 2007 report predicted that by 2012 the country would be short of approximately 30,000 or more artisans, 22,000 engineers, and significant (but unspecified) numbers of town and regional planners. To further address these gaps, the Department of Home Affairs (2006, cited in Daniels 2007) has identified a number of "scarce and critical" skills—including urban planning, agricultural engineers, and, appropriately, population scientists—that should enable people to immigrate easily to South Africa. However, businesses regularly complain that inefficiencies within the Department of Home Affairs and the inflexibility and undercapacity of a number of South African accreditation bodies (notably the South African Qualifications Authority) have limited the number of people they have been able to recruit. That employing nonnationals—even African nonnationals—does not help companies achieve government-set Black Economic Empowerment targets further discourages the use of these options. Nonetheless South Africa is today in a rather Janus-faced position: it is one of the strongest voices against the plundering of highly sought-after skilled migrants by developed countries, while it stands accused of the very same sin by other African countries.

While South Africa struggles to fill its skills gaps through an approach reminiscent of (largely discredited) 1970s-era "manpower planning," it has increasing numbers of semi- to highly skilled immigrants moving spontaneously to the country from the rest of the continent (in particular from Zimbabwe, the DRC, Kenya, Uganda, Nigeria, and Ghana). The first wave of these came early and was composed of intermediate or highly skilled professionals from highly unstable countries (such as Congolese doctors and mine engineers and Zimbabwean teachers) who found employment in the former homelands. In the mid-1990s the globalized African elites (e.g., academics, bankers, consultants, journalists) also began applying for positions in South African firms or for postings in South Africa from within their organization and firms. Many of these were absorbed, but many others experienced severe downgrading in their skills when coming to South Africa. Southern African Development Community prohibitions on recruiting medical professionals from within the region have further limited the number of professionals in South Africa who are able to work in their desired position. A 2008 effort to regularize Zimbabwean teachers helped to address part of the gap in the education sector, but there are thousands of other skilled professionals who have arrived in the country who are unable to work or are underemployed due to lack of documents or certification.

MIGRATION AND LOCAL GOVERNANCE

Skills gaps and brain drain remain general concerns for South Africa and, indeed, for the southern African region. However, while global debates on migration and development have tended to speak in terms of national policy frameworks and aggregate economic and social effects, the South African case illustrates the importance of exploring subnational dynamics. It is at the level of the province or, more important, the municipality where the consequences of migration—positive and negative—are most acute. In previous decades, much of the international migration into South Africa concentrated in agricultural and mining areas. Since the early 1990s both international and domestic migrants are increasingly concentrated in the country's urban centers (see Figures 8.2 and 8.3). Indeed population movements—some predictable, some spontaneous; some voluntary, some forced—are now perennial features of South African cities (SACN 2004:36; see also Balbo and Marconi 2005; Provincial Government of the Western Cape 2002; Dorrington 2005). Constitutionally empowered to be a leading force for development, local governments have nevertheless been wary of addressing migration concerns. This partially stems from a belief among many policymakers (local and national) that immigration is exclusively a matter of national policy concern. Some have yet to recognize the degree to which migration is transforming their cities. Others naively hope that heightened human mobility is simply a temporary outgrowth of the country's democratic transition. In almost all instances, budgeting and planning exercises have largely excluded extended population projections. Indeed the budget allocation system used by the South African Treasury mostly relies on census data, which are not updated and, according to numerous interviewed municipal officials, are a far cry from the actual demographics in their localities. Those peri-urban municipalities face mobility rates of 20 percent and above (of annual newcomers) and consequently find it impossible to meet the targets set in their own integrated development plans. This creates a widely shared sense of constant failure and inadequacy between responsibilities and means among local government leaders and administrative staff. (For more on the consequences for municipal authorities, see Landau 2009.) Even in

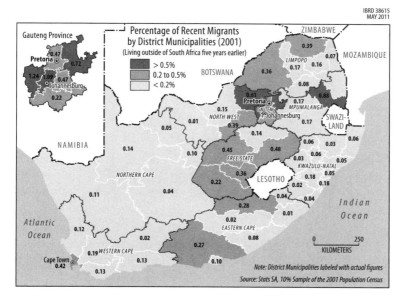

Figure 8.2   International migrants. Map developed by Forced Migration Studies at Wits with UNOCHA (Pretoria) using data from the 2001 national census.

slower growing municipalities, authorities often continue to plan for a slowly growing and largely stable population. The consequences of doing so include, among others, the inability to meet the demands for services among urban residents, including housing, health, and education. More fundamentally it means the resources and infrastructure are unavailable to provide water or transportation.

When viewed from the municipal level, migration is impressively and positively correlated with economic growth; this is evident with regard to domestic migrants and even more so in terms of international migration. Although there are clear endogeneity issues in trying to determine the causal relationships between mobility and growth, it is likely that some of the observed economic development is due to the arrival of new skills, investments, and trading connections. It is also undoubtedly the case that more prosperous and successful cities will continue to attract people from across the country and across the country's borders. However anxious urban planners may be about an ever-expanding population, South African cities, like those across the world, have little option but to prepare for an expanding population.

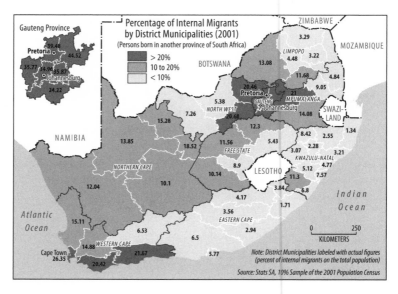

Figure 8.3   Internal migrants. Map developed by Forced Migration Studies at Wits with UNOCHA (Pretoria) using data from the 2001 national census.

Despite the undeniable relationship between economic growth and mobility, Table 8.2 offers a less sanguine reflection on the ties between mobility and human development (i.e., education, income, and life expectancy). While global evidence and ACMS research suggest that movements to cities offers the fastest route to individual socioeconomic improvement as well as economic development, the aggregate effects are less clear when observed at the municipal level (Bocquier 2009). Here we see an ambiguous, almost neutral effect that will require further research and fine-grained analysis to explain.

Despite the uncertainty of mobility's effects on human development, what is clear—although often unrecognized—is the important role local authorities can potentially play in maximizing migration's economic and human development potential. At the very least, local authorities are and will remain critical in managing the social and political tensions often associated with the movements of people. As decentralization continues across Africa—and elsewhere in the world—and cities seek to establish themselves as relatively autonomous global players, the challenges of migration and responsibilities of local authorities will only increase. The remainder of this chapter explores the local government's role in responding

Table 8.2 Relationship Between Urbanization and Human Development

	Percentage Recent Births	Percentage Recent Internal Migrants	Percentage Recent International Migrants	Percentage Recent Migrants	Growth	Human Development
Size	−0.154** (0.024)	0.099 (0.103)	0.177** (0.011)	0.124* (0.056)	0.167** (0.016)	0.403*** (0.000)
Percentage recent births	.	Correlated by def.	Correlated by def.	Correlated by def.	0.040 (0.305)	−0.069 (0.189)
Percentage recent internal migrants	.	.	Correlated by def.	Correlated by def.	0.137** (0.040)	−0.011 (0.444)
Percentage recent international migrants	.	.	.	Correlated by def.	0.233*** (0.001)	0.013 (0.434)
Percentage recent migrants	.	.	.	.	0.169** (0.015)	−0.007 (0.464)
Growth	.	.	.	.	.	0.022 (0.390)
Human development	.	.	.	.	.	.

***Significant at a 1% level; **significant at a 5% level; *significant at a 10% level.

Note: t-tests in parentheses.

to migration, some of the challenges associated with developing such a response, and the political hazards associated with current approaches. The discussion includes national trends with particular attention to South Africa's two primary cities: Cape Town and Johannesburg. Doing so highlights similarities and critical differences in the political calculus of migration management. We also pay considerable attention to non- and semiofficial responses to migration in the form of violence, discrimination, and economic exclusion. Whereas South Africa has taken conscious steps to institutionalize a human rights culture and the rule of law, these sharply contrast with these social and semiofficial responses. These include the privatization of violence and the spreading economies of corruption that are such unfortunate characteristics of countries across the continent.

Some within local government have seen increasing migration and diversity as a hugely positive sign of the cities' emergence, as trading and cultural centers and city planners in both Johannesburg and Cape Town have begun outlining strategies for recruiting and incorporating highly skilled migrants and refugees into the city's socioeconomic networks.[3] It is also evident, however, that many of the cities' leaders and citizens feel overwhelmed—if not threatened—by migration, and especially the movement of people south from the rest of the continent. In other places, the out-migration of the cities' skilled and affluent is raising the specter of economic decline and an ever-expanding underclass (SACN 2006). Elsewhere officials link migration with the expansion of drug syndicates, prostitution and human trafficking, unemployment, crime, and a range of other social and economic ills. Apart from a few exceptional cases, elected officials sense that urbanization and international migration raise the specter of economic and political fragmentation and urban degeneration (see Landau, et al. 2011; Beal et al. 2002).

Most of South Africa's metropolitan areas are now accepting that new arrivals are part of their populations. (Elsewhere there is the slow recognition that urban populations are being transformed by out-migration, a dynamic whose effects have yet to be fully explored.) Part of the shift in policy comes from the slow recognition among *some* officials in local government that without apartheid-style measures to control movements— measures that for reasons of intention and incapacity never achieved 100 percent effectiveness—cities can do little to alter regional migration dynamics (Collinson et al. 2006). In the words of one Johannesburg city councilor, "As much as we might not want them here, we cannot simply wish these people away" (personal communication, July 13, 2005). ACMS research reveals similar perspectives among planners and planning documents in Cape Town and elsewhere (see Landau, et al. 2011).[4]

However, this recognition does not come without considerable trepidation, and most local governments have thus far failed to develop empirically informed and proactive policy responses to international migration. Rather than replacing existing divisions with shared rules of economic and social engagement, discrimination against noncitizens threatens further fragmentation and social marginalization. There is a real possibility that exclusion based on nationality or community of origin effects initiatives, "to achieve a shared vision, amongst all sectors of our society, for the achievement of our goal of improving the quality of life for all citizens" (Gauteng Provincial Government 2005). Although there are slow changes in government, many officials continue to react to the presence of foreign migrants by implicitly denying their presence, excluding them from developmental plans, or allowing discrimination throughout the government bureaucracy and police. In both Cape Town and Johannesburg, internal and domestic migrants continue to be seen largely as a drain on public resources rather than as potential resources or, more neutrally, as the people government is dedicated to serve (see Provincial Government of the Western Cape 2002). Even those who wish to more proactively absorb new, often poor and vulnerable populations face considerable challenges in determining how to do so.

CHALLENGES OF DEVELOPING EFFECTIVE LOCAL GOVERNMENT RESPONSES TO MIGRATION

Recognizing the imperative to address migration in building inclusive, safe, and prosperous communities does not necessarily mean that officials have the information or tools to do this effectively. Perhaps the most fundamental challenge to local governments charged with creating inclusive cities is the elusive *meaning of inclusion* for South Africa's highly diverse and fragmented urban communities (see Tomlinson et al. 2003). With the end of apartheid-era pass laws and the country's full reintegration into regional politics and trade, previously "forbidden" cities have become the destination—if not the terminus—for peoples from throughout South Africa and the African continent. In many instances, these inward movements have been accompanied by the flight of affluent residents from the inner cities. As a result, the populations of Cape Town, Durban, and especially Johannesburg are new, and in many neighborhoods it is difficult to speak of an indigenous community or dominant culture or ethos. This is most visible in central Johannesburg, an area almost completely composed of new arrivals (see Table 8.3). In this context, it is difficult to develop a clear understanding of what cities currently look like, how groups interact, and what policies might achieve desired ends. To date, most urban planning models have been drawn from European, North American, and (to some extent) Latin American experiences. These may be valuable, but only when modified to consider South Africa's fundamentally different historical and social contexts (Winkler 2006).

For cities that have experienced rapid rates of urbanization, it is almost impossible to speak about integration or creating unified urban communities. Multiculturalism is a fact, but there are no guarantees that the interactions will be peaceful, productive, or characterized by mutual respect. In many instances, the opposite has been true (see Misago et al. 2009). The atomization and fragmentation of South African cities stand in sharp contrast with the vision of a self-identified urban population invested in cities' futures.

Negotiating a common basis of belonging is made all the more difficult by the nature of the cities' new populations. Many who come to the city

Table 8.3   Time in South Africa or Johannesburg

	Citizens	Noncitizens
Less than 1 year	5.2	13.0
1–2 years	3.6	12.8
2–3 years	8.9	10.6
3–4 years	6.3	10.6
4–5 years	3.6	8.4
5–6 years	5.2	8.1
6–7 years	7.3	5.8
7–8 years	3.6	5.6
8–9 years	2.6	3.1
9–10 years	7.8	4.8
More than 10 years	43.8	13.9
n	192	640

Note: Citizens were asked how long they had been in Johannesburg. Foreigners were asked how long they had been in the Republic of South Africa. As most foreigners go quickly to Johannesburg, this may be a good indication of how long they have been in the city.

Source: FMSP Data, African Cities Data on Johannesburg.

do not expect to stay there for long. According to Statistics South Africa, "The temporary nature of rural-to-urban migration in South Africa may add insight into the persistence of overcrowding and poor living conditions in urban townships. Migrants may employ a calculated strategy to maximise the benefits to their household of origin, rather than for their own benefit or the benefit of residential units in the urban setting" (in City of Johannesburg 2006:28). Critically, journeys home or onward often remain practically elusive for reasons of money, safety, or social status. This leaves almost two-thirds of Johannesburg's nonnational population effectively marooned in the city but not wishing to take root or invest in it. We also see evidence of this extralocal orientation in the levels of remittances being sent out of the city to both rural communities and other countries.

The fact that the little local governments know about the people living in their cities presents a further challenge of responding to migration. Whereas national governments have the relative luxury of developing generalized policy frameworks, local governments and service providers are responsible for more focused and context-specific interventions. For many of the reasons discussed earlier, in almost no instances are city governments able to draw on a nuanced and dynamic understanding of their constituencies. This is generally true regarding the urban poor and all the more so with geographically mobile people. Efforts to map "poverty pockets" (Cross et al. 2005) and review both national and localized migration data represent some of the first concerted efforts to understand South Africa's urban population dynamics (see Dorrington 2005; Bekker 2002; Kok and Collinson, 2006; SACN 2006; Landau and Gindrey 2008). However, many of these studies are based on admittedly incomplete census data—particularly inaccurate regarding foreign-born populations—and are often purely descriptive. While the Department of Provincial and Local Government now recognized that there is a need for improving cross-border and multinodal planning, including greater consideration of population mobility, planners are effectively unable to understand cities' functional economic geography or its region and how various components relate to each other (SACN 2006). In this context, local planners continue to be influenced by stereotypes and misreadings or incomplete readings of data.

The inability to effectively understand and predict urban populations poses significant risks to local governments' ability to meet their obligations and developmental objectives. Perhaps most obviously, the invisibility of large segments of the urban population can result in much greater demand for services than predicted, reducing service quality and outstripping budgetary allocations. In many instances, these are hidden costs: public and private infrastructure, water, and other services that are not accessed individually. The degradation of the housing stock due to high-population densities—a consequence of new migrants minimizing costs while maximizing centrality—also has long-term cost implications for cities that collect taxes on the bases of building values. Higher populations do not, however, necessarily result in higher costs to local government in receiving areas. Because many of South Africa's internal migrants are young men, they may remain relatively healthy, autonomous, and productive in urban areas, and hence levy few costs. Moreover, while they may not invest in property, much of their consumption of food and consumer goods is in urban areas. In such instances, sending communities may lose the benefits of their labor while being saddled with the costs of educating their children and providing for them in their old age. Many of these costs are paid centrally or via the provinces, but others are the responsibility of local government.

While both sending and receiving communities are influenced by the significant costs and benefits associated with migration, these calculations have rarely figured into the distribution of national resources by the South African Treasury. Since the promulgation of the new constitution in 1996, the Treasury has distributed money to the provinces (and subsequently to the metropolitan areas) based almost exclusively on current population estimates. Such practices are problematic for at least three reasons. First, the population estimates often significantly misrepresent where people actually live. Someone may own a house and vote in a rural community but live elsewhere for eleven months of the year (Department of Housing 2006). Second, people's presence in a particular locality is not necessarily a good predictor of their costs to local or provincial government. Third, infrastructure and social service planning requires long-term investments based on predictions of population in five to fifteen years' time; without reliable estimates, cities are unable to prepare for their population's future needs. In late September 2006 the South African Fiscal Commission convened a seminar to try to come to grips with these issues in order to better advise the Treasury on resource distribution. In 2008 the Treasury again met—with World Bank support—to discuss resource allocation. However, planning continues to be based on current rather than projected population distributions and all but ignores undocumented migrants.

Perhaps most worrying is that many planners remain unaware of such an approach's frailty in a country with such high rates of mobility. This is likely to become particularly problematic as South Africa begins implementing its national spatial development framework.[5]

The lack of coordination among government departments further exaggerates the partial and often ill-informed responses to human mobility. In our discussions with planners in both Johannesburg and Cape Town, they repeatedly expressed frustration regarding their efforts to foster collaboration within local government departments and, more important, between local governments and South Africa's other two governmental spheres (provincial and national). However, due to migration's spatial dynamics, effectively responding to human mobility is not something that any single governmental body or sphere can address as it requires coordination and planning that transcends the boundaries of metropolitan areas and encompasses a wider area connected by commuter flows, economic linkages, and shared facilities.

The paucity of collaboration is visible in a variety of potentially critical areas. Perhaps most obviously, the Department of Home Affairs (DHA) has been either reluctant or unable to share its data with city planners. These include the number not only of foreigners legally entering the country, but also of registered moves, deaths, and births. The most probable cause is lack of capacity within the DHA, although there is undoubtedly also a general reluctance to freely share information. It is, of course, not only the DHA that has shown a reluctance to work with local government, but the lack of coordination between DHA and local government is probably the most significant gap.

CONSEQUENCES FOR URBAN GOVERNANCE AND DEVELOPMENT

If not addressed, the challenges outlined above will have significant impacts on South Africa's ability to improve the welfare of all urban residents regardless of origins. As noted earlier, South Africa has a substantial skills gap that the government hopes to fill by spending millions of Rand on skills training (Department of Labour 2005; see also Ellis 2008). However, few employers (including the government) capitalize on the economic potential of those already in their cities or who are likely to come in the near future, including international migrants. Instead of positively exploiting the presence of foreigners who are often well educated and experienced, current policy criminalizes migrants and drives processes of informalization and illegality. In efforts to protect the rights and livelihoods of citizens, immigration policy has de facto promoted the illegal hiring of nonnationals in ways that continue to undermine the unions and suppress the wages paid to all workers. Moreover by encouraging nonnationals (and those who hire them) to work in the informal sector or shadow economy, the government deprives itself of an important source of revenue and helps create networks of corruption and illegality that will be difficult to eradicate.

Migrants' inability to access secure banking also has manifold consequences that extend beyond those excluded from service. Perhaps most obviously, lack of access to financial services (particularly credit) discourages migrants from investing in the cities in which they live (although those included in the ACMS Johannesburg survey are still more likely to hire people to work for them—often South Africans—than South African entrepreneurs; see Leggett 2003; Jacobsen and Bailey 2004; Simone 2004; Hunter and Skinner 2003). Such obstacles can only aggravate infrastructural decay, limit job creation, and prevent a kind of "rooting" through investment that can help stabilize communities and promote long-term planning. Given the migrants' general entrepreneurialism, their exclusion from business will have disproportionate effects. Keeping migrants and those they hire in the informal economy also denies the government a source of direct revenues (from taxes and licensing fees) and means that much of the business that takes place is, to a greater or lesser degree, illegal. This, in turn, weakens the law's (and the state's) legitimacy and regulatory power.

Education and health care are central to any population's economic and physical health (see Annan 1999). In transforming urban settings, education serves a dual role. The first is to provide children and youth with the technical and analytical training they need to compete in and contribute to a specialized, skills-based economy. Obstacles to any group acquiring those skills will consequently project existing inequalities into future generations and limit the country's ability to adapt to new economic opportunities. Education serves a second, but no less critical role: forging communities among strangers. Through the sustained interactions within the classroom, diverse groups learn common sets of rules, how to exercise civil rights, and mutual respect. Exclusion from education therefore can create a subset of the population without the knowledge or skills to interact productively within the city. Given the extraordinary degree to which

South African cities are fragmented and transient, this role is especially critical.

While the inability to access education may have delayed effects, denying migrants access to health services has both immediate and long-term consequences. In the short term, it puts them at physical risk and endangers the welfare of those who depend on them. Denying basic health services also raises the specter of public health crises, as the 2008 cholera outbreaks in Musina illustrate (IRIN 2008). While medical staff may discriminate between citizens and nonnationals, infectious agents are far less discerning. As long as migrants and South Africans continue to share space—often living in close proximity—those unable to access treatment become a danger to all those around them. A workforce already weakened by the scourge of HIV/AIDS is in no position to accept such an additional threat.

Informal responses and arbitrary policing are also developing their own dynamics and momentum that limit leaders' abilities to retain the power of law. Citizens and nonnationals alike now face threats to the legal protections the law ostensibly guarantees. However, if the police cannot be trusted, people have little choice but to develop alternative mechanisms to ensure their safety. Although many South Africans support the police's strategy of targeting foreigners on the assumption that they are behind most of the country's criminal activity, such actions are largely ineffective in establishing order or security. For one, there is no evidence that foreigners are disproportionately prone to criminal activity (Harris 2001). An obsession with them consequently distracts police from where they are needed (see Palmary 2002; Palmary et al. 2003; Vigneswaran and Hornberger 2009). Moreover the general ineffectiveness of such policing strategies is leading citizens to accept criminal activity as part of their social landscape. Many South Africans we have interviewed, for example, no longer classify mugging as a crime unless it involves the use of a firearm. In this context, people are seeking alternative means to manage crime. In some cases, this includes turning to groups like Mapogo a Mathamaga, a national investigation and "goods recovery" company that works largely outside the law but regularly draws on police information and backup.[6] These linkages "de-legalize" the criminal justice system, robbing the state of one of its most primitive functions and placing all of its urbanites at risk.

The arrest of people trading on the street, whether South African or foreign, or conducting other small business also affects the livelihoods of those arrested and their dependents. Cities must promote entry into trading

markets rather than close this avenue to those who have few other options, a category of people well represented in inner-city Johannesburg.
For migrants who lack the documentation or capital to find work in the
formal sector (despite many having skills to make contributions in this
area), regularly targeting this subset of the population for by-law infrac-
tions only drives trade further underground and increases the likelihood
that they will turn to irregular, illegal, or dangerous economic activities.
The kind of corruption and informal vigilantism seen against migrants in
Cape Town, Johannesburg, and elsewhere across the country also presents
a fundamental challenge to South Africa's legitimacy and risks institutionalizing patterns of violence and corruption in essential state agencies
and departments.

South Africa's economic and political success hinges on accountable
institutions that foster a set of overlapping goals among city residents.
Discrimination based on national or community origins, like other arbitrary forms of exclusion, undermines this objective in two primary ways.
First, for reasons discussed earlier, people who do not feel welcome in
South Africa's urban society are less likely to respect the rules and institutions dedicated to governing it. This may become visible in efforts to
dodge tax regulations, avoid census takers, or actively subvert regulatory
agencies they feel are more likely to prey on than promote their interests.
When not given the right to work or documents needed to secure housing, it may also result in building hijackings, criminal activity, or other
antisocial behaviors. Those who feel excluded are also unlikely to participate in planning exercises (e.g., the integrated development planning process). Such self-exclusion makes government policies all the less likely to
address city residents' priorities and needs and may, in time, harm public
institutions' efficacy and legitimacy (Winkler 2006).

There are also broader issues at stake regarding the relationships among
residents and both local and national government. As a senior strategist
for the City of Johannesburg notes, "The legitimacy of the South African
government is founded on overturning past patterns of discrimination
and exclusion. We have a proactive responsibility to absorb the poor and
promote social mobility."[7] For him and a few others at elite levels of local
government, refugees, immigrants, and migrants are simply another category of the vulnerable and poor. Indeed this is the position taken by Johannesburg's Human Development Strategy. The ability of Johannesburg
to implement such a program is, in the words of the same official, critical

to the "integrity of the city." As the mayor of Johannesburg recently stated, "It's an issue that you can't ignore" (Reuters 2006).

However, anti-outsider sentiments and scapegoating continue, challenging cities' legitimacy and their ability to establish accountable, socially embedded institutions. In the words of one immigrant now living in Johannesburg, "rumours are continuously spread by everyone that foreigners are responsible for whatever is wrong. It is like, 'thank you, foreigners that you are here, now we can blame you for everything.' South Africans do not look at their own—they just ignore their own problems and pretend that foreigners cause all their problems" (Beal et al. 2002:124). Although such attitudes are not universal, the presence of a convenient scapegoat prevents South Africans from holding their public institutions responsible for their shortcomings and failed promises. Although there have only been few instances in which local politicians have overtly manipulated an immigrant or migrant presence for electoral gain, there is a specter of the kind of public political scapegoating seen in Europe and elsewhere in a context where recourse to political violence is much more common.

CONCLUSIONS AND THE WAY FORWARD

There is little definite or final to say about migration and development in southern and South Africa. Population movements and their consequences are equally the result of long-term global and local political transformations and unpredictable natural and political crises. With every election cycle, policy responses to migration are equally uncertain. However, given the effects of the global economic crisis and populist and nativist pressures, it is unlikely that policy reforms will achieve positive, long-term, and regional development outcomes. If they do, it will be a result of good fortune instead of good planning.

In such a context, a chapter like this can end only by raising issues that will—or should—shape population and political dynamics and responses to them. To that end, there is a need to rethink three divisions: between documented and undocumented migrants, between voluntary and forced migrants, and between international and domestic migration. As elsewhere in the world, these are analytical categories that are closely tied with specific legislations and implementing bodies. This has tended to produce policy silos with little coordination among agencies charged with law enforcement, status determination, documentation, social assistance, or local development. In almost no instances do such firm distinctions make logical sense. This is all the more true in South Africa, where there are mixed migration flows and few bureaucratic mechanisms to distinguish among the various migrant categories. If there is to be substantive and effective reform in any one of these areas—asylum, migration, border management, or urban development—all must be considered together as part of a national and regional policy framework to address human mobility. In January 2009 Gauteng Province's Department of Local Government convened a special seminar on "migration mainstreaming" that sought to address just these concerns. While innovative and the first such initiative for the country's most migrant-rich province, many of the proposed measures relied on highly sophisticated collection, dissemination, and use of statistics that are yet unavailable. A more immediately feasible proposal includes regular coordination meetings that would bring together senior officials from across local government to review broad migration trends, identify information paucities, and consider potential mechanisms for incorporating migration into their annual and long-term plans.

There is also a need to introduce a spatial component in considering future policy directions and research. Perhaps more than many policy areas, national governments are automatically assigned comprehensive responsibility for matters affecting immigration and emigration. While national government has an important role, there is a need to move beyond the nation-state framework. Migration's most immediate effects are felt locally in both sending and receiving communities. Local government must necessarily be involved to ensure that these effects are developmentally positive. Moreover, because migration necessarily involves at least two distinct geographic locales, the developmental effects are, by definition, regional. As such, both analysis and policy debates must work toward a regional approach. What we must now begin is a new spatial analysis of migration that breaks from a long-standing epistemological nationalism. Any discussion of migration and development should hereafter consider local, national, and regional impacts and policy options.

In considering the possibility for positive policy reform, we must also consider the policy climate and institutional frameworks present in southern and South Africa. As we have detailed, the South African Department of Home Affairs has shown little interest or ability in developing and implementing sound and effective migration policy. Elsewhere in government, there has been little planning or consideration of human mobility both domestic and international. As such, there is little reason to believe that South Africa will independently shift its current security- and control-based policies to policies that are more developmentally oriented. At the local and regional levels, the capacity to evaluate, monitor, and address migration is almost totally absent. A small number of municipalities have begun to recognize human mobility as a significant issue, but few have undertaken substantive initiatives to address it. While the Southern African Development Community's secretariat is ostensibly responsible for developing a regional approach to migration, there is no one in the secretariat specifically charged with migration matters. Even were these bodies to develop effective policy, the inability to implement them will also mean that the effects may be more negative than positive.

We must also question the role that non-African actors are playing in pushing particular policy agendas. Although the International Organization for Migration (IOM) has played a positive role in training officials and assisting in the repatriation of refugees, their hyperbolic antitrafficking agenda has helped ensure that migration continues to be framed as a humanitarian and law-enforcement—and not development—concern. Despite the relatively few people affected by the horrors of human trafficking, the IOM and its partners have managed to push for policy reform, while the faulty asylum system remains relatively untouched. The European Union is also playing an important if more sophisticated role in South Africa's immigration regime. Through political dialogues and capacity building, they are gradually winning allies in their ongoing campaign to legitimize tightened border controls.

Finally, this chapter argues that global debates over governance and development have much to offer as policymakers across the developing world grapple with future migration policy directions. With a move away from a singularly prescriptive approach to governance, the United Nations Development Programme's 1997 human development concept, the European Commission's 2006 Strategic Paper on Governance, and even the World Bank Group's *Engagement on Governance and Anti-Corruption* (GAC) suggsest the need to develop policies based on a country's specificities. This suggests the need for a South (and southern) Africa migration management system that considers the region's population dynamics, economic needs, and institutional capacities. But as domestic and international support grows for supporting the governance of service delivery, migration continues to be governed largely as a security concern divorced from the broader social and economic issues with which it intersects. If nothing else, this chapter suggests that foreign assistance and domestic policy reforms push for "migration mainstreaming" into all aspects of governance. In a country where international and domestic mobility remains so demographically and politically important, the success of any development initiative must overtly consider the country's population dynamics. As part of this process, the government should identify and understand the root causes of the negative by-products of human mobility—corruption, human rights abuses, labor competition—and begin developing ways to help reduce them rather than rely on the fantasy that it should and can totally control mobility itself.

Any effort to incorporate migration into long-term policy and governance process will require better data and their integration into planning processes. This will become particularly important as South Africa embraces a spatial development model. As this chapter demonstrates, foreigners' presence and responses to outsiders may be driven by global processes but must be understood within specific, highly localized contexts. While it is useful to develop aggregated trends, reactions and attitudes may be shaped by the particular racial, economic, and political history of a single neighborhood. All this will require heightening capacity for statistical, institutional, and social analyses. While this is critical at the national level, all spheres of government should be encouraged to collaborate and develop the capacity for data collection and analysis at all levels. Last, mechanisms should be created to ensure that these analyses, if they eventually become available, are fed into decision-making processes. Doing otherwise will ensure policy failure and may help realize many planners' current fears about the effects of human mobility on prosperity, security, and development.

REFERENCES

Allison, S. 2012. "South Africa, The Asylum-Seeker's Paradise." *Daily Maverick* (11 September).

Annan, K. 1999. Foreword to *UNICEF-Education: The State of the World's Children*. New York: UNICEF.

Balbo, M., and G. Marconi. 2005. "Governing International Migration in the City of the South." Global Migration Perspectives #38. Global Commission for International Migration, Geneva.

Beal, J., O. Crankshaw, and S. Parnell. 2002. *Uniting a Divided City: Governance and Social Exclusion in Johannesburg.* London: Earthscan.

Bekker, S.B. 2002. "Main Report: Migration Study in the Western Cape 2001." Cape Town: Department of Planning, Local Government and Housing of the Provincial Administration of the Western Cape.

Bocquier, P. 2009. "Urbanization and Migration in Africa: Can Cities Grow without Slums?" Paper presented at the FMSP Migration and Society Seminar, University of Witwatersrand, Johannesburg, South Africa.

Bourgouin, France. 2006. "The Emergence and Success of Elite African Immigration to South Africa." Paper presented at the Sixteenth World Congress of Sociology, Durban.

Brown, Kyle G. 2010. "Anti-Immigrant Tensions Rise Again in South Africa," National Public Radio, August 15. Accessed at http://www.npr.org/templates/story/story.php?storyId=129038858&ft=1&f=1001.

Chikanda, A. 2007. "Medical Migration from Zimbabwe: Magnitude, Causes and Impact on the Poor." *Development Southern Africa* 24, no. 1: 47–60.

City of Johannesburg. 2006. *Johannesburg Growth and Development Strategy 2006.* Johannesburg: City of Johannesburg.

Collinson, M., P. Kok, and M. Garenne. 2006. "Migration and Changing Settlement Patterns: Multilevel Data for Policy." Report No. 03-04-01, Human Sciences Research Council, Pretoria.

Consortium for Refugees and Migrants in South Africa. 2009. *Protecting Refugees and Migrants in South Africa.* Johannesburg: Consortium for Refugees and Migrants in South Africa.

Cross, C., et al. 2005. "Poverty Pockets in Gauteng: How Migration Impacts Poverty." Report to the Gauteng Intersectoral Development Unit, Human Sciences Research Council, Pretoria.

Crush, Jonathan. 2007. "The Perfect Storm: The Realities of Xenophobia in Contemporary South Africa." Migration Policy Series No. 50, Southern African Migration Project, Cape Town.

Daniels, R. C. 2007. "Skills Shortages in South Africa: A Literature Review." University of Cape Town Development Policy Research Unit Working Paper 07/121. Cape Town, South Africa.

Department of Home Affairs. 2012. *Annual Report 2012.*

Department of Home Affairs. 1992–99. *Annual Reports.*

———. 1990–2004. *Annual Reports.*

———. 2006. *Government Gazette,* February.

Department of Housing. 2006. "Investigation into Urbanisation Trends in South Africa and the Implications for Housing." Presentation to the National Finance Commission, Midrand, South Africa, September 29.

Department of Labour. 2005. "National Skills Development Strategy, 1 April 2005– 31 March 2010." South African Department of Labour, Pretoria.

Dorrington, R. 2005. "Projection of the Population of the City of Cape Town 2001– 2021." Report prepared for the City of Cape Town, Centre for Actuarial Research, University of Cape Town.

Ellis, Steven. 2008. "South Africa and International Migration: The Role of Skilled Labour." In *Migration in Post-Apartheid South Africa: Challenges and Questions to*

Policy-Makers, edited by A. Wa Kabwe-Segatti and L. Landau. Paris: Agence Française de Développement.

Gauteng Provincial Government. 2005. *A Growth and Development Strategy (GDS) for the Gauteng Province.* Accessed at http://www.gautengonline.gov.za/Business/Documents/Growth%20and%20Development%20Strategy.pdf .

Harries, Patrick. 1994. *Work, Culture, and Identity: Migrant Labourers in Mozambique and South Africa, c. 1860–1910.* Johannesburg: Wits University Press.

Harris, B. 2001. *A Foreign Experience: Violence, Crime, and Xenophobia during South Africa's Transition.* Johannesburg: Centre for the Studies of Violence and Reconciliation.

Heckman, James, and Bo E. Honore. 1990. "The Empirical Content of the Roy Model." *Econometrica* 58 no. 5: 1121–49.

Hunter, N., and C. Skinner. 2003. "Foreigners Working on the Streets of Durban: Local Government Policy Challenges." *Urban Forum* 14, no. 4: 301–19.

IRIN. 2008. "South Africa–Zimbabwe: The Politics of Cholera." November 21. Accessed at http://www.irinnews.org/report.aspx?ReportID=81616.

Jacobsen, K., and S. Bailey. 2004. "Micro-Credit and Banking for Refugees in Johannesburg." In *Forced Migrants in the New Johannesburg: Towards a Local Government Response*, edited by L. B. Landau. Johannesburg: Forced Migration Studies Programme.

Joint Initiative on Priority Skills Acquisition (JIPSA). 2007. Report of the Secretariat on the Joint Initiative on Priority Skills Acquisition Meeting of the Joint Task Team, Cape Town, March 22.

Kok, P., and M. Collinson. 2006. "Migration and Urbanisation in South Africa." Report No. 03-04-02, Statistics South Africa, Pretoria.

Landau, L. B. 2009. "Changing Local Government Responses to Migration in South Africa." Paper delivered to Conference on Urban-Rural Linkages and Migration, Dortmund, September 17. Accessed at http://www.raumplanung.uni-dortmund.de/rel/typo3/fileadmin/download/Conference/programme/Landau_Changing%20local%20government%20responses%20to%20%20migration_17.09.09.pdf.

——. 2011. "Positive Values and the Politics of Outsiderness." In *Exorcising the Demons Within: Xenophobia, Violence and Statecraft in Contemporary South Africa*, edited by L.B. Landau. Johannesburg: Wits University Press.

Landau, L. B., and V. Gindrey. 2008. "Migration and Population Trends in Gauteng Province 1996–2055." Forced Migration Studies Programme Working Paper No. 42. Accessed at www.migration.org.za.

Landau, L. B., and A. Segatti, with J. P. Misago. 2011. *Governing Migration & Urbanisation in South African Municipalities: Developing Approaches to Counter Poverty and Social Fragmentation.* Pretoria: South African Local Government Association.

Leggett, T. 2003. *Rainbow Tenement: Crime and Policing in Inner Johannesburg.* Pretoria: Institute for Security Studies.

Levinsohn, J. 2008. "Two Policies to Alleviate Employment in South Africa." Working Paper No. 166, Harvard Center for International Development, May.

Maphosa, F. 2007. "Remittances and Development: The Impact of Migration to South Africa on Rural Livelihoods in Southern Zimbabwe." *Development Southern Africa* 24, no. 1: 123–36.

Misago, Jean Pierre, Loren B. Landau, and Tamlyn Monson. 2009. "Towards Tolerance, Law, and Dignity: Addressing Violence against Foreign Nationals in South Africa." International Organisation of Migration Regional Office for Southern Africa Report 01/2009. Pretoria, South Africa.

Palmary, I. 2002. *Refugees, Safety and Xenophobia in South African Cities: The Role of Local Government.* Johannesburg: Centre for the Study of Violence and Reconciliation.

Palmary, I., J. Rauch, and G. Simpson. 2003. "Violent Crime in Johannesburg." In *Emerging Johannesburg: Perspectives on the Postapartheid City,* edited by R. Tomlinson, R. Beauregard, L. Bremner, and X. Mangcu. New York: Routledge.

Pendleton W., J. Crush, E. Campbell, T. Green, H. Simelane, et al. 2006. "Migration, Remittances and Development in Southern Africa." Migration Policy Series Report No. 44. Cape Town, South Africa: Southern African Migration Project.

Posel, Deborah. 1997. *The Making of Apartheid 1948–1961: Conflict and Compromise.* Oxford: Clarendon Paperbacks. First published 1991.

Provincial Government of the Western Cape. 2002. *Migration Study in the Western Cape.* Compiled by Simon B. Bekker. Cape Town: Provincial Government of the Western Cape.

Republic of South Africa. 1999. *White Paper on International Migration.* Pretoria. Accessed at http://www.info.gov.za/whitepapers/1999/migrate.htm.

Reuters. 2006. "Johannesburg Mayor Plans Migrant-Friendly Drive." *Reuters Alert-Net,* August 22. Accessed at http://www.alertnet.org/thenews/newsdesk/L23422828.htm.

Segatti, A., and L. B. Landau, eds. 2011. *Contemporary Migration to South Africa: A Regional Development Challenge.* African Development Forum Series. Washington, D.C.: World Bank, Agence Française de Développement.

Simone, A. 2004. *For the City Yet to Come: Changing African Life in Four Cities.* Durham, N.C.: Duke University Press.

South African Cities Network (SACN). 2004. *State of the Cities Report 2004.* Johannesburg: SACN.

——. 2006. *State of the Cities Report 2006.* Johannesburg: SACN.

Southern African Migration Project. N.d. "Thinking about the Brain Drain in Southern Africa." Migration Policy Brief No. 8. Kingston, Ontario, Canada.

Statistics South Africa. 2001. *National Census 2001.* Pretoria: Statistics South Africa.

——. 2003. "Documented Migration 2003." Report no. 03-51-03, Statistics South Africa, Pretoria.

——. 2007. *Community Survey 2007.* Pretoria: Statistics South Africa.

——. 2012. *Census 2011: Statistical Release.* Pretoria: Statistics South Africa.

Tomlinson, R., R. Beauregard, L. Bremner, and X. Mangcu. 2003. "The Postapartheid Struggle for an Integrated Johannesburg." In *Emerging Johannesburg: Perspectives on the Postapartheid City,* edited by R. Tomlinson, R. Beauregard, L. Bremner, and X. Mangcu. New York: Routledge, 2003.

United Nations Development Programme. 2009. *Overcoming Barriers: Human Mobility and Development*. Houndsmill, U.K.: Palgrave Macmillan.

Vigneswaran, D., and J. Hornberger, eds. 2009. *Beyond "Good Cop" / "Bad Cop": Understanding Informality and Police Corruption in South Africa*. Johannesburg: Forced Migration Studies Programme.

Winkler, T. 2006. "Kwere Kwere Journeys into Strangeness: Reimagining Inner-City Regeneration in Hillbrow, Johannesburg." Ph.D. thesis, University of British Columbia, Vancouver.

CHAPTER 9

Migration Between the Asia-Pacific and Australia

A DEVELOPMENT PERSPECTIVE

Graeme Hugo

Of all the economic, social, and demographic changes that have swept across Asia and the Pacific in the past three decades, none has been as significant as the increase in personal mobility, which has been both a cause and a consequence of wider economic, social, and political transformation. In the past decade there has been heightened awareness of the complex relationship between mobility and two areas of key importance in the region: economic and social development on the one hand, and national and regional security on the other. This interest has been sharpened in the case of the latter by events such as September 11 and the Bali bombing, while the former has become a major focus of multilateral development assistance agencies, especially by the World Bank (2006), the Asian Development Bank (2004), the United Nations Population Division (2006a), and the Department for International Development (U.K. House of Commons 2004). The focus of this new interest in the migration and development relationship has seen a shift in global discourse which previously concentrated almost entirely on "brain drain" losses of human capital caused by the emigration of skilled people from less developed countries toward emphasis on the positive effects that migration can and does have on origin nations. As the former secretary general of the United Nations put it: "The potential for migrants to help transform their native countries has captured the imaginations of national and local authorities, international institutions and the private sector. There is an emerging consensus that countries can co-operate to create triple wins, for migrants, for their countries of origin and for the societies that receive them" (United Nations 2006a:5).

This shift has seen renewed activity, both within Asia and the Pacific and outside it, regarding the potential positive benefits to be gained from migration for poverty reduction and the betterment of the lives of people in poor countries. Yet the empirical base of the "triple win" thinking is very meager; this especially applies to the Asia-Pacific region which, by virtue of the fact that it has 55 percent of the global population and some of its most dynamic economies, must loom large. The dearth of knowledge regarding the complex migration and development relationship is in part a function of the lack of comprehensive data relating to mobility within most of the region. This chapter overcomes this problem by viewing Asia-Pacific mobility from the perspective of Australia.[1] Australia has one of the most comprehensive migration data systems of any country, which captures all flows into and out of the country as well as the stocks of migrants every five years at its population census. The census includes a large number of migration-related questions (Hugo 2004a). Of course, this perspective does not provide insights into several elements of international migration in the region, which do not impinge on Australia to any major extent. This particularly involves the massive unskilled labor migration between Asia-Pacific countries and the Middle East (Hugo and Young 2008). However, as will be shown, the Australian perspective provides a unique insight into south–north migration.

Hence this chapter seeks to review some of the consequences of migration between the countries of the Asia-Pacific region and Australia for development of origin countries. I begin with an examination of scale, composition, and trends in population mobility between Australia and Asia-Pacific countries. I demonstrate that it is more realistic to depict Australia's migration relationship with Asia and the Pacific as a system involving a complex of two-way movements than as the north–south displacement that is conventionally employed in the migration and development discourse. I also show that there has been an exponential increase in movement to Australia from Asia and the Pacific in recent years, but this has been overwhelmingly selective of highly skilled groups, and it was only in 2008 that Australia announced a pilot scheme to bring in temporary seasonal agricultural workers from the region. The consequences of the two-way movement for development in origin countries remain unclear since there has been little examination of these impacts. I assess the limited information that is available and conclude that, thus far, the impacts have been limited. I argue, however, that the strong circular dimension within the migration system opens up considerable potential for the positive development effects of migration to be enhanced. Migration can in no way be seen as a "silver bullet" solution to poverty and lagging development in the region and is not a substitute for good governance and sound development policy. Nevertheless it can play a positive supporting and facilitating role in improving economic and social development in origin areas. Moreover in several of the small and vulnerable countries in the region, migration can play a major role. However, for this to be achieved there needs to be a substantial shift in migration policy and thinking regarding migration, not only in the origin countries but also in Australia.

SOME DATA CONSIDERATIONS

There has been a strong bias in migration research toward immigration and its impact at the destination (usually a high-income country), while emigration and the impact on the origin (usually a less developed nation) remain neglected. This bias has been highlighted by the increasing policy interest in the impact of emigration on development in less developed economies. There has also been a bias toward what Ley and Kobayaski (2005:112) term the "narrative of departure, arrival and assimilation." The focus has been on permanent settlement at the destination. However, the paradigm shift in international migration research from permanent settlement to transnationalism has seen greater attention being paid to return and to circular migration between origin and destination. Nowhere is the bias toward immigration and permanent settlement at the destination more evident than in international migration *data collection*. In most countries the data collected relate only to immigration and not emigration and also focus on permanent movement (Dumont and Lemaitre 2005; Schachter 2006).

Australia and New Zealand are rare exceptions with respect to both these issues. All persons entering and leaving Australia are asked questions about country of birth, date of birth, gender, occupation, country of origin and destination, intended and actual length of residence in Australia (or in the case of Australians leaving, abroad), and reasons for moving.[2] The Australian Department of Immigration and Citizenship divides them into three categories according to the length of time they intend to stay in Australia for arrivals or be away from Australia for departures:

- *Short-term movements.* Australian residents and citizens who intend to stay abroad less than twelve months and foreign visitors who intend to stay in Australia less than twelve months.

- *Long-term movements.* Australian residents and citizens who depart but intend to return but with the intended length of stay abroad being twelve months or more and foreign visitors with temporary residence who intend to leave Australia but after a period of more than twelve months.
- *Permanent movements.* Australian residents and citizens (including former settlers) departing with the stated intention of residing abroad permanently and foreigners arriving with the stated intention of remaining permanently in Australia.

Of course, people's intentions do not always eventuate, and they can change their minds as to the degree of permanency of their move. Osborne (2004), for example, examined the mobility of people who indicated they had left Australia "permanently" in 1998–99, yet by mid-2003 some 24 percent had returned. Clearly this would be counterbalanced to some extent by those who indicated they were leaving on a long-term basis but in fact changed their mind and stayed away permanently. Nevertheless the Australian data do provide a good indication of the totality of permanent and temporary migration to and from Australia, while in other countries the data refer only to immigration.

An additional dimension of Australian arrival and departure data is that, as of July 1998, a personal identifier number has been assigned to every individual moving to and from the country. This enables the movement history of individuals into and out of Australia to be traced. In the context of the present chapter, data were obtained on all Asia-born individuals arriving to and departing from Australia over the 1998–2006 period, which show all the moves those individuals subsequently make. This has allowed us to construct the migration history of those individuals over the period. Hence we can establish the extent to which permanent arrivals from Asia have returned on a permanent or temporary basis to their homeland and the extent to which they have moved to third countries.

PERMANENT SETTLEMENT MIGRATION FROM ASIA AND THE PACIFIC TO AUSTRALIA

Since the abolition of the last vestiges of the infamous White Australia Policy in the 1950s, there has been an increase in permanent settlement of Asians in Australia. There has been a permanent settler immigration of more than 500,000 Asians to Australia from the 1990s till the end of the previous decade. The relative significance of the four Asian subregions has fluctuated over the period, with South Asians recording the most rapid increase in recent years. Asian countries account for seven of the ten top birthplace countries of migrant settlers, with China, India, and the Philippines as the top three.

Australia's permanent settlement program for immigrants has four components—skill, family, refugee-humanitarian, and special migration—and the proportions of policy categories among settler arrivals from Asia has changed over the past few years. While in the mid-1990s family-reunification migrants outnumbered skilled migrants in the Asian intake, there are now more than two skilled Asian migrants for every family migration settler (*DIAC Immigration Update*, various issues).

Almost half of recent Asian arrivals were in the workforce during the period, compared with one-third of the entire settler intake. The composition of the flow has also changed. Two-thirds of those arriving in the mid-1990s to the late 2000s were professionals or managers, in comparison to more than half of the total intake. Hence overall, at a time when the skill profile of Australian permanent settlers has increased substantially, the skill profile of the Asian intake has been higher than that of total settler arrivals. From a development perspective, then, there is increased potential for brain drain effects due to increased loss of skilled human capital from poorer Asia-Pacific countries.

CIRCULAR MIGRATION TO AUSTRALIA FROM ASIA

The permanent settlement program, however, reflects only part of Asia-Pacific skilled migration to Australia. Perhaps the most striking change in Australian immigration over the past decades has been the increased non-permanent immigration of workers (Hugo 1999). Hitherto Australia's immigration policy had eschewed temporary worker migration in favor of an overwhelming focus on permanent settlement in which Asia has been an important source of such arrivals. As is the case with permanent arrivals, the long-term migrants from Asia have a high skill profile. Around 75 percent of long-term arrivals from Asia were in the top three occupational categories, compared with 70 percent of the total intake over the past two decades. Hence the increased intake of skilled workers from Asia in the past decade or so has not only been in the traditionally important permanent migration program but has been supplemented by a large intake of skilled temporary residents.

One of the largest categories of skilled temporary residents with the right to work are foreign students. There has been a rapid increase in the number of foreigners moving to Australia to study, and Asians have made up around three-quarters of them. Of the largest ten countries of origin, eight are Asian: India, China, Korea, Malaysia, Hong Kong, Thailand, Indonesia, and Japan.

Asians, in contrast, are not as prominent among Business Long Stay Visa residents (457) as among students.[3] Four out of ten arrivals are Asians, and of the top ten origin nations, four are Asian (India, Philippines, China, and Japan). Over this period, more than 350,000 Short Term Business Visas were granted, with China being the largest origin country, followed by Japan, India, Thailand, Indonesia, and Singapore (DIMA 2007:62). It is important to point out that eligibility for a 457 Visa requires the applicant to have an occupation in the top four Australian Standard Classification of Occupation categories (managers and administrators, professionals, associate professionals, and tradespersons), so again strong skill selectivity applies.

An important emerging feature of Australian skilled immigration is the strong nexus that has developed between temporary migration and permanent settlement. Since around 2000 the proportion of persons granted permanent residence as settlers who are made up of "onshore" candidates, people already in Australia, or those having some form of temporary visa increased to almost one-third during the last years of the previous decade. In this context it can be observed that Asians make the transition from temporary to permanent residence in greater numbers than other birthplace groups. As Australia moves toward a system whereby a large proportion of settlers initially enter the country as temporary migrants of one kind or another (as is already the case in New Zealand and the United States), this new pattern is stronger among Asians than among immigrants from other regions. Over the past decade, almost a third of all Asian permanent additions to the Australian population were onshore settlers. It is also important to point out that skilled migrants are more prominent among Asian onshore settlers than they are among settler arrivals.

During the past decade, skilled migrants made up around 75 percent of onshore migrants from Asia, compared with 56 percent of the offshore permanent arrivals. Hence the growing onshore component of Asia–Australia migration is even more skill-focused than the long-standing offshore settlement part (*DIAC Immigration Updates*, various years).

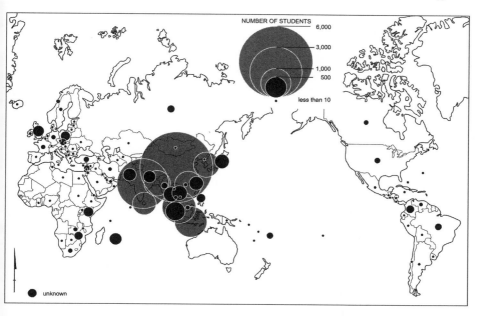

Figure 9.1   Overseas students transferring to permanent residence in Australia, by country of citizenship, 2005–6.

Source: DIAC unpublished data.

Since 1999 a number of changes in regulations have favored temporary migrants becoming permanent residents. Changes have included regulations that have made it possible for some foreigners on student visas to gain permanent residence without returning to their origin country. Almost 90 percent of these students were from Asia (see Figure 9.1).

The nexus between student migration and eventual permanent settlement is becoming an increasingly important process in skilled migration, not only in Australia but throughout the OECD region. Ongoing research is showing that the possibility of eventually obtaining permanent residence in Australia is increasingly a motivation for Asian students choosing to study there (Hugo and Tan 2007).

The link between studying in Australia and eventually establishing permanent settlement is not confined to students seeking permanent residence immediately after completing their studies. The Australian Points Assessment Scheme for selection of skilled settlers now gives points for having an Australian qualification, so large numbers of former students who studied in Australia and then returned to their origin country have subsequently

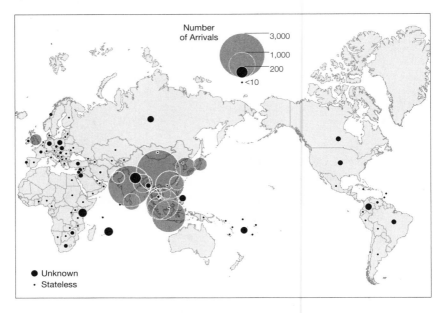

Figure 9.2   Number of skilled stream outcome principles with points for Australian qualification by citizenship, 2004–5.

Source: Unpublished data supplied by DIAC.

come back to Australia as settlers. Asians were again dominant in this category, accounting for almost 90 percent of such arrivals (see Figure 9.2).

A MORE COMPLEX PROCESS:
THE ROLE OF RETURN MIGRATION

Too often so-called south–north skilled migration is depicted as a one-way flow from less developed countries in regions like Asia to OECD countries; however, there are three important processes that emphatically negate this view. First, there is considerable *intraregional* south–south skilled migration within Asia, not only from less developed to more developed countries in the region but in the opposite direction as well. There are increasing numbers of skilled migrants moving between countries. South Korea, for example, has almost 1 million resident foreigners from a variety of national origins (see Figure 9.3). Singapore too is a major destination for skilled Asians. Although it does not release data on its immigrants (Fong 2006), it is estimated that of its 4.7 million residents, around

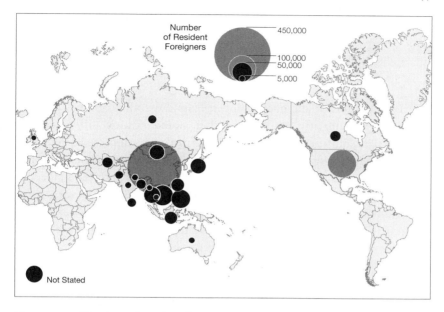

Figure 9.3   Number of resident foreigners in Korea by country of origin, May 31, 2007.

Source: Korea Immigration Service, Ministry of Justice.

1.7 million are foreigners, of whom around 1 million are permanent residents and 700,000 temporary workers. Skilled workers are dominant in the first group and make up about half of the second. China's rapid economic growth has attracted skilled workers from all over Asia, with Taiwan expressing concern regarding the brain drain to the mainland.

The second element of complexity in Asian skilled migration is the counterflow to the predominant trend of migration of skilled persons from Asia to OECD nations like Australia. As Dumont and Lemaitre (2005) have pointed out, analysts and policymakers have significantly underestimated the size and influence of this flow largely because there are few or no data on its scale. Australia is an exception since information is collected on all who leave the nation and can provide some insights into this flow, which can be divided into two groups:

- The foreign-born, who mainly represent *return migration* and *third-country migration* of former settlers (61 percent of the migrants from Australia to Asia).

- The Australia-born, some of whom are the Australia-born children of return migrants but who are predominantly Australian citizens of long-standing migration movements for one reason or another to an Asian country (39 percent), as the reciprocal migration referred to earlier.

The migration of the overseas-born from Australia to Asian destinations is predominantly return migration. Some striking differences between Asian countries in the extent of return migration are in evidence, but there are interesting contrasts between the three Asian regional groupings of countries. North East Asian countries, equivalent to 38.3 percent of arrivals, represent a return rate of over one in three immigrants. Most important here are Hong Kong returnees, which is part of a wider pattern of circulation of Hong Kong immigrants to Australia, with their homeland involving "astronauting" (Pe Pua et al. 1996). It also is associated with significant numbers of Hong Kongers taking out Australian citizenship before the 1997 handover to China (Skeldon 1994) and significant numbers subsequently returning to China. Similar patterns have been observed and analyzed in Canada (Ley and Kobayashi 2005). There is also a substantial return migration to Japan, which is a long-standing feature of Australia–Asia migration (Hugo 1994), with many Japanese coming to Australia on long-term company transfers with the intention of returning home on completion of that assignment (Iguchi 2008). Perhaps more surprising is the large proportion of Chinese and, to a lesser extent, South Koreans who have returned home. With 75,563 permanent arrivals between 1994 and 2006, the China-born have been the largest Asia–Australia migration flow. However, despite the relative recency of the large China flows, the return flow is substantial, equivalent to 21 percent of the inflow. For South Koreans it is 30 percent. It is clear from fieldwork that this reflects a considerable amount of dual-locality, with many Chinese- and South Korean–origin Australians maintaining work, family, and housing in both countries and circulating between them.

For South East Asia overall, the amount of return migration has been somewhat lower, equivalent to 15 percent of the inflow. It nevertheless has been significant, especially in Singapore, Indonesia, Malaysia, and Thailand. Even for Vietnam there has been a significant backflow. This is a recent phenomenon; much of the Vietnamese migration to Australia was of refugee-humanitarian migrants and occurred in the first fifteen years following reunification in 1975 (Viviani 1996), when it was characterized by a very low rate of return migration (Hugo 1994). However, with *doi moi,* namely, the economic reforms initiated in Vietnam in 1986 with the goal of creating a socialist-oriented market economy and the opening of the Vietnamese economy, it is apparent that an increasing number of Vietnamese Australians have returned to their birthplace and taken advantage of the liberalization of the economy to invest and set up businesses.

Perhaps the most striking figures are for South Asia, where rates of return are extremely low, especially for India, where there have been fifty-two immigrants for every returnee. This may be partly a function of the recency of much of the South Asian, especially Indian, immigration to Australia, but it still contrasts greatly with the flows from China, which also are mainly quite recent.

If we focus only on the 1997–2008 period, there were 209,496 Asia-born workers who migrated permanently to Australia, but 59,931 Asia-born (equivalent to 29 percent) who moved in the opposite direction. The breakdown by occupation of arrivals and departures indicates that while Australia experienced a substantial net gain in the high-skill categories, the flow of skill in the opposite direction is by no means insignificant.

Return migration is a long-standing feature of Australia's international migration. Hugo (1994) estimated that about a quarter of settler arrivals in post–World War II Australia subsequently reemigrated. Much of the return movement occurs within the first seven years of settlement. Hence in examining the pattern of Asian return migration, it is important to recognize that there are considerable differences between origin countries in the timing of migration to Australia. For example, in the 2001–6 intercensal period, the proportion is quite low for Vietnamese because much of the community arrived in Australia in the 1970s and 1980s as refugee-humanitarian migrants (Hugo 1990). On the other hand, for India, China, Korea, and Japan, the proportion arriving in recent years is very large, reflecting the increased focus on skill in the Australian migration program at the expense of family migration.

A third stream of migrants between Asia and Australia that needs to be considered is the Australia-born. Over the 1994–95 to 2005–6 period, there were 54,264 Australia-born permanent departures from Australia to Asian countries, equivalent to 13 percent of permanent arrivals from those countries. Of course, one important element in this group is the children of return migrants to Asian countries who were born to them during the time they resided in Australia. Nevertheless it is also apparent that there is increasing skilled migration of Australians with no family linkage with Asian countries who are motivated by career and economic factors. This is evident from the fact that almost 50 percent of the Australia-born flow was directed to the city-states of Singapore and Hong Kong. There is also significant movement of skilled Australians to Thailand, Indonesia, Malaysia, and Japan associated with the internationalization of skilled labor markets in the Asian region. Around 60 percent of Australia-born people leaving permanently for Asian destinations over the 1997–2007 period were in the workforce and were strongly concentrated in the high-skill occupations.

Overall there were around 184,000 Asian permanent arrivals who were employed in the workforce, but 93,300 permanent migrants who were working who moved to Asian destinations. There was, however, a net gain in all occupational categories except in unskilled labor. It is interesting to note that the net gain of managers and administrators was only 10 percent as large as the permanent arrivals in this occupational category, indicating a high degree of circularity in the movement. On the other hand, the net gain of professional workers was over a third the size of the permanent intake; hence the data do show that there is a significant north-to-south

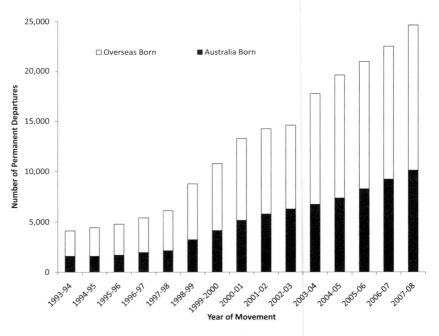

Figure 9.4   Permanent departures to Asia of Australia- and overseas-born, 1993–94 to 2007–08.

Source: DIAC unpublished data.

flow of skilled workers from Australia to Asia. The substantial increase that has occurred over the past fifteen years in both the return flow of Asians and the flow of Australians to Asia is depicted in Figure 9.4.

While the dominant permanent flow is toward Australia, there is a smaller but nevertheless significant counterflow. Over the 1990s and 2000s, over half a million Asians settled in Australia, but a sixth returned to Asia and there were around 73,000 Australia-born persons who moved permanently to Asia. Hence the net migration gain was approximately 390,000, representing a migration efficiency percentage of 53; that is, it takes two immigrants to get a net migration gain of one migrant (see Table 9.1). It is also relevant to see how the net migration pattern is distributed across particular occupations. This indicates that both Asia-born settlers and permanent departures are concentrated in the high-skill areas (managers and administrators, professionals and associate professionals). What is striking is that while professionals represent just over 50 percent of the settlers, they make up 82 percent of the net gain, indicating that there is a below-average rate of return for this group. On the other hand, almost half of managers and administrators return. The pattern is clear, however, that even though the gradient is toward Australia, there is a substantial flow of skilled migrants in the other direction.

A further element in the complexity of the migration relationship between Australia and Asia is the movement of Asians to Australia on a permanent basis, who subsequently move permanently elsewhere in a "third-country migration." Biao (2004:164) has explained, "In the international migration of the highly skilled, 'brain bypass' has become a new phenomenon. The term refers to the movement of skilled migrants from the South to countries such as Canada and Australia, where using experience acquired in those countries as leverage, they then move onto other countries, particularly the USA."

Biao (2004) found that there is a significant pattern among Indian information technology immigrants who study and settle in Australia, gain permanent residence, and then migrate to the United States. He explains that the immigrants use complex strategies to assess that they have a

Table 9.1   Permanent Migration in and out of Australia, 1993–94 to 2007–8

Asia-born moving to Australia	560,111
Asia-born moving from Australia to Asia	97,552
Australia-born moving from Australia to Asia	72,773
Net migration	389,786

Source: Department of Immigration and Citizenship (DIAC) unpublished data.

greater chance of migration to the United States from Australia than from India. Moreover their Australian permanent residence status can serve as insurance should they not be successful in the United States or in the case of a downturn in the U.S. IT economy.

Table 9.2 shows the proportions of departures of Asian birthplace groups from Australia between 1993 and 2007 that was directed toward the country of birth. Again there are some striking intercountry differences: the South Asia vs. East Asia contrast is apparent. Among East Asian countries, not only are the ratios of immigrants to emigrants much smaller and the outflows more substantial but the proportions returning to their birthplace are considerably greater. This is apparent in the two largest countries of origin: China and India. Table 9.2 shows that of the 25,919 China-born Australian residents who indicated they were leaving Australia permanently, 57.4 percent returned to China. Moreover more than another 25 percent went to Hong Kong. This pattern, observed by Zweig and Hand (2007), also applies for the China-born leaving the United States and Canada.

Table 9.2 Permanent Departures of Asia-Born from Australia According to Whether They Return to Their Birthplace or a Different Country, 1993–2007

Country of Birth	Arrivals	Departures	Percentage Returning to Country of Birth	Ratio of Arrivals to Departures
China	107,339	25,919	57.4	4.1
India	82,447	3,631	22.0	22.7
Singapore	19,354	3,075	53.0	6.3
Hong Kong	30,227	20,700	84.6	1.5
Philippines	51,540	3,395	44.5	15.2
Malaysia	27,881	5,350	34.4	5.2
Vietnam	39,351	8,874	57.1	4.4
Indonesia	31,768	6,359	74.6	5.0
Taiwan	18,073	8,350	80.3	2.2
Burma	5,977	277	10.5	21.6
Cambodia	9,618	1,013	29.1	9.5
Laos	465	173	28.0	2.7
Thailand	13,171	2,517	74.8	5.2
Japan	8,456	2,864	77.8	3.0
South Korea	14,802	3,811	74.9	3.9
Bangladesh	8,665	228	25.4	38.0
Nepal	2,250	37	8.1	60.8
Pakistan	12,163	520	31.3	23.4
Sri Lanka	25,052	1,285	24.0	19.5
Afghanistan	13,643	254	12.2	53.7

Source: DIAC unpublished data.

CIRCULAR MIGRATION FROM AUSTRALIA TO ASIA

Most of the literature on return migration and its impact on development in origin countries is focused on permanent return. Yet nonpermanent return can also impinge upon development. Returnees can bring with them not only money and equipment but also new ideas and new ways of doing things. It is apparent that settlement of Asian groups has resulted in an upswing of *nonpermanent* return migration out of Australia. Figures 9.5 and 9.6 show how long-term and short-term movement from Australia to Asian countries has greatly increased in recent years. Moreover it is apparent that the Asian-born have been an important component in that temporary movement out of Australia. Clearly the permanent settlement of Asians in Australia is creating a significant temporary flow back to countries of origin in which former settlers are an important component. This is especially the case in long-term movement in which the overseas-born make up an increasing majority of the flow from Australia to Asia.

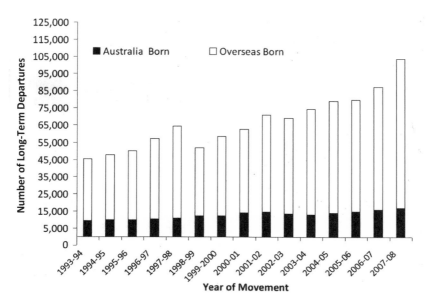

Figure 9.5   Long-term departures to Asia of Australia- and overseas-born, 1993–94 to 2007–08.

Source: DIAC unpublished data.

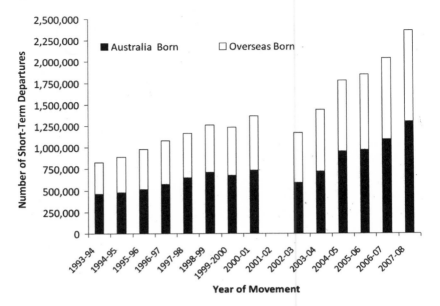

Figure 9.6   Short-term resident departures to Asia of Australia- and overseas-born, 1993–94 to 2007–08.

Source: DIAC unpublished data. Note: Data not available for 2001–2.

The special data set created using the personal identifiers of all persons moving into and out of Australia allows us to establish the extent to which this temporary movement out of Australia into Asia involves former settlers. Table 9.3 shows the average number of return trips made into and out of Australia over the 1998–2006 period by different Asian birthplace groups. They are differentiated according to their visa status granted by the Department of Immigration and Citizenship. To take China-born persons as an example, the data in the table can be interpreted as follows:

- China-born settler arrivals made an average of 2.4 return trips to Australia in the period before coming to settle.
- China-born visitors made an average of 4.4 trips per person.
- China-born residents of Australia made an average of 6.4 return trips during the reference period.

This clearly shows both that there is considerable circulation between Australian and Asian contexts of former settlers and also that there are significant numbers of China-born (based in China) who circulate fre-

Table 9.3   Country of Birth by Type of Movement: Average Number of Return Trips by Individuals, 1998–2006

Birthplace of Mover	Status of Mover					
	Settler Arrival	Visitor Arrival	Resident Return	Visitor Departure	Resident Temporary Departure	Resident Permanent Departure
	Average Number of Return Trips					
Burma (Myanmar)	1.0	3.6	5.8	4.4	5.9	4.1
Cambodia	1.3	4.8	4.0	5.2	4.0	4.1
Laos	1.2	3.2	5.2	3.5	5.6	4.3
Thailand	2.4	4.9	5.9	5.3	6.2	5.0
Vietnam	1.4	3.9	4.7	4.4	4.8	4.3
Brunei Darussalam	4.1	7.3	8.8	7.6	9.1	7.3
Indonesia	4.8	6.1	10.5	6.4	10.3	9.2
Malaysia	4.0	5.9	9.4	6.1	9.4	6.9
Philippines	1.5	3.9	4.8	4.7	5.0	4.1
Singapore	3.7	6.4	10.2	6.5	10.2	5.9
China	2.4	4.4	6.2	4.8	6.1	5.9
Hong Kong	3.5	5.4	6.4	5.6	6.7	5.1
Macau	3.2	5.1	6.2	5.3	6.4	4.8
Mongolia	1.6	2.5	4.7	3.1	4.4	0.0
Taiwan	5.1	5.8	8.7	6.0	8.9	8.0
Japan	4.0	5.4	8.3	5.6	8.5	6.3
Bangladesh	1.7	2.4	4.1	3.1	4.0	3.4
Bhutan	1.3	1.7	3.7	2.0	3.8	0.0
India	1.9	3.7	5.7	4.7	5.5	4.6
Maldives	2.6	4.6	13.0	5.0	12.1	0.0
Nepal	1.6	2.2	5.1	3.2	4.9	5.1
Pakistan	1.6	3.5	5.0	4.3	4.9	4.5
Sri Lanka	1.9	3.8	6.2	4.7	6.2	6.2
Afghanistan	0.6	2.2	2.4	3.3	2.3	3.4
Korea	2.5	3.7	7.5	4.2	7.5	6.4

Source: Special data set received by DIAC.

quently to Australia. In both cases the potential for significant development impacts in China is considerable.

The rate of resident return is especially high for those born in Singapore, Indonesia, Taiwan, Japan, Korea, and Malaysia, indicating a high level of business interaction with their homelands by Australian-based immigrants from these countries. Clearly immigrant Asians set up very active circuits of movement between Asian countries and Australia. Obviously a significant amount of this movement is family-based visitation; however, it is also apparent that much of the movement involves other motives. A study of Chinese academics in Australia (Hugo 2005) showed clearly that almost all maintained strong linkages with Chinese universities with joint research

Table 9.4   Asia-Born Australian Resident Short-Term Departures by Country of Destination (Asia) by Reason for Travel, 2007–8

Reason for Travel	Number	Percent
Exhibition	888	0.1
Convention/conference	10,072	1.5
Business	80,004	11.8
Visiting friends/relatives	332,834	49.1
Holiday	215,176	31.8
Employment	15,617	2.3
Education	5,393	0.8
Other	17,661	2.6
Not stated	31,766	
Total	**709,410**	**100.0**

Source: DIAC unpublished data.

projects and regular teaching stints in China, with knowledge exchange being substantial. These circuits already are powerful conduits for the flow of money, goods, and expertise into origin countries. Perhaps more important, they have the potential for becoming even more significant channels to facilitate development in an appropriate policy setting.

The long-term arrival and departure information for Australia does not include information on the reasons for movement, but this is available for short-term movement.[4] Table 9.4 shows the dominance of motivations in visiting friends and relatives among the Australian Asia-born residents making short-term visits back into Asia. This indicates that in 2007–8 there were 709,410 short-term visits made by Australians who were born in Asia. Of these, 32 percent were for holidays and 49 percent were to visit family and friends. It is undoubtedly the case, however, that many of those who nominated visiting family and friends as their main reason for travel in this visit actually combined it also with business activity and, in their interaction with friends, and to a lesser extent family, passed on knowledge and information gained in Australia.

Notwithstanding, one in five Asia-born Australians visiting Asia did so for a reason *other than* to visit family or friends or to vacation. Hence it is apparent that short-term home visiting of this group is already a significant mechanism of business activity and knowledge transfer. Moreover Table 9.5 shows that there is considerable variation between Asian countries in the extent to which return visiting is associated with business and other nonholiday family visitation. Table 9.5 indicates that in the largest single destination, China, 29 percent of all visitors had motives other than to vacation or visit family and friends. Similarly high proportions applied

Table 9.5 Asia-Born Australian Residents Making Short-Term
Visits to Asia by Country of Destination and Reason, 2007–8

Country of Destination	Total Number of Visits	Percent Not Visiting Family/ Friends Holiday
China	124,423	29.1
Hong Kong	86,956	25.3
Malaysia	67,640	22.9
India	64,311	14.8
Vietnam	57,896	11.5
Singapore	57,126	34.6
Philippines	45,377	15.8
Indonesia	45,051	26.7
Thailand	32,289	13.4
Japan	32,260	22.4
Taiwan	26,919	21.7
Korea	19,477	31.9
Sri Lanka	15,227	15.7
Pakistan	8,270	14.8
Cambodia	7,644	10.1
Bangladesh	6,562	12.6
Brunei	2,153	31.3
Macao SAR	2,139	27.3
Burma	2,094	11.4
Nepal	1,784	7.2
East Timor	1,231	62.3
Laos	1,226	6.7
Afghanistan	919	7.7
Maldives	146	10.3
Total	709,414	19.1

Source: DIAC unpublished data.

in other East Asian destinations as well as Singapore and Brunei. The proportions were lower in South Asia and in other countries that were sources of refugee migrants to Australia.

IMPLICATIONS FOR DEVELOPMENT IN ORIGIN COUNTRIES

The Australian international migration flow data analyzed here have demonstrated conclusively that the Asia–Australia migration system is characterized by a high degree of complexity and circularity. This stands in sharp distinction to the conventional depiction of the flow as south–north migration, wherein it is assumed, at least implicitly, that the overwhelming dominant pattern is of permanent redistribution of highly skilled people from poorer to better-off countries. While the explosion of this myth of south–

north migration is important for the Australian case, the only difference between it and most other OECD destinations of south–north migration is the fact that it has a more comprehensive data collection system that allows the inherent circularity and complexity in the system to be quantified. Australia is not a special case; such patterns are characteristic of south–north migration in most cases, but the data limitations simply conceal it. I argue that circularity, reciprocity, and complexity are structural features of the Asia–Australia migration system; they are not peripheral or ephemeral. The material analyzed here points to a pressing need to reconceptualize the whole concept of south–north migration so that it recognizes the fundamental complexity of the population flows that are involved. It also points to the urgency of improving our migration data collection systems, which in many countries remain grounded on the outmoded settlement migration model and are biased toward migration-receiving countries and considerations.

Another of the striking findings regarding Asia–Australia international migration relates to the substantial blurring between permanent and nonpermanent migration. It is apparent that categorizing international movers as either permanent or temporary is becoming increasingly problematic. It has long been the case that this dimension of mobility is more appropriately conceptualized as a continuum than as a binary dichotomy, but the overlap has increased in recent times. Many ways in which permanent and temporary migration are linked have been demonstrated in the Asia–Australia case. These include:

- Persons arriving in Australia as temporary migrants (e.g., students, temporary business migrants) becoming permanent residents of Australia.
- Persons arriving as permanent settlers in Australia but subsequently returning to their homeland or on to a third nation on a permanent basis.
- Persons arriving as permanent settlers in Australia but then returning to their homeland on a temporary basis, in many cases frequently traveling between Australia and their Asian homeland. Hence there is an important connection between permanent and temporary movement.
- Enhanced flows of Australians to Asia, not only returnees, but also it is apparent that the linkages fostered by permanent settlement migration have led to enhanced flows of tourists, businesspeople, and others into Asia.

Some of the most significant implications of the findings presented here, however, relate to the increasing global discourse on migration and development (GCIM 2005; United Nations 2006a; World Bank 2006).

BRAIN DRAIN

I showed earlier that although there is significant circularity in the migration between Asia-Pacific countries and Australia, there is a significant net migration gain of skilled people by Australia and a net loss for the origin countries. While in recent years there has been a shift in the discourse on migration and development away from an overwhelming focus on brain drain toward acknowledgment that the effects of migration can be more complex and have net positive impacts in origin areas, there are at least two reasons why brain drain needs to be considered an issue of significance in the Australian context. The first relates to the fact that many of the origin nations, especially in the Pacific region, are quite small. The second relates to the specific issue of the emigration of medical personnel from Asia-Pacific countries to Australia.

OECD research has indicated that 88 percent of immigrants from southern to northern nations have secondary education or higher qualifications, but that except in relatively small nations, southern countries do not lose a high proportion of their highly skilled persons to OECD nations.[5] Hence for large nations in the region such as China, India, Indonesia, Bangladesh, and Pakistan, the OECD analysis shows that, despite some losses, the bulk of highly educated groups remain at home. In the Australian context, however, several of the origin countries of migrants, especially in the Pacific, are quite small nations where "brain drain" can have a devastating quantitative and qualitative impact in robbing the country of the talent most likely to facilitate economic and social development. In Pacific Island countries there is now an intensive debate on brain drain. Fiji has lost half of its middle- to high-level labor through emigration since 1987 (Fiji National Planning Office 2005), and Voigt Graf (2003, and Voigt Graf et al. 2007) has demonstrated that significant migration losses of experienced and highly qualified teachers, health personnel, accountants, and bureaucrats have been a barrier to development. Moreover there are losses of skill in tourism, construction, and a range of professional services that also have had a damaging impact. Connell (2003) argues the following points:

- "Brain drain" has been excessive in several small Pacific Island countries such as the Cook Islands, Tonga, Fiji, and Samoa, where it has hindered development and reduced the welfare and bargaining position of those countries.

- Ironically some of these migrants become part of a "brain loss" or "brain waste" because their qualifications, despite getting them entry, are not recognized by appropriate occupational licensing bodies in the destination country.
- Although data are poor or nonexistent, he considers return migration to be very limited.
- It is unusually difficult to replace the skilled migrants in small island states because of the duration of training involved and the limited local demand for particular skills.

A second area of concern, however, relates to the impact of skilled migration in particular *sectors* of origin economies that can have a damaging effect on the well-being of local populations as well as in the development effort. This is especially apparent in the sector of medicine and health. At the 2006 census, 32 percent of the total Australian medical workforce was born in a foreign country, compared to less than 25 percent of the total workforce. Among doctors, 59 percent were born overseas; among nurses the rate was 29 percent. Between the 2001 and 2006 censuses there was an increase of 28 percent in the overseas-born medical workforce, compared to 11 percent in Australian-born medical workers. Table 9.6 shows that Asia and the Pacific have made a major contribution to the gain of medical workers over the 2001–6 period. At the 2006 census, Asia- and Pacific-born people made up 12 percent of the total Australian medical workforce: 27 percent of the doctors and 11 percent of nurses.

It has been argued that a more ethical approach to recruitment of health workers needs to be adopted in Australia (Scott et al. 2004). However, like other OECD nations, Australia has, through its contemporary immigration policies, encouraged the flow of skilled personnel from less developed nations. Under the Colombo Plan and later programs to train students from Asia and Africa in Australia, students were compelled to return to their homeland for at least two years following completion of their studies. This is no longer the case; indeed in recent years, Australia has helped foreign students in some skill areas to gain permanent residence in Australia without returning home. Moreover the increased skill focus in the migration program has encouraged the outflow of skilled workers from less developed nations. The recent WHO Global Code of Practice on the International Recruitment of Health Personnel passed at the Sixty-third World Health Assembly addresses some of these issues by establishing and promoting *voluntary* principles and practices for the

Table 9.6 Change in Australian Medical Workforce from Asia and the Pacific, 2001–6

Region	Total Medical Workforce			Doctors			Nurses		
	2001	2006	Change	2001	2006	Change	2001	2006	Change
Pacific	2,577	3,303	28.2	368	453	23.1	4,651	5,691	22.4
SE Asia	14,046	18,097	28.8	3,780	4,649	23.0	6,630	8,479	27.9
NE Asia	5,758	8,724	51.5	1,604	2,076	29.4	1,996	3,281	64.4
S Asia	5,132	8,708	69.7	2,855	4,849	69.8	1,328	2,284	72.0
Total	**27,487**	**38,832**	**41.3**	**8,607**	**12,027**	**39.7**	**14,605**	**19,735**	**35.1**

Source: Calculated from unpublished data from the ABS Australian Censuses.

recruitment of health personnel and discouraging active recruitment of health personnel from developing countries facing critical shortages of health workers. As an illustration, Table 9.7 shows the arrivals and departures of doctors and nurses for Australia over the 1993–2006 period according to region of origin and destination. Some interesting patterns are in evidence:

• There is a high degree of circularity in evidence. Over the period there were 2,918 permanent arrivals of doctors from the Asia-Pacific and 1,032 permanent departures to the region; comparable figures for nurses were 4,130 and 1,050. This indicates a moderate to high "efficiency" of migration of 48 and 63 percent, respectively.[6] This means that for every net permanent addition of 1 doctor and 1 nurse to the Australian doctor and nurse population by migration from Asia and the Pacific there needs to be an immigration of 2 doctors and 1.6 nurses, respectively.

• This contrasts with the relationship Australia has with Europe and the United Kingdom and, to a lesser extent, New Zealand. These also are significant origins of doctors and nurses permanently settling in Australia, but there are also significant numbers moving in the opposite direction so that the migration has very low efficiency. Indeed for North America there are more permanent departures than arrivals, resulting in a net migration loss. In the case of Europe and the United Kingdom, there needs to be 6.6 doctor settlers to achieve a net gain of a single doctor; for nurses the number is 4.8.

• It will be noted that the data for Africa show a greater "effectiveness" of permanent migration of doctors and nurses than is the case for Asia, with only 1.2 doctor and nurse settler arrivals to get permanent gains of 1 doctor and nurse.

• Hence although there is a substantial net gain of doctors and nurses from Asia, there are smaller but still significant flows in the other direction. In the Pacific ("Other Oceania" in the table), the migration is less effective and with a greater degree of circularity in the movement than is the case for Asia.

• Turning to long-term movement,[7] it is apparent that the migration is much less effective than we would expect because the arrivals enter Australia under temporary resident visas. Nevertheless Table 9.7 shows that the net gains are in fact larger than for those entering under permanent settler visas: 8,182 compared to 3,435 doctors and 9,682 compared to 6,141 nurses.

Table 9.7 Arrivals to and Departures from Australia of Skilled Health Workers, 1993–2006

Doctors	Permanent				Long Term			
	Arrivals	Departures	Migration Effectiveness	Net	Arrivals	Departures	Migration Effectiveness	Net
Africa (not including N. Africa)	340	28	84.7	312	1,702	824	34.8	878
Asia	2,812	989	48.0	1,823	9,376	6,254	20.0	3,122
New Zealand	1,788	773	39.6	1,015	1,631	950	26.4	681
Other Oceania	106	43	42.3	63	531	638	−9.2	−107
Europe and U.K.	1,491	1,097	15.2	394	11,608	8,224	17.1	3,384
North America	215	437	−39.0	−222	2,547	2,378	3.4	169
South America	72	22	53.2	50	194	139	16.5	55

Nurses	Permanent				Long Term			
	Arrivals	Departures	Migration Effectiveness	Net	Arrivals	Departures	Migration Effectiveness	Net
Africa (not including N. Africa)	892	80	83.5	812	2,560	975	44.8	1,585
Asia	3,758	825	62.6	2,933	7,041	5,897	8.8	1,144
New Zealand	4,104	2,799	18.9	1,305	3,392	2,333	18.5	1,059
Other Oceania	372	225	24.6	147	630	1,123	−28.1	−493
Europe and U.K.	5,861	3,792	21.4	2,069	23,904	18,458	12.9	5,446
North America	576	1,690	−49.1	−1,114	3,982	2,980	14.4	1,003
South America	47	58	−10.5	−11	192	254	−13.9	−62

Source: DIAC unpublished data.

- The low levels of effectiveness of long-term migration providing doctors permanently for Australia is evident in the fact that it takes 5 long-term arrivals from Asia to get a single person addition. For nurses the number is 18.1, indicating a high degree of circularity. There are net losses to the Pacific.
- Again, it is noticeable that for Africa there is much less circularity in evidence and a significant brain drain effect is in evidence.

Clearly there has been an increase in the tempo of migration of medical personnel from Asia and the Pacific to Australia in recent years. Many of these doctors and nurses go to rural and remote areas in Australia, where there is an overall shortage of medical personnel (Australian Institute of Health and Welfare 2003). This has led to a debate within Australia about the ethics of such movement and raises such issues as:

- Developing an Australian code of conduct for ethical recruitment independent of the WHO's and the Commonwealth's code of practice for the international recruitment of health workers.
- The possible reimbursement of the sending country for costs incurred in training of personnel.
- The need for more training of health workers in Australia.
- Selectively limiting proactive recruitment of skilled health professionals.
- Better supporting health care training systems in less developed countries.
- Encouraging the return of these doctors after they complete a term in Australia. (Reid 2002; Scott et al. 2004)

It is not feasible for Australia to unilaterally selectively disallow immigration of particular skilled people like doctors and nurses from Asia and Africa. However, there appear to be some other policy options. For example, receiving countries could make an investment in training and education in the less developed countries of origin of skilled migrants, in recognition of the costs invested by those origin nations in the development of the human capital encapsulated by the migrants. This, of course, would forge a link between immigration and development assistance policies and ministries in Australia. Such investments might be only for the creation of training institutions to produce future migrant settlers for Australia. However, the raison d'être of these investments should be the recognition that destination nations have a responsibility to meet development costs of human capital paid for in origin nations. Thus the investment could be "tied aid" in the sense that it is targeted to particular areas of activity in the origin nation. In some ways, this is analogous to the levies at present placed on migrant workers by some immigrant counties. Singapore, for example, imposes such a levy to be paid by the employers of skilled foreign workers, and the funds generated are put into the training and education of Singaporeans so that skill shortages in the long term can be met internally. It is not too large a jump to envisage a similar payment to and investment in the training and education system in origin countries. Moreover the work of Stark and Fan (2007) suggests that, while enhancing education can indeed lead to greater emigration, it also has substantial spillover effects in that some of those educated remain at home.

CIRCULAR LOW-SKILLED LABOR MIGRATION

One of the major planks of the contemporary argument that migration can be positive for development in origin countries relates to circular migration of low-skilled workers (GCIM 2005; Vertovec 2004). It is argued that low-skilled workers who migrate from less to more developed countries remit a high proportion of their earnings home and are more likely to return to their homeland because they have a higher level of commitment to their origins than do permanent workers. On the other hand, opponents contend that such movement tends to be exploitative of migrants and results in high levels of overstaying among the migrants (Castles 2003).

In the Australian government there has been long-standing bipartisan agreement that low-skilled temporary migration has no place in the country's international migration program. Both permanent and temporary migration elements are strongly oriented to highly skilled groups, and it is only under the increasingly restricted family and refugee-humanitarian programs that low-skilled workers can enter Australia to work. However, there has been a view increasing in popularity that there may be a growing mismatch between immigration policies focused on skill and a tightening labor market, with demand for labor across a broader skill spectrum. While such temporary low-skilled emigration can in no way substitute for better education, training, and labor force policies in less developed nations, it can relieve "labor surplus" situations in particular areas, especially in small economies like those in the Pacific and in East Timor. In short, there would appear to be a case to look at the full gamut of labor force needs in more developed nations and not just focus on skill and talent search in considering migration.

In recent years falling unemployment levels in Australia have seen a tightening of the labor market, which has created demand not only for skilled labor but also for unskilled and semiskilled workers. A specific case in point is growth sectors within agriculture. Labor shortages are felt most strongly in the horticultural sector, which is having increasing difficulty attracting sufficient labor to properly harvest their crops (National Harvest Trust Working Group 2000; National Farmers Federation 2008). The National Farmers Federation estimates that the Australian agricultural sector will need an additional 100,000 workers as it emerges from drought. Ironically, although Australia has eschewed bringing in migrant labor for agriculture, the horticultural industry has relied significantly on migration to supply its workforce. More than a third of the workforces are "backpackers," young European tourists; most of them arrive in Australia under the Working Holiday Program followed by the local workforce.

The shortage of harvesting workers has resulted in many petitions to the minister of immigration for programs similar to those in nations like the United States, the United Kingdom, and Canada to bring in guest workers on a temporary basis. Until recently the government rejected these proposals using the following arguments:

- The high level of unemployment in Australia would suggest that growers are not paying adequate wages or providing appropriate conditions for workers.
- It would undermine the integrity of Australia's immigration program in that:
  (a) It involves unskilled workers.
  (b) It is discriminatory in that it is available only to people from one region.
- It has been questioned whether the Pacific Island workers would indeed gain from the migration because of the high costs of travel in relation to the type and amount of work available and the wages paid.
- The loss of human resources would have a negative impact on the economies of home nations.

There also has been some opposition from the Australian Workers Union against the use of migrant workers in harvesting (*The Age*, February 14, 2000). Recently the Australian government undertook a seasonal worker program that was built on the Pacific seasonal worker scheme opened to employers in the horticultural industry and seasonal workers from East Timor, Kiribati, Nauru, Papua New Guinea, Samoa, the Solomon Islands, Tonga, Tuvalu, and Vanuatu. The government also undertook a small-scale three-year trial of seasonal worker arrangements with cotton and cane growers, aquaculture ventures, and hotel owners in the tourism industry.

REMITTANCES

There is a burgeoning literature on the significance of the flow of remittances from OECD nations to less developed countries and their role in poverty reduction (Adams 2003; Hugo 2003; Asian Development Bank 2004; Johnson and Sedaca 2004; Terry and Wilson 2005; World Bank 2006; GCIM 2005). It is stressed that remittances have particular value as a transfer from more developed to less developed countries since they flow directly to families and hence can have an immediate impact on improvement of well-being at the grassroots level. The role of the destination countries here is in the realm of facilitating these flows; reducing the degree of rent taking exacted on remittance flows by intermediaries; and ensuring that there are safe, quick, and reliable channels for migrants to make remittances to their families in less developed countries. Efforts to reduce the transfer costs imposed by intermediaries are needed if the full benefits of remittances are to be realized.

Australia had some 5,253,852 foreign-born persons in 2007; 1,527,650 were born in Asia, 234,253 were born in sub-Saharan Africa (excluding South Africa), and 127,098 were born in Oceania (excluding New Zealand and Australia). This represents, potentially at least, a significant opportunity for the development of diaspora communities within Australia that are connected to less developed countries and provide conduits for flows of remittances, investment, technology, and knowledge to them. Although, as my colleagues have pointed out numerous times in this volume, without the right economic, social, and political policies in place, remittances and migration cannot do much and may even hurt countries of origin. With the important exception of the Pacific, there has been little research in Australia on the relationship between Australian-based immigrant communities that are resident in Australia and their home countries, and on the flow of remittances they send. However, again with the important exception of the Pacific, the level of outward remittance flow from Australia would seem to be small. Among the reasons for this is the fact that the increasing emphasis on skill in the Australian migration program means that the families from which many migrants come are among the better-off groups in their home countries, so there will not be a pressing need for migrants to remit funds. Indeed, for some the opposite is the case. Obviously the inflow of funding from Asian countries to Australia from families supporting foreign higher education students studying in Australia is substantial (137,000 students in 2003, 85 percent from Asia). It is estimated that in 2007–8 international education activity contributed A$14.2 billion in export income to the Australian economy,[8] the largest services export industry ahead of tourism. The main contributors are China (A$3.1 billion), India (A$2 billion), Korea (A$1 billion), Malaysia (A$0.7 billion), Hong Kong and Thailand (A$0.6 billion), Indonesia (A$0.5 billion), Vietnam (A$0.4 billion), and Japan (A$0.3 billion). This export income grew by 23.4 percent over the previous year.

Remittance flows appear to be greater among some groups of migrants than others. Unfortunately there are few data available relating to this in Australia, but the Longitudinal Survey of Immigrants in Australia, which involved two groups of migrants arriving in 1993–95 and 1999–2000 who were reinterviewed twice in the first case and once in the second (Hugo 2004a), has some information. Table 9.8 shows that when the first survey migrants were interviewed within a few months after arrival in Australia, fewer than 8 percent sent remittances back to relatives. This, of course, is understandable given that it takes time for immigrants to become established. When interviewed for a third time (1998–99), a larger proportion had sent remittances home to relatives. It will be noted that the largest proportions sending remittances were the refugee-humanitarian migrants, who also are the poorest group with the highest level of unemployment and greatest reliance on benefits (Richardson et al. 2001).[9] The highest proportions of birthplace groups sending back remittances were drawn from regions made up of mostly less developed countries: Pacific (41.4 percent), South Asia (47.5), South East Asia (42.3), Middle East (33.1), and Africa (31.8).

These large-scale surveys are notoriously poor in detecting remittances; in detailed fieldwork it is evident that among some groups there are substantial flows of remittances. This has been especially demonstrated for immigrants from Tonga, Samoa, and Fiji in Australia (e.g., Connell and Brown 2004). More recent data (Brown 2008) shows the high level of remittances in Fiji and Tonga (Table 9.9). Brown (2008) shows that in Tonga, remittances have important poverty-alleviation effects.

Table 9.8   Remittances Sent to Relatives by Immigrants in Australia According to Visa Category of Arrival

	None	Less than $1,000	$1,000–$5,000	$5,001–$10,000	$10,001 +
Family					
1st interview	97.6	6.2	1.0	0.1	0.1
3rd interview	72.1	12.7	11.9	1.9	1.3
Skill					
1st interview	92.0	5.1	2.4	0.2	0.1
3rd interview	69.6	6.0	14.4	4.6	4.5
Humanitarian					
1st interview	90.5	8.8	0.7	-	-
3rd interview	55.4	21.1	18.1	3.0	2.5
Total					
1st interview	92.1	6.3	1.3	0.2	0.1
3rd interview	68.9	12.3	13.6	2.8	2.3

Source: Longitudinal Survey of Immigrants to Australia, unpublished data.

Table 9.9   Fiji and Tonga Estimates of Total Remittances, 2004 (US$)

	Fiji	Tonga
Remittances received per capita	$370.88	$753.02
Population	836,002	98,322
Percent who are recipients	42	90.9
Total remittances (US 000$)	$130,343	$67,330
As percent of GDP	6.2	41.8
As percent of exports	8.3	154.2

Source: Brown 2008a.

Recent fieldwork among recently arrived groups from the Horn of Africa (Eritrea, Sudan, Somalia, and Ethiopia) indicates substantial flows of remittances being sent back, despite recent arrival and high levels of unemployment. Table 9.10 shows the very low incomes that this group has in Australia, a result of high levels of unemployment and reliance on unemployment benefits. Nevertheless, despite their low incomes, the proportion remitting is high and the amounts remitted are a significant proportion of their incomes.

Another issue is that until recently, Australia eschewed temporary worker migration and focused almost totally on permanent settlement of families in migration. This may have had a dampening impact on remittances (Ryan 2005). High levels of remittances tend to be associated with temporary migration, whereby migrants leave their families behind in the

Table 9.10 Survey of Horn of Africa Settlers in Melbourne and Adelaide: Income and Remittances in A\$, 2008

Annual Income	Number	Percent Not Remitting	Average Annual Remittance (A\$)
Less than \$10,000	105	74.2	1,500
10,000–20,000	70	91.4	4,039
20,001–30,000	51	90.2	3,815
30,001–40,000	60	96.7	3,543
40,001–50,000	30	96.7	3,190
Over 50,000	20	90.0	4,083

Source: Wege 2010.

origin country and those families are often almost totally dependent on remittances for their day-to-day existence. For most of the post–World War II period, Australia's immigration program favored permanent settlement, and the family migration section of the migration program facilitated the "reunion" of families in Australia. Ryan (2005) argues that this is the main explanation for remittances out of Australia being low. He shows how Australia's Balance of Payments on Current Account includes remittances in an "Other Sectors" item. This item has been around \$3.5 billion in recent years (World Bank). Given that Australia now hosts a significant influx of temporary skilled workers and that a minority are from southern nations (Hugo 2003),[10] the north–south flow of remittances from Australia would seem to be limited.

In the Pacific, particularly the Polynesian countries, remittances are a more significant factor in local economies than in any other part of the world (Bertram and Watters 1985). As Crocombe (2001: 66) points out, "Of the two million Polynesians in the world, only 14 per cent live in independent Polynesian nations." Remittances contributed 20 percent of Tonga's GDP and 25 percent of Samoa's in 2010 (World Bank 2011). It is apparent too that remittances are increasingly important in Fiji's economy. In the Melanesian Pacific countries there is little emigration, although internal mobility levels are high. The potential for future high levels of worker outmigration from nations like Papua New Guinea is high because of high levels of unemployment and underemployment coupled with significant population growth. Remittances from Australia to southern countries have undoubtedly been significant, although the nature of migration to Australia, both in terms of its historical emphasis on family settlement and more recently on skilled temporary migration, has not been conducive to the initiation of large flows, many of which go directly to impoverished families in migrant-origin nations. However, in line with a total focus in Australia on international migration impact on Australia and a lack of intent in the effort on origin countries, there are no reliable representative data available on remittances. Nevertheless there is new concern regarding migration's impact on the development in origin countries (within both the Development Assistance Agency and the Department of Immigration and Citizenship).

OTHER DEVELOPMENT-RELATED FUNCTIONS FOR THE DIASPORA

In Australia the recent emergence of the discussion on migration and development has focused strongly on remittances. However, it is recognized that expatriates can have other beneficial impacts on development in their home countries. The key to this is the development of network linkages between the expatriate community and the homeland. This often involves organization of diaspora communities at the destination and interaction with family and others in the homeland, a phenomenon with a long history but that is greatly facilitated by modern information and communication technology (Hugo 2004b). Since the 1970s Australia has espoused a policy of multiculturalism, which, among other things, stipulated that "every person should be able to maintain his or her culture without prejudice or disadvantage" (Jupp 2002:87).

Although Australian multiculturalism policy places less emphasis on cultural maintenance than that in Canada (Jupp 2002:84), this has meant that the development of diaspora organizations has not been hindered and in some cases has been enhanced by government policy. Until recently immigrants were required to renounce their prior citizenship before they could become Australian citizens. Dual citizenship was introduced in 2002 largely due to lobbying by Australian expatriates (Hugo 2004b).

There is growing evidence that some diasporas often continue to have strong family and professional linkages with their homelands and that these can have beneficial development impacts (Newland and Patrick 2004). It should be noted, however, that all diasporas do not have such effects or might not be interested in having such linkages. Nevertheless it is relevant that Australia has strong expatriate communities from all Asia-Pacific nations, as is shown in Figure 9.7. In the United Kingdom, the

Department for International Development undertook in 2007 to "build on the skills and talents of migrants and other ethnic minorities within the U.K. to promote the development of their countries of origin" (DFID 2007:23; DFID 1997). These activities need to be considered with a view to the possibility of some such initiatives being undertaken in the Australian context since Figure 9.7 shows there are substantial Australian-based communities of Asia-Pacific origin groups.

The extent to which migrants have formed groups in Australia through residential concentration, development of ethnic- or nationality-based media, formation of formal ethnic or nationality organizations, and maintaining linkages with home nations has varied considerably between origin groups. There are no Australian government policies or programs seeking to enhance or support linkages between expatriates and their homelands, although destination countries like the Philippines have a suite of organizations and structures to maintain and sustain linkages with their diaspora. There is little research available regarding the role of those linkages in the development of origin communities and nations.

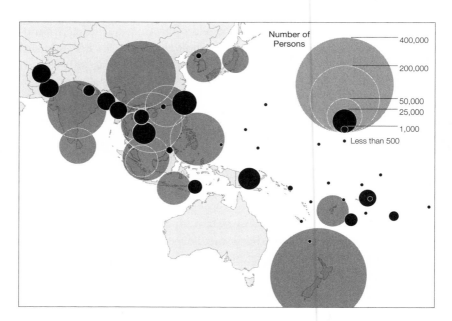

Figure 9.7   Persons living in Australia born in the Asia-Pacific by country of birth, 2006.

Source: ABS 2006 Census.

Undoubtedly Australia's Chinese and Vietnamese communities have been substantial contributors to the massive influx of investment into their homelands in recent years. The increased availability of goods from Asia in Australia may in small part be associated with the bridgehead markets established by expatriate communities and their involvement in trade. There have been a number of nationality-based chambers of commerce developed in Australia to facilitate trade between Australian and Pacific nations in which the diaspora has played a role. Undoubtedly the development of diaspora communities has encouraged the flow of people (mainly tourists and businesspeople) between their homelands and Australia.

One issue about which little is known is the role of the diaspora in knowledge transfer and the spread of ideas. However, as discussed by Levitt and Lamba-Nieves (this volume), social remittances and the transfer of culture shape how developmental outcomes are understood and indirectly shape how these outcomes, through the implementation of public policies, will be achieved. There is considerable interest in the emergence of networks of academics, researchers, scientists, and technologists in the spread of knowledge and in countries maintaining a competitive edge in global innovation and trade (Meyer and Brown 1999; Hugo 2008a). The potential for such channels of communication to facilitate knowledge transfer is substantial. There has been increasing recognition in the literature that the existence of a diaspora of researchers, scientists, and technologists can provide a "brain gain option," providing avenues for technology transfers, information spread, and training for people in their home country so that these professionals need not return to their home nation (Barré et al. 2003; Meyer et al. 1997, 2001; Meyer 2001a, 2001b). China has used administrative means to encourage such networking (Biao 2006). The potential of "virtual return" through the use of modern information and communication technology has led to a significant change in China's official policy toward the high-skill people in its diaspora. Wescott (2005) has pointed out that the policy has changed from *huiuo fuw* (return and serve the motherland) to *weiguo fuwu* (serve the motherland) in recognition of the increasing ability of the diaspora to deliver benefits to the homeland while abroad.

RETURN MIGRATION

One of the ways the effects of brain drain can be negated is when the outflow of skilled workers from less developed countries is circular and not

permanent. Hence removal of barriers to return migration at both destination and origin is important. This includes not only making available a
range of both permanent and temporary migration options to immigrants
but also ensuring the portability of benefits and savings accumulated
while the migrants are in the destination. Indeed one could argue that a
circular pattern of south–north migration could have significant advantages not only to the southern nations but also to the northern. One of the
major areas of concern in such nations is the aging of their populations. It
is apparent from research on the effect of migration on aging that its impact
is marginal because migrants themselves age and contribute to the aging
problem (United Nations 2000). However, if a pattern of circular migration is established, the migrant workforce is maintained with a young profile because the return outflow of older workers is replaced by an inflow of
younger workers.

In an immigration nation such as Australia, it is often overlooked that
there is a substantial element of return migration among settlers. It is estimated (Hugo 1994; Hugo et al. 2001) that up to a quarter of all settlers to
Australia in the postwar period have subsequently emigrated from Australia, although the rates of return vary greatly among birthplace groups.
It was shown earlier that the ratio of permanent departures to permanent
arrivals for several Asian- and Pacific-born settler migrants coming to
Australia is considerable. However, there are some important exceptions;
there is generally a low rate of return migration among immigrants to
Australia from the poorest country origins. On the other hand, there is a
very high rate of return among immigrants from more developed countries like New Zealand, the United States, Canada, Japan, and the United
Kingdom (Hugo 1994; Hugo et al. 2001). It is also a consistent finding in
Australia that return rates are lowest among settlers who come under the
refugee-humanitarian criteria. Another consistent pattern is that patterns
of onward migration are greatest for skilled persons and least for unskilled.
The meanings of these findings for development impacts in origins need
to be fully explored.

Australia does not have a policy of encouraging skilled settlers from
less developed nations to return to their home nation. Indeed the raison
d'être of Australia's postwar migration policy, at least until the mid-
1990s, was to eschew "guest worker" migration, and the emphasis was
exclusively on permanent settlement. In the 1960s, 1970s, and 1980s there
was some concern among Australian immigration officials at what was

seen as a significant "settler loss" (Hugo 1994). The fact that up to a quarter of settlers to Australia eventually left the country was seen by some as a failure of the immigration settlement system, although many (especially those who are highly skilled) never had any intention of settling permanently in Australia. Up to the early 1990s there was a substantial investment of government resources into "postarrival services" to facilitate the adjustment of migrants and to reduce the chance that they would return to their home nation (Jupp 2002). Hence it would take a substantial conceptual leap for the Australian government to develop policies to encourage return migration of skilled settlers to their home country.

A DEVELOPMENT-SENSITIVE MIGRATION POLICY FOR AUSTRALIA?

Australia has been a world leader in the development and management of migration policies that are not discriminatory along religious, ethnic, national, or racial lines and that have a mix of humanitarian, economic, and family elements. While these policies have had an important humanitarian component and recognized national responsibilities to the international refugee problem, they have been developed with Australian national interests (especially labor interests) being the overwhelming consideration (Ryan 2005; Hugo 2005). The new thinking on international migration and development, however, suggests that it is possible to develop immigration policies in migration destinations that have win-win-win outcomes for the destination country, the migrants themselves, and the origin communities. Injecting an element of development sensitivity into destination-country policies need not require the sacrifice of any gains the country experiences from migration or of the autonomy of that country. This presents a major challenge to the international community in a public policy arena that is already highly sensitive.

The implication of the contemporary discourse on migration and development (United Nations 2006a) is that there needs to be a conceptual change among migration policymakers not only in origin countries but also in destinations if the potential for win-win-win is to be realized. From the perspective of a destination country like Australia, what would be involved in a *development-sensitive migration policy?* To begin with, such a policy should *not* involve:

- Any loss of national sovereignty and/or reduction in control over who can enter or settle in Australia.
- Any sacrifice of the undoubted benefits of international migration to Australian economy, society, and culture.

Can Australia develop effective policies to assist in migration from Asia and the Pacific in order to play a positive role in development and poverty reduction without any loss of the gains being delivered by current immigration policy? What are the elements in a destination-country immigration policy that can deliver benefits to an origin country? Such questions are being increasingly raised in Europe and North America (DFID 2007), but there are a number of elements that can be put forward in a preliminary way:

- Fundamentally it involves examining and considering the benefits and impacts of a particular migration policy, not only from the perspective of the destination country but also from that of the origin countries.
- One consideration relates to issues of brain drain, especially that of medical workers. The potential for such elements as codes of practice or providing medical training development assistance to origin areas needs to be considered in a pragmatic and realistic way. It needs to be recognized that not all skilled emigration is negative in its effects on low-income countries, but where this is the case, effective, workable ways of counterbalancing negative effects need to be considered. Undoubtedly some coordination of migration and development assistance policy in education and training needs to be investigated.
- Another consideration relates to circular migration. Australia has developed one of the most effective temporary migration programs in the world for skilled and recently for agricultural workers (Khoo et al. 2003). Although there have been abuses of the program, it has overwhelmingly had a positive impact in Australia (Khoo et al. 2003). Only time will tell if the newly minted seasonal worker program for the agricultural sector is equally efficient.

Seasonal worker programs in Australia need to be comprehensively and authoritatively investigated. It needs to be established whether there are real sectoral labor shortages for unskilled or semiskilled workers who do not meet the criteria for temporary entry or permanent settlement. If so, in what areas? Moreover this analysis should not be confined to the contemporary situation but should be projected over the next two decades in light of the aging workforce and structural changes in the Australian economy. It has been shown, for example (Hugo 2007), that Australia faces an increase in the number of paid care workers of 3 percent per annum between 2001 and 2011 and 3.2 and 3.9 percent per annum over the next two decades. In all, over the next three decades there will be an extra 69,954 workers needed in the residential area and 136,457 in the nonresidential area. This investigation needs to look at the *past* experience of temporary labor migration schemes but also at the potential for Australia to develop best practices in such schemes using all of the tools available in migration management and governance in the twenty-first century. The question needs to be asked whether all unskilled temporary labor migration is bad, or whether it is the way such schemes have been managed in the past that has caused the negative effects. The fact is that such schemes are often beneficial to the migrants and their families.

As has already been discussed, consideration needs to be given to how positive diaspora linkages with home nations can be facilitated. This would involve examining and perhaps revising dual citizenship laws, portability of entitlements, facilitating joint activities in business and research, involving the migrant diasporas in planning the effective delivery of development assistance in the origin countries, as well as many other initiatives. Consideration should also be given to whether Australia should extend its policy of multiculturalism to encourage dual nationality so that immigrants from low-income countries are encouraged to be fully involved with their home country, not just maintaining their culture, language, and heritage. Indeed their participation in development of their origin nations could be encouraged.

With respect to remittances, the World Bank (2006; Terry and Wilson 2005) is placing considerable emphasis on the development of policies to maximize the amount of money remitted by migrants to their home area and the effective capturing of these resources to facilitate poverty reduction and development at home. There would seem to be potential for Australia to play a role in this effort in the Asia-Pacific region. In cooperation with other multilateral agencies and partner governments Australia could be encouraged to:

- Improve access to safe, fair, transparent remittance service providers.
- Reduce the excessive rent-taking in remittances and maximize the amount received by the recipient.

- Link remittances to other mainstream financial services (banks, etc.) so that senders and receivers gain access to a wider range of such services.
- Develop ways of increasing the effectiveness of remittances in poverty reduction and development.

CONCLUSION

The involvement of development-assistance agencies in high-income nations in migration and development initiatives is a new phenomenon (DFID 2007:1). However, the growing evidence of the positive role that migration can and does play in the reduction of poverty and facilitation of economic and social development (World Bank 2006) has meant that multilateral and national development agencies are now seriously considering how they can direct resources to "increase the benefits and reduce the risks of migration for poor people" (DFID 2007:1) and for people in low-income countries. It is necessary, however, to make a few cautionary remarks:

- Migration cannot be seen as a substitute for good governance and the development of a sound economic development policy within Asia-Pacific countries. Its role is purely subsidiary and facilitating in the development process.
- Migration is a sensitive issue in Asia and the Pacific (as it is elsewhere), and there are real sensitivities about the involvement of foreign nations in matters relating to the movement of people into countries. Over a long period this has been a barrier to developing meaningful dialogue between pairs of sending and receiving countries in the region.
- In the Australian context, migration issues have been addressed by a single government department (currently the Department of Immigration and Citizenship) for almost the entire postwar period. The DIC has developed a substantial body of experience and capacity in migration, but that experience has not related at all to the development impact of migration on origin economies. Formulation of more development-sensitive migration policies would involve partnership with a wider range of government institutions, especially the Development Assistance Agency.
- Consideration of migration and development initiatives involves, potentially at least, activities not only in low-income nations but also in destination countries, which differentiates these from most development assistance programs.

Nevertheless three basic points also need to be made:

- The movement of people has increased, and is increasing, in Asia and the Pacific.
- The weight of empirical evidence is that this mobility can potentially be harnessed to facilitate and assist in poverty reduction and positive developmental outcomes, although it is not a substitute for good governance and sound economic policy.
- Australia is better placed than almost any other high-income nation to provide development assistance relating to migration because of its long experience with migration and its highly developed knowledge of migration, migration policy, and management and their impacts.

Australia is an important destination for both permanent and temporary migration from low-income Asian and Pacific nations. Like most destination nations, its immigration policy is overwhelmingly formulated in terms of its own national interest, which in the past has involved little or no consideration of the impact of migration on origin nations. This may change, however, partly because of the global discussion on the migration-development nexus but also because it increasingly can be seen as being within Australia's national interest to do so. Since September 11 there has been a rethinking of security considerations in Australia as there has been elsewhere in the world. This has involved a reevaluation of the nation's relationship with neighboring nations and the realization that enhancing the security, stability, and well-being of those nations is fundamental to Australia's security. There have been significant increases in investment, capacity building, and strategic interest in those countries. Hence, whereas in the past migration and development considerations may have been minor elements in the formulation of migration policy and practice, this may well change in the future.

At present, however, it would take a substantial conceptual leap for destination governments like Australia to factor in the impacts in origin countries as a major element shaping immigration and settlement policy. Migration to Australia is not the answer to remedying low development levels in origin nations, but it can potentially contribute to some improvement of the situation in origin areas; however, it will take policy intervention to maximize such impacts. At the very least, there needs to be development of a more substantial evidence base on which to consider policy formulation in this area. Moreover, if recommendations are to be considered by government, then the implications of migration and development policy for the national interest at the destination needs to be considered. In the post–September 11 world it could be argued, for example, that the Australian national interest would be served if neighboring countries are stable and secure and have populations whose well-being is improving. To the extent that migration can play a role in achieving this it needs to be seen as part of this effort. It is probable that achievements in this area will be slow and incremental rather than massive and dramatic, as win-win-win scenarios can be formulated that enhance the well-being of migrants and their families, serve the labor market needs of Australia, and have a net positive development effect in the home country.

REFERENCES

Adams, R. H. 2003. "International Migration, Remittances, and the Brain Drain: A Study of 24 Labor-Exporting Countries." World Bank Policy Research Working Paper 2069, June.

Asian Development Bank. 2004. "Developing the Diaspora." Paper presented at Third Co-ordination Meeting on International Migration, Population Division, Department of Economic and Social Affairs, United Nations Secretariat, New York, October 27–28.

Australia Bureau of Statistics (ABS). "Population Census." Canberra, 2006.

Australian Institute of Health and Welfare. 2003. "Health and Community Services Labour Force 2001." National Health Labour Force Series No. 27, AIHW, Canberra.

Australian Senate Standing Committee on Employment, Workforce Relations and Employment. 2006. *Perspectives on the Future of the Harvest Labour Force*. Canberra: Senate Printing Unit, Department of the Senate, Parliament House.

Barré, R., V. Hernandez, J.-B. Meyer, and D. Vinck. 2003. *Diasporas Scientifiques /Scientific Diasporas*. Paris: IRD Editions.

Bertram, G., and Watters, R. F. 1985. "The MIRAB Economy in South Pacific Microstates." *Pacific Viewpoint*, 26, no. 3: 497–519.

Biao, X. 2004. "Indian Information Technology Professionals' World System: The Nation and the Transition in Individuals' Migration Strategies." In *State/Nation /Transnation: Perspectives on Transnationalism in the Asia/Pacific*, edited by B. S. A. Yeoh and K. Willis. London: Routledge.

——. 2006. "Towards Sustainable 'Brain Circulation': What India and China Can Learn from Each Other." Paper presented at the International Conference on Population and Development in Asia: Critical Issues for a Sustainable Future, Phuket, Thailand, 20–22 March.

Bowen, C. 2008. "Visa for Pacific Island Seasonal Worker Scheme." September 23. Accessed at http://www.minister.immi.gov.au/media/media-releases/2008/ceo8090.htm.

Brown, R. P. C. 2008. "Migration, Remittances and Human Development: Impacts on Some MDG Goals." Paper prepared for the UNDP/World Bank Meeting, Sydney, November 3–4.

Castles, S. 2003. "Migrant Settlement, Transnational Communities and State Region." In *Migration in the Asia Pacific: Population, Settlement and Citizenship Issues*, edited by R. I. C. Hawksley and S. Castles. Cheltenham: Edward Elgar.

Castles, S., and M. J. Miller. 2003. *The Age of Migration*. 3rd ed. London: Macmillan.

Cobb-Clark, D. A., and S. E. Khoo. 2006. *Public Policy and Immigrant Settlement*. Cheltenham: Edward Elgar.

Connell, J. 2003. "Losing Ground? Tuvalu, the Greenhouse Effect and the Garbage Can." *Asia Pacific Viewpoint* 44, no. 2.

Connell, J., and R. P. C. Brown. 1995. "Migration and Remittances in the South Pacific: Towards New Perspectives." *Asian and Pacific Migration Journal* 4, no. 1: 1–33.

——. 2004. "The Remittances of Migrant Tongan and Samoan Nurses from Australia." *Human Resources for Health* 2, no. 2: 1–21.

Crocombe, R. 2001. *The South Pacific 2001*. Fiji: Institute of Pacific Studies, University of the South Pacific.

Department for International Development (DFID). 1997. "Eliminating World Poverty: A Challenge for the 21st Century." White Paper on International Development. London, United Kingdom.

——. 2007. "Moving out of Poverty—Making Migration Work Better for Poor People," Policy Paper, DFID, London.

Department of Immigration and Multicultural Affairs (DIMIA). 2007. "Population Flows: Immigration Aspects." Canberra: Australian Government Publishing Service.

Dumont, J., and G. Lemaitre. 2005. "Counting Immigrants and Expatriates in OECD Countries: A New Perspective." Paper prepared for the Conference on Competing for Global Talent, Singapore Management University, January 13–14.

Fiji National Planning Office. 2005. "Key Issues of Labour Market Operations." Accessed at http://www.fijichris.gov.fj.

Fong, P. E. 2006. "Foreign Talent and Development in Singapore." In *Competing for Global Talent*, edited by C. Kuptsch and Pang Eng Fong. Geneva: International Labour Organization.

Global Commission on International Migration (GCIM). 2005. *Migration in an Interconnected World: New Directions for Action*. Geneva: GCIM.

Hammond, J., and J. Connell. 2008. "The New Blackbirds? Vanuatu Guestworkers in New Zealand." Unpublished manuscript.

Hugo, G. J. 1990. "Adaptation of Vietnamese in Australia: An Assessment Based on 1986 Census Results." *Southeast Asian Journal of Social Sciences* 18, no. 1: 182–210.

——. 1994. *The Economic Implications of Emigration from Australia*. Canberra: Australian Government Publishing Service.

——. 2003. "Migration and Development: A Perspective from Asia." *IOM Migration Research Series* 14: 1–45.

——. 2004a. "Australia's Most Recent Immigrants." Australian Census Analytic Program Report 2053.0. Canberra: Australian Bureau of Statistics.

——. 2004b. "The Longitudinal Survey of Immigrants to Australia (LSIA)." Paper prepared for IRSS Workshop on Longitudinal Surveys and Cross Cultural Survey Design, Home Office, London, May 11–12.

——. 2004c. "Some Dimensions of Australia's Diaspora." Paper prepared for the Second International Population Geographies Conference, St. Andrews, Scotland, August 11–14.

——. 2005. "The New International Migration in Asia: Challenges for Population Research." *Asian Population Studies* 1, no. 1: 93–120.

——. 2008a. "The Indian and Chinese Academic Diaspora in Australia: A Comparison." Paper prepared for Twentieth Conference of the International Association of Historians of Asia, Jawaharlal Nehru University, New Delhi, November 16.

——. 2008b. "Some Emerging Demographic Issues on Australia's Teaching Academic Workforce." *Higher Education Policy* 18, no. 3: 207–30.

Hugo, G. J., D. Rudd, and K. Harris. 2001. *Emigration from Australia: Economic Implications*. Committee for Economic Development of Australia (CEDA). Information Paper No. 77. Melbourne: CEDA.

——. 2003. "Australia's Diaspora: Its Size, Nature and Policy Implications." (CEDA). Information Paper No. 80. Melbourne: CEDA.

Hugo, G. J., and G. Tan. 2007. "Transnational Education, Migration and Regional Development: The Case of South Australia." Paper presented to Workshop on Transnational Education and Migration in Globalising Cities, Asian Research Institute, National University of Singapore, July 3–4.

——. 2007. "Contextualising the 'Crisis in Aged Care' in Australia: A Demographic Perspective." *Australian Journal of Social Issues* 42, no. 2: 169–82.

Hugo, G. J., and S. Young, eds. 2008. *Labour Mobility in the Asia-Pacific Region*. Singapore: Institute of Southeast Asian Studies.

Iguchi, Y. 2004. "International Migration and Labor Market in Japan: Growing Intra-Regional Trade, Investment and Migration." Paper presented at workshop on International Migration and Labour Market in Asia organized by the Japan Institute for Labour Policy and Training, Tokyo, February 5–6.

——. 2008. "Declining Population, Structural Change in the Labor Market and Migration Policy in Japan." Paper presented at the Conference on Demographic Change and International Labor Mobility in the Asia Pacific Region: Implications for Business and Cooperation, Seoul, March 25–27.

Johnson, B., and S. Sedaca. 2004. *Diasporas, Emigrés and Development: Economic Linkages and Programmatic Responses*. Special Study of the U.S. Agency for International Development, Carana Corporation, March.

Jupp, J. 2002. *From White Australia to Woomera: The Story of Australian Immigration*. Cambridge: Cambridge University Press.

Khoo, S. E., C. Voigt-Graf, G. Hugo, and P. McDonald. 2003. "Temporary Skilled Migration to Australia: The 457 Visa Sub-Class." *People and Place* 11, no. 4: 27–40.

Ley, D., and A. Kobayashi. 2005. "Back to Hong Kong: Return Migration or Transnational Sojourn?" *Global Networks* 5: 111–28.

Maclellan, N. 2008. "Workers for all Seasons? Issues from New Zealand's Recognised Seasonal Employer (RSE) Program." Institute for Social Research, Swinburn University of Technology Report, Hawthorn, Australia.

Maclellan, N., and P. Mares. 2006. "Remittances and Labour Mobility in the Pacific." Working paper on seasonal work programs in Australia for Pacific Islanders, Institute for Social Research, Swinburne University of Technology, Victoria.

Meyer, J., and M. Brown. 1999. "Scientific Diaspora: A New Approach to the Brain Drain." World Conference on Science Discussion Paper No. 41, UNESCO–ICSU, Budapest, Hungary, June 26–July 1.

Meyer, J. B. 2001a. "Network Approach versus Brain Drain: Lessons from the Diaspora." *International Migration* 39, no. 5: 91–110.

——. 2001b. "Les diasporas de la Connaissance: Atout Inédit de la Compétitivité du Sud." *La Revue Internationale et Stratégique* 55: 69–76.

Meyer, J. B., J. Charum, D. Bernal, J. Gaillard, J. Garnes, J. Leon, A. Montenegro, A. Morales, N. Narvaez-Berthelemot, L. Stella-Parrado, and B. Schlemmer. 1997. "Turning Brain Drain into Brain Gain: The Colombian Experience of the Diaspora Option." *Science, Technology and Society* 2, no. 2: 285–317.

Millbank, A. 2006. "A Seasonal Guest-Worker Program for Australia?" Research Brief No. 16, Canberra: Parliamentary Library.

National Farmers' Federation. 2008. "Workforce from Abroad Employment Scheme Proposed Pilot Programme." April, Canberra, Australia.

National Harvest Trail Working Group. 2008. "Harvesting Australia." Report of the National Harvest Trail Working Group, Canberra.

Newland, K., and E. Patrick. 2004. *Beyond Remittances: The Role of Diaspora in Poverty Reduction in Their Countries of Origin*. Washington, D.C.: Migration Policy Institute.

Osborne, D. 2004. "Analysing Traveller Movement Patterns: Stated Intentions and Subsequent Behaviour." *People and Place* 12, no. 4: 38–41.

Pe-Pua, R., C. Mitchell, R. Iredale, and S. Castles. 1996. "Astronaut Families and Parachute Children: The Cycle of Migration Between Hong Kong and Australia." Canberra: AGPS.

Ramasamy, S., V. Krishnan, and C. Bedford. 2008. "The Recognised Seasonal Employer Policy: Seeking the Elusive Triple Wins for Development through International Migration." *Pacific Economic Bulletin* 23, no. 3: 171–86.

Reid, S. 2002. "Health Professional Migration: A Call to Action." Paper presented at ARRWAG National Conference, Adelaide, April 24.

Richardson, S., F. Robertson, and D. Ilsley. 2001. "The Labour Force Experience of New Migrants." Department of Immigration and Multicultural Affairs Report. Canberra: Department of Immigration and Multicultural Affairs.

Ryan, J. F. 2005. "Migration, Remittances and Economic Development. Case Study: Australia." Paper presented at Workshop on International Migration and Labour Markets in Asia, Japan Institute for Labour Policy and Training, Tokyo, January 20–21.

Schachter, J. P. 2006. "The Potential of Using Household Surveys to Improve the Measurement of International Migrant Remittance Data." Joint UN Commission for Europe (UNECE)/Eurostat Working Paper 8. Edinburgh. Accessed at http:///www.unece.org/stats/documents/ece/ces/ge.10/2006/wp.8.e.doc.

Scott, M. L., A. Whelan, J. Dewdney, and A. B. Zwi. 2004. "'Brian Drain' or Ethical Recruitment? Solving Health Workforce Shortages with Professionals from Developing Countries." *Medical Journal of Australia* 180: 174–76.

Skeldon, R. 1994. "Turning Points in Labor Migration: The Case of Hong Kong." *Asian and Pacific Migration Journal* 3, no. 1: 93–118.

Stark, O., and C. S. Fan. 2007. "Losses and Gains to Developing Countries from the Migration of Educated Workers: An Overview of Recent Research and New Reflections." Center for Development Research, ZEF Discussion Paper No. 116. Bonn, Germany.

Terry, D. F., and S. R. Wilson, eds. 2005. *Beyond Small Change: Making Migrant Remittances Count.* Washington, D.C.: Inter-American Development Bank.

U.K. House of Commons. 2004. *Migration and Development: How to Make Migration Work for Poverty Reduction.* London: Stationery Office.

United Nations. 2000. *Replacement Migration: Is It a Solution to Declining and Ageing Populations?* New York: United Nations.

United Nations. 2005. *Protocol to Prevent, Suppress and Punish Trafficking in Persons, Especially Women and Children.* Supplement to the UN Convention Against Transnational Organised Crime, Annex II, United Nations Document A/55/383.

——. 2006a. "International Migration and Development: Report of the Secretary-General." Sixtieth session, Globalization and Interdependence: International Migration and Development, May 18.

——. 2006b. *World Population Policies 2005.* New York: United Nations.

Vertovec, S. 2004. "Migrant Transnationalism and Modes of Transformation." *International Migration Review* 38, no. 3: 970–1001.

Viviani, N. 1996. *The Indochinese in Australia 1975–1995: From Burnt Boats to Barbecues.* Melbourne: Oxford University Press.

Voigt-Graf, C. 2003. "Fijian Teachers on the Move: Causes, Implications and Policies." *Asia Pacific Viewpoint* 44, no. 2: 163–74.

——. 2007. "Pacific Islanders and the Rim: Linked by Migration." *Asian and Pacific Migration Journal* 16, no. 2: 143–56.

Voigt-Graf, C., R. Iredale, and S. E. Khoo. 2007. "Teaching at Home or Overseas: Teacher Migration from Fiji and the Cook Islands." *Asian and Pacific Migration Journal*, 16, no. 2: 199–223.

Wege, M. 2010. "Horn of Africa Migrants in Adelaide and Melbourne: An Emerging Diaspora." Ph.D. dissertation, University of Adelaide.

Wescott, C. 2005. "Promoting Exchanges Through Diasporas." Paper presented at the G-20 Workshop on Demographic Challenges and Migration, Sydney, August 27–28.

World Bank. 2006. *Global Economic Prospects 2006: Economic Implications of Remittances and Migration.* Washington, D.C.: World Bank.

——. 2011. *Migration and Remittances Factbook.* Washington, D.C.: World Bank.

Zweig, D., and D. Han. 2007. "Chinese Research Students and Scholars in Japan: The Impact on Sino-Japanese Relations." Japan External Trade Organization Report. Tokyo.

CHAPTER 10

Asian Migration to the United States

DEVELOPMENT IMPLICATIONS FOR ASIA

Philip Martin

This chapter reviews the consequences of Asian migration to the United States for the development of the migrants' countries of origin. There are three distinct types of Asian migrants: students and professionals with temporary and immigrant visas in North America, Europe, and Oceania; low-skilled migrant workers, most of whom remain in Asia; and a diverse mix of family unification, economic, refugee, and other migrants, some of whom remain in Asia and some of whom leave the region.

China, India, the Philippines, and Vietnam are the most important Asian sources of migrants and immigrants for the United States and Canada. Each source country has unique attributes. Migration from the Philippines, a former U.S. colony, is well established; only a third of the Filipino-born U.S. residents in 2000 arrived in the 1990s, according to the census.[1] China, the number-two source of Asian migrants to the United States, began sending large number of migrants more recently; almost half of the 1.2 million Chinese in the United States arrived in the 1990s.[2] The third leading Asian source of migrants, India, also began to send migrants recently; 55 percent of the 1 million Indians in the United States in 2000 arrived in the 1990s.[3] The fourth leading Asian source of immigrants, Vietnam, is different; only 45 percent arrived in the 1990s.[4]

It is very hard to determine the effects on the development of their countries of origin caused by the migration to the United States of 1 percent of Filipinos and Vietnamese and 0.1 percent of Chinese and Indians:

1. The Philippines, the major migrant-sending nation in Asia, is the country most dependent on remittances to sustain many families and

communities. Remittances are over 10 percent of GDP, and so many young people educate themselves for overseas jobs that migration may be a substitute for development.

2. Vietnam began sending migrants to the United States as a result of the Vietnam War. First-wave migrants were often well-educated and English-speaking; later waves included large numbers of refugees with little education, followed by family unification migrants. Only 19 percent of Vietnamese adults in the United States in 2000 had a college degree.

3. Most Chinese migrants in the United States arrived after the 1989 Tiananmen Square incident. The result is a bimodal distribution of Chinese migrants: many have relatively little education and live in or near Chinatowns in cities such as New York and San Francisco, while others have high levels of education and are spread throughout the United States.

4. Indian immigrants most closely fit the stereotype of the successful Asian immigrant. Over half of those in the United States in 2000 arrived since 1990, and 70 percent of Indian adults in the United States in 2000 had a college degree.

Migration to the United States may have had the most significant development impacts on the Philippines, where the migration safety valve may have reduced the need to make fundamental economic reforms. Development in Vietnam, China, and India appears to be driven more by internal policy changes than by migration. The exception may be the Indian IT outsourcing industry, which is closely linked to migration.

ASIAN MIGRANTS TO THE UNITED STATES

Between 2000 and 2010, 34 percent of the 11.3 million immigrants admitted to the United States were from Asia; in FY10 alone, around 410,000 of the 1 million immigrants were from Asia (39 percent). Three countries—India, China, and the Philippines—accounted for half of the 3.9 million Asian immigrants between 2000 and 2010 (see Table 10.1).

Migrants from Asia differ from other immigrants in several ways. First, a higher share of Asian immigrants is admitted for employment than for family reunification and other reasons. About 14 percent of all U.S. immigrants and 20 percent of Asian immigrants (including family members) were admitted in FY10 for employment reasons. By contrast, only 8 percent

Table 10.1   Immigration to the United States, 1820–2010 (in Millions)

	Total	Before 1970	Since 1970	Share Since 1970 (%)
World	76.4	44.8	31.6	41
Europe	39.7	35.4	4.3	11
Asia	12.1	1.6	10.5	87
Americas	21.9	7.3	14.6	67
Africa	1.5	0.1	1.4	95
	FY10	**FY00–10**		
Asia	410,209	3,881,044		
China	67,634	659,345		
India	66,185	656,649		
Philippines	56,399	601,862		
Top 3	190,218	1,917,856		
Top 3	46%	49%		

Source: 2010 *Yearbook of Immigration Statistics*, Table 2, http://www.dhs.gov/files/statistics/publications/yearbook.shtm.

of immigrants from Mexico were admitted under the economic and employment priorities for issuing immigrant visas. Second, Asians dominate among some types of temporary workers; 55 percent of the 339,000 H-1B admissions in FY09 (the latest data point available) were Asians.[5] Third, Asians do not loom large in U.S. enforcement data; they accounted for about 2 percent of the foreigners apprehended in FY10, led by 1,900 Chinese, and 5,100 of the 387,000 foreigners formally removed from the United States in FY10, less than 2 percent.

The United States had 40 million foreign-born residents in 2010, according to the American Community Survey (U.S. Census Bureau 2011), including 17.5 million who were naturalized U.S. citizens.[6] The foreign-born differed from the U.S.-born in many characteristics significant for earnings, including average age (forty-one for the foreign-born, thirty-six for the U.S.-born), education (almost a third of foreign-born adults, 32 percent, did not complete high school, vs. 12 percent of the U.S.-born), and language (52 percent of the foreign-born speak English less than very well vs. 2 percent of the U.S.-born).

The U.S. foreign-born population is bimodal in attributes that affect earnings, as illustrated by comparisons between Asian-born and Latin American–born U.S. residents in the 2000 census. The 8.2 million U.S. residents in 2000 who were born in Asia were 26 percent of the 31.1 million foreign-born residents. They had a median age of thirty-nine, 43 percent of Asian adults had a college degree or more, and 48 percent reported speaking English less than very well. By contrast, the 16 million U.S. residents in 2000 who were born in Latin America had a median age of thirty-four, 10 percent of adults had a college degree or more, and 62 percent reported speaking English less than very well.

The United States is not the only destination for Asian migrants. Most immigrants and many temporary workers entering Canada are Asian, and Asians also migrate to Europe and Oceania. Most assertions about the impacts of migration to a particular country on the development of a migrant's country of origin are based on anecdote, especially in countries where migrants are diffused over many destinations.

ASIAN MIGRATION IN PERSPECTIVE

The Asia-Pacific region, home to almost 60 percent of the world's population, is unusual in dealing with migration in three major respects. First, there is a widespread sense inside and outside the region that Asia is different. There are many reasons for this belief, including the Asian economic miracle that catapulted several countries from poorer to richer in a relatively short time (World Bank 1993).[7] This economic success may encourage Asian leaders to believe that they can achieve another success in managing internal and international labor migration to achieve goals that include protecting migrants and local workers, enhancing cooperation between governments in labor-sending and -receiving areas to better manage migration, and ensuring that migration promotes development in labor-sending areas.

Second, there is more diversity in national labor migration policies than in national economic policies. The policy extremes can be approximated by a triangle. Singapore lies at one corner, welcoming professionals to settle with their families, while rotating less-skilled foreign workers in and out of the country. Japan lies at another corner, allowing but not recruiting foreign professionals and preferring ethnic Japanese over Latin American and foreign trainees, students, and unauthorized workers to guest-work with full labor market rights. The Gulf Cooperation Council countries represent a third corner, relying on migrants for over 90 percent of private-sector workers, requiring migrants to have citizen sponsors, and recently announcing policies to cooperate with migrant-sending countries to assure returns. The contrast between the similar investment-intensive and export-led economic policies of East and South East Asian nations, and the dissimilar labor migration policies, is striking.

Third, there appears to be convergence in the migration policies of labor-sending governments in the region. Most want to send more workers abroad, to increase the share of skilled workers among migrants, and to diversify the destinations of migrants to include more European and North American destinations. To achieve these marketing, up-skilling, and diversification goals, many Asian governments have established ministries or agencies to promote and protect migrants, with promotion accomplished by ministerial visits and protection via regulation of private-sector recruiters and predeparture reviews of the contracts they offer to migrants.[8] The evolving migrant promotion and protection infrastructure often assumes that development is a natural or inevitable outgrowth of sending more workers abroad, so that remittances can serve as the major indicator of migration's development impacts.

In 2010 Asian nations had about 61 million migrants, or 29 percent of the 214 million global migrant stock (United Nations 2011). The number of migrants in East Asia doubled between 1975 and 2010, to 6.5 million, but East Asia accounts for only 11 percent of Asia's migrants. The number of migrants declined in Southern and Central Asia, largely because of the shrinking number of persons resettled after wars for independence on the Indian subcontinent, and rose slower in South East Asia than in East Asia. The most rapid growth in migrants has been in Western Asia, where the migrant stock increased by 75 percent between 1990 and 2010 (see Table 10.2).

Migration from Asia to traditional immigration countries was largely blocked until the mid-1960s, when policy reforms in Canada and the

Table 10.2   International Migrant Stock, Asia and World, 1990–2010 (in Millions)

	1990	2000	2010
World	**155.5**	**178.5**	**213.9**
More developed regions	82.4	104.4	127.7
Less developed regions	73.2	74.1	86.2
Asia	**50.9**	**51.9**	**61.3**
Central Asia	6.6	5.2	5.0
East Asia	4.5	5.7	6.5
South East Asia	3.1	4.8	6.7
Southern Asia	20.2	15.7	14.3
Western Asia	16.5	20.5	28.8
Asian World Share	32.7%	29.1%	28.7%

Source: United Nations, Department of Economic and Social Affairs 2011, Trends in International Migrant Stock: Migrants by Sex and Age (United Nations database, POP/DB/MIG/Stock/Rev.2010).

United States eased entry for Asian professionals who were offered jobs by Canadian and U.S. employers. These professionals usually arrived with their families, and most quickly climbed the economic ladder in the receiving countries. Indeed an analysis of immigrant men in the United States in 1970 found that their earnings caught up to those of American men of the same age and education within thirteen years, and then exceeded the earnings of similar U.S.-born men, suggesting that the extra drive and ambition that prompts migration can expand the economy and raise average earnings (Chiswick 1978).[9]

Asian migration to traditional immigration destinations for employment and family unification has made Asian nations a major source of immigrants in Australia, Canada, New Zealand, and the United States. After the Vietnam War ended in 1975, a million South East Asian refugees were resettled in Canada and the United States, forging new migration networks that continue to add immigrants, mostly through family unification. With affluence, there are more Asian students studying in traditional immigration destinations. Many remain to work, and some eventually settle and form or unite families.

However, most international labor migration in Asia involves workers moving from one Asian nation to another for temporary employment. The first significant flows of workers in the Asia-Pacific region began after oil price hikes in 1973–74, when Gulf oil exporters turned to foreign contractors who hired foreign workers to build infrastructure projects such as roads and bridges. As the demand for labor shifted from construction to services and from men to women, there were predictions that Arab migrants would replace Asians for language and cultural reasons (Birks and Sinclair 1980). This did not happen. Indeed, despite efforts to "nationalize" Gulf workforces by prohibiting foreigners from filling some jobs, migrant workers (most from South and South East Asia) continue to fill over 90 percent of private sector jobs in most Gulf Cooperation Council countries.

There is also migration from one nearby Asian country to another, as exemplified by Indonesian workers in Malaysia and Burmese in Thailand. Many of these migrants are unauthorized despite periodic efforts to legalize them. Policy in the countries that send workers abroad and receive migrants is in flux. The Malaysian government announced plans to reduce the employment of migrants, while the Thai government is devolving more responsibility for managing migration onto provincial governments.

MIGRATION AND DEVELOPMENT: THE 3RS

Voluntary migration between poorer and richer areas should be self-stopping, as wages rise in migrant-sending areas and rise more slowly or fall in migrant-receiving areas. Eventually there should be convergence in wages and levels of economic development, reducing the incentive to migrate for economic opportunity.

However, there is no automatic link between more migration and faster development. Migration can accelerate development in countries poised to grow, such as the Southern European countries in the 1960s and 1970s, or perpetuate underdevelopment, as in many island countries today.

The effects of migration on development are often grouped under the 3R channels of recruitment, remittances, and returns. *Recruitment* refers to who goes abroad; international migration is generally most beneficial to developing countries if low-skilled workers who would have been unemployed or underemployed at home are recruited for jobs abroad. *Remittances* are that portion of the monies earned by migrants abroad that are sent home; with higher wages abroad, remittances usually exceed what migrants would have earned at home, so that migration can improve living standards for migrant families and provide additional capital to developing countries. *Returns* focus on what migrants do after a period of employment abroad, asking whether they acquired new skills that are useful for development or whether they return to rest and retire.

RECRUITMENT: VIRTUOUS AND VICIOUS CIRCLES

The impacts of recruitment on development can be captured by extreme examples summarized as virtuous or vicious circles (Martin et al. 2006:chapter 3). Sending Indian IT workers abroad is an oft-cited example of a virtuous migration and development circle, while the emigration of African doctors and nurses is often considered an example of a vicious circle. Virtuous circles are more likely if migrants are abroad for only a short time, they send home significant remittances, and they return with new skills and links to destination countries that increase trade and investment. Vicious circles can be the outcome of migrants fleeing countries perceived to be sinking ships.

The Indian IT case began with multinationals that recognized their talented Indian employees and moved them to subsidiaries outside India.

Eventually Indian firms that specialized in moving IT workers to foreign jobs evolved, especially during the late 1990s IT boom, when there were fears of so-called Y2K problems with computers.

Indians abroad learned what clients there expected, and this experience allowed some to return to India to perform work for foreign clients, creating jobs in India (Kapur 2007). Between 1985 and 2005 the number of IT workers in India ballooned, from 7,000 to over 700,000; Indian IT workers gained a global reputation for high-quality and low-cost work, and the quality of IT services in India improved since there was no reason not to provide the same quality of service to local as to foreign clients, accelerating India's development. The Indian government bolstered the IT industry by reducing barriers to imports of computers, helped to ensure a reliable communications infrastructure, and allowed the state-supported Indian Institutes of Technologies to set quality benchmarks for IT education. This virtuous circle created new jobs in India as well as a new source of export earnings.[10]

The Indian government supported and encouraged this migration. The governments of many African countries, by contrast, highlight that the recruitment of health care professionals by public and private health services by their former colonial rulers has led to a vicious circle in which a lack of health care slows economic development.

In the late 1990s the British National Health Service (NHS) hired more doctors and nurses to reduce patient waiting times, including some from former African colonies. This prompted several African governments to complain that the United Kingdom was recruiting doctors and nurses who had been trained at taxpayer expense, lowering the quality of health care in developing countries strained by AIDS. Some African countries demanded compensation for the recruitment of their health care professionals, and some withheld the final licenses usually needed to find jobs abroad until doctors and nurses trained at government expense completed a period of service, often in a rural area.[11]

These complaints of a health care brain drain led to ethical recruitment initiatives. For example, the U.K. Code of Practice for the International Recruitment of Healthcare Professionals, developed in 2001 and revised in 2004, applicable only to the NHS, asserts that "international recruitment is a sound and legitimate contribution to the development of the healthcare workforce," but advises the NHS not to target developing countries for recruitment of health care personnel "unless there is an explicit government-to-government agreement with the U.K. to support recruitment activities" (Department of Health 2004:7).[12] The World Health Organization at its 63rd World Health Assembly adopted a Global Code of Practice on the International Recruitment of Health Personnel, which establishes and promotes voluntary principles and practices for the ethical recruitment of health care workers and to facilitate the strengthening of health care systems. Like the U.K. Code of Practice, the Global Code discourages governments from active recruitment of health workers from developing countries facing critical shortages of health care personnel.

The health care professional worker migration issue is complex. First, government-set salaries for doctors and nurses have not increased significantly despite the exodus. Second, there are human rights concerns about restricting the right of health care workers to leave a country. Physicians for Human Rights, winner of the Nobel Peace Prize in 1997 for its work to ban land mines, issued a report in July 2004 that called on industrialized nations to reimburse African countries for the loss of health professionals educated at government expense. However, PHR also emphasized that there is a trade-off between the rights of African health professionals to seek a better life abroad and the rights of people in their home countries to decent health care.[13] Clemens (2007) agrees that the interactions of health care deficiencies and migration are complex, but concludes that solutions to health care workforce issues in many African countries lie inside the country. For example, many developing countries do not sufficiently compensate doctors and nurses assigned to rural areas, and some prohibit the establishment of private health care training institutions.

The vicious cycle in which out-migration leads to slower development is an example of brain-drain concerns that have been recognized for decades (Adams 1968). However, there has been no agreement on a global response. Bhagwati (1976) would have migrant-receiving countries compensate migrant-sending developing countries for the cost of the migrants' education, but this proposal has suffered from practical implementation problems, including deciding how to collect extra or normal taxes paid by migrants in industrial countries and how to distribute such compensation to their countries of origin.

In recent years compensation has been downplayed, in part because of the brain-gain via brain-drain theory. The governments of countries that send educated workers abroad "lose" the investment made in their education and may suffer slower growth as a result; this is the classic brain drain. However, the brain-gain via brain-drain theory holds that, because some developing country professionals go abroad and enjoy higher earnings, the average earnings of all professionals in a developing country rise and encourage more young people to go to school (Mountford 1997; Beine et al. 2001). However, not all of those who acquire health care or other professional qualifications will emigrate, for personal and other reasons, so the sending country winds up with more nurses than if it prohibited the recruitment of "essential workers." A moment's reflection suggests that the brain-gain via brain-drain theory is not widely applicable in the contemporary world, with the possible exception of Cuba and North Korea.

The complexity of the brain-drain debate is heightened by the contrast between the mostly African countries demanding compensation for the recruitment of their health care workers and countries such as the Philippines, which has government agencies to promote the out-migration of professionals, including nurses. Most Filipino health care workers who emigrate are trained in private, tuition-charging schools, and most nursing students take out loans to cover the cost of their education. The Filipino experience suggests that changes in policies unrelated to migration, such as how education is financed, may be more important than trying to manage the brain-drain via migration and compensation policies.

The recruitment experiences of most migrant-sending countries lie between the virtuous and vicious migration and development extremes. Indeed governments in migrant-sending countries often have little control over who is selected to fill foreign jobs, since employers abroad normally determine who to hire. Employers want the best worker they can recruit to fill vacant jobs, even if that means an engineer from a low-wage country winds up filling a low-skill job abroad, resulting in "brain waste."

REMITTANCES: SHORTCUT FOR DEVELOPMENT?

Most migrants remit some of their foreign earnings to family and friends at home. During the 1990s, when remittances to developing countries doubled, sending-country governments and development institutions became aware of rising remittances, which often provided the foreign exchange essential to cover balance-of-payments deficits and sustain economic development policies (Ratha 2003). Leaders of major labor-sending countries began to acknowledge the importance of remittances by symbolically welcoming home some returning migrants at Christmas each year, as in the Philippines, or calling migrants "foreign exchange heroes," as did former Mexican president Vicente Fox.

Remittances pose several migration and development challenges. Many national governments as well as international organizations such as the World Bank want to increase remittances, which can be accomplished by sending more workers over national borders and ensuring that they earn, save, and remit. Governments and international organizations want to reduce the costs of sending money through formal channels, which should reduce the use of informal channels for remittances and minimize the opportunity for terrorists to use such channels.

The World Bank reported that global remittances totaled $440 billion in 2010, after a quick recovery to the level in 2008. The top five recipients of remittances are India, which received $55 billion in 2010; China, $51 billion; Mexico, $23 billion; the Philippines, $23 billion; and France, $16 billion. The major sources of remittances were countries with the most migrants: the United States, $48 billion; Saudi Arabia, $26 billion; Switzerland, $20 billion; the Russian Federation, $19 billion; and Germany, $16 billion. In 2010, seventy-two countries received more than $1 billion in remittances, and in twenty-four countries remittances represented 10 percent or more of GDP (Ratha, Aga, and Silwal 2012).[14]

Most migrants are from developing countries, and 74 percent of global remittances went to developing countries; the $325 billion received by developing countries in 2010 was four times the $81 billion they received in 2000 (Ratha, Aga, and Silwal 2012). There are several reasons for rapidly rising remittances, including better reporting after the September 11, 2001, terrorist attacks,[15] lower costs to remit through banks (which are more likely to report remittances), and the depreciation of the dollar, which raises the dollar value of remittances transferred in other currencies (World Bank 2006:xiii).[16]

The major migration and development challenge over the past decade has been to reduce the cost of sending small sums over borders through regulated financial institutions. There are three steps involved in a typical remittance transfer: the migrant pays the remittance to a money transfer firm, such as Western Union, in one country; the money transfer firm instructs its agent in another country to deliver the remittance; and the agent pays the recipient.[17] These three steps are sometimes called the first mile, the intermediary stage, and the last mile, and they involve three major costs. First is the fee paid by the sender, typically $10 to $30 to send the usual $200 remittance. Second is the exchange rate difference, as when dollars are converted to pesos at a rate less favorable than the interbank exchange rate. Third are fees that may be charged to recipients when they collect their funds. (In many cases, remittance pickup points are located in stores or other outlets that encourage recipients to spend some of the money received.) There may also be an interest rate float if there is a time lag between paying and receiving remittances.

The second remittance-related migration and development challenge is to ensure that the spending of remittances accelerates development in migrant-sending areas. Most studies suggest that each $1 in remittances generates a $2 increase in economic activity, as the spending of remittances on housing, education, and health care creates jobs (Taylor and Martin 2001; Yang and Martinez 2006). Most remittances are spent on daily needs, as would be expected because foreign earnings replace money that would have been earned locally. However, remittances often exceed what would have been earned at home, and after basic consumption needs are satisfied, remaining remittances are often used to build or improve housing, educate and provide health care to children, and expand or launch new businesses.

Remittances can speed up development if macroeconomic fundamentals are correct. Sound economic policies give all residents, migrants and nonmigrants, incentives to save and invest (World Bank 2006). One policy question is whether governments should have special policies to encourage migrants to send remittances, such as matching remittances that are contributed to develop migrant areas of origin. Mexico's 3x1 matching program is perhaps the best known. It provides $3 in federal, state, and local funds for each $1 contributed by migrants abroad for improvements in their areas of origin.[18] However, the 3x1 program has limited impacts on development because it is small, reflects migrant priorities that may be different from those of nonmigrants, and reduces funds available for other projects. Mexican migrants contributed $30 million under the 3x1 program in 2010, which was around 0.1 percent of Mexico's $23 billion in remittances. Spending the total $120 million available was sometimes problematic, since migrants may want to improve the local church for weddings and festivals, while nonmigrants may want water and sanitation system improvements. Matching funds come from government development budgets, so migrant contributions effectively "leverage" development funds for purposes that may run counter to the priorities of nonmigrants.

The best way for a migrant-sending country to maximize remittances and their impacts on development is to get the economic fundamentals correct, which means having an economy that is growing, an appropriate exchange rate, and a climate that fosters small investments. Migrants can sometimes have other impacts that speed development, as when they steer investments to, and persuade their (foreign) employers to buy products from, their countries of origin. Migration increases travel and tourism between countries, as well as trade in ethnic foods and goods that migrants became familiar with while abroad.

RETURNS: ENTREPRENEURS OR RETIREES?

The third R in the migration and development equation is *returns*. Migrants who have been abroad can return with new energy, ideas, and entrepreneurial vigor that can accelerate development in their countries of origin. Migrants are generally drawn from the ranks of the risk takers, and a combination of their remittance savings and skills acquired abroad can speed development, as in Southern Europe and Korea. On the other hand, if migrants settle abroad and cut ties to their countries of origin, or if they return only to rest and retire, there may be few development-accelerating impacts, as in many Pacific and Caribbean islands. There is also the possibility of back-and-forth circulation, which under some conditions can contribute to economic growth in both countries. (See, e.g., Hugo in this volume for a discussion of the Asia-Pacific migration to Australia.)

A desirable outcome is migrant-led development, meaning that migrants accelerate development upon their return. Taiwan provides an example. Government policy encouraged out-migration during the 1960s and 1970s and return migration in the 1980s and 1990s. During the 1960s and 1970s, most government educational spending was for primary and secondary education, so Taiwanese often went abroad for university education, and over 90 percent of the graduates remained overseas.[19] When Taiwan's economy began to grow rapidly in the late 1970s, the government established the Hinschu Science-Based Industrial Park to encourage Taiwanese abroad to return by offering financial incentives and subsidized Western-style housing (Luo and Wang 2002). Hinschu, begun in 1980, became a major success by 2000, when over 100,000 workers were employed by three hundred companies, half headed by returned migrants. Many local governments in China have followed a similar strategy of subsidizing the return of migrants to speed economic development.[20]

It is much harder to persuade migrants who have been successful overseas to return and contribute to the development of countries that are not taking off economically. There is often little need for Taiwanese-style return subsidies if a developing country grows rapidly, as is evident from Ireland to China. But if prospects for development at home are uncertain, even subsidies may be insufficient to persuade migrants settled abroad to return. Several international organizations operate return-of-talent programs, offering to cover the cost of travel and housing for professionals settled abroad who return to work in government or educational institutions. However, the contribution of such programs to development appears to be very modest (Keely 1986), since human capital cannot reverse the effects of deficient development policies.

Rising interest in migration and development have prompted more governments to recognize that migrants abroad may be a key to development at home. Many migrant-sending governments have enacted legislation that permits or encourages dual nationality or dual citizenship in an effort to maintain links to citizens abroad. Some researchers believe that, in a globalizing world, dual nationality can be the keystone for "a Diaspora model [of development], which integrates past and present citizens into a web of rights and obligations in the extended community defined with the home country as the center" (Bhagwati 2003).

MIGRATION AND DEVELOPMENT IN ASIA

PHILIPPINES

The Philippines sends more workers abroad each year than any other Asian country. According to the government, there are 83 million Filipinos at home and 8 million abroad.[21] Filipino migrants remitted $1.75 billion a month in 2010, a total of $21 billion that year, equivalent to 12 percent of the country's GDP. In recognition of the importance to the economy of migrants and remittances, the Filipino president welcomes some returning migrants at Christmas in a *Pamaskong Handog sa OFWs* (welcome home overseas foreign workers) ceremony.[22]

Around 1.6 million Filipinos went abroad legally to work in 2010, an average of more than 4,500 a day, the seating capacity of almost eleven 747s; a similar 1.4 million Filipino migrants were deployed in 2009 (POEA 2010). Some 1.1 million were land-based, and 347,150 were sea-based workers, totaling 30 percent of those staffing the world's ships. Most of the land-based migrants, 70 percent, had been abroad before, in jobs ranging from domestic helper to driver to construction worker and in countries from Saudi Arabia to Canada (see Table 10.3).[23]

Table 10.3   Philippine Migrant Deployments in 2006–9

	2010	2009	2008	2007	2006
Total	**1,470,826**	**1,422,586**	**1,236,013**	**1,077,623**	**1,062,567**
Land-based	1,123,676	1,092,162	974,399	811,070	788,070
Rehires	781,710	742,447	597,426	533,098	489,528
Share	70%	68%	61%	66%	62%
Sea-based	347,150	330,424	261,614	266,553	274,497
Destinations					
Saudi Arabia	293,049	291,419	275,933	238,419	223,459
UAE	201,214	196,815	193,810	120,657	99,212
Hong Kong	101,340	100,142	78,345	59,169	96,929
Qatar	87,813	89,290	84,342	56,277	45,795
Singapore	70,251	54,421	41,678	49,431	28,369

Source: POEA 2009.

In 1974 President Ferdinand Marcos issued Decree 442 to ensure "the careful selection of Filipino workers for the overseas labor market to protect the good name of the Philippines abroad." Decree 1412 in 1978 discussed strengthening worker recruitment for local and foreign jobs "to serve national development objectives." The Philippine Overseas Employment Administration (POEA) was created in 1982 to promote the migration of workers and to protect them during recruitment at home and employment abroad.

Over half of the migrants leaving the Philippines are women, and some are vulnerable to abuse in the private households in which they work. In 1995 Flor Contemplacion, a Filipina domestic helper in Singapore, was hanged after killing another Filipina maid and a Singaporean child.[24] President Fidel Ramos was unable to win additional time to investigate the case, prompting the enactment of Republic Act 8042, the so-called Filipino migrant workers' Magna Carta, which obliges the government to take steps to protect migrants abroad.

The POEA sends workers abroad, regulates private recruitment agencies, and checks the contracts that recruiters provide to migrants (www.poea.gov.ph). It had a 295-million peso ($7 million) budget in 2009 and more than five hundred employees, and its costs were around 200 pesos ($5) for each migrant deployed. The POEA directly sent 3,192 workers abroad in 2009; of this figure 2,296 were under its Government Hiring Facility program, 403 were under the Taiwan Special Hiring Program, 210 were under the EPS-Korea Special Hiring Program, and 283 were under the Japan Special Hiring Program (POEA 2009).

Israeli-Lebanon fighting in summer 2006 resulted in the return of Filipina domestic helpers in those countries who complained of mistreatment.[25] The government responded with the "Supermaid" program that, beginning in January 2007, requires Filipina domestic helpers abroad to receive training in emergency health care before departure and to be paid at least $400 a month. Subsequently the number of Filipinas deployed as domestic helpers fell sharply; there were 91,000 newly hired household service workers in 2006 and 48,000 in 2007. In 2010 the figure rose to 96,500 household service works deployed. POEA suspects that some may leave as gardeners or other types of workers not covered by the $400 a month minimum wage, which may prompt a minimum wage for all those going abroad.

The Philippine government believes it is managing labor migration effectively, citing more workers leaving legally and fewer licensed recruitment agencies. (Agencies that violate rules are closed.) There were 1,349 licensed recruiters in 2009, including 980 land-based recruiters and 369 staffing firms that provide seamen to shipping companies. The POEA, which has a hard-to-enter, easy-to-go policy toward recruiters, requires them to post bonds of 2 million pesos ($45,000) and to be jointly liable with foreign employers if the contracts of migrant workers are violated.

Joint liability is a potential best practice that may be useful to protect migrants in other countries. First-time migrants may not know much about the foreign jobs they are leaving to fill, and Philippine law makes Filipino recruiters jointly liable with foreign employers to fulfill the terms of the contracts signed by the foreign employer, the Filipino recruiter, and the migrant. Migrants abroad often have limited access to redress for contract violations, but when they return to the Philippines, they can turn to the POEA for assistance if there were violations of contract terms, and Filipino recruiters must pay judgments against the foreign employer.

The Philippines deployed 50,000 workers to foreign jobs in 1975. The number rose to 500,000 a year in the late 1980s, and today tops the 1-million-a-year target set by the government for the 2004–10 period. The major debate among Filipino economists is whether labor out-migration will be self-stopping, as migrants send home remittances that are spent and invested to fuel economic and job growth, or whether some migration will create conditions that lead to more migration.

Remittances reduce poverty. Adams and Page (2005) find that a 10 percent increase in the share of migrants in a country's population is associated with a 1.9 percent decrease in the share of residents living in poverty, defined as living on less than $1 a day, and that a 10 percent increase in the share of remittances in a country's GDP is associated with a 1.6 percent reduction in poverty nationwide. However, with most remittances accruing to wealthier households, migration does not significantly reduce inequality in the Philippines (Rodriguez 1998).

Indeed, instead of being better off because of remittances, poor nonmigrants may be worse off because of "Dutch disease," as remittances increase the value of the peso and shrink the number of jobs in garment and other export-oriented manufacturing industries. Acosta (2007) finds this result for El Salvador, where remittances reduced the supply of labor and increased the demand for nontradable goods, which in turn increased the value of the currency and reduced jobs in the export sector. The Philippines Central Bank in 2007 pointed to evidence of Dutch disease, including the appreciation of the peso, the loss of jobs in export industries, and the rising price of nontradable compared to tradable goods, including housing.[26]

The social effects of remittances are also uneven. The so-called complacency effect may reduce the work efforts of members of families with a migrant abroad. Pernia (2008) concluded that migration and remittances have very mixed effects on the Philippines, as the "remittance windfall may have a moral hazard effect as the government softens in pursuing policy reform or improving governance while people are lulled into complacency, as appears to be happening in the Philippines" (2008:6). He added, "Labor export cannot be relied upon as a policy for reducing poverty, redressing income inequality and, for that matter, fostering the country's long-run development" (21).

A culture of migration reportedly prompts many children to plan to follow their parents abroad to work and may lessen their interest in education and the local labor market. Labor migration has been called a "civil religion," with teens considering where to go abroad, TV shows exploring the tensions associated with family separation, and the Central Bank displaying remittance numbers on a billboard at Christmas. The evangelist Rick Warren calls Filipino guest workers the Josephs of today, toiling in the homes of modern pharaohs to liberate Filipinos at home.[27]

INDIA

India sends primarily low- and semiskilled workers to the Gulf oil-exporting states. However, according to the 2010 American Community

Survey (U.S. Census Bureau 2011), there were 1.7 million U.S. residents born in India. Their median age was thirty-five, almost 70 percent were college graduates, and 25 percent reported speaking English less than very well.

As in the Philippines, it may be that the relatively small number of Indian migrants in the United States has more development impact in India than the much larger number of Indians in the Gulf States. Migration from India to the Gulf is primarily from southern India; Kerala and Tamil Nedu each contribute 20 percent (see Rajan and Zachariah this volume). However, the development impacts of this migration are mixed. For example, some 1.8 million Kerala residents are abroad, and their remittances of $5 billion a year are equivalent to 20 percent of Kerala state's GDP.[28] About a quarter of remittances to Kerala are spent on education, and educating residents who cannot find jobs locally reportedly spurs emigration, as unemployment in Kerala is almost 20 percent. Kerala is a state of 32 million with a per capita income of $675, below the $730 average for India.

A survey of Indian migrants found that 80 percent learned of foreign jobs from friends and relatives; they paid an average $1,200 to migrate, and a third turned to moneylenders to cover these predeparture costs. Migrants using recruitment agents paid more, an average of $2,000, to cover the cost of the foreign work visa, passport, medical tests, insurance, and airfare. About 60 percent of the jobs held by the Indians in the Gulf paid $200 a month, making recruitment costs equivalent to six to ten months' earnings.

CHINA

There were 1.4 million U.S. residents born in China (excluding Taiwan and Hong Kong), according to the 2010 American Community Survey (U.S. Census Bureau 2011). Their median age was forty-one, 43 percent were college graduates, and 64 percent reported speaking English less than very well.

At least 10 percent of Chinese—some 130 million—are internal migrants, meaning they are living and working away from the place in which they are registered. Most migrants have moved from rural areas in the center and western parts of China to cities and coastal provinces in the east.

The Chinese government introduced the *hukou* household registration system in the 1950s, first to allocate grain and later to regulate internal

migration (Chan and Zhang 1999). As a result, Chinese are generally registered in their place of birth, and it is often difficult to change registration from one place to another. Especially low-skilled migrants may find
it difficult to access government services, ranging from housing to education and health care, as access to public services is generally confined to
the place in which the *hukou* says the individual is registered.

In 1978, before market reforms began, about 70 percent of Chinese
were employed in agriculture, which generated 28 percent of GDP. By
2006 only 43 percent of the 760 million Chinese workers were employed
in agriculture, which generated 12 percent of GDP. Most estimates find
that up to half of the 327 million agricultural workers in China are redun-
dant. However, many "surplus rural workers" are over forty and less attractive to urban employers. In 2006 urban residents in China had an
average income of 10,500 yuan ($1,400), compared with 3,300 yuan ($440)
for those in rural areas.

About 350 million Chinese, a quarter of the population, had urban
*hukou*s in 2008, while 950 million had rural *hukou*s. However, the Ministry of Housing and Urban-Rural Construction reported that 45 percent of
Chinese, about 600 million, lived in cities in 2008, reflecting significant
rural–urban migration. Not all of those who are living in urban places
while registered in rural places are workers; estimates in 2008 ranged
from 150 million to 200 million. The number of rural–urban migrant
workers has been rising; it was about 30 million in 1982, 54 million in 1995,
and 140 million in 2004.

Most of the 110 million workers employed in Chinese manufacturing
are internal rural–urban migrants, as are most of China's construction
workers. About 70 percent of internal migrants are between fifteen and
thirty-five and earn lower wages than urban residents, an average 540 yuan
($80) a month in 2004, compared to 1,350 yuan for registered urban resi-
dents. Remittances from urban to rural China are estimated to exceed
$80 billion a year. With more couples migrating, more children are left
with relatives in rural areas. In 2008 an estimated 58 million children
under seventeen lived in rural areas without either parent.

The Chinese central government has been debating whether to loosen
or abolish the *hukou* system. In January 2008 the National Development
and Reform Commission recommended that the household registration
(hukou) system be ended within five years so that internal Chinese migrants have the same benefits in employment, education, health care, and
housing as local residents. The Commission, which said a "free flow" of

migrants from rural to urban areas would maintain rapid economic growth, estimated that 43 percent of China's 1.3 billion residents live in cities, including 200 million rural–urban migrants.

The most recent review by the Ministry of Public Security in 2005 concluded that local governments would have to extend to migrants the right to housing, education, and health care, which would cost money. The central government recently ordered urban schools to accept migrant children and not charge fees for K–9 education. However, some urban schools levy other fees, prompting some migrant parents not to enroll their children in regular public schools.[29] Cui Chuanyi, a rural development researcher at the State Council, China's Cabinet, said in 2007, "Very few migrants sever their ties to the farm, not because they don't want to move but because their human rights in the cities are not protected" (*Migration News,* 2007).

Some local governments are making it easier for rural–urban migrants. Shenzhen, which has 2.1 million registered residents and 8 million migrant workers, in July 2008 became the first Chinese city to offer "citizenship" to migrants. Residents ages sixteen to sixty who have been living in the area at least thirty days but are registered elsewhere can obtain ten-year residence certificate smart cards that allow them to apply for driving licenses and business visas to visit Hong Kong or Macao. Children of residence certificate card holders will be able to go to local public schools, and their families can apply to live in low-cost public housing.

OTHER ASIAN COUNTRIES

Vietnam is the fourth-largest source of Asian migrants. According to the 2010 American Community Survey (U.S. Census Bureau 2011), there were 1 million U.S. residents born in Vietnam. Their median age was thirty-seven, 19 percent were college graduates, and 70 reported speaking English less than very well.

Like Cubans, Vietnamese arrived in the United States in waves. The first wave was dominated by those who worked with the U.S. military, many of whom had an education and spoke English. Later waves included primarily refugees and family members, many of whom had little education, helping to explain the bimodal character of those born in Vietnam.

Most Vietnamese who migrate to work abroad do not come to the United States. Before 1989 Vietnam had labor cooperation agreements with several Eastern European countries, including East Germany, under which workers were sent abroad to repay debts incurred by the government. Since 1993 Vietnam has allowed and increasingly promoted labor emigration; in 2006 it sent 400,000 migrant workers to forty countries, including 100,000 in Malaysia and 90,000 in Taiwan (Anh Nguyen 2008:4–5).

Vietnamese migrants have some of the highest debts when they go abroad, often exceeding the earnings they expect in the first year of typically three-year contracts. As a result, up to 25 percent run away from the employer to whom they were assigned, since they can earn more as unauthorized workers than as legal workers with debt deductions from their wages. In response, the Vietnamese government has proposed punishing runaways when they return to Vietnam.

Most Vietnamese migrants have three-year contracts, and their expected earnings as well as the cost of migrating vary significantly by destination. Migrants to Malaysia earn the least, $10,800 over three years, while migrants to South Korea earn the most, $30,600 over three years. The costs of migrating abroad are lowest for those going to South Korea, $700, or 2 percent of expected earnings, but Korean employers expect migrants to work up to ten hours a day, and abuse of migrants is reported to be common. Malaysia accepts twice as many Vietnamese migrants as Korea but at wages that are only a third of Korean levels, so that migrants in Malaysia have far lower savings and remittances.

Vietnam had a 5 percent tax on remittances until 1997; when this tax was removed, formal remittances rose (World Bank 2006:93). Like many other countries that send workers abroad, Vietnam allows migrants to import some goods duty-free when they return. In 2006 Vietnam taxed those earning more than 5 million dong ($315) a month but was considering lowering the income threshold to raise more taxes from lower earners, including migrants.

Bangladesh and Indonesia are examples of countries that send large numbers of workers abroad but few to the United States. There were 151,000 Bangladeshi-born U.S. residents according to the 2010 American Community Survey (U.S. Census Bureau 2011), and 90,000 born in Indonesia. Both immigrant groups are young and well educated; the median age of Bangladeshi-born U.S. residents was thirty-three, and 46 percent were college graduates, while the median age of Indonesian-born U.S. residents was thirty-seven, and 46 percent were college graduates.

CONCLUSIONS

Long-distance migration often has a Darwinian quality: the harder it is to migrate to another country, the more human capital is required of those who succeed in entering and settling. It has been harder for Asians to immigrate to the United States than for Latin Americans, and most U.S. residents born in Asia have more human capital than those born in Latin America.

The Philippines, India, and China present three very different cases of migration to the United States and their consequences for development at home. There are an estimated 8 million Filipinos abroad, including 1.8 million in the United States in 2010, the major source of remittances to the Philippines. Philippine-born U.S. residents were slightly older than U.S.-born residents in 2010, a median forty-two versus thirty-six, and relatively well educated: 87 percent of adults were high school graduates and 45 percent were college graduates. Filipinos in the United States are less than 20 percent of the total number of Filipinos abroad, but they account for over half of remittances to the Philippines.[30]

There were 1.4 million Chinese-born U.S. residents in 2000, and over half arrived before 1990. Most had high levels of education: 43 percent of the Chinese adults in the United States in 2000 were college graduates. By contrast, 70 percent of the Indian adults in the United States in 2000 were college graduates, one reason why Indians are more often associated with IT and other industries and occupations requiring high levels of education.

Migration alone will not solve the region's developmental challenges; however, even though there is no automatic link between more migration and faster growth, migration can accelerate development in countries ready to grow. (See the introduction to this volume and Hein de Haas in this volume for a discussion focusing on Morocco.) Virtuous cycles, remittances, and migrants' entrepreneurial activities will have a significant impact on development in their home country only if the conditions exist for migrants to invest their remittances and their human capital. Sound economic policies give migrants and nonmigrants incentives to save and invest, thus increasing countries' developmental potentials.

On the other hand, migration can also perpetuate underdevelopment by reducing the need to make fundamental economic reforms. As remittances pour in, governments may have an incentive not to invest in certain areas such as health and education since presumably some of the monies sent from abroad are destined for such purposes.

A policy question that still needs further debate is whether governments should have special policies to encourage migrants to send remittances. However, the best way for migrant countries to encourage migrants to send remittances and maximize their impact on development is to have an economy that is growing, an appropriate exchange rate, and a climate that fosters small investments such as those by returning migrants. The evidence reviewed in this chapter seems to suggest that the combination of sound economic policies with migrants' human capital and entrepreneurial skills creates virtuous migration cycles, which encourages development.

REFERENCES

Abella, Manolo. 1995. "Asian Labor Migration: Past, Present and Future." *ASEAN Economic Bulletin* 12, no. 2: 125–38.

——. 1997. *Sending Workers Abroad*. Geneva: International Labor Office.

Acosta, Pablo. 2007. "Entrepreneurship, Labor Markets, and International Remittances: Evidence from El Salvador." In *International Migration, Economic Development and Policy*, edited by Caglar Ozden and Maurice Schiff. New York: Palgrave MacMillan.

Adams, Richard H., and John Page. 2005. "Do International Migration and Remittances Reduce Poverty in Developing Countries?" In *World Development* 33: 1645–69.

Adams, Walter, ed. 1968. *The Brain Drain*. New York: Macmillan.

Anh Nguyen, Dang. 2008. "Labour Migration from Viet Nam: Issues of Policy and Practice" International Labour Organization. ILO Asian Regional Programme on Governance of Labour Migration Working Paper No. 4. Bangkok. Accessed at http://www.ilo.org/wcmsp5/groups/public/—asia/—ro-bangkok/documents/publication/wcms_099172.pdf.

Beine, Michel, Frederic Docquier, and Hillel Rapoport. 2001. "Brain Drain and Economic Growth: Theory and Evidence." *Journal of Development Economics* 64, no 1: 275–89.

Bhagwati, Jagdish, ed. 1976. *The Brain Drain and Taxation: Theory and Empirical Analysis*. Amsterdam: North-Holland, 1976.

——. 2003. "Borders Beyond Control." *Foreign Affairs,* March/April. Accessed at www.foreignaffairs.org/20030101faessay10225/jagdish-bhagwati/borders-beyond-control.html.

Birks, J. S., and C. A. Sinclair. 1980. *International Migration and Development in the Arab Region*. Geneva: International Labour Organization.

Borjas, George J. 1994. "The Economics of Immigration." *Journal of Economic Literature* 32, no. 4: 1667–1717.

Buchan, James. 2002. "International Recruitment of Nurses: Policy and Practice in the United Kingdom." *Health Services Research* 42, no. 3: 1321–35.

Castles, Stephen, and Mark Miller. 2003. *The Age of Migration: International Population Movements in the Modern World*. London: Palgrave Macmillan.

Chan, Kam Wing, and Li Zhang. 1999. "The Hukou System and Rural-Urban Migration in China: Processes and Changes." *The China Quarterly*. 160: 818–55.

Chanda, Rupa. 2004. "Movement and Presence of Natural Persons and Developing Countries: Issues and Proposals for the GATS Negotiations." South Centre Working Paper 19, May. Accessed at www.southcentre.org.

Chaudhuri, Sumanta, Aaditya Mattoo, and Richard Self. 2004. "Moving People to Deliver Services: How Can the WTO Help?" *Journal of World Trade* 38, no. 3: 363–94.

Chiswick, Barry R. 1978. The Effect of Americanization on the Earnings of Foreign-Born Men. *Journal of Political Economy* 86: 897–922.

Clemens, Michael. 2007. "Do Visas Kill? Health Effects of African Health Professional Emigration." CGD Working Paper 114. Accessed at www.cgdev.org/content/publications/detail/13123.

Commission on Immigration Reform. 1995. "Legal Immigration: Setting Priorities." July. Accessed at http://migration.ucdavis.edu/mn/cir/95Report1/Titlepages/Title pages2.htm.

Cornelius, Wayne A., Takeyuki Tsuda, Philip L. Martin, and James F. Hollifield, eds. 2004. *Controlling Immigration: A Global Perspective*. Stanford: Stanford University Press.

Department of Health. 2004. "Code of Practice for the International Recruitment of Healthcare Professionals." Leeds: Department of Health Workforce Directorate.

Dollar, David, and Aart Kraay. 2003. "Spreading the Wealth." *Foreign Affairs*, January/February. Accessed at www.foreignaffairs.org/20020101faessay6561/david-dollar-aart-kraay/spreading-the-wealth.html.

Economist. 2002. "Do Developing Countries Gain or Lose When Their Brightest Talents Go Abroad?" September 26.

Escobar, Agustin. 2008. "Can Migration Foster Development in Mexico?" Mimeo, September.

Faini, Riccardo, and Alessandra Venturini. 1993. "Trade, Aid, and Migration: Some Basic Policy Issues." *European Economic Review* 37, nos. 2–3: 435–42.

Galson, David. 1981. *White Servitude in Colonial America: An Economic Analysis*. Cambridge: Cambridge University Press.

Hailbronner, Kay. 1997. "New Techniques for Rendering Asylum Manageable." In *Immigration Controls: The Search for Workable Policies in Germany and the United States*, edited by Kay Hailbronner, David Martin, and Hiroshi Motomura. New York: Berghahn Books.

Hatton, Timothy J., and Jeffrey G. Williamson. 1998. *The Age of Mass Migration: Causes and Economic Impact*. New York: Oxford University Press.

———. 2006. *Global Migration and the World Economy: Two Centuries of Policy and Performance*. Cambridge, Mass.: The MIT Press.

Henderson, David. 2006. "The Negative Effects of the Minimum Wage." National Center for Policy Analysis. Accessed at http://www.ncpa.org/pub/ba550.

Hollifield, James. 1992. *Immigrants, Markets, and States*. Cambridge: Harvard University Press.

Kapur, Devesh. 2007. "The Economic Impact of International Migration from India." In *Movement of Global Talent: The Impact of High Skill Labor Flows from India and China*, edited by Udai Tambar. Policy Research Institute for the Region. Princeton.

Kapur, Devesh, and John McHale. 2006. "Give Us Your Best and Brightest: The Global Hunt for Talent and Its Impact on the Developing World." Center for Global Development. Washington, D.C.

Keely, Charles. 1986. "Return of Talent Programs: Rationale and Evaluation Criteria for Programs to Ameliorate a Brain Drain." *International Migration* 24, no. 1: 179–89.

Khadria, Binod. 1999. *The Migration of Knowledge Workers: Second-Generation Effects of India's Brain Drain*. New Delhi: Sage.

Kuptsch, Christiane, ed. 2006. *Merchants of Labor*. Geneva: ILO.

Kyle, David, and Rey Koslowski, eds. 2001. *Global Human Smuggling: Comparative Perspectives*. Baltimore: Johns Hopkins University Press.

Lee, Joseph. 2004. "The Development of Taiwan's Economy and Its Labor Market in 2003." Mimeo.

Lemert, Charles C. 2005. *Social Things: An Introduction to the Sociological Life*. Lanham, Md.: Rowman and Littlefield.

Lowell, B. Lindsay. 2002. "Some Developmental Effects of the International Migration of Highly Skilled Persons." International Migration Papers (IMP-46). International Labour Organization. Geneva, Switzerland.

Lowell, B. Lindsay, and Alan M Findlay. 2002. "Migration of Highly Skilled Persons from Developing Countries: Impact and Policy Responses." International Migration Papers (IMP-44). International Labour Organization. Geneva, Switzerland.

Lucas, Robert. 2005. *International Migration Regimes and Economic Development*. London: Edward Elgar.

Luo, Yu-Ling, and Wei-Jen Wang. 2002. "High-Skill Migration and Chinese Taipei's Industrial Development." In *International Mobility of the Highly Skilled*. Paris: OECD.

Martin, Phillip. 1993. *Trade and Migration: NAFTA and Agriculture*. Washington, D.C.: Institute for International Economics.

——. 1994. "Good Intentions Gone Awry: IRCA and U.S. Agriculture." *Annals of the Academy of Political and Social Science* 534 (July): 44–57.

——. 2003a. *Bordering on Control: A Comparison of Measures to Combat Irregular Migration in North America and Europe*. Geneva: International Organization for Migration.

——. 2003b. *Promise Unfulfilled: Unions, Immigration, and Farm Workers*. Ithaca, N.Y.: Cornell University Press.

——. 2004. "Germany: Managing Migration in the 21st Century." In *Controlling Immigration: A Global Perspective*, edited by Wayne A. Cornelius, Takeyuki Tsuda, Philip L. Martin, and James F. Hollifield. Stanford: Stanford University Press.

——. 2005a. "Merchants of Labor: Agents of the Evolving Migration Infrastructure." International Institute for Labour Studies DP/158/2005, Geneva.

——. 2005b. "Mexico-U.S. Migration." In *NAFTA Revisited: Achievements and Challenges*, edited by Gary Hufbauer and Jeffrey Schott. Institute for International Economics. Washington, D.C.

Martin, Philip, Manolo Abella, and Christiane Kuptsch. 2006. *Managing Labor Migration in the Twenty-First Century*. New Haven: Yale University Press.

Martin, Philip, Susan Martin, and Sarah Cross. 2007. "High-Level Dialogue on Migration and Development." *International Migration* 45, no. 1: 7–25.

Martin, Philip L., and Edward Taylor. 1996. "The Anatomy of a Migration Hump." In *Development Strategy, Employment, and Migration: Insights from Models*, edited by Edward Taylor. Paris: OECD.

Martin, Philip L., and Gottfried Zuercher. 2008. "Managing Migration: The Global Challenge." *Washington D.C. Population Reference Bureau* 63, no 1. Accessed at www.prb.org/Publications/PopulationBulletins/2008/managingmigration.aspx.

Massey, Douglas S., et al. 1998. *Worlds in Motion: Understanding International Migration at the End of the Millennium*. New York: Oxford University Press.

Migration News. 2007. "China: Migrants, Environment" 14, no. 1, January. Accessed at http://migration.ucdavis.edu/mn/more.php?id=3258_0_3_0.

Mountford, Andrew. 1997. "Can a Brain Drain Be Good for Growth in the Source Economy?" *Journal of Development Economics* 52, no. 2: 287–303.

OECD. 2002. *International Mobility of the Highly Skilled: From Statistical Analysis to the Formulation of Policies*. Paris: OECD.

——. 2005. *Migration, Remittances and Development*. Paris: OECD.

——. 2005–2010. *Trends in International Migration (SOPEMI)*. Annual. Paris: OCED.

——. 2007. *Policy Coherence for Development: Migration and Developing Countries*. Paris: Development Center, OECD.

Papademetriou, Demetrios, and Philip Martin, eds. 1991. *Unsettled Relationship: Labor Migration and Economic Development*. Contributions in Labor Studies, No. 33. Westport: Greenwood.

Pernia, Ernesto M. 2008. "Migration, Remittances, Poverty and Inequality: The Philippines." School of Economics University of the Philippines Discussion Paper No. 0801. Manila.

Philippine Overseas Worker Administration (POEA). 2009–2010. *Annual Reports*. Manila.

Ratha, Dilip. 2003. "Workers' Remittances: An Important and Stable Source of External Development Finance." In *Global Development Finance 2003*. Washington, D.C.: World Bank.

Ratha, Dilip, Gemechu A. Aga, and Anil Silwal. 2012. Remittance Flows in 2011—An Update. World Bank. April 23. Accessed at http://web.worldbank.org/WBSITE/EXTERNAL/TOPICS/0,,contentMDK:21924020~pagePK:5105988~piPK:360975~theSitePK:214971,00.html.

Rodriguez, Edgard R. 1998. "International Migration and Income Distribution in the Philippines." *Economic Development and Cultural Change* 48: 329–50.

Ruhs, Martin, and Philip Martin. 2008. "Numbers vs. Rights: Trade-offs and Guest Worker Programs." *International Migration Review* 42, no. 1: 249–65.

Skeldon, Ronald. 1997. *Migration and Development: A Global Perspective.* Essex, U.K.: Longman.

Straubhaar, Thomas. 1988. *On the Economics of International Labor Migration.* Bern: Haupt.

Taylor, Alan, and Jeffrey Williamson. 1997. "Convergence in the Age of Mass Migration." *European Review of Economic History* 1, no 1: 27–63.

Taylor, J. Edward, and Philip L. Martin. 2001. "Human Capital: Migration and Rural Population Change." In *Handbook of Agricultural Economics,* vol. 1, edited by Bruce Gardener and Gordon Rausser. Amsterdam: Elsevier Science.

United Nations, Department of Economic and Social Affairs, Population Division (DESA). 2006. "International Migration Report 2005." ST/ESA/SER.A/220. Accessed at www.un.org/esa/population/publications/2006Migration_Chart/2006Itt Mig_chart.htm.

———. 2011. Trends in International Migrant Stock: Migrants by Age and Sex. POP/DB/MIG/Stock/Rev. 2011: New York: United Nations.

U.S. Census Bureau. 2011. American Community Survey. Washington, D.C.

U.S. Department of Homeland Security. Annual. *Immigration Statistics.* Accessed at www.dhs.gov/immigrationstatistics.

World Bank. 1993. *The East Asian Miracle: Economic Growth and Public Policy.* New York: Oxford University Press.

———. 2006. Global Economic Prospects. The Economic Implications of Remittances and Migration. Accessed at http://go.worldbank.org/oG6XW1UPP0.

———. 2008. *World Development Indicators.* Washington, D.C.: World Bank.

Yang, Dean, and Claudia A. Martinez. 2006. "Remittances and Poverty in Migrants' Home Areas: Evidence from the Philippines." In *International Migration, Remittances, and the Brain Drain,* edited by Caglar Ozden and Maurice Schiff. Washington, D.C.: World Bank.

CHAPTER 11

Indian Migrants to the Gulf

THE KERALA EXPERIENCE

S. Irudaya Rajan and K. C. Zachariah

"Migration is a product not of discrete and unconnected factors in the sending and the receiving countries, but of historical connections between the countries. It is not fortuitous; it is systematic" (Cheng and Bonacich 1984:41). Indian emigration has been taking place since the beginning of modern India, but never has the country witnessed such massive movements of people to other parts of the world as in the nineteenth and twentieth centuries (Tinker 1974; Cohen 1995). In one of our recent works, we reviewed the historical patterns of Indian emigrants over a long period of time (Irudaya Rajan and Kumar 2010). Though no firm estimates are available on international migration from India, today the number is quite low relative to India's billion-plus population.

ESTIMATES OF INTERNATIONAL MIGRATION FROM INDIA

The first crude estimate by the first Global Convention of People of Indian Origin, held in New York in 1989, puts the figure at 20 million (Jagat 1994). The High Level Committee on the Indian diaspora wrote in December 2001 in the foreword to its report that "the population of Indian Diaspora is estimated to be around 20 million" (Ministry of External Affairs 2001:3).[1] However, countrywide estimates provided in the same report give the approximate number of Indians settled throughout the world in 133 countries as 16.9 million.[2] Of these, 51 percent are people of Indian origin.[3]

There are about 10,000 Indians or more in forty-eight countries, and more than half a million persons of Indian descent in eleven countries. Among the emigrants of diverse nationalities, overseas Indians constitute a sizable segment. According to the Ministry of Overseas Indian Affairs (MOIA 2008), India has the second-largest diaspora in the world. Of this group, around 500,000 Indians were reported as a stateless population in eleven countries: Brunei Darussalam, Canada, Finland, Kenya, Madagascar, Malaysia, Myanmar, Netherlands, Philippines, Switzerland, and Venezuela.[4] The highest stateless Indian population is in Myanmar, with 400,000. The breakdown of India's population into three categories (people of Indian origin, Indian citizens, and stateless Indians) is not available for three countries: the United States (1.7 million total Indian population), the United Kingdom (1.2 million), and South Africa (1.0 million).

The nonresident Indians,[5] according to the report, are estimated at around 3.9 million, excluding those reported in South Africa, the United Kingdom, and the United States. Interestingly, around 3.3 million Indians (about 85 percent) live in six countries in the Middle East: Bahrain, Kuwait, Oman, Qatar, Saudi Arabia, and United Arab Emirates.

Table 11.1 summarizes the estimated number of people of Indian origin in countries with more than 100,000 Indians. Out of twenty-three coun-

Table 11.1   Countries with Estimated Indian Population over 100,000, 2001

Country	People of Indian Origin	Indian Citizens	Stateless	Total
Australia	160,000	30,000	0	190,000
Bahrain	0	130,000	0	130,000
Canada	700,000	150,000	1000	851,000
Fiji	336,579	250	0	336,829
Guyana	395,250	100	0	395,350
Kenya	85,000	15,000	2500	102,500
Kuwait	1,000	294,000	0	295,000
Malaysia	1,600,000	15,000	50000	1,665,000
Mauritius	704,640	11,116	0	715,756
Myanmar	2,500,000	2,000	400000	2,902,000
Netherlands	200,000	15,000	2000	217,000
Oman	1,000	311,000	0	312,000
Qatar	1,000	130,000	0	131,000
Réunion Island	220,000	55	0	220,055
Saudi Arabia	0	1,500,000	0	1,500,000
Singapore	217,000	90,000	0	307,000
South Africa	0	0	0	1,000,000
Suriname	150,306	150	0	150,456
Trinidad and Tobago	500,000	600	0	500,600
United Arab Emirates	50,000	900,000	0	950,000
United Kingdom	0	0	0	1,200,000
United States of America	0	0	0	1,678,765
Yemen	100,000	900	0	100,900

Source: Ministry of External Affairs 2001.

tries, only six report having more than 1 million Indians (Malaysia, Myanmar, Saudi Arabia, South Africa, United Kingdom, and United States). Incidentally, People of Indian origin contribute minimal remittances to the Indian economy, as they stay with their family members (spouse and children); thus they do not transfer cash to their home country to support their families. This is not true of Indian citizens who work as contract laborers or other professionals in most of the countries in the Gulf region. Among the Gulf countries, Saudi Arabia leads with 1.5 million Indians, followed by United Arab Emirates (900,000), Kuwait and Oman (300,000 each), and Qatar and Bahrain (100,000 each). No breakdown exists by gender at an all-Indian level. However, the latest MOIA (2008) annual report states that the overseas Indian community abroad is over 25 million.

LABOR MIGRATION

Migration of workers from India to other countries is not a new phenomenon. The Ministry of Overseas Indian Affairs maintains records of individuals who obtain emigration clearance to work abroad.[6] Earlier, the destination of Indian workers was mainly to the United States, the United Kingdom, and Canada. Indian migration to the Gulf has a history of several centuries, but it received a fillip only with the discovery of oil and the commencement of oil drilling on a commercial basis. The oil price hike of October 1973 marked a major watershed in the migration process. The massive demand for labor was accounted for by the sudden growth in the construction industry as the Gulf countries, which became immensely wealthy overnight, embarked on a construction frenzy, building roads, ports, and airports, as well as schools, colleges, and administrative blocks, all symbols of the new wealth. For the additional labor required, they turned to more distant, non-Arab countries such as India.

The number of workers that emigrated from India as contractual employment workers over the past several years is presented in Figure 11.1. The numbers are very small compared to the total emigrants reported earlier because many emigrants do not require emigration clearance from the government. As per the Emigration Act of 1983, seventeen categories of persons have been exempted from emigration clearance (see Table 11.2). The initial flow of contractual labor from India started with a low profile of just 160,000 in 1985, reached a peak of 440,000 in 1993, then slowly declined and is currently on an increasing trend, with 370,000 in 2002 and reaching a peak of 840,000 in 2008. A decline due to the global financial and economic crisis was evident in 2009 and 2010.

Out-migration from India can be classified into four distinct phases. The first phase covers the period between 1985 and 1991, which witnessed the annual volume of emigration ranging between 110,000 and 200,000. The second phase covers the first half of the 1990s (1992–97), when the annual flow of labor was more than 400,000. The third phase started after 1998, when a heavy fall in emigration took place in the annual outflow of the labor (Irudaya Rajan 2004). The last phase started at the beginning of the twenty-first century, when the annual flow was on the rise, reaching close to 900,000 million in 2008 and again declining due to economic conditions in Gulf countries.

Table 11.2 Categories of Individuals Who Do Not Require Emigration Clearance in India, 2010

1	All holders of diplomatic/official passports.
2	All gazetted government servants.
3	All income-tax payers (including agricultural income-tax payers) in respect of their individual capacity.
4	All professional degree holders, such as doctors holding M.B.B.S. degrees or degrees in ayurveda or homoeopathy; accredited journalists; engineers; chartered accountants; lecturers; teachers; scientists; advocates, etc.
5	Spouses and dependent children of category of persons, listed from (2) to (4).
6	Persons holding class 10 qualification or higher degrees.
7	Seamen who are in possession of Continuous Discharge Certificate (CDC) or sea cadets, desk cadets (i) who have passed final examination of three years B.Sc. Nautical Sciences Courses at T. S. Chanakya, Mumbai; and (ii) who have undergone three months pre-sea training at any of the government-approved training institutes such as T. S. Chanakya, T. S. Rehman, T. S. Jawahar, MTI(SCI) and NIPM, Chennai after production of identity cards issued by the shipping master, Mumbai/Kolkata/Chennai.
8	Persons holding permanent Immigration visas, such as in UK, USA, and Australia.
9	Persons possessing two years' diploma from any institute recognized by the national Council for Vocational Training (NCVT) or State Council of Vocational Training (SCVT) or persons holding three years' diploma/equivalent degree from institutions like polytechnics recognized by central/state governments.
10	Nurses possessing qualification recognized under the Indian Nursing Council Act, 1947.
11	All persons over the age of 50 years.
12	All persons who have been staying abroad for more than three years (the period of three years could be either in one stretch or broken) and spouses.
13	Children under 18 years of age.

Source: MOIA annual report 2009–10.

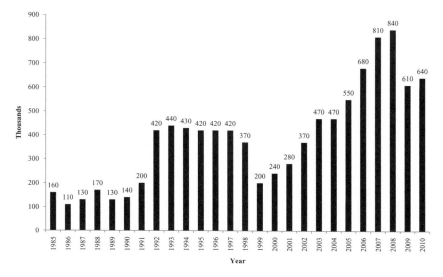

Figure 11.1   Trends in workers emigrated from India, 1985–2010.

Source: Compiled from various annual reports of the Ministry of Labor and Ministry of Overseas Indian Affairs, Government of India.

Where did Indian migrants go? Our analysis indicates that around 95 percent of labor migration reached six destinations in the Middle East: Saudi Arabia, United Arab Emirates, Bahrain, Kuwait, Oman, and Qatar (see Table 11.3). This trend continued until 2010 with around 75 percent of migrants going to this region. In 1994 Saudi Arabia led with 65 percent annual labor outflow from India, followed by the United Arab Emirates. Even in absolute numbers, except in 1999 Saudi Arabia attracted large numbers of Indian laborers. The available labor outflow reveals that Gulf countries became an important destination for Indians.

Where do migrants come from? Statewise breakdown of the number of workers granted emigration clearance is available for the years 1993–2010 (see Table 11.4). There has been a continuous decline in the number of emigration of workers in almost all states under study until 1999, followed by a slow increase. Kerala accounts for the largest number of workers, recently being surpassed by Uttar Pradesh. Some of the other states having a sizable number of labor emigrants are Karnataka, Maharashtra, Punjab, and Rajasthan. One of the reasons for the low labor migration in Kerala is that persons holding secondary-level education are exempted

Table 11.3   Labor Outflows from India by Destination, 1988–2010

Year	Bahrain	Kuwait	Oman	Saudi Arabia	United Arab Emirates	Others	Total
1988	8,219	9,653	18,696	85,289	34,029	9,348	165,234
1989	8,520	5,679	16,574	49,710	28,189	11,786	120,458
1990	6,782	1,077	34,267	79,473	11,962	6,300	139,861
1991	8,630	7,044	22,333	130,928	15,446	7,121	191,502
1992	16,458	19,782	40,900	265,180	60,493	13,971	416,784
1993	15,622	26,981	29,056	269,639	77,066	19,974	438,338
1994	13,806	24,324	25,142	265,875	75,762	20,476	425,385
1995	11,235	16,439	22,338	256,782	79,674	28,866	415,334
1996	16,647	14,580	30,113	214,068	112,644	26,162	414,214
1997	17,944	13,170	29,994	214,420	110,945	29,951	416,424
1998	16,997	22,462	20,774	105,239	134,740	54,952	355,164
1999	14,905	19,149	16,101	27,160	79,269	42,968	199,552
2000	15,909	31,082	25,155	59,722	55,099	56,215	243,182
2001	16,382	39,751	30,985	78,048	53,673	59,825	278,664
2002	20,807	4,859	41,209	99,453	95,034	106,301	367,663
2003	24,778	54,434	36,816	121,431	143,804	44,044	466,456
2004	22,980	52,064	33,275	123,522	175,262	10,715	474,960
2005	30,060	39,124	40,931	99,879	194,412	15,945	548,853
2006	37,688	47,449	67,992	134,059	254,774	14,175	676,912
2007	29,966	48,467	95,462	195,437	312,695	3,550	809,453
2008	31,924	35,562	89,659	228,406	349,827	113,223	848,601
2009	17,541	42,091	74,963	281,110	130,302	64,265	610,272
2010	15,101	37,667	105,807	275,172	130,910	76,699	641,356

Source: Compiled from various annual reports of the Ministry of Labor, Government of India, and Ministry of Overseas Indian Affairs, Government of India.

from emigration clearance. Southern states such as Kerala, Tamil Nadu, and West Bengal have the highest number of educated Indians in the country.

WORKERS' REMITTANCES

The money that migrants send home is important not only to their families but also to their country's balance of payments. In many developing countries, remittances represent a significant proportion of their GDP as well as of their foreign exchange earnings. Remittances in India represented around 3 percent of its GDP in 2011 (World Bank 2011). In terms of the proportion of remittances to GDP, Philippines ranks first among the Asian countries (with 8.8 percent), followed by Sri Lanka. Seven of the twenty countries listed are in Asia: India, Sri Lanka, Pakistan, Bangladesh (South and South West Asia), Indonesia, Philippines, and Thailand

Table 11.4 Workers Granted Emigration Clearances by Major States, 1993–2010

Year	Andhra Pradesh	Karnataka	Kerala	Maharashtra	Punjab	Rajasthan	Tamil Nadu	Uttar Pradesh	Others	Total
1993	35,578	34,380	155,208	35,248	14,212	25,243	70,313	—	68,156	438,338
1994	34,508	32,266	154,407	32,178	12,445	27,418	70,525	—	61,638	425,385
1995	30,284	33,496	165,629	26,312	11,852	28,374	65,737	—	53,650	415,334
1996	29,995	33,761	167,325	25,214	11,751	18,221	64,991	—	62,956	414,214
1997	38,278	40,396	156,102	25,146	12,414	28,242	63,672	—	52,174	416,424
1998	30,599	11,535	91,720	24,657	26,876	19,824	69,793	—	80,160	355,164
1999	18,983	5,287	60,445	9,871	15,167	9,809	47,402	—	32,588	199,552
2000	29,999	10,927	69,630	13,346	10,025	10,170	63,878	—	35,207	243,182
2001	37,331	10,095	61,548	22,713	12,422	14,993	61,649	—	57,913	278,664
2002	38,417	14,061	81,950	25,477	19,638	23,254	79,165	—	85,701	367,663
2003	65,971	22,641	92,044	29,350	24,963	37,693	89,464	—	104,330	466,456
2004	72,580	19,237	63,512	28,670	25,302	35,108	108,964	27,428	94,159	474,960
2005	48,498	75,384	125,075	29,289	24,088	21,899	117,050	22,558	85,012	548,853
2006	97,680	24,362	120,083	15,356	39,311	50,236	155,631	66,131	108,122	676,912
2007	105,044	27,014	150,475	21,496	53,942	70,896	150,842	91,613	138,131	809,453
2008	97,530	22,413	180,703	24,786	54,469	64,601	128,791	139,254	136,054	848,601
2009	69,233	18,565	119,384	19,128	27,291	30,974	78,841	125,783	121,073	610,272
2010	72,220	17,295	104,101	18,123	44,744	47,803	84,510	140,826	111,734	641,356

Source: Compiled from various annual reports of the Ministry of Labor and Ministry of Overseas Indian Affairs, Government of India.

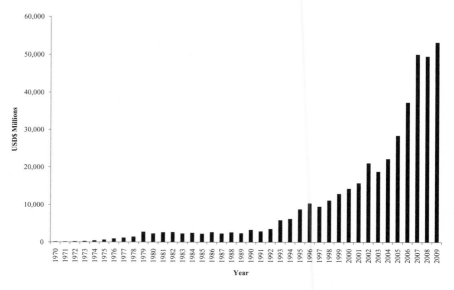

Figure 11.2   Remittances to India, 1970–2010.

Source: World Bank 2011.

(South East Asia). In Yemen and Jordan, remittances contribute one-fifth of the GDP.

Figure 11.2 shows the trends in remittances for India over the past forty years. According to the estimates of the World Bank, remittances to the country have grown steadily, from US$120 million in 1970, to US$2.76 billion in 1980, US$3.29 billion in 1991, US$12.89 billion in 2000, and about US$54 billion in 2010. Similarly the percentage of remittances to GDP has increased, from 0.14 in 1970, 2.50 in 2000, and 4.2 in 2007—a significant contribution to the Indian economy.

The Indian economy has benefited directly by the liberalization of the foreign exchange regime since 1991. According to one estimate, this "windfall" gain varied from nearly Rs500,000 in 1991–92 to Rs3.34 billion in 1999–2000 (Kannan and Hari 2002). In 2007 emigrants transferred around Rs578 million to India, the equivalent of US$12.13 billion in foreign exchange reserves in India. However, no systematic study exists to assess the impact on remittances on the Indian economy and society. There is some evidence at the state level (Zachariah, Mathew, and Irudaya Rajan 2003; Zachariah and Irudaya Rajan 2004, 2009a, 2009b), which is further explored in the next section.

THE KERALA EXPERIENCE

In order to make an assessment of the emigrants from Kerala to the Gulf, the Centre for Development Studies conducted four large-scale surveys over ten years, in 1998, 2003, 2007, and 2008. The findings presented in this section are based on the Kerala Migration Survey (KMS) in 2008, funded by the Department of Non-Resident Keralite Affairs and the Ministry of Overseas Indian Affairs (Zachariah and Irudaya Rajan 2010). In this survey, the sample size was enhanced to 15,000 households from 10,000 households in the three earlier migration surveys. The increase in sample size—with a minimum of 1,000 households in every district of Kerala—is expected to yield reliable migration estimates at the district and *taluk* (a taluk is the smallest administrative unit in India, about four or five *taluk*s constitute a district) levels in Kerala (for more details, see Zachariah and Irudya Rajan 2010).

These estimates are made on the basis of answers to the following questions: Has any person who was a usual resident of this household migrated out of Kerala and is still living outside India? Those who are still living outside India are called emigrants. Similarly those who worked abroad and returned to Kerala are called return emigrants.

The sample consists of three hundred localities (*panchayat*s, or municipal wards). From each locality, fifty households (HHs) were selected for canvassing. Estimation is done at the *taluk* level. Thus for a *taluk* we have:

r_i = Number of emigrants in the sample households in the ith locality
h_i = Number of sample HHs in the ith locality (50)
H_i = Total number of HHs in the sample locality in 2008
H = Total number of HHs in the *taluk* in 2008

Table 11.5 presents the estimates of the number of Kerala migrants living outside India. In 2008 the number of migrants was estimated around

Table 11.5 Number of Emigrants, Return Emigrants, and Nonresident Keralites from Kerala, 1998–2008

Kerala	Number		Increase	Per 100 Households	
	2008	1998	1998-08	2008	1998
Emigrants	2,193,412	1,36,1919	831,493	29.0	21.4
Return emigrants	1,157,127	739,245	417,882	15.3	11.6
Nonresident Keralites	3,350,539	2,101,164	1,249,375	44.3	33.0

2.2 million. The corresponding number in 1998 was 1.3 million. During the ten-year period from 1998 to 2008, the number of emigrants from Kerala has increased by 832,000.

Migration begets migration; emigration begets return emigration. The greater the extent of emigration, the greater would be the extent of return migration. Return emigration is a built-in aspect of the emigration process. This is particularly true of Gulf migration, where almost all emigration is of short duration and temporary in nature. Return emigration statistics derived from the KMS surveys suggest that this is in fact the case. The number of return emigrants rose from 739,245 in 1998 to 1,157,127 in 2008, the net increase being 417,882 during the period 1998–2008. The number of nonresident Keralites (NRKs) in 2008 was 3,350,539, while the corresponding number in 1998 was 2,101,164. Thus the number of NRKs increased by 1,249,375 during 1998–2008. The number of emigrants per 100 households increased from 21.4 percent in 1998 to 29.0 percent in 2008. Similarly the number of return emigrants per 100 households increased from 11.6 percent in 1998 to 15.1 percent in 2008 (see Figure 11.3). Figure 11.4 illustrates out-migration trends from Kerala using previous waves from the KMS.

Estimates of the number of emigrants by district is much more reliable in the last wave of the KMS-2008 given its superior size. Figure 11.5 indicates that Malappuram district had the largest number of emigrants from

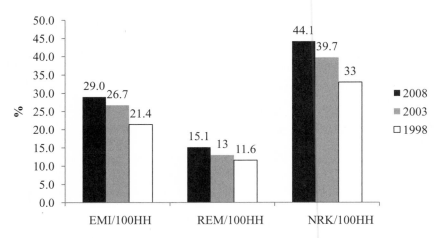

Figure 11.3   Emigrants (EMI), return emigrants (REM), and nonresident Keralites (NRK) per 100 households in Kerala, 1998–2008.

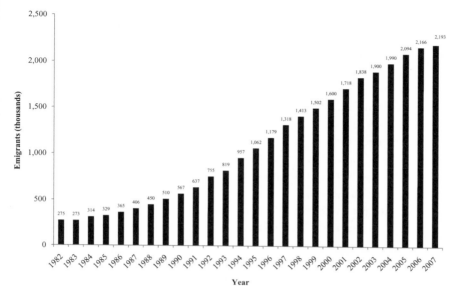

Figure 11.4   Trends in emigration from Kerala, 1982–2008.

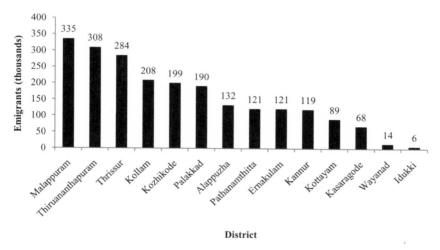

Figure 11.5   Number of emigrants by districts in Kerala, 2008.

Kerala, 335,000 out of a total of 2,193,412 for Kerala as a whole (15.3 percent).

Kerala witnessed accelerated emigration at the start of the 1970s, and from then on the Gulf countries have absorbed most of the out-migration from this region. For instance, in 1998, 94 percent of migrants coming out from Kerala went to a Gulf country; this figure declined to 89 percent in 2008.

The changes within the Gulf region resemble a more dramatic contrast. Saudi Arabia was the principal destination in 1998, with 37.5 percent of Kerala's emigrants (Table 11.6). The proportion of emigrants from Kerala to Saudi Arabia declined to 26.7 percent in 2003 and further to 23.0 percent in 2008. However, the number of Kerala emigrants in Saudi Arabia has remained stable; it has not declined at all during the ten-year period. On the other hand, the United Arab Emirates (UAE) has received a rising proportion of Kerala emigrants, from 31.0 percent in 1998 to 41.9 percent in 2008 (see Table 11.6).

According to the 2001 Census, 56.3 percent of Kerala's population is Hindu, 19.0 percent is Christian, and 24.7 percent is Muslim. However, Muslims make up the majority of the emigrants at 41.1 percent, followed by Hindus with 37.7 percent and Christians with 21.2 percent (Table 11.7).

Religion is an important factor related to emigration in Kerala. The proportion of households with emigrants (EMI), return emigrants (REM), or nonresident Keralite (NRK) is highest among the Muslims and lowest among the Hindus. For example, the proportion of households

Table 11.6 Emigrants by Country of Residence, 1998–2008

	Numbers			Percentage		
Countries	2008	2003	1998	2008	2003	1998
United Arab Emirates	918,122	670,150	421,959	41.9	36.5	31.0
Saudi Arabia	503,433	489,988	510,895	23.0	26.7	37.5
Oman	167,628	152,865	139,571	7.6	8.3	10.2
Kuwait	129,282	113,967	68,163	5.9	6.2	5.0
Bahrain	101,344	108,507	74,654	4.6	5.9	5.5
Qatar	121,613	98,953	62,969	5.5	5.4	4.6
Gulf Region	1,941,422	1,636,477	1,278,211	88.5	88.9	93.9
Other countries	251,990	204,048	83,708	11.5	11.1	6.1
Total	**2,193,415**	**1,838,478**	**1,361,955**	**100.0**	**100.0**	**100.0**

Table 11.7 Emigrants and Emigrants per 100 Households by Religion, 2008

	Percentage Distribution			Emigrants per 100 Households	
Religion	1998	2003	2008	2003	2008
Hindus	29.5	31.2	37.7	14.6	18.7
Christians	19.8	25.1	21.2	31.4	29.9
Muslims	50.7	43.7	41.1	56.1	56.4

with either an emigrant or a return emigrant among Muslims is as much as 52.9 percent (one out of every two households), compared with only 18 percent among Hindus. The broad distribution of households by the number of EMI, REM, and NRK by religion is given in Table 11.8.

In 2008 about 18 percent of the Kerala households had a member living as an emigrant outside India. The corresponding number in 2003 was slightly higher, at 19 percent. Similarly 11.8 percent of the households had a return emigrant, and 26.5 percent had either an emigrant, a return emigrant, or both. These proportions have not changed much since 2003, although there was considerable increase in the number of emigrants, return emigrants, and nonresident Keralites. Migrants per 100 households also increased considerably during this period. Yet the proportion of households with at least one emigrant did not increase significantly. These statistics seem to imply that emigrants from Kerala are not randomly selected. When a new person emigrates, it is likely that he or she comes from a household that already had sent out an emigrant in the past (Table 11.9).

The majority of the migrants in Kerala are males. The proportion of female emigrants from Kerala rose from 9.3 percent in 1998 to 14.6 percent in 2008. Emigration from Kerala has been and still is dominated by males. Among the emigrants from Kerala in 2008, the proportion of females was only 14.6 percent. Although this proportion is much higher than that in 1998 (9.3 percent), it was lower than that in 2003. Surprisingly there was a decline in the proportion of women emigrants between 2003 and 2008; the proportion of females among the return emigrants was only 11.8 percent, down from 15.3 in 2003.

Table 11.8 Percentage of Households with One or More Migrants by Religion, 2008

Religion	Emigrant	Returned Emigrant	Nonresident Keralite
Hindus	12.4	7.2	18.1
Christians	16.3	11.0	24.6
Muslims	36.4	25.7	52.9
Average	18.0	11.8	26.5

Table 11.9 Percentage of Households with One or More Migrants, 2003–8

Year	Emigrant	Retruned Emigrant	Nonresident Keralite
2008	18.0	11.8	26.5
2003	18.9	11.2	25.8

Figure 11.6 provides the trends in remittances to Kerala over a long period of time; it indicates a continuous growth of such remittances. The
flow of about Rs43,288 crores (432.88 trillion rupees, which is around
US$900 million) into the Kerala economy in 2008 by way of remittances
did have a very significant impact on the state's economy and the living
conditions of its citizens. It is important to state that 88.5 percent of emigrants from Kerala went to the Gulf, and as such they contributed a major
chunk of remittance flows into Kerala.

For a total population of 33.71 million in Kerala in 2008, the remittance
of Rs43,288 crores meant an average per capita remittance of Rs12,841
(US$260 in 2008); for an average household, it was Rs57,227 (US$1,150 in
2008) per year. Remittances thus make a substantial contribution to the
annual income of the households in Kerala.

Remittances are also associated with the macroeconomic indicators of
the state. To begin with, remittances in Kerala in 2008 were around a
third (31 percent) of Kerala's NSDP (Net State Domestic Product). The
per capita income of the state excluding remittances stood at Rs41,814
(US$841) but was as much as Rs54,664 (US$1,100) when remittances were
also included (Table 11.10).

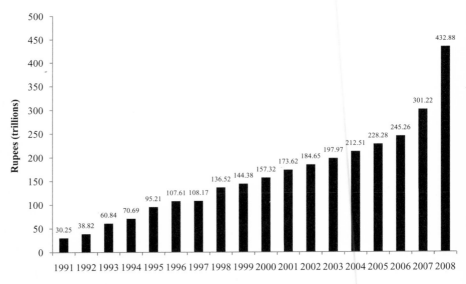

Figure 11.6   Estimated remittances to Kerala, 1991–2008.

Source: Zachariah and Irudaya Rajan 2009b.

Table 11.10   Macroeconomic Impact of Remittances on the Kerala Economy, 1998–2008

Indicators	1998	2003	2008
Remittances (Rs crores)	13,652	18,465	43,288
NSDP (Rs crores)	53,552	83,783	140,889
Per capita income (Rs)	16,062	25,764	41,814
Modified NSDP (Rs crores)	67,204	102,248	184,177
Revenue receipt of government	7,198	10,634	24,936
Transfer from central government	1,991	2,653	7,861
Government nonplanned expenditure	5,855	9,908	18,934
State debt (Rs crores)	15,700	31,060	61,653
Receipt from cashew export	1,317	1,217	1,198
Receipt from marine products	817	995	1,431
Modified per capita income	20,157	31,442	54,664
Remittances as percent of NSDP (%)	25.49	22.04	30.73
Remittances as ratio of revenue receipt	1.90	1.74	1.74
Remittances as ratio of transfer from centre	6.86	6.96	5.51
Remittances as ratio of government expenditure	2.33	1.84	2.29
Remittances as ratio of state debt	0.87	0.59	0.70
Remittances as ratio of receipt from cashew export	19.37	15.17	36.13
Remittances as ratio of receipt from marine export	16.71	18.56	30.25

Source: Zachariah and Irudaya Rajan 2009a.

Other statistics also indicate the importance of remittances in Kerala's economy. Remittances were 1.74 times the revenue receipt of the state. Remittances in Kerala were 5.5 times the subsidies Kerala got from the central government and 2.3 times the annual nonplanned expenditure of the Kerala government. In 2008 remittances were sufficient to wipe out 70 percent of the state's debt and 36 times the export earnings from cashew products and 30 times that from marine products.

Looking at the breakup of the total remittance of Rs43,288 crores (US$870) by household type, we found that Rs16,493 crores (US$332) was received by Hindu households, Rs7,800 crores (US$157) was received by Christian households, and Rs18,995 crores (US$382) was received by Muslim households. The average remittances per household was Rs37,385 (US$752) among Hindus, Rs50,107 (US$1,008) among Christians, and as much as Rs119,004 (US$2,394) among Muslims (Table 11.11 and Figure 11.6).

In 2008 the emigration rate per 100 households was 29 percent, but only 18 percent of the households had an emigrant member because some had more than one emigrant. The proportion of households that received remittances was even smaller. The 2008 Kerala Migration Survey estimated that only 17.1 percent of the households had received cash remittances

Table 11.11   Total Remittances and Remittances per Household by Religion

Religion	Remittances (in Crores)		Remittances per HH (in Crores)	
	2003	2008	2003	2008
Hindus	5,475	16,493	6,134	37,385
Christians	4,679	7,800	13,760	50,107
Muslims	8,311	18,995	24,351	119,004
Total average	**18,465**	**43,288**	**11,586**	**57.227**

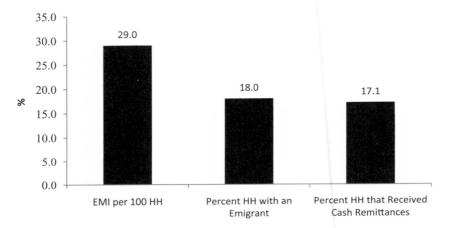

Figure 11.7   **Percentage of households that received cash remittances with EMI.**

(Figure 11.7). Muslim households received the largest proportion of remittances, while Hindu households received the smallest (Figure 11.8).

Total remittances by district are given in Figure 11.9. Remittances vary considerably among districts. Malappuram district leads with a total of Rs6,486 crores. Following are Thrissur district with remittances amounting to Rs5,961 crores and Thiruvananthapuram district with Rs4,801 crores. Idukki and Wayanad come last. While Malappuram accounts for 15 percent of the state's remittances, Idukki accounts for less than 0.5 percent.

The average remittance per household in Malappuram was around Rs103,585 which is nearly double the state average (Rs57,227). The other districts with high average remittance per household were Thrissur, Pathanamthitta, Kollam, and Kozhikode. The average remittances per household in Idukki district were less than a tenth of the state average for Pathanamthitta, Kollam, and Kozhikode. The average remittances per household in Idukki district were less than a tenth of the state average.

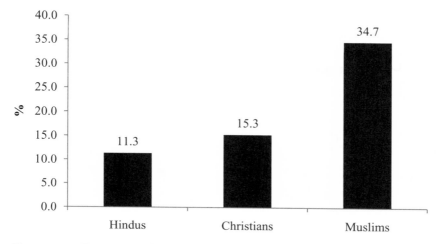

Figure 11.8   Percentage of households that received remittances by religion.

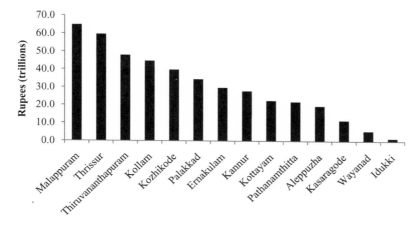

Figure 11.9   Total remittances by districts, 2008 (trillions of rupees).

The impact of remittances on Kerala are manifest in household consumption, saving and investment, quality of houses, and possession of modern consumer durables. Remittances also play a major role in enhancing the quality of life and contribute to a high human development index for Kerala in terms of education and health, along with reduction in poverty and unemployment.

Kerala's Gulf connection is so strong that even at the time of the global crisis, both emigration and remittances seemed to be resilient. According to our recent study conducted for the government of Kerala (Zachariah and Irudaya Rajan 2009a), even at the peak of the recession in the Gulf, when 173,000 emigrants returned to Kerala, 239,000 emigrants left Kerala to work in the Gulf, resulting in a net migration of 66,000. Similarly the total cash remittances that Kerala households received in 2009 registered a modest increase of 7 percent.

DISCUSSION

What implications does our analysis have for development? Over the past decade remittances, as a direct by-product of migration, have had positive effects in reducing poverty as well as unemployment in Kerala. For instance, the unemployment rate before migration among future migrants has been estimated around 30 percent and only approximately 7 percent among return migrants (Rajan and Zachariah 2003).

Migration, on the other hand, also creates new challenges that permeate throughout Kerala's society. Given the influx of remittances into the region, new tensions have emerged between the old and new economic elites as well as certain imbalances regarding income distribution given that Gulf migration from Kerala is not a prevalent phenomenon among all Kerala households, as is often assumed (around 25 percent of Kerala households have an NRK). An interesting pattern, which will have important implications for the future, is the fact that Muslims are more likely to migrate than any other religious group: almost half the number of migrants migrating to the Gulf were Muslim, that is, one out of every two Muslim households had an NRK, in contrast to the Hindu community, in which only 18 percent of households had an NRK. The implications in terms of social and economic inequalities based on religion need to be further explored; however, the potential to exacerbate some old and new inequalities is latent. Perhaps the new migrant destinations beyond the Middle East, such as the United States and the United Kingdom, will cancel out the potentials for conflict if Hindus or Christians tend to self-select at higher rates than Muslims to those destinations.

Even though migration from Kerala over the past three decades has increased in absolute numbers, its growth has been increasing at decreasing rates (see Figure 11.10). A plausible explanation of this phenomenon is given by the expansion of employment opportunities within the state. Data from the KMS and official state sources seem to suggest that in recent years, remittances to Kerala are being invested more productively,

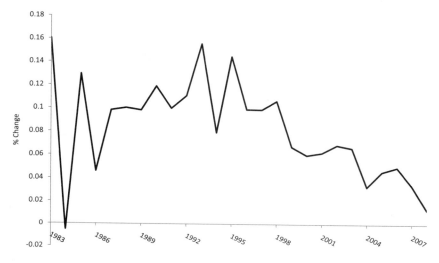

Figure 11.10   Migration rate change, 1982–2008.

generating an increase in the demand for labor, which to some extent has reduced the need to migrate in search of employment, coupled with the economic downturn experienced in the Gulf.

Previous experiences in the state illustrate how developments in the agricultural industry, especially those in the rice and coconut businesses, gave way to the development of the rubber-based industry by providing investment capital. Migrant remittances also have the potential to spur development. The emergence of India as an economic superpower will necessarily potentiate remittances' impact in particular states such as Kerala; however, the country as a whole and Kerala state in particular need to raise basic educational standards, increase the number of and access to universities, and improve the state's agricultural productivity, infrastructure, and environmental quality before migration can accelerate development.

REFERENCES

Cheng, L., and E. Bonacich, eds. 1984. *Labour Immigration under Capitalism: Asian Workers in the United States before World War II*. Berkeley: University of California Press.

Cohen, R., ed. 1995. *The Cambridge Survey of World Migration*. Cambridge: Cambridge University Press.

Irudaya, Rajan, S. 2004. "From Kerala to the Gulf: Impacts of Labour Migration." *Asia Pacific Migration Journal* 13, no. 4: 497–509.

———, ed. 2010. *Governance and Labour Migration: India Migration Report 2010*. New Delhi: Routledge India.

Irudaya Rajan, S., and P. R. Gopinathan Nair. 2006. "Saudi Arabia, Oman and the Gulf States." In *The Encyclopedia of the Indian Diaspora*, edited by Brij V. Lal. Singapore: Editions Didier Millet.

Irudaya Rajan, S., and Prabhat Kumar. 2010. "Historical Overview of International Migration." In *Governance and Labour Migration: India Migration Report 2010*, edited by S. Irudaya Rajan. New Delhi: Routledge India.

Irudaya Rajan, S., and D. Narayana. 2010. "The Financial Crisis in the Gulf and Its Impact on South Asian Migrant Workers." Report submitted to the Asian Development Bank and the Ministry of Overseas Indian Affairs, Government of India.

Irudaya Rajan, S., and Remya G. Prabha. 2008. "India." *Asia Pacific Migration Journal* 17, nos. 3–4: 277–86.

Irudaya Rajan, S., and B. A. Prakash. 2009. "Migration and Development Linkages Re-Examined in the Context of the Global Economic Crisis." Invited paper for the Civil Society Days of the Third Global Forum on Migration and Development, November 2–3, Athens.

Irudaya Rajan, S., V. J. Varghese, and M. S. Jayakumar. 2010. "Looking Beyond the Emigration Act 1983: Revisiting the Recruitment Practices in India." In *Governance and Labour Migration: India Migration Report 2010*, edited by S. Irudaya Rajan. New Delhi: Routledge India.

Jagat, K. Motwani. 1994. "Twenty Million Global Indians: An Overview." In *Manorama Year Book 1994*. Kerala: Kottayam.

Kannan, K. P., and K. S. Hari. 2002. "Kerala's Gulf Connection: Remittances and Their Macroeconomic Impact." In *Kerala's Gulf Connection: CDS Studies on International Labour Migration from Kerala State in India*, edited by K. C. Zachariah, K. P. Kannan, and S. Irudaya Rajan. Thiruvananthapuram, India: Centre for Development Studies.

Ministry of External Affairs. 2001. *Report of the High Level Committee on the Indian Diaspora*. New Delhi: Government of India.

Ministry of Overseas Indian Affairs. 2008. *Annual Report 2007–08*. New Delhi.

Tinker, H. 1974. *A New System of Slavery: The Export of Indian Labour Overseas, 1830–1920*. London: Oxford University Press.

World Bank. 2008. *Migration and Development Brief 8. Outlook for Remittance Flows 2008–2010: Growth Expected to Moderate Significantly, but Flows to Remain Resilient*. Washington, D.C.: World Bank.

———. 2009. *Migration and Development Brief 11. Migration and Remittance Trends 2009: A Better-than-Expected Outcome So Far, but Significant Risks Ahead*. Washington, D.C.: World Bank.

———. 2011. *Migration and Remittances Factbook 2011*. Washington, D.C.: World Bank, 2011.

———. 2011. *Remittances Data Inflows 2010*. Washington, D.C.: World Bank.

Zachariah, K. C., P. R. Gopinathan Nair, and S. Irudaya Rajan. 2006. *Return Emigrants in Kerala: Welfare, Rehabilitation and Development*. New Delhi: Manohar.

Zachariah, K. C., E. T. Mathew, and S. Irudaya Rajan. 2003. *Dynamics of Migration in Kerala: Dimensions, Determinants and Consequences.* Hyderabad: Orient Longman.

Zachariah, K. C., B. A. Prakash, and S. Irudaya Rajan. 2003. "The Impact of Immigration Policy on Indian Contract Migrants: The Case of the United Arab Emirates." *International Migration* 41, no. 4: 161–72.

———. 2004. "Indian Workers in UAE: Employment, Wages and Working Conditions." *Economic and Political Weekly* 39, no. 22: 2227–34.

Zachariah, K. C., and S. Irudaya Rajan. 2009a. "Impact of the Global Recession on Migration and Remittances in Kerala: New Evidences from the Return Migration Survey 2009." Research Report, Centre for Development Studies, Thirivananthapuram, India.

———. 2009b. *Migration and Development: The Kerala Experience.* New Delhi: Daanish.

———. 2010. "Migration Monitoring Study, 2008: Emigration and Remittances in the Context of Surge in Oil Prices." Centre for Development Studies Working Paper 424, Thiruvananthapuram, India.

———. 2011. *Diasporas in Kerala's Development.* New Delhi: Daanish.

NOTES

INTRODUCTION

1. The GFMD (2011) is a nonbinding, voluntary, and government-led process that seeks to address the migration and development interconnections in practical and action-oriented ways.

2. The GMG (2011) is an interagency conglomerate bringing together heads of U.N. agencies and international organizations to promote the wider application of all relevant international and regional instruments and norms relating to migration and to encourage the adoption of more coherent, comprehensive, and better coordinated approaches to the issues of international migration.

3. RCPs bring together representatives of states, international organizations, and nongovernmental organizations for informal and nonbinding dialogue and information exchange on migration-related issues of common interest and concern (IOM 2011).

1. DEVELOPMENT AND MIGRATION

1. The International Committee on Migration and Development Research of the Social Science Research Council organized a conference, Migration and Development: Future Directions for Research and Policy, in New York City February 28–March 1, 2008, to address central theoretical and practical issues that would benefit from future internationally comparative and interconnective research. The project proposed here grows in part out of the papers and discussions at that conference (http://essays.ssrc.org/developmentpapers/?page_id=3).

2. In contrast to our use of *transition* to indicate universal migratory and developmental transformations, Castles and Miller (2009) use the term to describe the process by which temporary migrants become permanent settlers.

3. This chapter is based on data that can serve as indicators for all four transitions in 2005, the most recent year for which contemporaneous national indicators are available for a large majority of nations in all regions of the world. Although the national data come from the United Nations, we have not compiled the national data into precisely the same subregions used by that organization

(particularly in Europe). In examining more recent but less evenly available national data for the same indicators, we have found no substantive differences in the results.

4. While not particularly interesting theoretically, some exceptions seem to result from data inconsistencies. For example, United Nations data indicate that Western Europe is less urbanized than Northern Europe, but this may be the result of countries in the two subregions defining *urban* differently. In Western Europe, for example, Switzerland defines communes with more than 10,000 persons as urban, while Belgium and Austria reserve the label for locations with more than 5,000 persons, and France more than 3,000; in Northern Europe, Norway, Denmark, and Sweden define as urban those locations that have as few as 200 people (United Nations 2007d).

5. Easterlin's (1961) article, "Essays in the Quantitative Study of Economic Growth," appeared in a special issue of the journal *Economic Development and Cultural Change*, which was presented to Simon Kuznets on his sixtieth birthday by his students and friends.

6. Another theoretical approach that examines linkages between development and international migration focuses on the global impact of labor markets (e.g., Petras 1981; Cohen 1987; Potts 1990; Williamson 2005; Pritchett 2006). We do not examine here this approach's important contributions because of space limitations and because the dynamics of centralized labor markets do not seem as analytically relevant as world-systems to the analysis of regional development and migration transitions.

3. BRINGING CULTURE BACK IN

1. This chapter is based on our ongoing individual and joint fieldwork during the past twenty years. We draw on examples from Latin America and South Asia to illustrate our points. For a more in-depth discussion of study methods and findings, see Levitt 2001, 2007.

5. FAMILY AND SCHOOL RECONFIGURATION

1. The twentieth Constitution of the Republic of Ecuador, Article 416, "advocates the beginning of universal citizenship, free mobility of all inhabitants of the planet and the progressive ending of the foreigner condition"; Article 7 "demands respect for human rights, in particular for the rights of migrants" (Constitución de la República del Ecuador 2009: 183). Moreover both section 3, "Human Mobility," and section 10, "Population and Human Mobility," emphasize the right to migrate and to ask for refugee status and appeal to the principle of universal citizenship. With this constitutional proposal, Ecuador bets on a new conception of citizenship that points toward the principle of free informed mobility, entry in receiving countries, and local and regional development due to the free movement of persons.

2. It is estimated that for the corresponding year, while poverty in rural areas remained stable, in urban areas it increased by 100 percent on the coast and by 80 percent in the cities of the Sierra region (Vela 2006:25).

3. During 1999 Ecuador experienced one of the most severe impoverishments in the history of Latin America. Between 1990 and 2001 national poverty increased from 39 to 65 percent (Rojas 2007:3). It was also accompanied by a higher concentration of wealth: in 1999 the poorest 20 percent received 4.6 percent of the income, and by 2000 they received less than 2.5 percent. On the other hand, the richest 20 percent of the population had 52 percent of the wealth in 1990, and by 2000 they had 61 percent. Also, the GDP fell dramatically, by 30 percent, compared to 1998, and the unemployment rate reached 14 percent in 1999 (Acosta 2006:10–11).

4. One of the defining features of Calderón, as well as of the Oyacoto commune, is that since the 1970s it has been a receiving point for the internal flow of migrants; since the end of the 1990s it has also received an inflow of international immigrants coming from Colombia, Peru, and recently from Cuba. As a matter of fact, 24.2 percent of Calderon's population is immigrant in origin, mostly from other provinces in the Ecuadorian highlands (PROREDES 2006b:2–6; INEC 2001). In the case of Cañar, this locality has been living with migratory behavior for more than forty years. First, the 1960s experienced an important outflow of its inhabitants to the nation's coast; then, since the 1970s, international emigration to the United States started to predominate. Finally, in the past decade, the international destinations have diversified to include Spain. It is estimated that currently four out of ten households are involved in migratory practices (Escobar 2008).

5. Before our ethnographic research was undertaken in Oyacoto (February 2007), there were no quantitative or qualitative data about the life conditions in this community or more relevant information about emigration processes that affected it. The data available refer to the urban parish where this community is located: Calderón, one of the parishes that form the Metropolitan District of Quito (MDQ), capital of Pichincha Province and of Ecuador. The population of the parish is 84,219; 39.54 percent are poor with unsatisfied basic needs, and 11.99 percent live in extreme poverty. While migratory density in Calderón is 6.6 percent, MDQ's varies between 3.1 and 6 percent of the population. Hence Calderón is the parish with the highest migration rate in the capital city (INEC 2001). Therefore, the following findings emerge from an ethnographic immersion in the community and in-depth interviews with local spokespersons.

6. WOMEN, CHILDREN, AND MIGRATION

1. Women as refugees and as asylum seekers.

2. Based on the marital status of women at the time of migration and on their employment status, Thadani and Todaro (1984) identified four variants of female migration: (1) married women in search of employment, (2) unmarried women in search of employment or for marital reasons, (3) unmarried women migrating for marital reasons, and (4) married women migrating for family reunification with no thought of employment.

3. It can be argued that "migration" from Mexico to the United States started as early as 1848 with the signing of the Treaty of Guadalupe Hidalgo that ended the Mexican-American War (1846–48) and by which Mexico lost more than half of its prewar territory to the United States.

4. Recently governments and international organizations have been devoting a lot of attention and resources to the potential link between remittances and development. One issue, however, that has not been fully discussed by governments or international organizations is the fact that remittances constitute a transfer between individuals for very specific purposes. How can we turn these monies into what is commonly known as development?

7. MIGRATION AND DEVELOPMENT

1. Until recently women migrated almost exclusively in the context of family migration. However, it should be noted that, since the 1990s, an increasing proportion of independent labor migrants to Europe and North America are female, which also seems to be the result of general cultural change.

8. THE SOUTHERN CROSSROADS

Portions of this paper were originally prepared in support of the United Nations Development Programme's 2009 Human Development Report and have been previously published as Loren B. Landau and Aurelia Wa Kabwe Segatti, "Human Development Impacts of Migration: South African Case Study," Human Development Research Paper 2009/5, United Nations Development Programme, New York, December 2008. The authors are grateful for feedback we received during this process from Jenny Klugman and others. We are also grateful to Véronique Gindrey for invaluable assistance in the statistical analysis included in this chapter.

1. More information on the 2001 census and the 2007 community survey are available from the Statistics South Africa website (http://www.statssa.gov.za/publications/populationstats.asp).

2. Author interview with Martine Schaffer, director, Homecoming Revolution, Johannesburg, December 19, 2009.

3. In 2005 Cape Town conducted a skills audit of its refugee population to better develop policies to capitalize on their presence in the city. Johannesburg has yet to follow suit but has recently officially recognized the potential contributions migrants make to the city.

4. Johannesburg metropolitan government has slowly begun to consider migrants as a vulnerable group, although it is unclear whether any efforts to include migrants in local decision-making priorities are being made.

5. For more on the country's spatial development perspective, visit http://www.thepresidency.gov.za/pebble.asp?relid=514.

6. Interview with Cecil van Schalwyk, director of Midrand office of Mapogo a Mathamaga, July 25, 2003.

7. Interview with Graeme Götz, Strategic Planning Unit, City of Johannesburg, July 18, 2008.

9. MIGRATION BETWEEN THE ASIA-PACIFIC AND AUSTRALIA

1. With a quarter of the population born in a foreign country and nearly half the population at any one time being immigrants, the children of immigrants, or temporary migrants, Australia is one of the nations most influenced by international migration.

2. The island nature of Australia means that clandestine international migration is extremely minor.

3. This visa category is analogous to the HB1 visa in the United States.

4. That is, for temporary migrants for whom the intended length of stay is less than twelve months.

5. See http://www.oecd.org/edu/educationeconomyandsociety/44824375.pdf.

6. Migration efficiency is obtained by dividing net migration (in minus out) by gross migration (in plus out) and is a measure of the effectiveness of migration in increasing the numbers of medical workers.

7. That is, people indicating on arrival in Australia they will be staying longer than one year, when in fact they intend *not* to stay permanently.

8. $A1 = US$0.71 as of January 2009.

9. Moreover Cobb-Clark and Cook (2006) have shown that the refugee-humanitarian migrants were the only visa category to experience a worsening of labor market conditions over the time between the two interviews.

10. Except in the foreign students category.

10. ASIAN MIGRATION TO THE UNITED STATES

1. The United States had 1.4 million Filipino-born residents in 2000, including two-thirds who arrived before 1990; 45 percent of the Filipino adults in the United States in 2000 were college graduates.

2. There were 1.2 million Chinese-born U.S. residents in 2000, including 53 percent who arrived before 1990; 43 percent of the Chinese adults in the United States in 2000 were college graduates.

3. There were 1 million Indian U.S. residents in 2000, including 45 percent who arrived before 1990; 70 percent of the Indian adults in the United States in 2000 were college graduates.

4. There were 1 million Vietnamese U.S. residents in 2000, including 55 percent who arrived before 1990; 19 percent of Vietnamese adults in the United States in 2000 were college graduates.

5. Admissions record events, not unique individuals, so a foreigner holding an H-1B visa is "admitted" each time he or she reenters the United States.

6. U.S. Census Bureau, "Selected Characteristics of the Foreign-Born Population by Region of Birth: Africa, Northern America, and Oceania," 2010. Accessed at http://factfinder2.census.gov/faces/tableservices/jsf/pages/productview.xhtml?pid=ACS_10_1YR_S0504&prodType=table.

7. The East Asian economic miracle stands in sharp contrast to the lack of similar African and Latin American investment- and export-led growth success stories.

8. Despite the desires of many labor-sending countries, relatively few Asian migrants move under the terms of bilateral agreements and Memoranda of Understanding.

9. Borjas (1994) reexamined Chiswick's findings and concluded they applied to the unique set of circumstances that accompanied the lifting of barriers to Asian immigration in the mid-1960s.

10. Khadria (1999) questions the extent of the virtuous circle from Indians settled abroad, finding that nonresident Indian investments in India benefit primarily the investors rather than India as a whole because the nonresident Indian investors do little to directly improve the Indian education and health care systems.

11. For example, South Africa graduates about 1,300 doctors and 2,500 nurses a year; those who receive government support for their education must serve two years in rural areas before receiving their license to practice. South Africa complained that it spent $1 billion educating health workers who emigrated in the 1990s, equivalent to a third of the development aid it received from the end of apartheid in 1994 to 2000.

12. The International Council of Nurses issued similar recruitment guidelines in 2001 (www.icn.ch/psrecruit01.htm).

13. Celia W. Dugger, "In Africa, an Exodus of Nurses," *New York Times*, July 12, 2004. PHR did not recommend that African governments try to prevent the emigration of health care workers, but did recommend that industrialized countries not recruit actively in Africa.

14. Escobar (2008:Table 2) compares remittances per capita and GDP per capita in 2003 for selected Lain American countries, finding that in very poor countries such as Haiti and Bolivia remittances per capita from Haitians and Bolivians in the United States were over four times larger than GDP per capita, e.g., $2,000 per U.S. Haitian in remittances versus $500 in GDP per capita. However, in richer countries such as Mexico, remittances per capita were less than GDP per capita.

15. The World Bank reported that some migrants in rich countries remitted more funds after September 11, 2001, so they would have funds at home if they were deported. Such "defensive remittances" may help to explain the tripling of remittances to Pakistan between 2001 and 2003 (World Bank 2006:92).

16. Another factor increasing formal remittances is the spread of banks from migrant countries of origin to migrant destinations, where they offer services in the migrant's language as well as ancillary services to migrant relatives at home.

17. Agents in the two countries periodically settle their credit and debit accounts, often via a commercial bank.

18. The World Bank's (2006:95) *Global Economic Prospects* concluded that most Hometown Associations (HTAs) raise and invest less than $10,000 in their communities of origin, and that the effects of such investments are "poorly documented." In particular, *Global Economic Prospects* asserts that Mexico's 3x1 program, begun in 1997, established projects worth $44 million by 2002, but concludes that "HTAs have not been very successful" in part because diasporas may not have good information on local needs or have different priorities for infrastructure improvements.

19. These students were highly motivated to pursue advanced studies. Before they could do so abroad, however, they had to complete two years of military service and obtain private or overseas financing.

20. Shanghai reportedly had 30,000 returned professionals in 2002, 90 percent of whom had M.S. or Ph.D. degrees earned abroad. Jonathan Kaufman, "China Reforms Bring Back Executives Schooled in U.S.," *Wall Street Journal*, March 6, 2003; Rone Tempest, "China Tries to Woo Its Tech Talent Back Home," *Los Angeles Times*, November 25, 2002.

21. The Population Reference Bureau (PRB.org) puts the Philippine population at 90 million in 2008, with a projected 150 million in 2050.

22. An account of the December 22, 2011, welcome is at http://www.gov.ph/2011 /12/22/pamaskong-handog-sa-ofws-december-22-2011.

23. Of the 811,000 land-based migrants leaving in 2007, almost 30 percent went to Saudi Arabia, 15 percent went to the UAE, and about 6 percent each went to Hong Kong, Qatar, and Singapore. These five countries absorbed two-thirds of the land-based Filipinos deployed in 2007.

24. The events surrounding this case are covered in "A Death in the Family," *Asia Week*, December 29, 1995. Accessed at http://edition.cnn.com/ASIANOW/asiaweek /95/1229/feat3.html.

25. Fighting between Israel and Hezbollah in mid-2006 resulted in 6,000 Filipinos, mostly domestic helpers, being flown home; two-thirds were undocumented. Between 1990 and 2005 migration to Lebanon was banned because of frequent mistreatment of domestic helpers. That ban was lifted in 2005 and reimposed in 2006.

26. Ernesto B. Calucag, "The Symptoms of Dutch Disease," *Business World*, February 22, 2008, www.bworldonline.com/Research/populareconomics.php?id=0074.

27. Jason DeParle, "A Good Provider Is One Who Leaves," *New York Times*, April 22, 2007.

28. A driver from Kerala employed in Qatar reported earning $375 a month, five times the $75 a month he earned in Kerala, but lamented that he sees his family only during one three-week vacation a year. Jason DeParle, "Jobs Abroad Support 'Model' State in India," *New York Times*, September 7, 2007.

29. Fees for unofficial primary schools in urban areas are often $25 or $50 a month. Current law requires high school students seeking to attend college to take entrance exams in the place they are registered to live. Most children who move to urban areas with their parents reportedly drop out of school.

30. Some $7.6 billion of the $14.4 billion in remittances reported by the Philippine Central Bank in 2007 was recorded as coming from the United States; Saudi Arabia was the second leading source of remittances, at $1.1 billion in 2007. The U.S. share of remittances may be inflated by migrants in, e.g., Hong Kong using U.S. banks to transfer remittances (www.bsp.gov.ph/statistics/keystat/ofw.htm).

11. INDIAN MIGRANTS TO THE GULF

1. The Ministry of External Affairs, Government of India, with the approval of the prime minister of India, decided to appoint a high-level committee on the Indian

diaspora with five members to review the status of persons of Indian origin (POI) and nonresident Indians (NRI) on August 18, 2000. The committee submitted its report on December 19, 2001.

2. Estimates published in the report of the High Level Committee on the Indian Diaspora submitted to the Ministry of External Affairs, New Delhi. Please note that this is not an accurate figure but an underestimate. Unfortunately the government of India has no regular mechanisms to assess the number of Indians living abroad. Most often, high commissioners in respective countries provide the data on Indians living in their countries by request from the Ministry of External Affairs from time to time.

3. A person who, at any time, has held an Indian passport or anyone, either of whose parents or whose grandparents or great-grandparents was born in and was permanently resident in India as defined in the Government of India Act 1935 and other territories that became part of India thereafter, provided he or she was not at any time a citizen of the countries referred in part 2 (b) of Ministry of Home Affairs notification No. 26011/4/98-IC.1 dated March 30, 1999, or the spouse of a citizen of India or person of Indian origin covered in the above categories of PIO. Most of them have taken citizenship of their country of residence, and the strength of their ties with India dies with the passage of time.

4. *Stateless population* is defined as Indians who stay without valid travel documents in their respective countries.

5. NRIs are Indian citizens holding Indian passports and residing abroad for an indefinite period, whether for employment or for carrying on any business or vacation or for any other purpose.

6. All Indian passport holders need emigration clearance to visit Emigration Check Required (ECR) countries for work abroad. As of this writing, seventeen countries require emigration clearance for ECR passport holders, and the government of India has exempted 174 countries as of 2009 (Irudaya Rajan, Varghese, and Jayakumar 2010). However, few categories of individuals receive a passport with emigration check not required (see Table 11.2 in this book).

INDEX

Abella, Manolo, 8
Accelerated and Shared Growth
    Initiative for South Africa, 206
Acosta, Pablo, 292
Adams, Richard H., 291–92
African Centre for Migration Studies
    (ACMS), 199, 203–4, 210
ageing, 264, 267
agency, culture as, 76
age of mobility, xv
agriculture: agricultural economies, 1, 7,
    9; National Farmers Federation, 256;
    South Africa migration, 208
Amnesty International, 93
amnesty programs, 93, 105
apartheid, 200, 203, 212–13
Appadurai, Arjun, 69
Arizpe, Lourdes, 68–69
Asia-Australia migration, 266;
    Australia-born, 238, 239–40;
    Australian Workers Union, 256; from
    Australia to Asia, *243*, 243–47, *244*,
    245, *246*, *247*; backpackers, 256; brain
    drain and, 266; categories, 231–32;
    China and, 244–45; circular
    migration, 233–36, 248, 266;
    complexity, 248; conclusion, 268–70;
    data considerations, 231–32;
    development-sensitive policies,
    265–70; education activity, 258;
    family reunification, 233, 260;
foreign-born, 237, *237*, 238–39, *240*,
    257, *262*; guest workers, 264; labor
    market, 256; long-term movements,
    232; migration-development nexus
    and, 269; multiculturism, 261, 267;
    National Farmers Federation, 256;
    onshore migrants, 234; permanent
    departures, 241–42, *242*; permanent
    settlements, 232–35, *235*; postarrival
    services, 265; poverty and, 268–69;
    reciprocity, 248; refugee-humanitarian
    migrants, 233, 238, 255, 258, 264,
    329n9; return migration, 236–43;
    seasonal worker programs, 266–67;
    sensitivity of, 268; short-term
    movements, 231, 246, *246*, *247*, 266;
    skilled migrants, 233–34, *236*, 258, 266;
    students, 235–36; third-country
    migration, 241; two-way movement,
    230; White Australia Policy, 232;
    Working Holiday Program, 256
Asia-Australia migration, development
    implications: brain drain, 249–55;
    cultural maintenance, 261; diaspora
    organizations, 261–62, 267; dual
    citizenship, 261, 267; investment
    opportunities, 263; knowledge
    transfer, 263; low-skilled labor,
    255–57; overview, 247–48;
    remittances, 257–61, *259*, 267–68;
    return migration, 263–65

118–23; cultural closeness, 121–22;
decline, 121, 122; family
reconfiguration in, 124–28; family
reunification and, 112, 221; financial
crisis and, 221; frequency, 120; from
macro to micro, 123–28; overview,
111–14; regularization process, 122;
remittances, 113, 123; school changes
and, 128–33; scope of, 111–12;
theoretical approach, 114–18; as
tourists, 121
education: activity in Asia-Australia
migration, 258; Morocco migration
and, 183–84; South Africa migration
and, 218–19. *See also* schools
El Salvador, 57, 71
emigration, 56, 305; acceleration, 12; to
immigration, 10, 14, 31; India-Gulf
migration, Kerala experience, *311*,
311–13, *312, 313*; India-Gulf migration
and, *306, 309*, 332n6;
institutionalizing, 57; societies, 1, 9
Emigration Act of 1983, 305
employment, 30; Philippine Overseas
Employment Administration, 101,
290–91; regulating, 104–6;
self-employment, 50; wages, 18. *See
also* unemployment
*Engagement on Governance and
Anti-Corruption*, 223
Erikson, Thomas Hylland, 22
"Essays in the Quantitative Study of
Economic Growth," 326n5
ethnicity, 68
European Commission Strategic Paper
on Governance, 2006, 223
European Court of Justice, 150
European Union (EU), 121, 149–50;
codevelopment policies, 172; new
citizens, 152
Europe migration: causal relations in
transitions, 13–17; historical
evidence, 14–17; progression, 17;
push pull factors, 18; states and, 20
exclusion, 213, 220

exode rurale, 183
expulsion protection, 150

family: economies, 15; formation, 174;
migration and, 54–56; norms, 186;
nuclear, 185; remittances and, 260;
role of, 115–16; schools as ally, 134;
transnational, 116; in transnational
migration, 135
family reconfiguration, 116; children's
emotional wounds, 126–27, 129, 134;
in Ecuador-Spain migration, 124–28;
female migration and, 145; schools
and, 133
family reunification, 94, 109; Asia-
Australia migration, 233, 260;
byproducts and benefits, 159;
Ecuador-Spain migration and, 112,
221; Germany controlling, 151–52;
Immigration Reform and Control
Act and, 156; Morocco migration
and, 173–74; negative effects, 159;
process, 129; women and, 141–42
Fan, C. S., 255
female migration, 109, 116, 120, 328n1;
categories, 144; family
reconfiguration and, 145; numbers,
139–40, *140, 141*; overview, 139–42;
policy implications, 159–60; reasons
for, 142–45; remittances and, 142,
144–45; research and analysis,
140–41; types, 327n2
Ferenczi, Imre, 18
fertility levels, 7, 8; decline, 9, 16, 31;
high to low, 10; income and, 19–20;
low rates, 14
fiesta patronal, 73–74, 77–78
Fiji, 258, *259*
financial crises, 47, 106; Ecuador-Spain
migration and, 221; migrant workers
and, 96
Fondation Hassan II pour les
Marocains Résidant a l'É tranger,
177–78
forced labor, 96